Managerial Economics

The beauty of a book on managerial economics is that it can be used as a way of introducing business and management students to economic concepts as well as providing economics students with a clear grasp of how to use the skills they will need in the world of business.

The concepts of strategy, the underlying motivations of all the agents involved in a particular economic situation, and the interdependence of actions taken by agents are the primary focus of this text, unlike many previous books in the area which have covered strategy and motivation very briefly.

Topics considered include:

- product differentiation and advertising

- price discrimination

- hiring and training workers

- labor–management relations

- international trade

A host of key learning features are employed to add color to the text such as case studies, examples, and exercises. Some of the many specific cases considered include a discussion of how to choose a mobile phone plan, advertising competition in the US beer industry, competition between Internet Service Providers, and incentives in PGA golf tournaments.

Timothy C. G. Fisher is Associate Professor of Economics at Wilfrid Laurier University, Canada.

Robert G. Waschik is Senior Lecturer in the Department of Economics and Finance at La Trobe University, Australia.

Managerial Economics

A game theoretic approach

Timothy C. G. Fisher

and

Robert G. Waschik

London and New York

First published 2002
by Routledge
11 New Fetter Lane, London EC4P 4EE

Simultaneously published in the USA and Canada
by Routledge
29 West 35th Street, New York, NY 10001

Routledge is an imprint of the Taylor & Francis Group

Typeset in Times by
Integra Software Services Pvt. Ltd, Pondicherry, India
Printed and bound in Great Britain by
T. J. International Ltd, Padstow, Cornwall

British Library Cataloguing in Publication Data
A catalogue record for this book is available from the British Library

Library of Congress Cataloging in Publication Data
A catalog record for this book is available from the Library of Congress

ISBN 0–415–27288–2 (hbk)
ISBN 0–415–27289–0 (pbk)

Contents

Figures

Tables

Preface

· ·

Business is a game – the greatest game in the world if you know how to play it.

Thomas J. Watson, founder of IBM

This book represents a completely new approach to managerial economics by focusing on two of the major recent advances in economics: game theory and imperfect competition. Game theory is used to highlight the role of strategy in business decisions. Imperfect competition theory is used to explain how strategies interact in modern industries.

- Brings together two of the major recent developments in microeconomics: game theory and imperfect competition.

- Emphasis on strategic interaction between firms and on strategies for managers.

- Key points illustrated throughout the text with the use of business cases.

- Examples bring theory closer to the real world.

- End-of-chapter exercises test grasp of the theory.

Acknowledgments

···

We would like to thank all of the people who have spent considerable time and effort reading, reviewing, and commenting on various versions of this book, including:

Maria Gallego, *Wilfrid Laurier University*
Joe Kushner, *Brock University*
Steven Law, *University of New Brunswick*
A. Matadeen, *Simon Fraser University*
Robert Morrison, *McGill University*
Ingrid Peters-Fransen, *Wilfrid Laurier University*

Abdul Rahman, *University of Ottawa*
Tom Ross, *University of British Columbia*

A great many undergraduate and graduate students at Wilfrid Laurier University were exposed to the material in this text at varying levels of sophistication over the years. We're sure that much was learned by all involved, and that this is a better text for the many comments which were received from these students.

Chapter 1

Introduction

••

On August 27, 2001, Northwest Airlines, the fourth largest US carrier, announced it was reducing fares on domestic and international flights by as much as 25 percent. For example, the price of a round-trip ticket from Detroit to Paris fell from $679 to $512. Not only were fares reduced, but the normal 21-day advance purchase requirement for the cheap fares was cut to 14 days and tickets purchased over the web were eligible for an additional 5 percent discount. This was obviously a boon to travelers. But imagine what the situation was like at Northwest's main rivals: American Airlines, United Airlines, and Delta Air Lines. The cut in fares was significant and Northwest had advertised that it was going to last for at least four months. The other airlines had to react quickly or risk losing business to Northwest.[1] Given the slim profit margins enjoyed by airlines in 2001, it's probably not overstating the case too much to say that a quick and sensible reaction to Northwest's fare-cutting was vital to the profitability of the other airlines.

Moreover, imagine the situation at Northwest when someone first came up with the idea of a fare cut. One of their main concerns would have been: how are the other airlines going to react? Because Northwest's managers are well aware that the other airlines are operating on the brink of profitability, they must have expected that American, United, and Delta were going to react to the fare reductions offered by Northwest. Thus, when deciding to cut fares, Northwest's managers also must have taken into consideration how rival airlines would react.

There is nothing particularly special about this example. It merely serves to illustrate a central theme of this book: planning ahead and anticipating how rivals might react – in other words *strategy* – is a vital component of business. Anyone who plays a sport or takes part in a competition intuitively knows strategy is important. Business is no different. How firms react to things their rivals do is a critical part of decision-making within any firm.

A more common-place example takes place in almost every major city on every continent several times a year: gasoline price wars. If you drive a car, you will be especially aware of the price of gasoline and you will have noticed how the price fluctuates from one week to the next. For example, in Sydney, Australia, the price of petrol may vary by up to 20 percent in any given month. It is unlikely that the underlying cost of drilling, transporting, refining, and distributing the product varies by anything like as much as 20 percent a month. The price changes are much more likely to be the result of competition between firms for market share.

But the same underlying forces are at work here as in the air fares example. Each time a firm decides to cut (or raise) its price, it has to take into account how its competitors are going to react. In other words, firms have to take into account how their competitors are going to react to their decisions, and, as a result, firms have to come up with ways of dealing with their competitors' reaction. Put another way: strategy is vital to firms in a competitive business environment.

Both examples presented so far have been about the strategic aspects of pricing. But strategic issues are not confined to decisions about prices. Advertising is used heavily in some industries, especially beer and detergent retailing. We shall see that advertising plays a strategic role in positioning a firm's product relative to rival products. Investment, too, has a strategic element. Toyota Canada recently completed construction on a C$500 million expansion to its Cambridge, Ontario, factory where the Corolla model is produced. This signals to Toyota's competitors that the firm is committed to producing more Canadian-built cars in the foreseeable future, which has implications for pricing and production levels for any firm that produces a product to rival the Toyota Corolla. Mergers and acquisitions have a strategic element as well, as do research and development. All these strategic issues are discussed in various chapters of this book.

1.1 The use of game theory

Any student of economics knows about the demand and supply model. This simple yet remarkably powerful set of tools describes how markets made up of participants acting purely in their own self interest determine overall prices and production levels. On the demand side of the market, *consumers* make decisions about how to allocate a fixed set of resources to consume goods and services to make themselves as well off as possible. On the supply side of the market, *firms* produce goods and services. Firms are assumed to minimize costs and maximize profits, given the structure of competition. The simplest markets describe firms with no market power (*perfect competition*) or one firm with complete market power (*monopoly*).

But very few firms fit this description of the supply side of the market. It is certainly not the case that Northwest Airlines or United Airlines, Shell or BP, or Toyota or General Motors operate in a market where they have either no market power or complete market power. If we want to describe how decisions made by managers to maximize profits or minimize costs in any of these companies are made, we need to expand our demand and supply model to allow us to consider the strategic effect that decisions made by managers have on the market. The missing element from the simple demand and supply model is the fact that what a manager in one firm does will affect the behavior of other managers in the same market. All managers know this. Managers at Northwest know that managers at United and other airlines will respond to their pricing strategy, and an important part of their job is understanding how United will respond to their pricing strategy.

We have argued that strategy is at the center of important business decisions. Now you might think that there are probably as many strategies as there are business situations. This, after all, is the implicit view of case study analysis employed by many business schools. A case study is deliberately anecdotal: cases tell a story, and every story is different. Since every story is different, it might seem very difficult to come up with any general system of analyzing business situations.

But this is precisely what we will attempt to accomplish through the use of *game theory*, the mathematical science of conflict and cooperation. We will show that many business situations can be deconstructed to a few basic conditions that can be systematically analyzed. We will also see how it is possible to break down strategy into component parts and analyze the role played by each part. Thus, through game theory we will develop a general approach to understanding what strategy is and how choices of strategy effect the outcome of certain situations. Theoretical analysis is all very well in the classroom, but it will never completely take the place of experience. That is why each chapter in the book contains several cases to illustrate and expand on the theoretical material and to tie it in to the real world.

1.2 Traditional managerial economics

What is so special about our approach to managerial economics? The answer is simple: the focus on strategy. Traditionally, managerial economics has simply been treated as intermediate microeconomics adapted for business students. This approach does not take into account a major development in economics that has taken place in the last 20 years: the use of game theory.

Ignoring game theory in economics is a bit like analyzing a successful professional sports team and focusing on the physical fitness of the athletes. Certainly, physical fitness is an important element of success in sport. But in the modern era where each team has the ability to ensure all its players are at the peak of their physical condition, physical fitness surely is not the key to the difference between winning and losing. Successful teams

are those that have the best strategies, whether it be a strategy for getting players, a strategy for trading players, or strategy (tactics) employed during the game. Sir Alex Ferguson of Manchester United and Fabio Capello of AS Roma don't command the highest salaries because they know how to get their soccer players into shape. They are well paid because their strategies for success have been shown to work.

1.3 Overview of the book

This book is divided into three parts: basic theory, applications of game theory to interactions *between* firms, and applications of game theory to interactions *within* the firm. The first part, comprising Chapters 1–4, covers the basic economic tools of the firm. The second part, comprising Chapters 5–12, introduces game theory, which is our basic tool for analyzing strategic behavior, and applications of the tools to strategic interaction between firms. The third part of the book, comprising Chapters 13–16, analyzes strategic interaction within a firm.

In Chapter 2, we step back from the manager's role at the firm and examine the question of why firms exist in the first place. Obviously, if we have no idea why firms exist it will be difficult to figure out what the firm is supposed to do and, therefore, impossible to figure out what the manager is supposed to do. By analyzing the main reasons why firms exist we can begin to think about what sorts of problems the manager is likely to face and the strategies that are likely to come into play.

Chapter 3 serves two purposes. First, to provide some basic tools that will be used in the book. Second, to serve as a brief review of introductory economics and re-acquaint readers with terms that will be used in the book. The chapter is one of the few parts of the book that looks like a conventional managerial economics text. Here we analyze the two extreme competitive situations a firm can find itself in: a very large number of rivals (perfect competition) and no rivals (monopoly). These polar opposite cases are useful for introducing terminology about firms that will be used in the book. They are also useful because they represent cases where strategy plays a relatively minor role, meaning we can focus on the more mundane aspects of the firm's operation.

Chapter 4 continues with the analysis of a monopoly firm in order to introduce the notion of price discrimination. In particular, we look at various pricing methods that firms may use in order to squeeze more revenue from their customers. The many clever pricing practices that firms use are discussed here.

Chapter 5 introduces game theory. Here we define what is meant by a "game," what is meant by "strategy," and so on. We also introduce various types of games that will appear, in different contexts, throughout the book. This chapter is the core building block for much of the material that follows in the book.

Chapter 6 contains our first analysis of strategy in a business setting. We examine the relatively straightforward case of an industry that contains two firms. Here we begin to stretch our analysis beyond the two extremes of market structure by examining a special case where there are only two firms in an industry, which is called a duopoly. The chapter analyzes strategies of the firms in two cases: determining what price to charge, and determining how much output to produce. Thus, Chapter 6 presents the first concrete application of game theory.

Chapter 7 examines the issues surrounding product positioning. Suppose a firm is considering entering a market which is new to the firm. Should it design its new product to compete directly with existing products, or could profits be maximized by positioning the new product so that consumers view it as being distinct and different from those already available in the market? The strategic response from rival firms will be different in each case, but can be anticipated by a manager.

Chapter 8 discusses the role of advertising. With the large number of consumer goods available, and with new goods being introduced all the time, advertising plays an important role in informing consumers about the characteristics of a firm's products. But there is also a strategic role played by advertising. A manager may be able to increase demand for the firm's products by increasing advertising expenditures, thereby changing the perception of consumers. But increases in advertising expenditures are costly, so the positive effects of advertising on demand must balance the negative effects on cost. In Chapter 8, we consider the ways in which advertising can affect the structure of competition in a market and how advertising can be used to affect market demand and profits.

Chapter 9 looks at the role of information. Firms sometimes cannot be sure about the characteristics of their customers and this information might be extremely important. For example, a major problem faced by insurance companies is the possibility that too many of their customers end up to be bad risks. But there are ways insurance firms can design policies in order to minimize the risk of this happening. On the other side of the coin, consumers may not be certain about the characteristics of the firm they are thinking about buying from. Again, information on, say, the reliability of a firm's products, might be very important to the prospective buyer. We will discuss ways firms can use to convince consumers that they are worth buying from.

At any point in time, a firm earning high profits must face the potential threat of entry by other firms seeking to capture some of these profits. In Chapter 10, we analyze how a firm might respond to the threat of entry by other firms. Might the firms want to deter entry, or would the firm be better off by accommodating entry by other firms and securing its market position? On the other hand, what market conditions might lead a firm to enter a market where there exists a well-defined structure of competition?

Most businesses resent government interference. But there are compelling reasons in favor of government regulation, which is discussed in Chapter 11. There, we look at the basic rationale for government regulation. We discuss issues of regulation that arise in monopolies, intellectual property, unfair business practices, and the environment.

Chapter 12 turns our attention away from the workings of firms in a single country and looks at the wider implications of increased global trade. We briefly examine the arguments for and against free trade. We then look at the recent formation of the World Trade Organization (WTO) and its implications for firms. There is a case study of a trade dispute between Australia and the United States over automobile parts.

The last part of the book focuses on strategic issues that arise within the firm itself. Chapter 13 looks at the multidivisional firm. Firms with divisions producing rival products and firms with divisions that produce goods or services used by other divisions within the firm must be careful that incentives are structured so that the goal of overall profit maximization at the firm is accom-

plished. One of the key issues in the area is that of transfer pricing. In order to maximize overall profits, it is crucial that the prices placed on transactions between divisions within the firm are priced correctly.

The last three chapters turn to a central problem within the firm: the management of human resources. Chapter 14 covers the basic model of a perfectly competitive labor market. This is useful for introducing things like the basic hiring rule that firms will follow and the way labor markets work to determine the wages firms have to pay.

But, just like the standard model was found inadequate in explaining most interactions in the product market, the standard model is not really an accurate description of hiring and compensation practices at modern corporations. The key issue is how to motivate employees to give the optimal amount of effort in their jobs when observing the employees actions might be difficult and costly. Chapter 15 looks at how firms structure human resource policies so as to get the right amount of work from their employees at minimum cost. We also discuss executive and management compensation schemes.[2]

Chapter 16 looks at the issues that arise when a firm's workers belong to a union. It contains a brief comparison of the three kinds of industrial relations system found in developed economies. The chapter goes on to discuss the theory of wage bargaining, union power, strikes, and the effects of unions on firms.

1.4 Partial equilibrium and general equilibrium

Before we get to our analysis of competition and monopoly we need to make a final point. A national economy is made up of thousands of firms and millions of consumers. In some small way, the actions of each firm or consumer have an impact on all the other firms and consumers.

For example, when Northwest Airlines changes its fares, some consumers will change their travel plans. Obviously, Northwest is hoping that a lot of people who would not otherwise have flown with them will now decide to take a trip to visit family or friends. And this will certainly happen to some degree. The consumers who decide to take trips will change how they spend the rest of their income. Perhaps by taking a trip they will postpone buying a new car, or a new washing machine, or maybe they will just not go out to restaurants for a month or two. Each decision has repercussions for firms in the economy. Car sales might drop off, which has an impact on new-car dealers and on car producers. Sales of washing machines might fall, which affects department stores and producers of appliances. Restaurants will be less busy, and so on. As a result, restaurants, retailers, and goods-producing firms might cut back the hours of their employees. In turn, these workers will adjust their spending decisions, which has further implications for other firms and people in the economy.

What we have just described is the behavior of an economy in *general equilibrium*. A change in the behavior of one market in an economy will generally have impacts in markets throughout the whole economy. Sometimes these effects will be very small. Nevertheless it is important to acknowledge that these inter-market effects are present, and may be significant.

By and large, we will concentrate on the relation between firms and their immediate competitors. In the language of economics, we say that the analysis is *partial equilibrium* in nature. We will concentrate on the effects of a manager's strategic decision-making problem only on the market in which the manager operates. Northwest may drop its price on air travel, and this may cause such an increase in demand for air travel that local travel agents find they have to hire more people to handle the phones. The manager at Northwest is concerned only with the effect that the pricing strategy has on the firm's market, and does not take into account the effect on the market for travel agents. Partial equilibrium considers the determination of equilibrium in one single market at a time.

1.5 The role of the consumer

This book is about the behavior of managers running firms. Basically, firms produce goods or services to be sold to consumers. In the language of economics, firms *supply* goods or services that consumers *demand*. The exchange of goods or services takes place in a *market*. By and large, this book will completely ignore the role played by consumers in the market. We will simply summarize the behavior of consumers with a demand curve, which we will assume accurately represents the preferences of all consumers interested in buying a specific good or service. Mathematically, the demand curve is written:

$$q = D(p)$$

where q stands for the amount of the good or service that consumers demand and p stands for the price. Sometimes it is more convenient to express the demand equation with price on the left-hand side, in which case we have the inverse demand function, which is written:

$$p = P(q)$$

Often we will work with linear demand curves which have the basic form $q = a - bp$. Solving for p we have $p = (a/b) - (1/b)q$, which is the inverse demand curve.

An important concept related to a demand curve is the *price elasticity of demand.* The price elasticity, as it is often called for short, measures how responsive is quantity demanded to price changes. The price elasticity for a good or service is:

$$\varepsilon = \frac{\%\ \text{change in quantity demanded}}{\%\ \text{change in price}} \quad (1.1)$$

We shall use the symbol ε to stand for price elasticity throughout the book. In calculus, the price elasticity formula is:[3]

$$\varepsilon = -\frac{dq/q}{dp/p}$$

Why is there a minus sign here? Since the demand curve is downward sloping, an increase in price will result in a decrease in quantity demanded. In other words, if the denominator is positive, then the numerator will be negative, implying the ratio is negative. The convention is to report the price elasticity as a positive number, so the ratio is multiplied by minus one.

Another way of writing the price elasticity equation is:

$$\varepsilon = -\left(\frac{dq}{dp}\right)\frac{p}{q} = -\left(\frac{dp}{dq}\right)^{-1}\frac{p}{q}$$

The first equality shows that the price elasticity for a given value of p and q can be calculated as the derivative of the demand function times the ratio of p and q. The second equality shows that the elasticity can also be calculated as one over the slope of the inverse demand function times the ratio of p and q. If $\varepsilon < 1$, demand is *inelastic*, i.e. relatively unresponsive to price changes. If $\varepsilon > 1$, demand is *elastic*, i.e. relatively responsive to price changes.

Example

Suppose the demand function is $q = a - bp$, for $a > 0$ and $b > 0$. Then $dq/dp = -b$ and $\varepsilon = -(-bp/q) = bp/q$ for any point (q, p). Since $q = a - bp$, we could also write $\varepsilon = bp/(a - bp)$.

Summary

- A list of actions a firm may undertake to approach a market, or to react to actions by other firms in the same market is collectively referred to as the firm's strategy. Almost any business situation from output levels, to pricing, to marketing, to research, and so on, has a strategic element.
- Demand and supply analysis ignores strategy altogether, because in a competitive market prices and output decisions are made by the market and not by any individual firm.
- Traditional managerial economics largely ignores the role of strategy and the main tool economics has developed to deal with strategy, namely game theory. This book stresses strategic aspects of decision-making within the firm, using game theory as its primary tool of analysis.
- General equilibrium analysis considers the effect a change in one market has on every other market in the economy. Partial equilibrium analysis focuses on one market at a time, ignoring the spillover effects in other markets.

Summary contd

- The collective purchasing decisions of consumers for a specific good or service are summarized in a demand curve. In principle, a demand curve exists for every good or service in the economy. The inverse demand curve presents the same information as the demand curve but with price, rather than quantity demanded, as the dependent variable.

Notes

1 In fact, within hours, the rival airlines matched the fare cuts, the web discount, and the shorter advance purchase requirement announced by Northwest.

2 It seems fitting in book about managerial economics that we discuss the manager's pay at some point!

3 The numerator is the proportionate change in q or, if multiplied by 100, the percentage change in q. Similarly, the denominator is the proportionate change in p or, when multiplied by 100, the percentage change in p. Taking the ratio, therefore, is equivalent to (1.1).

Exercises

1 Given the following two equations:

$$P = 5 - 0.05\,Q$$
$$P = 0.75 + 0.0125\,Q$$

(a) Identify which of the two equations is the demand function and which is the supply function.

(b) Calculate the equilibrium price and quantity.

(c) Calculate the price elasticity of demand at the equilibrium price and quantity. Is demand elastic at this point?

(d) Suppose a tax of $0.25 per unit is levied on this good and that producers are required to collect the tax. Calculate the new equilibrium price and quantity in the market. (Hint: Before the tax was imposed, producers were willing to supply 100 units when $P = \$2$. After the tax is imposed, they

will require a price of $2.25 to supply 100 units.)

(e) Calculate the percent of the tax that is shifted to the consumer and the percent that is borne by the producer.

(f) Sketch the pre-tax and post-tax equilibria on a diagram showing the demand and supply curves, the prices paid by the consumer, the prices received by the producer, and the tax.

2 Suppose demand and supply for a product are given:

$$Q = 0.001\,Y - 0.5\,P$$
$$Q = 0.5\,P$$

where Y stands for average household income.

(a) If average household income is $40,000, calculate the equilibrium price and quantity.

(b) Suppose a tax of 25 percent of the purchase price is applied to the good and that producers are required to collect the tax. (Assume income remains at $40,000.) Determine the new equilibrium price and quantity.

(c) Graph the supply function and the demand function before and after the tax is imposed. Show on the diagram the equilibrium prices with and without the tax.

(d) Determine tax revenue and tax incidence on producers and consumers.

3 Suppose demand and supply for a product are given:

$$P = 100 - 0.05\,Q$$
$$P = -200 + 0.25\,Q$$

(a) Calculate equilibrium price and quantity.

(b) If the government sets a price ceiling at $40, determine the excess demand that occurs.

(c) Assuming black marketeers buy the entire legal output, find the black-market price and, hence, determine the profits of the black marketeers.

(d) Sketch a diagram illustrating equilibrium before the price ceiling is imposed and showing the black-market price, quantity, and profits.

4 Suppose the daily demand for milk in your local town is given:

$$Q = 10 - 0.1\,P$$

where units are millions of liters. The national supply curve of milk is given:

$$Q = 4.9\,P$$

Suppose that the world price of milk is $1 per liter.

(a) Calculate the equilibrium price, output, and demand when foreign milk is allowed into the domestic market. How much milk will be imported in this case?

(b) Suppose imports of milk are banned. Calculate equilibrium price and output.

(c) Suppose farmers successfully lobby to have a price-support scheme implemented and that the support price is set at $3 per liter. Determine domestic demand, output, and, hence, calculate the daily addition to storage required by the excess production of milk.

(d) Suppose the government proposes a quota system to deal with the over-supply arising from the price support scheme. Assuming one quota per 100,000 liters of milk, how many quotas will be issued to yield a price of $3 per liter?

(e) Which scheme – price support or quota – will farmers prefer, if any? Explain.

Part I

Theory

....

Chapter 2

The manager and the firm

• •

When you are finished with this chapter you should understand:

- Why firms exist, and why firms exist in a particular form
- Some of the factors which limit the size of firms
- The *agency problem* between owners of a firm, and managers and workers at a firm
- Why profit-sharing plans may or may not alleviate the agency problem
- What are the factors affecting the environment within which a firm operates

In order to understand what the manager of a firm does, it is first necessary to understand exactly what we mean by the term *firm*. This being the case, we might as well start at the beginning and ask why firms exist in the first place. Once we've answered this question we'll have a better idea where managers fit into the picture and, therefore, we'll be able to come up with a clear definition of the role of the manager. And once the role of the manager is defined we can start analyzing what it is that managers do, which, of course, is the purpose of the book.

Thus, the first section of this chapter looks at the various reasons why firms exist. And wrapped up with the existence issue is the question of why do firms exist in a particular form. Given that there are reasons for firms to exist, the next logical question is why do firms take a particular form. For example, Microsoft is a very large software company with revenue in 1999 of US$19.7 billion (€19.3 billion).[1] Yet there are literally thousands of small software companies all over the world.

The question is, how can so many small companies compete with such a vast corporation. Put another way, we could ask why it is that one company is so large and another is so small. But this is just one aspect of the question: why do firms exist in a particular form? In other words, if we understand how small firms and large firms come into being we can begin to understand how these firms might compete with one another.

The second section of the chapter outlines the task of the manager. Basically, it's quite simple: we assume the manager will try to maximize the firm's profits. Thus the question arises how the owners, who presumably want the maximum return on their investment, guarantee that the managers actually running the firm do what the owners want.

2.1 Why do firms exist?

Before we look at different reasons why firms exist, we must first be clear that we understand what we mean when we talk about firms. So we'll start with a general definition of a firm:

Definition

A *firm* is a group of workers and managers, collectively called *labor*, and a group of physical assets, like machinery in a manufacturing operation or computers in a service sector firm, collectively called *capital*, which produce goods and/or services.

The main argument for the existence of firms is the presence of *increasing returns to scale*. Returns to scale is a concept directly related to the productivity of factors of production. Suppose that some amount of labor and capital can be used by a firm to produce a particular amount of output. Now imagine that the level of usage of all capital and labor increases by 1 percent. If total output increases by *more than 1 percent*, then there exist increasing returns to scale.

We can construct a very simple example of increasing returns to scale to motivate the existence of a firm. Suppose that you own a piano which you want to move from one part of your residence to another. The piano is too heavy and awkward for you to move by yourself. Your productivity in moving the piano by yourself is equal to zero. But two people working together would be able to move the piano. In this case, there exist increasing returns to scale, since the productivity per person or *average productivity increases* when the number of people moving the piano increases from one to two. You will probably have to compensate another person to help you move the piano, or you may just hire the services of a company which specializes in moving pianos. But either way, we now have labor being employed to perform a service, and that is an activity which implies the existence of a firm.

There are three potential sources of increasing returns in labor: *division of labor*, *specialization*, and *learning-by-doing*. Division of labor arises when it is more productive to divide work among a group of workers. For example, if you have ever worked on a group project, you probably have found out that the work gets done more quickly if divided among the group members: someone to do the research, someone to do the writing, someone to do the typing, and so on. At the very least, division of labor prevents tasks from being repeated, like two people in the group discovering the same reference for a project. And it doesn't make much sense to have two people typing at the same keyboard!

Related to division of labor is specialization: when the work is divided up so that people carry out different tasks, people will get better at performing their individual task. As a result, individual productivity will increase. Lastly, related to specialization is learning-by-doing.

Thus, because of increasing returns to labor, more workers may be able to produce more output working together than they would if they worked alone. This creates an incentive for workers to join together, which in turn results in the formation of firms.

Increasing returns alone would seem to suggest that firms could grow very, very large because worker productivity increases for ever. In practice, however, increasing returns have limits. A good example here is to consider the production of some good which takes place along an assembly line, like a car. Imagine a complete assembly line from beginning to end. The initial stage of the line would be the construction of the chassis of the car. Farther down the line, various parts would be welded onto the chassis at appropriate points. The engine would be bolted in, and so on. Now you can imagine that cars could be produced with only a single worker (a very talented worker) staffing the entire assembly line. But if we added more workers to the line, productivity of each worker would increase, because of the benefits of division of labor (as each worker can concentrate on a particular task), specialization, and learning-by-doing (as workers get better at their assigned tasks with experience). But there will come a point where adding more workers to the assembly line will not increase efficiency, and will ultimately reduce efficiency, as workers get in each others way. This characteristic of production technology is typically captured by assuming that the *marginal product of labor is eventually diminishing*.

There is a further problem which we can identify here, and it is directly related to the issue of the size of a firm. With only one worker on the assembly line, it is a simple matter to evaluate the worker's performance. All that needs to be done is to divide the number of completed cars by the number of hours the worker has spent producing those cars. But if we have many workers along the same assembly line, evaluating performance becomes more difficult. Some workers may work harder, while others may shirk. Having more workers along the line may be a good thing, because the production process benefits from increasing returns. However, the firm now needs to hire another type of labor, in order to manage and monitor the performance of workers on the line. So we've identified a cost to increases in the size of the firm: monitoring costs.[2]

Let's look more closely at this monitoring problem. Why does this problem arise in the first place? So far the only people in the firm who are involved in the production of cars are the workers on the assembly line. But there is another group of people who are also interested in the way that cars are produced along the assembly line: the owners of the firm. In fact, these two types of people or *economic agents* have very different incentives:

1 The owners of the car company include all of its shareholders, and their objective is to see that the firm is organized and run in such a way as to maximize their returns.
2 The workers along the assembly lines at the car company have as their objective to make as much money as possible for themselves. This income does not necessarily depend on how many cars are produced in a given period of time.

This is an important element in the definition of a firm: the distinction and relationship between ownership and control. It can help to determine the ultimate size of a firm, as well as the structure of a firm and how the firm operates. So to continue, we need to pay a bit more attention to the ultimate objective of the firm or the owners of the firm.

2.2 Objectives of the firm

The objective of the owners of a firm is to see that the value of the firm is maximized. An important factor affecting the value of the firm at any point in time is total profits earned by the firm. Profits at some time *t* are defined as the difference between total revenue earned from sales of output and total costs incurred during production. For some time period *t*, we will denote profits as π_t, total revenue as R_t, and total costs as C_t, so that:

$$\pi_t = R_t - C_t$$

So for our purposes, the objective of the owners of the firm will be to maximize profits earned by the firm.

We have defined a firm as a collection of groups of workers and managers, and physical assets which produce output. But how is it that the firm maximizes profits? On its own, a physical asset such as the building housing the assembly line cannot maximize profits. Workers and managers are directly involved with the production process, but the objective of these workers and managers is not necessarily to maximize profits. In economics, we typically treat these workers and managers as consumers, who seek to maximize their own well-being by spending income which is derived from selling their services to the labor market. So the objective of any worker or manager at the firm will generally be to see that he or she keeps his or her job, and earns as high a wage as possible. But none of these objectives need necessarily have anything to do with ensuring that cars are produced as efficiently as possible, or that the firm maximizes profits.

We've identified a problem here, due to the fact that the owners of the firm may not have the ability to directly maximize the profits of the firm, since they may not be directly involved in the production process of the firm. This problem is referred to as an *agency problem*. An agency problem exists when the objectives of the owners of the firm (shareholders who want to maximize profits) do not coincide with the objectives of their agents (workers and managers who want to keep their job and earn income). For example, I may own some shares of the car company, and as such I am interested in ensuring that the car company is maximizing profits. But I don't work on the assembly line, and I am not directly involved in the production of cars.

We can describe a general framework of the structure or organization of a firm, by describing the following hierarchy of decision-makers at a typical firm:

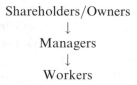

A firm may be small enough that it is owned and operated by the same person or persons. If the local piano moving company is owned and run by the same two individuals who also do all of the piano moving, then the owners of the firm are the same people who manage the firm, and are also the same people who directly produce output at the firm. In this case, an agency problem cannot occur. The objectives of the owners must be the same as the objectives of the workers, because they are all the same people. Another example might be your local corner store, which may be owned and operated by the same individual or family. On the other hand, a firm may be so large that there are many owners and many workers, but the owners do not operate the firm. If your local corner store is a Seven-Eleven, the worker who operates the store – the person behind the counter – is not the owner. Seven-Eleven is owned by Atlantic-Richfield, which is an oil company with millions of shareholders (traded on the New York Stock Exchange under the title ATR). The Seven-Eleven corner store has literally millions of owners and it is highly unlikely that the operators or workers will ever even be aware of meeting one of their owners.

How can the owners of the Seven-Eleven ensure that the operators of all their stores do a good job? You could say that they simply hire managers to keep the operators in line. But this only begs another question: how then do the owners ensure that the managers do a good job? When you think about it, the whole organization of Seven-Eleven, from the

Profit-Sharing and the Agency Problem

A recent "Economics Focus" article in *The Economist** describes a number of interesting aspects of profit-sharing plans in OECD countries. Approximately 12–14 percent of workers in Canada and the United States participate in some sort of profit-sharing scheme. But there are significant differences between countries in participation in profit-sharing schemes, from a high of more than 25 percent of workers in France to less than 7 percent in Italy and Germany and less than 5 percent in Australia.

How can these plans work as a mechanism to resolve the *agency problem* between owners of a firm and workers? Workers are paid a share of their wages out of profits which the firm earns. Since workers earn more if the company is more profitable, they have an incentive to work harder, to ensure that the company earns higher profits. In fact, there are a number of studies which conclude that profit-sharing plans can increase productivity by as much as 10 percent. Such increases in productivity contribute to higher profitability, which is in the interest of both the owners of the firm and workers who earn a share of their income from profits.

There are other mechanisms which the firm can use in order to resolve this agency problem. We will look more closely at how these plans can be in the interest of both the owner and the employee when we discuss how firms motivate workers and managers in Chapter 15.

* See the November 30, 1996 issue of the *The Economist*.

chief executive at the head of the corporation to the operators handling customers are all agents of the owners – they all are supposed to be acting in the interest of the owners. But how can the owners be sure this is the case?

One way is to base the manager's pay on the firm's profit. For example, the manager (and any other employees for that matter) could be paid a share of the firm's profit. In this case, the manager's pay is higher the higher are the firm's profits, which brings the goals of management in line with the goals of the firm's owners. The only problem is that pay based on profit is very risky for the manager. In a year when profits are low (or negative) – due to a recession, for example – the manager might not get paid anything at all, even though the manager worked to the peak of her ability. Thus there is a need to balance the needs of the owners to ensure performance from management against the desire for managers to have a reasonably secure income. For the time being we will ignore the issue of performance and assume that some scheme is in place at the firm which ensures managers act in the interests of the firm's owners. We will return to the issue of management performance in Chapter 15.

2.3 The market environment

We've had a good look inside the firm, and we've seen some of the issues that concern the operation of the firm, the structure and size of the firm, and ultimately why a firm might exist at all. Now let's take a step back and look at the environment within which the firm operates: the market.

We can neatly summarize the market within which a firm operates in Figure 2.1.[3] The firm itself is inside the box in the center of Figure 2.1. It has competitors which produce goods or services which compete directly

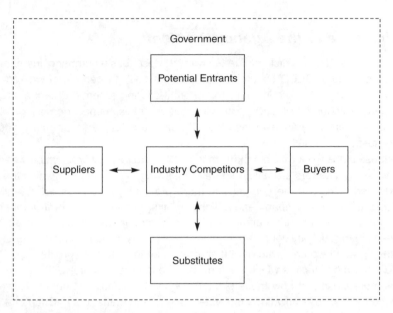

Figure 2.1 The market environment

with those produced by the firm. If we look across horizontally, the firm interacts on the one side with suppliers, and on the other side with buyers. If we look below the firm, we see that the firm faces competition from other firms which produce and sell goods which are substitutes for those produced by the firm. Above the firm, the threat of entry into the firm's market by other firms can affect the market in which the firm operates. In order to maximize profits, the manager of the firm must take into account all factors affecting all of these cells, and evaluate the importance of each.

For example, consider a firm producing and supplying power using coal-fired generators. It needs a supply of coal to produce its output. Thus it may be very important for the firm to negotiate some sort of alliance with one of its suppliers. In fact, we may see this firm setting up its production facility right next to a coal mine.

On the other hand, the relationship between a car maker and the supplier of tires for auto-mobiles may not be as important to the car maker, since there exist many different tire makers competing for the business of the car company. However, automobile manufac-turers in North America have had to pay sig-nificant attention to the behavior of entrants into the car industry from Japan and South Korea. So the manager in a car company might have to pay more attention to the beha-vior and structure of potential entrants.

By understanding all of the inter-relation-ships described in Figure 2.1, and determining which are the most important to a firm in a particular market, the manager gains import-ant insight into how managerial decisions affect the profitability of the firm.

2.4 *The role and effect of government*

There is one element of Figure 2.1 which we haven't discussed yet: encircling the market environment of the firm is the *government*. The modern corporation may be affected by the government in many different respects.

There may be regulations on the quality of the product or service sold by the firm, like building standards in the construction of houses, or licensing procedures for the manufacture of pharmaceuticals. There are regulations affecting how firms can dispose of wastes produced as a by-product of operations. There are regulations affecting how the firm treats its workers. And, of course, there are taxes that firms have to pay, such as the Goods and Services Tax (GST) and the Corporate Income Tax.

There is a broader issue which is important when considering the role of government. Suppose we look at the behavior of a particular market where there is no government intervention at all. Is there any scope for the government to step into this market and change the behavior of economic agents in this market in some way, so that the market outcome is in some way superior?

For example, suppose there were no regulations regarding the disposal of hazardous waste by a pulp and paper mill, and suppose we looked at the behavior of the pulp and paper market. The relevant agents in this market may be the pulp and paper mill, and consumers of its products. The interaction between agents in this market may well result in a market outcome where the firms produce pulp and paper which is purchased by consumers. But production of pulp and paper implies the production of hazardous waste, and it is costly for the pulp and paper mill to dispose of this waste. While consumers are better off because there is pulp and paper which they can consume, there is a negative element or *externality* associated with this outcome: the pollution implied by the improper disposal of hazardous waste. We may find that there is a role for the government to step into this market and regulate the way in which the firm disposes of hazardous waste. This disposal will be costly, so the firm would probably raise the price of pulp and paper. But consumers may be willing to pay this price if the elimination of the pollution is worth the extra cost.

On the other hand, we may describe a market outcome where the behavior or intervention of the government actually makes things worse. Government regulations exist in a number of different markets, and can take a number of different forms. For example, the government enforces a minimum price below which no firm can sell beer. This has the effect of limiting price competition in the beer market. The effects of government telecommunications regulators in Australia (Australian Communications Authority), France (L'Autorité de Régulation des Télécommunications), and Canada (the Canadian Radio-television and Telecommunications Commission or CRTC) have significant implications for the types of television and radio programming that is available to consumers in those countries.

In general, we will be interested in finding out if there are actions that a government can take which improve on a market outcome, or if there are actions which a government is taking which can be changed so as to improve on a market outcome.

Summary

- A firm is defined as a collection of groups of labor and capital which produce goods or services.
- Firms exist to take advantage of the benefits of increasing returns to scale.

> ***Summary contd***
>
> - There are organizational costs associated with increases in the size of a firm, including monitoring costs and eventually decreasing productivity of labor.
> - Decision-making within a firm must be consistent with the objectives of the firm, which include the maximization of profits.
> - An *agency problem* exists between owners of the firm and managers and workers when the objectives of owners are not consistent with the actions of managers and workers.
> - A simple profit-sharing plan can alleviate this agency problem.
> - The manager at the firm must understand the relative importance of all factors affecting the environment within which a firm operates (including competitors, suppliers of inputs, consumers, potential entrants, producers of close substitutes, and the role of the government) when formulating an appropriate business strategy.

Notes

1 See Microsoft Corporation Income Statement (1999) at http://www.microsoft.com/msft/ar99/income.htm.
2 There are many excellent references which discuss the relative benefits of team production versus the inherent monitoring costs. For example, see Alchian and Demsetz (1972) and Tirole (1988), Chapter 1, and the references therein.
3 This is a modified version of Figure 1.1 in Porter, Michael E. *Competitive Strategy: Techniques for Analyzing Industries and Competitors* (New York: The Free Press, 1980), p. 4.

Exercises

1 Suppose that all Internet Service Providers (ISPs) were required to have a license issued by the government, for which the government charged a price $\hat{p}$. If the government made $\hat{p}$ very large, would you expect there to be very many or very few ISPs in the market? Would each individual ISP be large or small? What do you think would happen to the size of the average ISP and the number of ISPs if the government reduced $\hat{p}$ by 95 percent?

2 In some large companies, managers are given the option of buying stock in their company at a pre-determined set price $\bar{s}$ per share.

(a) How might this strategy resolve the *agency problem* between owners and managers?

(b) What would happen if a crash in technology shares caused the stock price to fall below $\bar{s}$?

3 Use Figure 2.1 to identify the various factors affecting the market environment of:

(a) Microsoft Corporation

(b) Seagate Technology (manufacturer of hard disk drives)

(c) Qantas Airlines

(d) your favorite local Italian restaurant

In each case, which are the most important factors affecting a profit-maximizing manager's decision-making problem?

References

Alchian, A. and Demsetz, H. "Production, information costs, and economic organization." *American Economic Review*, 77 (1972), pp. 388–410.
Porter, Michael E. *Competitive Strategy: Techniques for Analyzing Industries and Competitors* (New York: The Free Press, 1980).
Tirole, Jean, *The Theory of Industrial Organization* (Cambridge, MA: The MIT Press, 1988), pp. 15–60.

Chapter 3

Monopoly and perfect competition

•••

When you are finished with this chapter you should understand:

- What is meant by the terms "market structure" and "market power"
- The difference between monopoly, oligopoly, and perfect competition
- Real-world examples of monopoly, oligopoly, and perfect competition
- The mathematical condition for profit maximization at a firm
- The relationship between average cost, average variable cost, average fixed cost curve, and marginal cost

This chapter serves two purposes. First, it is a starting point for our analysis of firms. Starting with Chapter 6, we are going to examine industries where there are just a few firms. In such industries each firm has to take into account the actions and reactions of its competitors. This is where strategy comes in. But analyzing strategy is complex, so we start in this chapter with two special cases where strategy doesn't come into play. This gives us an opportunity to introduce terms that will be used in subsequent chapters and it helps to put the subsequent material into perspective. A second purpose of the chapter is to provide a link back to introductory microeconomics courses. The two kinds of industry discussed in this chapter – monopoly and perfect competition – should be familiar to you from introductory microeconomics.

To put the material on monopoly and perfect competition into perspective, the first thing we do is look at the way economists classify markets or industries (the terms are more or less synonymous). This should provide you with a way of thinking about the material in the rest of the book. What you should get out of this section is the idea that, with the exception of monopoly and perfect competition, strategy is important in almost every other kind of industry. In developed economies, perfectly competitive and monopoly industries are extremely rare relative to other kinds of industries, which is why we spend much of the book looking at other industry types.

We then go on to discuss the fundamentals of a firm's profit maximization problem, which we talked about briefly in the last chapter. The point of the section is to get across the idea that firms, regardless of the kind of market in which they operate, all follow the same basic rules. We briefly digress into a discussion of the firm's cost function. Most of this material will be (vaguely?) familiar to you from your first-year course in economics. Once the cost curves are out of the way, we move on to discuss profit maximization. Then we look at the case of the monopoly firm, since it is perhaps the easiest case to analyze. When that is done we move on to perfect competition.

Many concepts used throughout the book are introduced in this chapter, so it is important that you understand the material here. And later on, if there is something you forget about cost or the basic rule of profit maximization, you can always come back to this chapter to jog your memory.

3.1 Classifying markets

All through the book we will use the terms *market* and *industry* synonymously. What do these terms mean? Roughly speaking, a market or industry is defined by the good or service being produced. We thus talk about the market for cars (or the car industry), or the market for legal services, or the market for labor services. This definition is very imprecise, but it will serve for the time being. In addition to the good or service being produced, economists classify an industry according to the *number of firms* the industry contains and the amount of *market power* possessed by each firm in the industry. The number of firms in an industry is a straightforward concept. Market power refers to the degree to which a firm controls the prices of the goods or services it produces.

The term "control" in the definition of market power is very significant. At first glance, you might think that every firm controls its own prices. But that ignores competition from other firms in the industry. In fact, owing to competition, most firms have only limited discretion over the prices they

set. For example, when General Motors (GM) sets the price of the Chevrolet Cavalier, it has to take into account the prices charged for cars that compete with the Cavalier, like the Ford Escort, the Toyota Corolla, the Honda Civic, and so on. Because GM competes with other firms, the price of the Cavalier is determined to some extent by the prices of models produced by other firms. Thus, economists say that GM does not have complete control over the price of the Cavalier. The same argument applies to any firm with at least one competitor: competition restricts the prices any one firm can charge, so the firm loses some discretion, or control, over its own price.

The market power of a firm is related to the number of firms in the industry. Roughly speaking, the more firms in an industry, the less control any single firm in the industry has over its prices. The smallest number of firms that can be in an industry is, obviously, one. You may recall from introductory microeconomics that an industry with one firm is called a *monopoly*. Examples of monopolies, especially in electricity generation and local telephone service, used to be commonplace in developed economies until the late 1980s. But waves of deregulation starting in the United States and the United Kingdom, and followed by other European countries, Canada, and Australia have removed monopoly power in power generation and telecommunications. Monopolies are more common in developing countries as in the case of Petróleos Mexicanos (Pemex), which is the monopoly supplier of gasoline in Mexico, or Telkom SA, which is the monopoly supplier of local telephone service in South Africa. Nowadays in developed countries, monopoly is more commonly found in the case of patents, which are legal monopolies created by government legislation. Because a monopoly has, by definition, no competitors, it is one of the few cases where the firm has complete control over its prices.[1]

The next smallest number of firms that can be in an industry is two, which is referred to as a *duopoly*. There are only two firms in the world, Boeing and Airbus, that produce large commercial airliners. Commercial airline manufacturing is, therefore, a duopoly. Firms in a duopoly have some control over their prices – after all they are only one firm away from a being monopoly – but neither firm can afford to ignore the prices charged by its rival. Thus, everything else being equal, the degree of price control for a duopoly firm is less than that of a monopoly firm.

Economists don't have different names for industries with three, or four, or other small numbers of firms – all are referred to as *oligopoly* industries. Oligopoly is by far the most common type of industry in most economies. Examples are automobile manufacturing, in which there are a dozen or so firms selling mass-produced cars worldwide (GM, Toyota, Ford, Chrysler, Mazda, Volkswagen, Honda, BMW, Mercedes–Benz, Hyundai, Renault), and cigarette manufacturing, in which there are half-a-dozen or so firms (British American Tobacco, RJ Reynolds, Philip Morris, Imperial Tobacco).

At the other end of the spectrum are industries with a very large number of firms. Generally speaking, these industries contain firms with little or no control over the prices they charge. In the case of perfect competition, an individual firm has absolutely no control over its price. Examples of perfectly competitive markets are typically found in financial markets and in markets for agricultural products. For example, individuals have no control over the price at which they lend (i.e. save) their money. A wheat farmer in Saskatchewan or South Australia has no control over the price

of durum semolina. Interest rates and wheat prices are set by market forces.

If a firm has some control over its price, price can be a strategic variable. That is, a firm with market power can manipulate its price, for example, to gain customers at the expense of rival firms. Under perfect competition, however, individual firms have no control whatsoever over the price, so a firm can't manipulate its price to gain an advantage over its competitors. If a firm can't set prices, how are prices determined? The answer is that price is determined in the market. In some ways, the absence of market power to firms in a perfectly competitive market is a lot like the absence of individual voter power in a democratic general election. The outcome of a democratic vote, i.e. which party is elected into government, is determined by the joint actions of all the individual voters and not by any one voter. Individual voters in a democracy lack any "market power" to dictate the outcome of the election in the same way that individual firms under perfect competition lack any market power to dictate the price.

Another aspect of market power is the degree of differentiation between products produced by competing firms in the same industry. We assume that firms in perfectly competitive industries produce identical or *homogeneous* products. If firms didn't produce identical products, then they could compete with one another on non-price aspects of their products, which would give them market power. But if firms produce an identical product, consumers will be indifferent between where they buy the product. Put another way, firms producing identical products cannot compete with one another in any aspect of their product except the price.

Homogeneous products are not unique to perfectly competitive industries: some

Table 3.1 Types of industry

Product	Number of firms		
	Many	*Several*	*One*
Homogeneous	Perfect competition (wheat farmers)	Homogeneous oligopoly (oil producers)	Monopoly (Pemex)
Differentiated	Monopolistic competition (restaurants)	Differentiated oligopoly (car producers)	

oligopoly industries produce homogeneous products. A good example is oil companies. They are a relatively small number of retail sellers of gasoline (and even fewer firms refining gasoline from crude oil). Most drivers are indifferent whether they buy their gas from, say, Shell or BP, implying they view the products to be homogeneous.

There is also a type of market structure that, like perfect competition, has a large number of firms, but unlike perfect competition the firms have some market power. This market structure is referred to as *monopolistic competition*. Market power arises because each of the firms are producing a slightly differentiated product. A good example is restaurants. Any medium-sized town has a large number of restaurants, all of which produce a slightly different product. Even if the type of cuisine is the same, restaurants can differentiate themselves by offering different quality food, a different ambience, or a different location. For example, think of the range of Italian restaurants where you live.

It is easy to see how an agricultural product, for example, is homogeneous. It would be impossible to identify which farm in South Australia was the origin of a specific grade of wheat in a grain elevator in Port Adelaide. However, most goods or services produced by firms in the same industry are not identical. For example, Heineken and Carlsberg go to great lengths, mainly through advertising,

to convince consumers that their beers are different. The degree of brand loyalty in the beer industry suggests that they are successful. Thus, consumers don't view Heineken and Carlsberg as identical products. And thousands of taste tests acclaim that Pepsi and Coke are not viewed as identical products either. We shall see later how *differentiated products*, as opposed to homogeneous products, play a critical strategic role.

The discussion of this section is summarized in Table 3.1. Really, there are only two things to remember. Market power increases as we move from left to right in the table, because, everything else equal, market power is inversely related to the number of firms in the industry. Market power also increases moving from top to bottom of the table, because, everything else equal, market power is greater for firms producing differentiated products. The table also gives examples of each market type.

3.2 The basic profit maximization problem

Pick a firm at random in the economy. It could be a large multinational like ExxonMobil, a small law firm in your local town, a regional chain of pizza restaurants, whatever. As we said in Chapter 2, the manager at any firm maximizes profit (π). It doesn't matter whether the firm operates in a perfectly competitive, an oligopoly, or a monopoly market: we assume profit maximization is the manager's goal. Because profit is revenue (r) minus cost (c), the manager's task is to maximize:

$$\pi = r - c$$

3.2.1 Profit

It is important to remember that π stands for *economic profit* and not any other measure of profit, such as accounting profit. The key difference is that economic profit measures the costs of production by current *opportunity costs*. The opportunity cost of something used for production is the price it could command in an alternative activity. In most cases, what the firm pays out for, say, labor, is also the opportunity cost. But problems can arise in the case of owner-operated businesses.

If someone works in their own business, economic profit measures the cost of their time by the wage they could earn elsewhere. By working in their own business, they have given up the opportunity of working somewhere else. Similarly, if someone invests money in their own business, economic profit treats the money as a loan to the business at the existing market rate of interest. By investing in the business, they have given up the opportunity of investing elsewhere.

Economic profit also rules out using historical costs. All costs are measured at the going rate, not what the firm originally paid. For example, suppose a taxi company purchased a million liters of gasoline at 60 cents per liter and thereafter the price rose to 75 cents a liter. In this case, the calculation of economic profit measures the cost of gasoline to the taxi company using the price of 75 cents a liter.

This isn't to say that accounting profit is "wrong" and economic profit is "right." Each measure serves different purposes. The idea of economic profit is to get an accurate measure of the ongoing viability of the business. Accounting measures may have other concerns like auditing, taxation, and so forth.

3.2.2 Revenue

Assuming (for now) that the firm is producing only one type of good, and that the firm is charging a single price for the good, revenue equals the amount produced times price at which it is sold:[2]

$$r = pq \tag{3.1}$$

Firms cannot set the price and expect to sell anything other than the amount that consumers are willing to purchase at that price. In other words, firms have to take demand for the product as given. Suppose the firm faces a demand curve $q = D(p)$ with inverse demand given by $p = P(q)$. Substituting for the price using inverse demand into (3.1) gives:

$$r = P(q)q$$

Revenue is thus a function of q times q, so may as well write it in a more compact form:

$$r = r(q) \tag{3.2}$$

which just says that revenue depends on q. The price is subsumed into the q term, as illustrated in the following example.

Example

Consider the inverse demand curve $p = a - bq$, which is just a standard linear demand curve. In this case, $r = pq = (a - bq)q = aq - bq^2$. After substituting for p, which is a function of q, the revenue function depends only on q.

3.2.3 Cost

Cost depends on the amounts of each of the *inputs* hired for production and their corresponding prices. Inputs are anything firms use in production like workers, raw materials, electricity, machinery, and so on. The amounts of the inputs hired in turn depend on the amount of output the firm produces.[3] We assume, for the time being, that input prices are fixed. Thus, cost is ultimately determined by the amount of output produced. Hence, for the purposes of the manager's problem, cost is simply a function of output:

$$c = c(q)$$

Example

A cost function that we will encounter frequently in examples throughout the book is linear in output: $c = a + bq$, where $a > 0$ and $b > 0$. Another commonly used cost function is a quadratic function of output $C = d + eq^2$, where $d > 0$ and $e > 0$. In both these examples, note that the firm incurs a cost even if it produces nothing. In the first case, $c = a$ when $q = 0$, and in the second case, $c = d$ when $q = 0$. We'll say more about this soon.

Before we solve the profit maximization problem, we shall briefly discuss more about the firm's costs. There are a couple of reasons for doing this. First, it is a logical place in the book to introduce cost concepts that will be used throughout the analysis. The material covered in this section applies to any firm. Second, a detailed discussion of costs is necessary in order to introduce diagrammatic analysis, something we use extensively in the book.

When we talk about the cost of production, it is important to distinguish between costs that can be changed immediately and those that can only be changed after a period of time. In the *short-run*, the firm may be stuck with a given size of office space, or warehouse facilities, because it isn't feasible to alter them immediately. Alternatively, the firm may have signed multi-year leases on property, machinery, or office equipment, none of which can be altered in the short run. In the short run, therefore, some inputs are fixed. The costs associated with these inputs are called *fixed costs*. Because the firm can't get rid of the fixed inputs in the short run, fixed costs have to be paid even if the firm produces no output at all.

Of course, not all inputs are fixed in the short run. For example, labor time can be varied from day to day according to the amount of work that has to be done. Costs associated with inputs that can be changed in the short run are called *variable costs*. The firm can always avoid paying variable costs by hiring no variable inputs. We assume that the firm cannot produce anything without variable inputs, and that, the more variable inputs that are hired, the more output produced. Thus, if the firm were to *shut down* (produce nothing) then variable costs will be zero.

In the *long run*, there are no fixed inputs by definition. Leases can be allowed to expire and leased equipment returned or upgraded. Likewise the firm can change its location by leasing or buying new property. And of course anything that can be changed in the short run can also be changed in the long run. In the long run, therefore, all costs are variable costs. By definition, fixed costs only show up in the short run.

The distinction between short run and long run simply has to do with whether the firm has any fixed inputs: in the short run some inputs are fixed, in the long run all inputs are variable. There is no specific time period applying to the short run or long run. The long run for a take-out pizza restaurant may be only a matter of months – as long as it takes to get out of the lease on the premises and move the ovens. But the long run for an automobile plant is likely to be a lot longer. In order to locate a car manufacturing plant, and then design, build, and bring the plant on line may take three or four years.

We can now write the firm's short run cost function as:

$$c(q) = c_F + c_V(q) \qquad (3.3)$$

where c_V stands for variable costs and c_F for fixed costs. Fixed costs are constant and, consequently, don't vary with the level of output.[4] Variable costs, on the other hand, vary according to the amount of output produced. More output requires more variable inputs, which increases variable costs. Total cost $c(q)$ is just the sum of fixed and variable costs.

Average cost curves

It turns out to be more useful to look, not at the total cost of production, as given in (3.3), but at the average costs of production. To do this, we simply divide equation (3.3) by the amount of output (q):

$$\frac{c(q)}{q} = \frac{c_F}{q} + \frac{c_V(q)}{q} \qquad (3.4)$$

On the left-hand side is the *average cost (AC)* of production. This is sometimes called the *unit cost* of production, because $c(q)/q$ is just the cost per unit of producing q units. The expressions on the right-hand side are called, respectively, *average fixed cost (AFC)* and *average variable cost (AVC)*, for obvious reasons. Thus, we can write:

$$AC = AFC + AVC$$

Figure 3.1 graphs the short run average cost curves. Average fixed cost always has the shape shown in the left-hand panel of Figure 3.1. When $q = 0$, average fixed cost is infinite, and as q increases from zero average fixed cost falls as the fixed costs c_F are divided by more and more units of output.

Average variable cost is shown as falling at first and then increasing. This may be regarded as a typical case, although it is also possible that average variable costs are constant and then increase. The important point is that average variable costs eventually increase. Why is this? Recall in the short run that there is at least one fixed input at the firm. Consider a firm that is producing, say, cars with workers and where the fixed input is the factory. In principle, output can be increased by adding more workers. As long as the factory is big enough, it should be possible to add, say, 10 percent more workers to get 10 percent more output. This would increase variable cost by 10 percent and leave the average variable cost unchanged, giving a flat region for the average variable cost function. In fact, if production could be set up more efficiently, meaning output goes up by more than 10 percent when 10 percent more workers are added, average variable costs might even fall initially, as shown.

But if the firm wanted to increase output further, eventually the fixed factory size would become a constraint. Adding more workers into a crowded factory will require even more workers than before to get the same increase in output. In other words, to get another, say, 10 percent in output might require 15 percent more workers. But this means that average variable cost increases. Thus, the presence of a fixed factor means that average variable costs eventually increase, as shown in Figure 3.1.

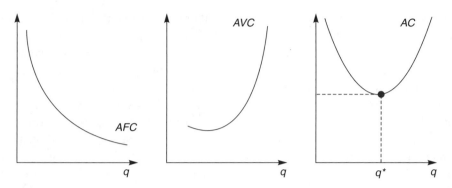

Figure 3.1 Average cost curves

Because average cost (*AC*) is the sum of average fixed cost and average variable cost, as is shown in equation (3.4), it should be clear from the two left-hand panels of Figure 3.1, that, when the two are added together, the average cost curve will have the U-shape depicted in the right-hand panel. The falling average fixed cost is eventually offset at higher levels of output by the rising average variable cost, implying the average cost curve first falls then rises.

As we have seen, average cost falls owing to the presence of fixed costs. When average costs fall, we say that there are *economies of scale* in production. Thus, the presence of fixed costs gives rise to economies of scale. In Figure 3.1, economies of scale exist for the range of output from $q = 0$ to $q = q^*$. Economies of scale are a very important concept that we'll encounter time and again throughout the book. Make sure you understand what economies of scale are and where they come from. Note also, that if there were no fixed costs, the average cost and average variable cost would be one and the same.

Marginal cost curve

There is one more cost curve that is very useful for analyzing a firm's costs. The *mar-*

ginal cost (*MC*) is defined as the derivative of the total cost with respect to the output level:

$$MC = \frac{dc(q)}{dq} \tag{3.5}$$

In words, marginal cost is the increase in cost resulting from an increase in output of one unit. It could also be called the incremental cost. Recall that, by definition, fixed cost does not change with the output level. It is equivalent to say, therefore, that marginal cost is the increase in variable cost resulting from an increase in output of one unit.

A typical marginal cost curve is shown in Figure 3.2 together with the average cost and

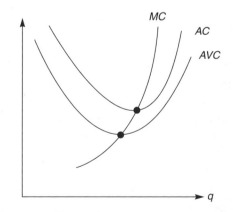

Figure 3.2 Marginal and average cost curves

average variable cost curve. As you can see, the marginal cost curve passes through the minimum point of both the average curves. This is no accident. To see why this is so, consider moving along the average variable cost curve. If the average variable cost curve is falling, it must be that the cost of the extra unit produced is below the average to that point. In order for the average to fall, additional units must cost less than the average. On the other hand, if the average is rising, it must be that the cost of an extra unit produced is above the average to that point. To bring the average up, additional units must cost more than the average.[5]

Putting the argument together, it follows that average variable cost is falling when marginal cost is below it, and rising when marginal cost is above it. Only when average variable cost is neither rising nor falling, i.e. when average variable cost is at its minimum, can marginal cost and average variable cost be equal. Thus, the marginal cost curve passes through the minimum point of the average variable cost curve. The same argument applies to the average cost curve: when it is falling, marginal cost lies below it, and when it is rising, marginal cost lies above it.

average variable cost: $AVC = a$
average cost: $AC = f/q + a$

Taking the derivative of the cost function with respect to q yields marginal cost:

marginal cost: $MC = a$

Figure 3.3 shows the average and marginal cost functions for this example. Notice that average variable cost is constant and equal to marginal cost. This special case will be used frequently through the book in order to illustrate examples.

In the next example, the cost function is a quadratic function of output:

$$c(q) = f + bq^2, \quad b > 0$$

Obviously, fixed cost and average fixed cost are the same as before. Also:

variable cost: $c_V = bq^2$
average variable cost: $AVC = bq$
average cost: $AC = f/q + bq$

Taking the derivative of the cost function with respect to q yields marginal cost:

marginal cost: $MC = 2bq$

Examples

To keep these concepts straight, let's look at a couple of examples. In the first case, let the firm's cost function be a linear function of output:

$$c(q) = f + aq, \quad a > 0$$

From this it is easy to determine:

fixed cost: $c_F = f$
average fixed cost: $AFC = f/q$
variable cost: $c_V = aq$

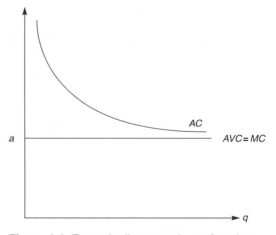

Figure 3.3 Example: linear total cost function

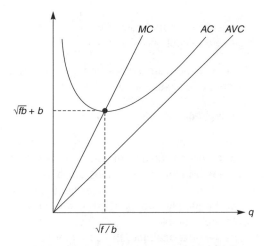

Figure 3.4   Example: quadratic total cost function

Figure 3.4 shows the average and marginal cost functions for this example. In this case, marginal cost and average cost are linear and increasing functions, with marginal cost rising twice as fast as average variable cost.

3.2.4 Profit maximization

We are now in a position to state formally the manager's profit maximization problem:

$$\max_{q} \pi = r(q) - c(q)$$

The problem is, therefore, to choose the level of output that maximizes the difference between revenue and cost. Recall that this problem is, basically, the same for any firm – large or small – operating in any kind of market – monopoly, perfect competition, or any of the other kinds of markets we will encounter through the book.

The first-order condition for this maximization problem gives:

$$\frac{dr(q)}{dq} - \frac{dc(q)}{dq} = 0 \qquad (3.6)$$

The second expression is the derivative of the cost function with respect to q, which is just marginal cost. The first expression is the derivative of the revenue function with respect to q, which, not surprisingly, is called *marginal revenue*. Adding marginal cost to both sides of (3.6) and using MR to stand for marginal revenue, the first-order condition may be written:

$$MR(q) = MC(q) \qquad (3.7)$$

This condition simply states that, in order to maximize profit, a firm will choose the level of output such that marginal revenue equals marginal cost. Equation (3.7) is probably the single most important condition in the book: it is the profit maximizing condition for any type of firm. Be sure you remember it.

It's easy to see the intuition for this result. Recall that marginal cost represents the addition to the firm's cost from increasing output one unit. Likewise, marginal revenue represents the addition to the firm's revenue from increasing output one unit. Now suppose the firm is producing at a level of output where $MR \neq MC$. It could be that $MR > MC$ or $MR < MC$.

If $MR > MC$, then by increasing output one unit, the firm will add more to revenue than to costs. This means that profit will go up if the extra unit is produced. In fact, as long as $MR > MC$, the firm can increase profit by increasing output. On the other hand, if $MR < MC$, the firm can increase profit by decreasing output: the cost savings from producing one less unit are larger than the revenue losses from not selling the unit. So, if $MR > MC$, the firm can increase profit by raising output, and if $MR < MC$, the firm can increase profit by decreasing output. It follows that profits are maximized when $MR = MC$.

With this knowledge behind us, let's now turn to two types of market you are probably familiar with from your first-year course: monopoly and perfect competition.

3.3 Monopoly

Monopolies may arise for a variety of reasons. In the case of De Beers, which controls over 80 percent of the world's diamond supply, monopoly arises from the control of a particular resource. Alternatively, a firm may develop a product or service that has never existed before. Until competing firms develop a rival product, the first firm has a monopoly. For example, when Sony developed the Walkman in the early 1980s, it was several months before Panasonic and JVC were able to bring personal stereos to the marketplace. In the meantime, Sony effectively had a monopoly in the personal stereo market. Similarly, when 3M developed the Post-It line of adhesive labels, it was several months before competing products appeared. Until the rival products appeared, 3M had a monopoly over the market for self-adhesive labels. In these examples, the monopoly lasts only a short time until rival firms enter the market. But sometimes when a firm develops a new product, it may be awarded a *patent* by the government. The patent effectively prevents rival firms from producing a similar product for a fixed period of time. For example, patent protection lasts 20 years in most countries that are members of the WTO.[6] Patent monopolies are common in the pharmaceutical industry, where they are granted for specific drugs like Prozac (Eli Lilly), and in agriculture, where they are granted for genetically modified crops like Round-Up Ready canola (Monsanto).

Another reason monopolies arise is because, in some cases, a single firm is the most cost-effective way to serve the market. Take the case of local telephone service. Before the advent of the cell (mobile) phone in the late 1980s, monopolies were the rule for local telephone service for this very reason. To see why, consider what would happen if there were two providers of local telephone service in a town. Since there wouldn't be much use having a telephone service that only allowed you to reach half the telephone numbers, every home and every office building would need to have access to both services. But this would mean two sets of telephone wires for every home and office building. From the standpoint of production, this is clearly less efficient than having everyone served by a single set of lines. In this example, a monopoly may be able to provide the same service at a lower cost to the community. Instances where costs are lower if there is only one firm in the industry are referred to as *natural monopolies*. As it turned out, the technological change represented by the cell phone allowed telephone networks to be established at much lower cost, since it is much cheaper to put up a few radio transmitters than it is to string wires into every home and office building. The result is that in many countries consumers now have a choice of which local phone company to use.[7] That is, the natural monopoly vanished following a change in technology.[8]

The source of monopoly power will make a difference to the strategy at the firm. For example, a firm with a patent, or a firm with a natural monopoly can ignore competition for a long period of time. A 20-year patent is a very long time to have protection from competing products. A natural monopoly has very little to fear from competition unless there is a technological breakthrough. Compared with firms introducing a new product, natural monopolies and firms with patents are insulated from competition. As stressed in the opening chapter, competition among rival firms means strategy comes into play. Our purpose is not to introduce any strategic considerations until Chapter 6. Thus, we focus here on a monopoly that is guaranteed for many years – either through patent or by way of a natural monopoly – and leave the case of the firm with a short-lived monopoly following the introduction of a new product until Chapter 10.

Let's summarize the above discussion by making the following monopoly assumptions:

- there is one firm in the industry
- firms are *not* free to enter the industry

The first assumption is just the definition of a monopoly. The second assumption guarantees that the monopoly will persist. If firms could enter a monopoly industry, i.e. produce the same good or service the monopoly is producing, the industry would cease to be a monopoly. For a firm to maintain a monopoly there must be *barriers to entry* that prevent other firms from entering the industry. Examples of barriers to entry have already been given: a patent or the presence of a natural monopoly prevents the entry of firms into a market and, thus, constitute barriers to entry.

3.3.1 Optimum at the firm

The profit maximization problem for the monopoly is just:

$$\max_q \pi = r(q) - c(q) \tag{3.8}$$

which is exactly the same as the basic problem we looked at above. We know the first-order condition to this problem gives the condition:

$$MR(q) = MC(q) \tag{3.9}$$

which states that the monopoly produces the output level where marginal revenue equals marginal cost.

We can actually be a little more specific about the profit maximization condition for a monopoly. To see this, write out the expression for the revenue of the monopoly. Recall revenue is $p \times q$. Also, since monopoly means there is only firm in the market, the demand curve for the monopoly firm is just the market demand curve $q = D(p)$. Thus, the monopoly has to determine its price from the inverse demand curve, so $p = P(q)$. The revenue function for a monopoly, therefore, is $r(q) = P(q)q$. Taking the derivative of the revenue function with respect to q gives marginal revenue. Thus, using chain rule of differentiation on the revenue function, the first-order condition (3.7) may be written:

$$P(q) + \frac{dP(q)}{dq}q = MC(q) \tag{3.10}$$

The expression on the left-hand side requires a little bit of discussion.

There are two effects on revenue when a monopoly increases output by one unit. First, revenue increases by the amount of the price that the extra unit can be sold to consumers. Second, in order to sell the extra unit, the monopoly has to cut the price it charges on the units it sold prior to the output increase. Each effect is shown on the left-hand side of equation (3.10). The increase in revenue on the extra unit sold is represented by the term $P(q)$. The cut in price is represented by the term $dP(q)/dq$. Hence, the decrease in revenue represented by the price cut applied to all q units sold prior to the output increase is equal to $dP(q)/dq$ times q, which is the second term. All that we've done here is break down the marginal revenue effect

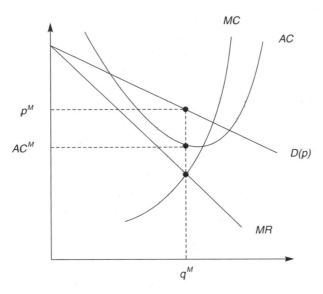

Figure 3.5 Optimum for a monopoly firm

into two components. Adding these two effects together gives the marginal revenue of production.

There is one other thing to see from equation (3.10). The first term is the price from the equation for the demand curve. Since the demand curve has a negative slope, $dP(q)/dq < 0$, which means that the second term is negative. Therefore, for any value of q, $MR(q)$ is less than $P(q)$. Geometrically, this means that $MR(q)$ lies below the demand curve $D(p)$.

The profit maximization solution for a monopoly can be illustrated graphically using our knowledge of cost curves and the maximization condition in (3.7). As you can see from Figure 3.5 the profit maximizing output level for the monopoly occurs at the output level where MR and MC intersect, reflecting (3.7). The monopoly determines its price from the demand curve. Given the output of q^M, price is p^M.

If the monopoly isn't making a profit at the output level q^M, it will leave the industry in the long run. The more likely case, how-

ever, is that the monopoly is making economic profits at q^M. This is illustrated in Figure 3.5. Notice that the price the monopoly charges p^M is greater than the average cost of production AC^M at the profit maximizing output level q^M. Thus $p^M > AC^M$, so multiplying both sides by q^M we have:

$$p^M q^M > AC^M q^M$$

The expression of the left-hand side is the revenue to the monopoly from selling q^M units, or $r(q^M)$. Using the definition of average cost, $AC^M = c(q^M)/q^M$, which implies $c(q^M) = AC^M q^M$. The expression on the right-hand side is, therefore, the cost of producing q^M units $c(q^M)$. Thus, $r(q^M) > c(q^M)$, and it follows that $\pi > 0$ for q^M units of output.

Ordinarily, positive economic profits would attract other firms to the industry. But, to keep things simple for now, we have assumed that other firms are not free to enter this industry. Since no other firms will enter this industry, the short run and long run for this monopoly look identical.[9] On the other hand, we'll see that in the case of perfect competition, there is an important distinction between the short run and the long run.

3.4 Perfect competition

Formally, a perfectly competitive industry is described by the following assumptions:

- there are many firms in the market
- firms have no market power
- firms produce homogeneous products
- firms are free to enter or exit the industry

Each of these assumptions is critical to the structure of perfect competition. It is important to understand the role of these assumptions, because they are linked to the ideas developed in the rest of the book. Basically, the purpose of the first three assumptions is to prevent any development of strategic behavior. As we discussed in the opening section of the chapter, large numbers of firms with no market power producing a homogeneous product mean that no one firm can dictate the price.

Freedom to enter or exit the industry ensures that there is no market power in the long run. Put another way, we say there are no barriers to entry or *barriers to exit*. As discussed before, barriers to entry may exist because of costs, regulation, or strategic behavior by firms already in the industry. Barriers to exit prevent firms from leaving an industry. For example, a power generation company may be forced by law to supply electricity to a remote community even though it is unprofitable for the company.[10]

3.4.1 Optimum at a firm

We can write the profit maximization problem for a firm in a perfectly competitive industry in the usual way:

$$\max_{q} \pi = r(q) - c(q) \tag{3.11}$$

and the first-order condition is the same as before. The firm sets output according to:

$$MR(q) = MC(q) \tag{3.12}$$

Foreign Exchange Markets

Roughly \$400 billion (€440) passes through foreign exchange markets in the world in *one day* To give you an idea of the magnitude of this figure, it is roughly equal to the total value of all the goods and services produced in the Australian economy in *one year*. So, when someone goes down to their local bank branch to buy some US dollars for a vacation in Florida, the resulting exchange of their currency for US dollars is a drop in the ocean compared with overall trading on the two currencies in any one day. Because individual transactions on foreign exchange markets are infinitesimal compared with the market as a whole, it follows that no one person can dictate the price at which the currencies are exchanged. Occasionally, governments intervene in foreign exchange markets and exert some influence on exchange rates through sheer size of purchasing power. But no private buyer or seller of foreign exchange has any such market power. In this case, the second assumption of a perfectly competitive market is satisfied.

Money is money the world around: one person's US dollars are treated the same as anyone else's, satisfying the third assumption. Lastly, in most developed economies there are no restrictions on who can buy or sell US dollars, satisfying the free entry and exit assumption. Thus, the market for US dollars satisfies the four assumptions of a perfectly competitive market.

Owing to the assumption that firms under perfect competition have no market power, each firm in the industry takes the price as given. In other words, each firm sets its price at the level p determined in the market. This means that the extra revenue the firm gets from selling one more unit of the good is just p, that is, $MR(q) = p$. The first-order condition, therefore, can be written:

$$p = MC(q) \qquad (3.13)$$

Equation (3.13) simply states that a firm under perfect competition produces output where market price equals marginal cost, as illustrated in Figure 3.6 for a market price of p^*. In this example, q^* is the profit-maximizing output. Note that this really isn't very different from the monopoly case: all that happens is marginal revenue is replaced by the price, which is fixed at the market level.

The condition (3.13) may be used to derive the firm's supply function. A different market price of p' simply changes the left-hand side of equation (3.13). The firm decreases production if $p' < p^*$ (or increases production if $p' > p^*$), until equality between marginal cost and price is re-established. But this means that marginal cost in Figure 3.6 traces out a relationship between price and production, which, by definition, is the firm's supply function.

Actually, there is a little bit more to the supply function than that. There are cases when the firm may not wish to supply anything at all. Suppose the firm is making a loss at the "profit-maximizing" output. It always has the option of shutting down. If it shuts down, the firm simply gets rid of all its variable inputs: it lays-off workers, turns off the power, cancels delivery of materials, and so on. So variable cost c_V drops to zero. But the firm still incurs the fixed cost. By definition, the firm is committed to paying the fixed cost – perhaps because of a contractual obligation arising from a lease, or loan repayments – regardless of whether it produces any output at all.

Given the firm is going to lose money if it shuts down and lose money if it operates, what should the firm do? The obvious answer is to choose the option that gives smaller losses. If the firm shuts down, profit equal the fixed cost, $-c_F$. If the firm operates, profit equals $pq - c_V - c_F$. The firm will shut down if:

$$pq - c_V - c_F < -c_F$$

Adding c_F to both sides and rearranging, the shut-down condition is:

$$pq < c_V$$

Dividing by q gives c_V/q on the right-hand side, which is just average variable cost. Thus, the firm will shut down if:

$$p < AVC$$

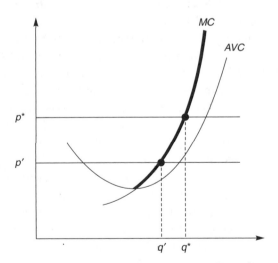

Figure 3.6 Optimum for a firm under perfect competition

As long as price is greater than average variable cost the firm will produce the level of output where $p = MC(q)$. If price is lower than average variable cost, the firm produces nothing. The firm's supply curve, therefore, is the marginal cost curve above the average variable cost curve, shown as the thick portion of the marginal cost curve in Figure 3.6.

3.4.2 Industry equilibrium in the short run

The question is: how is market price determined? An *equilibrium* in an industry is represented by the intersection of the market supply curve and the market demand curve. The market supply curve is simply the sum of all the supply curves (or marginal cost curves) for individual firms in the industry. Similarly, the market demand curve is just the demand curves of individual consumers summed across all consumers in the market.[11] As shown in Figure 3.7, the intersection of the supply curve S and the demand curve D determines the equilibrium price p^* and the equilibrium quantity q^*.

Price is determined by the joint actions of all the participants in the market – the firms and the consumers – with no single participant being able to dictate the outcome.

3.4.3 Industry equilibrium in the long run

The short-run equilibrium in the industry, shown in Figure 3.7, and the corresponding optimum for a representative firm, shown in Figure 3.6, is not necessarily the end of the story. Suppose that firms are making a profit

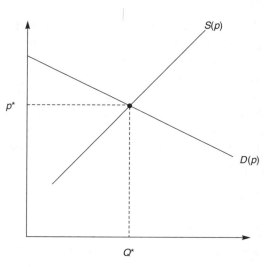

Figure 3.7 Market equilibrium under perfect competition

at the market price p^*. In other words, suppose that $p^* > AC^*$ at q^* units of output. This will attract the attention of firms outside the industry. Since firms are free to enter the industry, some of these outside firms will start producing the same good. Of course, as more firms enter the industry, supply increases and this will cause the price to fall from p^*. Eventually, the price will fall far enough to drive profit for all firms in the industry to zero. At this point new firms no longer have an incentive to start producing in the industry. Thus, long-run equilibrium is attained: the number of firms in the industry stops changing, and each firm makes zero profit.

If, conversely, the original firms in the industry are losing money at the price p^*, the whole process works in reverse. Losses induce some firms to leave the industry. As a result, the supply curve shifts to the left and the price rises. Eventually, the price rises far enough to eliminate losses, and the industry settles down to long-run equilibrium where all firms make zero profit.

Summary

- Monopoly and perfect competition are two limiting cases of market structure. Generally speaking, market power decreases with the number of firms in the industry and increases with the degree of product differentiation.
- The manager's objective is to maximize the economic profit of the firm, which implies producing the level of output at which marginal revenue equals marginal cost.
- The firm's costs are described using the average cost, average variable cost, and average fixed cost curve. The marginal cost curve passes through the minimum of the average cost and average variable cost curve.
- Monopoly can arise from new goods or services, patents, and for technological reasons. Only the latter two are likely to last for very long.
- A monopoly firm produces at the level of output at which marginal revenue equals marginal cost. Positive economic profits will persist for the monopoly in the long run if there are barriers to entry.
- Perfect competition is characterized by a large number of firms. No firm has any market power and price is determined by demand and supply. Positive or negative economic profits will not persist in the long run because firms will enter or exit the industry and the equilibrium market price will adjust so that zero profits eventually prevail.

Notes

1 Of course, this ignores the possibility that the prices the monopoly charges are regulated by a government agency. We go into this issue in more detail in Chapter 11, which discusses regulation.

2 To keep things simple, we assume that everything produced is sold, i.e. there is no unsold inventory.

3 The mathematical relationship between the amount of inputs and the resulting amount of output is represented by the production function, which is discussed in detail in Chapter 14.

4 The terms a and d in the cost function example represent fixed costs.

5 Think about a professor marking midterms. If the next exam has a lower grade than the average grade for the midterms already marked, the average including the newly marked exam must be lower. If the next exam has a higher grade than the average for those already marked, the average including the new exam must be higher.

6 Patents are discussed in more detail in Chapter 11.

7 Cable TV is similar natural monopoly that has been almost eliminated by technological change. The development of low-cost satellite television service is threatening the monopoly of the cable delivery services.

8 Natural monopolies are discussed in much more detail in Chapter 11.

9 Of course, demand may shift, and this would have an effect on the profit maximizing output.

10 In this case, the company uses the profits obtained from their other consumers to cover the loss. Thus, remote electricity consumers are effectively subsidized by other, non-remote users. Whether such cross-subsidization is beneficial for society as a whole is a question that we will not address here.

11 Adding supply curves across firms or demand curves across consumers must be done in terms of units of the good. Since Q is on the horizontal axis, adding supply curves and demand

curves across Q is referred to as *horizontal summation*.

Exercises

1 Fill in the five cells of Table 3.1 with examples of your own. That is, give examples of homogeneous products producing industries with many and a few firms, examples of differentiated products producing industries with many and a few firms, and a monopoly industry.

2 Suppose a firm faces an inverse demand given by $p = 10 - 2q$. Calculate the firm's revenue (r) function. Plot the revenue function by calculating the points on the function for $q = 0, 1, 2, 3, 4, 5$ and drawing a smooth line between the points.

3 Suppose a firm has a cost function given by $c = 5 + q$.

  (a) Is this a short-run or long-run cost function? Explain.

  (b) Determine the fixed cost (c_F) and variable cost (c_V) functions.

  (c) Determine the average fixed cost (AFC), average variable cost (AVC), and average cost (AC) functions.

  (d) Determine the marginal cost (MC) function.

4 Suppose a firm has a cost function given by $c = 2q^2$.

  (a) Is this a short-run or long-run cost function? Explain.

  (b) Determine the fixed cost (c_F) and variable cost (c_V) functions.

  (c) Determine the average fixed cost (AFC), average variable cost (AVC), and average cost (AC) functions.

  (d) Determine the marginal cost (MC) function.

5 Suppose a firm facing inverse demand curve $p = 10 - 2q$ has a cost function given by $c = 5 + q$.

  (a) Determine the firm's revenue (r) function.

  (b) Determine the firm's profit maximizing output level.

  (c) Determine the price the firm will choose to set.

  (d) Calculate the firm's cost, revenue, and profit at the profit maximizing output level.

6 Suppose a firm facing inverse demand curve $p = 10 - 2q$ has a cost function given by $c = 2q^2$.

  (a) Determine the firm's revenue function.

  (b) Determine the firm's profit maximizing output level.

  (c) Determine the price the firm will choose to set.

  (d) Calculate the firm's cost, revenue, and profit at the profit maximizing output level.

7 Suppose an industry has only one firm with a cost function given by $c = 100 + 9q^2$. The inverse demand curve for the industry is given by $p = 20 - q$.

  (a) Determine the profit maximizing output level for the monopoly.

  (b) Determine the price the firm will charge, and the profit level at the firm.

  (c) In the long run, will this firm choose to stay in the industry? Explain.

  (d) Will other firms be attracted to the industry? Explain.

8 Suppose a perfectly competitive industry is made up of 100 firms. Suppose each firm has a cost function given by $c = q^2$. Suppose also that the inverse demand curve *for the industry* is given by $p = 10 - 0.02Q$.

(a) Determine each firm's marginal cost curve.

(b) Determine the equation for each firm's supply curve.

(c) Determine the equation for the industry supply curve.

(d) Determine the equilibrium price and quantity in the industry.

(e) Determine the output and profits of each firm.

(f) Does this represent a long-run equilibrium in the industry? Explain.

References

Tirole, Jean. *The Theory of Industrial Organization* (Cambridge, MA: MIT Press, 1988).

Hal R. Varian. *Intermediate Microeconomics*, 5th edn (New York: W. W. Norton and Company, 1999).

Chapter 4

Price discrimination

●●

When you are finished with this chapter you should understand:

- What is meant by the term "price discrimination"
- The conditions under which a firm may practice price discrimination
- The difference between first-, second-, and third-degree price discrimination
- Real-world examples of price discrimination
- The inverse-elasticity rule of third-degree price discrimination
- How to use demand elasticities to solve for a firm's optimal price

The next time you get on a plane to fly somewhere, ask the persons next to you how much they paid for their ticket.[1] Chances are, what they paid for their ticket is not what you paid for yours. Even though both of you are flying to the same destination and receiving exactly the same kind of service, each has paid a different price. Whenever different prices are charged to different consumers for the same good or service, economists say that *price discrimination* has occurred. Examples of price discrimination are common. Apart from airline tickets, price discrimination is found for hotel rooms, car rentals, and rail tickets.[2]

The purpose of this chapter is to discuss the reasons for price discrimination and the different types of price discrimination. The basic reason firms practice price discrimination is to get extra revenue (and, therefore, profit) from customers that they would not be able to do if they charged the same price to everyone. At one extreme, firms may be able to charge different prices to every individual consumer in the market. This kind of price discrimination can only be practiced for small numbers of consumers, say in the market for dental services in a small remote community. In this case, a dentist may charge a high price for the richest consumer in town, a lower price for the next richest person, and so on. Of course, this requires a good deal of information on the part of the dentist, but it's the sort of information that might be well known (or at least easy to figure out) in a small community. The point is, by price discriminating, the dentist is able to get more revenue from her customers than if she simply charged the same price to everyone in town. If a *uniform price* were charged, she might lose some customers by setting too high a price, or not get enough payment from her richer customers if the price were set too low.

Another form of price discrimination is the *two-part tariff*. A two-part tariff exists when firms charge an initial fee for access to the good or service and an additional fee for each unit of the good or service that the customer buys. Many firms providing access to the Internet have a two-part tariff structure to their prices: a fixed monthly access fee together with a fee per minute of connect time. Another example of a two-part tariff is practiced by consumer warehouse companies like Costco that charge an annual membership fee. Once the fee is paid, customers can purchase as much of the discount-priced items carried by the chain as they wish. As we shall see, the purpose of a two-part tariff is the same as that of charging every single consumer a different price: getting more revenue from customers, and hence more profit, than could be achieved from charging a uniform price.

Yet another kind of price discrimination occurs when firms are able to discriminate among various types of consumers on the basis of observable characteristics of the consumers, such as their age, or their location. Charging business travelers different prices for the same class of seat than vacationers on an airline flight is one example of this kind of price discrimination. Business travelers are distinguished from vacationers because they typically buy their tickets at the last moment and don't want to stay over on a Saturday night. Airlines typically offer cheap fares only on reservations made three weeks in advance for travel including a stay over on a Saturday night. This way, the observable characteristic, namely how far in advance the ticket is purchased, effectively screens business travelers from vacationers. Once again, the purpose of different fares is to squeeze more revenue from travelers than could be accomplished by a uniform price.

We'll discuss each of these three types of price discrimination in this chapter. In each case, the underlying objective of price discrimination for the firm is to derive more revenue from its customers than it could achieve by charging the same price to everyone. In order to fix the concepts, the entire chapter will deal with the case of a monopoly firm. But the key factor required for a firm to practice price discrimination is that the firm has some market power. Price discrimination, therefore, is possible in any kind of market where firms have market power, and not just monopoly markets. In fact, price discrimination is ruled out only in a perfectly competitive market. As we shall see, there are many examples of price discrimination. Price discrimination is one of the most commonly practiced pricing strategies by all types of firms, whether monopoly or otherwise.

4.1 The basic idea behind price discrimination

As we pointed out in the introduction, the basic idea behind price discrimination of any sort is for the firm to increase the revenue it gets from its customers. It's easy to see why this is the case. Figure 4.1 displays a typical downward-sloping demand curve in any market. A firm selling to this market can set a price of p_1 in order to get sales of q_1 units.

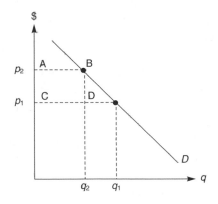

Figure 4.1 The reason for price discrimination

In this case, every customer in the market pays the same price. Up to this point in the book this is really the only option we have allowed the firm to consider. The revenue to the firm from charging a uniform price of p_1 is, obviously, $p_1 q_1$.[3]

Now suppose the firm is somehow able to price discriminate in the market by charging a price of p_2 to some of its customers and p_1 to the rest of its customers. In this case, the revenue to the firm from the customers paying the high price is $p_2 q_2$. The remainder of the market is served at the lower price p_1. Of the total q_1 units sold in the market, q_2 are sold at the higher price leaving $q_1 - q_2$ to be sold at the lower price. The revenue from the group served at the lower price is, therefore, $p_1(q_1 - q_2)$. Total revenue to the firm is thus $p_2 q_2 + p_1(q_1 - q_2)$, or, equivalently, $(p_2 - p_1) q_2 + p_1 q_1$. Because revenue from a uniform price of p_1 is $p_1 q_1$, revenue at the firm is $(p_2 - p_1) q_2$ higher by following price discrimination. In terms of Figure 4.1, therefore, price discrimination increases the firm's revenue by the area of the rectangle ABCD.

Whether a uniform price is charged or not, the firm produces a total of q_1 units. Thus, the total costs of production are the same under uniform pricing as under price discrimination. Because total costs are the same, but revenue is higher from price discrimination, it follows that the firm's profit is higher when it follows price discrimination. Not surprisingly, higher profits are the basic reason firms practice price discrimination. This being the case, you might wonder why price discrimination isn't practiced all the time. In fact, most goods are sold at uniform prices. The question is: why is price discrimination not more commonplace? There are two reasons.

The first reason is fairly obvious. In the example above, think about what will happen if the individuals who buy at the low price p_1 are able to re-sell their purchases to the people who pay the high price p_2. If this kind of re-selling, or *arbitrage* goes on, then price discrimination will ultimately fail. Consumers paying the low price will re-sell to those who would otherwise have paid the high price, cutting the firm's sales at the high price to nothing. The end result is that the manufacturer receives a uniform price of p_1. If arbitrage is possible, therefore, firm's cannot practice price discrimination.

Whether or not arbitrage is possible depends on *transactions costs*. For some services, like medical treatment or telephone calls it is difficult if not impossible for one consumer to re-sell the service to another. In such cases, price discrimination is clearly feasible. For retail goods, however, the transactions costs of arbitrage are relatively low. For example, someone who purchased a brand-new television at a low price could simply take out an advertisement in the local paper and expect to be inundated with calls from buyers facing higher prices. For this reason, price discrimination is rarely practiced for retail commodities.

The other reason that price discrimination may not be practiced is more subtle. For some goods and services, arbitrage may occur not between consumers, but between the types of good or service that any one consumer purchases. For example, consider first-class travel on an airplane. The airline may be well aware that a certain proportion of the traveling public are prepared to pay extra for the premium service offered in the first-class cabin. But the airline may not be able to identify these people easily. If the airline sets the price of first-class too high, even the people willing to pay extra may decide the high price is not worth their while and travel economy class. Even to those willing to pay a premium, the saving on the fare more than makes up for the inferior service of economy class. In this case, consumers willing to pay a high price end up buying at the lower-priced service. In other words, arbitrage by individual consumers between the type of service frustrates the airline's attempt at price discrimination.

From the airline's perspective, the problem is that consumers themselves choose which class to fly and that those willing to pay a high price cannot be identified from those who are not. Of course, airlines do successfully offer first-class service on many routes, so they have managed to solve this problem. The problem is really one of making each consumer buy the package that is intended for her rather than the package intended for someone else. Because consumers themselves choose which class to purchase, the airline has to make use of what are called *self-selection* devices that correctly sort consumers into high-fare and low-fare groups, as we shall see below.

To sum up, there are two reasons why price discrimination may be difficult for a firm to practice: arbitrage between consumers, and arbitrage by individual consumers between the types of good or service offered by the firm. The implications for price discrimination of the two kinds of arbitrage are quite different. The easier is arbitrage between consumers, the less likely is price discrimination. In contrast, more pronounced differences among consumers imply increased amount of arbitrage between types of service and may induce the firm to practice more price discrimination.

As the preceding examples may suggest, price discrimination is practiced in several different forms. Convention defines three classes of price discrimination. The case where each individual in the market is served at a different price, as in the example of the dentist in a small community, is referred to as *first-degree* price discrimination. The case where firms use self-selection devices to charge different prices to consumers with a different willingness to pay, as in the example of first-class air travel, is referred to as *second-degree* price discrimination. And the case where the firm uses observed signals about the consumers to charge them different prices, as in the example of how far in advance of the travel an airline ticket is purchased, is referred to as *third-degree* price discrimination. The key difference between the last two kinds of price discrimination is that the firm uses a signal about consumers to practice third-degree price discrimination, but when there is no signal and self-selection devices are used the firm practices second-degree price discrimination.

In the remainder of the chapter, we discuss first-, second-, and third-degree price discrimination. However, we shall not discuss them in numerical order. Because second-degree price discrimination is the most complex, it is discussed last.

4.2 First-degree price discrimination

A simple example of first-degree price discrimination occurs when all consumers purchase either one or zero unit of a good, like a daily newspaper. Suppose each consumer is willing to pay v_i for the good. Then first-degree price discrimination involves charging a set of personalized prices so that each consumer pays an amount equal to her willingness to pay, or in other words, $p_i = v_i$ for each consumer i. For example, one person is charged 30 cents for the paper, another is charged four cents, while another is charged $1.12, and so on, depending on how much they value the newspaper.

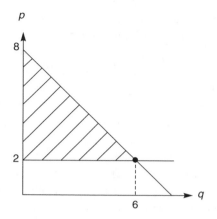

Figure 4.2 Consumer surplus and the two-part tariff

As another example, consider the case where there are n consumers with identical downward-sloping demand functions. Suppose each consumer's demand function is $q = 8 - p$, as shown in Figure 4.2. If the monopolist charges a uniform price of $p = 2$, as shown, each consumer will buy six units of the good. As we've already seen, price discrimination can increase the amount of revenue to the firm compared with a uniform price. But there is an upper limit to the amount of revenue the firm can take from consumers. This can be seen using the concept of *consumer surplus*, which is the difference between what the consumer is willing to pay for the good and what the consumer actually has to pay. The demand curve in Figure 4.2 shows what the consumer is willing to pay for the good. The price $p = 2$ shows what the consumer actually has to pay for the good. The shaded area, therefore, represents the consumer surplus from buying six units.

The consumer surplus represents the value of the good to the consumer that is not covered by the price. The consumer surplus, therefore, represents the upper limit on the amount of extra revenue the firm can take

from the consumer. In the example, the area of the shaded triangle implies that the consumer surplus from six units is $18.[4] Thus, the firm can charge the consumer $18 (or slightly less) for the right to purchase the good and then charge the consumer $2 per unit. This way, the entire consumer surplus is extracted from the consumer in the form of additional revenue to the firm. The consumer will not pay more than $18 for the right to purchase the good, because that would leave the consumer with a negative benefit from buying the good. The consumer can always do better than a negative benefit from buying the good by simply not buying the good at all, thereby getting zero consumer surplus.

This form of pricing scheme, where the firm charges consumers a fixed fee for the right to purchase a good in addition to a price for each unit purchased is referred to as a *two-part tariff*. Although initially two-part tariffs might seem bizarre, they are actually quite common. Taxis, for example, charge a fixed fee for getting in the cab (i.e. the meter does not start at zero) and then a charge varying according to distance traveled. Polaroid charges a fixed fee implicit in the purchase price of the camera and then a charge varying according to the number of units of film purchased. And telephone companies charge a fixed fee implicit in the monthly rental fee and a charge varying according to the number of telephones in the house.

This is all very well, but how does the firm set the per unit price? The firm sets the per unit price equal to the marginal cost of producing the last unit, as shown in Figure 4.3. Adding up the identical individual demand curves gives the market demand curve D and the firm's marginal cost curve is labeled MC. The total revenue to the firm is the area under the demand curve, and the area under

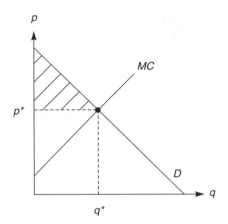

Figure 4.3 The optimal two-part tariff

the marginal cost curve is the total cost to the firm. Profit is, therefore, represented by the area above *MC* and below *D*, i.e. total revenue minus total cost. Profit is maximized when the per unit price is $p = p^*$. Once the per unit price is established, the fixed fee for the right to purchase the good is determined. The shaded area represents the total consumer surplus of all individuals in the market. Because consumers are identical, the fixed fee charged to each consumer is simply the total consumer surplus divided by the number of consumers.

To this point, we have assumed that every consumer has the same demand curve. Suppose instead that consumers have different demand curves and the monopolist knows each individual demand curve. In this case, the profit-maximizing per unit price is determined in the same way, where the per unit price is equal to the marginal cost of producing the last unit of the good. The fixed fee for the right to purchase the good is unique to each consumer and equal to the consumer surplus determined from the individual's demand curve at the optimal per unit price.

Having said all this, first-degree price discrimination is unlikely in practice. First,

there is the problem of arbitrage between consumers, where those paying a low fee for purchase rights re-sell purchasing rights to those being charged a higher fee. More important, there are obvious information problems: it is extremely unlikely that the firm knows the demand curves of all the consumers in the market. Moreover, individuals have no incentive to reveal this information to the firm. Everyone thinking of buying the product has an incentive to say that they do not value the product very highly so that the monopoly charges them a low fee for purchasing rights.

If first-degree price discrimination is rarely observed, why are two-part tariffs common? The reason is that two-part tariffs in themselves do not represent first-degree price discrimination. First-degree price discrimination means charging every consumer a unique individual price. Two-part tariffs may be used to do this, as we have shown in this section, but they can also be set so that the fee for purchasing rights is the same for everyone regardless of their willingness to pay. A uniform purchase rights fee, which applies to the examples of two-part tariffs given above, is clearly not a case of first-degree price discrimination. Thus, while two-part tariffs can be used to illustrate first-degree price discrimination, the real-world examples of two-part tariffs are not cases of the practice. We'll see that two-part tariffs are more commonly used in second-degree price discrimination.

4.3 Third-degree price discrimination

In the case of third-degree price discrimination, the monopoly firm has some exogenous information on its consumers that allows the firm to segment the market into several submarkets. For example, the firm can observe the age of consumers and offer discounts to seniors. Airline companies may observe how far in advance of the travel date tickets are purchased and offer discounts to those who buy tickets early. In Canada, VIA rail offers discounts on train travel to anyone with valid student identification. Computer companies often offer discounts to educational users and publishers offer discounts to first-time magazine subscribers. In all these cases, the firm uses observable information on the consumer to charge low prices to one group and high prices to another. That is, observable information is used by the firm in order to practice price discrimination.

To illustrate, suppose the monopoly serves two distinct sub-markets or groups of consumers. Each sub-market has a unique downward-sloping demand curve which is known to the firm. The quantity demanded in each of the two markets is written $q_1 = D_1(p_1)$ and $q_2 = D_2(p_2)$. Assume that arbitrage cannot occur between the groups. That is, someone in the group being charged a low price cannot turn around and re-sell the good to someone in the group paying a high price. Assume also that the monopoly cannot discriminate between individuals within any one group, even by using the self-selection devices we will discuss in the next section. Given these assumptions, the monopoly will have to charge everyone in the same group the same price, but prices may differ between the two groups. Total demand at the monopoly is given by:

$$q = q_1 + q_2$$

Let total cost of the monopoly be denoted $C(q) = C(q_1 + q_2)$. The profit-maximization problem for the monopoly is written:

$$\max_{p_1, p_2} p_1 q_1 + p_2 q_2 - C(q_1 + q_2)$$

which is just total revenue minus total costs, where total revenue is the sum of revenue in

the two sub-markets. Substituting $D_1(p_1)$ for q_1 and $D_2(p_2)$ for q_2 we have:

$$\max_{p_1, p_2} p_1 D_1(p_1) + p_2 D_2(p_2)$$
$$- C(D_1(p_1) + D_2(p_2)) \tag{4.1}$$

Since p_1 and p_2 appear symmetrically in this problem, let's focus on just one of the prices, say p_1. The first-order condition to the profit-maximization problem (4.1) for p_1 is:

$$p_1 \frac{\partial D_1}{\partial p_1} + D_1 - \frac{\partial C}{\partial D_1} \frac{\partial D_1}{\partial p_1} = 0$$

Now $\partial C/\partial D_1 = \partial C/\partial q_1$. Since p_2, and hence q_2, is held fixed in the first-order condition for p_1, it follows that $\partial C/\partial q_1 = \partial C/\partial q$. Using this fact, subtracting D_1 from both sides, and dividing by $\partial D_1/\partial p_1$ we have:

$$p_1 - \frac{\partial C}{\partial q} = -\frac{D_1}{\partial D_1/\partial p_1}$$

Since $\partial C/\partial q = MC$, after dividing through by p_1 the first-order condition becomes:

$$\frac{p_1 - MC}{p_1} = \frac{1}{\varepsilon_1} \tag{4.2}$$

where $\varepsilon_1 = -(p_1 \partial D_1/\partial p_1)/D_1$ is just the elasticity of demand in the first market. Owing to the symmetry in (4.1), the first-order for the second market is analogous:

$$\frac{p_2 - MC}{p_2} = \frac{1}{\varepsilon_2} \tag{4.3}$$

where $\varepsilon_2 = -(p_2 \partial D_2/\partial p_2)/D_2$ is just the elasticity of demand in the second market. The formulas (4.2) and (4.3) state that the price markup over marginal cost in each sub-market is equal to the inverse of the elasticity demand in that sub-market. For obvious reasons, these equations are called the *inverse-elasticity rule* for a monopoly.

To see the economics behind these equations assume, for the sake of argument, that

Eurostar Ticket Prices

Like many transportation businesses, the Eurostar rail service between London and Paris practices price discrimination with a vengeance. For example, the regular price of a one-way first-class ticket from London to Paris is $279, which is fully refundable up to two months before the date of travel. However, the price falls to $219 for a ticket that is only 50 percent refundable up to three days before the travel date. People over the age of 60 can purchase a 50 percent refundable ticket for $189. There is also a 50 percent refundable youth fare available, with suitable photo identification, of $165 for travelers under the age of 26. All of these discounts are examples of third-degree price discrimination, because they are based on an observable characteristic of people (their age) with different demand elasticities (seniors and young people, especially students, are probably more sensitive to price than other travelers).

Eurostar also offers a second (economy) class service. The one-way London–Paris journey costs $199, or $139 if the ticket is 50 percent refundable, with a youth fare of $79. Strictly speaking, the price differential between first and second class is not an example of third-degree price discrimination because the two classes represent different levels of service. First-class passengers get priority boarding, larger seats, a welcome drink, a three-course meal, newspapers, and a free taxi upon arrival. Nonetheless, there is an element of price discrimination inherent simply in making the first-class service available. As we shall see in the next section, Eurostar may offer the the first-class service in order to extract more consumer surplus (more revenue), and hence more profit, from richer customers.

$\varepsilon_1 < \varepsilon_2$. Thus, demand in market 1 is less elastic than demand in market 2. Equivalently, the consumers in the first sub-market are less responsive to price than the consumers in the second sub-market. If $\varepsilon_1 < \varepsilon_2$, it follows that $1/\varepsilon_1 > 1/\varepsilon_2$, and, therefore, the price markup is larger in the first market than in the second market. When you think about it, this makes perfect sense. The monopolist is just raising the price to the group that will reduce its quantity demanded less.

This rule explains why students and senior citizens are given price discounts. Students and seniors are more sensitive to price increases, so they are charged lower prices than other consumers. It is easy to price discriminate in these cases, because it is easy for firms to identify students (with a valid student ID card) and seniors (with the date of birth taken from a driver's license). The rule also explains why business travelers typically

pay more for air travel than vacationers. Business travel is more of a necessity than vacation travel, so vacationers are more responsive to airline prices and, hence, pay a lower price. The device airlines use to screen vacationers from business travelers, of course, is how far in advance of the travel date the ticket is purchased. This works on the assumption that most business travel is not planned very far in advance. The rule may also explain why prices for some consumer goods differ between Canada and the United States (when measured in the same currency). Different demand elasticities in the two countries may lead producers to price discriminate between Canadian and American consumers.

The following numbers from the airline industry give an example of how a firm might use information on elasticities to form prices using the inverse-elasticity rule.

A market study has shown that the elasticity of demand for air travel from the United States to Europe is 1.83 for tickets purchased at least 21 days before departure date and 1.30 for tickets purchased less than 21 days before departure.[5] From the preceding discussion, it is clear that the tickets purchased less than 21 days before travel will be more expensive, because they have a lower elasticity of demand. But how much more expensive will they be? Solving (4.2) for p_1 gives:

$$p_1 = \left(\frac{\varepsilon_1}{1 - \varepsilon_1}\right) MC$$

Similarly, solving (4.3) for p_2 gives:

$$p_2 = \left(\frac{\varepsilon_2}{1 - \varepsilon_2}\right) MC$$

Taking the ratio of these two equations:

$$\frac{p_1}{p_2} = \left(\frac{\varepsilon_1}{1 - \varepsilon_1}\right)\left(\frac{1 - \varepsilon_2}{\varepsilon_2}\right) \tag{4.4}$$

Let the tickets purchased less than 21 days in advance be called sub-market 1. Hence, $\varepsilon_1 = 1.30$ and $\varepsilon_2 = 1.83$. Plugging these values into (4.4), we find $p_1/p_2 = 1.97$. In other words, tickets purchased less than 21 days in advance will cost the consumer 97 percent more, that is almost double, than tickets purchased before the 21-day limit.

To fix the idea that the elasticity in a sub-market is inversely related to the price charged in that sub-market, consider the following example. A monopoly producer of hockey sticks has the following demand curves, for Canada and the United States:

Canada: $q_C = 500 - 20p_C$ (4.5)

United States: $q_U = 500 - 10p_U$ (4.6)

Suppose that the total cost of producing hockey sticks is $TC = 10q$, where $q = q_C + q_U$. It follows that marginal cost is

$MC = 10$ whatever the number of hockey sticks produced. From the first-order conditions (4.2) and (4.3), we know the prices in the two countries will be determined in part by the elasticities ε_C and ε_U where:

$$\varepsilon_C = -\left(\frac{\partial q_C}{\partial p_C}\right)\frac{p_C}{q_C} = -(-20)\frac{p_U}{500 - 20p_C}$$

$$= \frac{20p_C}{500 - 20p_C} \tag{4.7}$$

and:

$$\varepsilon_U = -\left(\frac{\partial q_U}{\partial p_U}\right)\frac{p_U}{q_U} = -(-10)\frac{p_U}{500 - 10p_U}$$

$$= \frac{10p_U}{500 - 10p_U} \tag{4.8}$$

Using the inverse-elasticity rule and the fact that $MC = 10$, we have for the Canadian market:

$$\frac{p_C - 10}{p_C} = \frac{500 - 20p_C}{20p_C}$$

$$20p_C - 200 = 500 - 20p_C$$

$$40p_C = 700$$

$$p_C = 17.5$$

Similarly, for the American market we have:

$$\frac{p_U - 10}{p_U} = \frac{500 - 10p_U}{10p_U}$$

$$10p_U - 100 = 500 - 10p_U$$

$$20p_U = 600$$

$$p_U = 30$$

The firm's optimal price for hockey sticks in Canada is $17.50 and in the United States is $30. Because the price in the United States is higher, the elasticity of demand must be lower in the United States. This is easy to check using the elasticity formulas. Substituting $p_C = 17.5$ into (4.7), reveals $\varepsilon_C = 2.33$. Likewise, substituting $p_U = 30$ into (4.8), reveals $\varepsilon_U = 1.5$. As expected, the United States has a lower elasticity of demand.

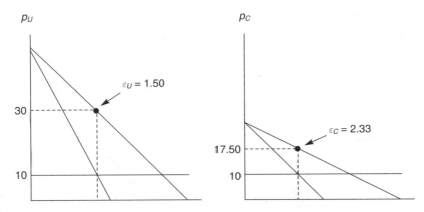

Figure 4.4 Optimal pricing in Canada and the United States

Figure 4.4 illustrates what's going on in this example another way. The left panel shows the US market and the right hand panel shows the market in Canada. To maximize profit, the firm sells where marginal cost $MC = 10$ equals marginal revenue in each market. Prices are then determined from the demand curve in each market. Demand in the United States is less elastic than demand in Canada, so price is higher in the United States.

4.4 Second-degree price discrimination[6]

In the last section, the monopolist was able to distinguish among different types of consumer using an observable characteristic of the consumer. For example, the monopolist was able to identify the demand elasticity of a consumer simply by determining her age or student status. In this section we look at what happens if there is an underlying difference between groups of consumers but the monopolist is not able to observe any characteristic that identifies the group a particular consumer belongs to. In other words, imagine the situation if there were no such thing as student ID cards. In this case, the monopoly would have no way of telling whether an

individual were a student. And don't forget, asking customers their student status won't provide the monopolist with any useful information. All consumers will claim to be students in order to get discounts.

For the sake of argument, suppose there are two groups of consumers: rich and poor. The firm does not observe the income of any particular individual, so it has no way of knowing if a person is rich or poor. But, because the rich consumer may be willing to pay more for the good or service offered by the firm, it may be in the interest of the monopoly to try to price discriminate among rich and poor consumers. You can think of the problem in terms of the monopolist designing one price-quantity bundle for the rich consumer and another price-quantity bundle for the poor consumer. This is done in such a way that the consumer will choose the "correct" bundle from the firm's point of view. That is, the rich consumer will buy the bundle the monopoly intends her to buy, and not the bundle intended for the poor consumer. Likewise, the poor consumer will buy the bundle intended for her, and not the bundle intended for the rich consumer. In this way, the bundles satisfy a self-selection criterion. The second-degree price discrimination problem is: how can the monopoly price discriminate among consumers even when it can't identify them?

We shall see that a two-part tariff is one such mechanism that solves the second-degree price discrimination problem. Recall a two-part tariff is made up of an up-front fee or premium for the right to purchase the good or service and a per unit charge for each unit the consumer buys. Thus, if a consumer buys q units at a per unit price of p, the total cost to the consumer is given by:

$$T = A + pq \qquad (4.9)$$

where A is the premium charged to the consumer for the right to purchase the good or service. As noted above, examples of two-part tariffs are taxi rides, Polaroid pictures, and telephone rentals.

To figure out how to solve this problem, we need to understand the purchasing behavior of the consumers. To understand purchasing behavior, we need to look at consumer preferences. The utility of each consumer depends on two things: the total cost, or tariff, T, and the quantity of the good purchased, q. Everything else being equal, a higher tariff (resulting from a higher price, or a higher premium) makes the consumer worse off, and a higher quantity makes the consumer better off. This is true whether the consumer is rich or poor. The preferences of an individual over the tariff and the amount purchased can be represented by indifference curves. An indifference curve simply connects all the T and q points that give the consumer the same level of utility.

Figure 4.5 shows representative indifference curves for a poor consumer. These indifference curves don't have the usual shape: as you can see from Figure 4.5 they have a positive slope. The positive slope is explained as follows. When T is increased, as shown for

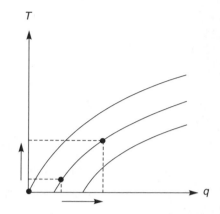

Figure 4.5 Indifference curves for a poor consumer

the middle indifference curve, the consumer is worse off. Therefore, q must be increased in order to return the consumer back to the level of utility where she started. In other words, to stay on a given indifference curve, q must increase when T increases, implying that the indifference curves have a positive slope. Another unusual feature of these indifference curves is that the curves closer to the horizontal axis represent *higher* utility levels. This follows because the consumer is better-off for lower T values and higher q values. Lastly, note that $q = 0$ and $T = 0$ when the consumer decides not to buy the good. Thus, the indifference curve through the origin represents combinations of T and q for which the consumer is indifferent between buying and not buying the good.

What about indifference curves for the rich consumers? Indifference curves for the rich consumers must also have a positive slope, because a lower T and higher q make consumers better off regardless of their income level. However, the indifference curves for rich consumers will be steeper than those of the poor consumers. This is illustrated in Figure 4.6, which shows just one indifference

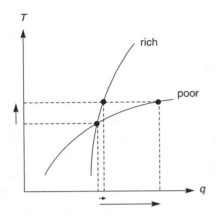

Figure 4.6 Indifference curves for rich and poor consumers

curve for the rich consumer and one for the poor consumer.

The reason indifference curves are steeper for the rich consumer is as follows. If T is increased, represented in Figure 4.6 by the arrow next to the vertical axis, both rich and poor consumers are worse off. But an increase in T is more damaging to the poor than it is to the rich: because the poor have lower incomes, money is "worth" more to them than it is to the rich. Technically, we are assuming that the marginal utility of income is decreasing. In other words, the increase in utility from an extra dollar is larger for poor consumers than it is for rich consumers. Alternatively, taking away a dollar from consumers (i.e. increasing T by $1), results in a greater loss of utility to poor consumers. For a given increase in T, therefore, the poor will have to be given more q than the rich in order to bring them back to the level of utility before the increase in T.

Don't be confused by the fact that the indifference curves appear to cross in Figure 4.6. Remember, since any one individual is either rich or poor, any one individual has either steep or flat indifference curves, not both. The indifference curves for any one

individual do not cross, as illustrated in Figure 4.5 for the poor consumers. You can imagine another diagram for the rich consumers that is analogous to Figure 4.5. The only difference, of course, would be that the indifference curves for the rich consumer would be steeper.

4.4.1 Two-part tariffs when consumer incomes are known

Now consider the two-part tariff charged by a monopolist serving this market. Suppose that the firm produces output at constant marginal cost, i.e. $MC = c$. And suppose, initially, the firm is able to identify the rich consumers from the poor. (Of course, this isn't the case we are really interested in, but it is a useful starting point.) When the firm knows which consumers it is facing, it can practice first-degree price discrimination, i.e. it can use individual prices. Since there are only two types of consumer – rich and poor – the firm needs only to come up with two sets of tariffs. Recall from the section on first-degree price discrimination that the profit-maximizing two-part tariff sets the price of the good equal to marginal cost, i.e. $p = c$, and the right-to-purchase fee equal to the consumer surplus of the individual.

Figure 4.7 shows the two-part tariff for the case of first-degree price discrimination. The two-part tariff for the poor consumer is A_P and the price the poor consumer pays is $p = c$. This is represented in Figure 4.7 by the straight line with equation $T = A_P + cq$. The two-part tariff for the rich consumer is A_R and the price the rich consumer pays is $p = c$. This is represented in Figure 4.7 by the straight line with equation $T = A_R + cq$. Since rich and poor consumers pay the same unit price, the slope of the two-part tariff lines are the same for the rich and the

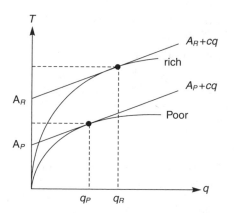

Figure 4.7 Two-part tariffs with first-degree price discrimination

poor. The right-to-purchase premiums are different, however, with A_R being higher than A_P.

Note that the indifference curves for the two consumer types in Figure 4.7 pass through the origin. This is no accident. Under first-degree price discrimination, the firm extracts all the consumer surplus from its customers. This means that all the consumers, rich and poor alike, will be just indifferent between buying the good and not buying it.

In fact, the indifference curves through the origin determine the size of the right-to-purchase fees for the rich and poor consumers. To see why this is the case, recall that the unit price p is set equal to the marginal cost of production, c. Since c is constant, the price is fixed as far as the monopolist is concerned.[7] Since p is fixed, the monopolist adjusts the right-to-purchase fee in order to extract all the consumer surplus. This amounts to choosing the fee so that the tariff line is as far up the vertical axis as possible while still leaving the consumer with just enough utility to keep them buying the good. In other words, the tariff lines are chosen to be tangent to the indifference curves through the

origin for each consumer type. Since the indifference curves for the rich consumer are steeper, tangency implies a higher fee for the rich consumer and that the rich consumer buys more than the poor consumer, as shown in Figure 4.7.

This is all very well, but in reality the monopolist does not know the income level of its customers. If it offers the two right-to-purchase fees A_R and A_P to consumers, all the consumers, regardless of their actual income level, will claim they are poor in order to avoid paying the higher fee A_R. And, even though the monopolist knows that some of its customers are lying about their income, it has no way of telling who is lying from who is not. The incentive for consumers to misrepresent their income can be illustrated using a diagram.

Figure 4.8 represents what would happen if the monopolist tried to practice first-degree price discrimination. The original equilibrium is shown, with the rich consumers paying a higher right-to-purchase fee than the poor consumers. Because the monopolist can't tell whether a customer is rich or poor, each customer has the option of choosing to pay either the high fee A_R or the low fee A_P.

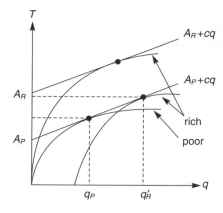

Figure 4.8 The incentive for rich consumers to lie

Obviously, both customers will choose to pay the lower fee. Basically, consumers are faced with two tariff schedules and choose the one that maximizes their utility. As Figure 4.8 shows, this leads both consumers to tangencies between their indifference curves and the $A_P + cq$ tariff schedule. Poor consumers are, therefore, in the same position as before. But rich consumers now "pretend" to be poor in the sense that they buy the good at the lower fee A_P.

Because the rich pay less, they must be better off. This can be seen from Figure 4.8. By paying the fee A_P, a rich consumer chooses to be on the lower tariff schedule $A_P + cq$ at the tangency to their indifference curve and consumes q'_R. Because this indifference curve is below their original indifference curve, the rich consumer is better off. Put another way, it is because the rich consumer can get on a higher indifference curve by paying A_P instead of A_R that the rich consumer has an incentive to lie. Note that the poor consumer has no such incentive. A poor consumer "pretending" to be rich would only make herself worse off. In fact, because the poor consumer is already indifferent between buying and not buying the good at the fee A_P, the poor consumer wouldn't even consider buying the good at the higher fee.

4.4.2 The standard monopoly price

The preceding argument shows that first-degree price discrimination will break down when the monopolist is unable to identify groups of consumers. What will the monopolist do in these cases? One option is to ignore the differences between rich and poor and simply treat the two types of consumer as one market. In this case, the monopoly sets the standard monopoly price and doesn't charge a right-to-purchase fee. That is, the

marginal revenue for the aggregate market is set equal to the marginal cost of production to determine the profit-maximizing output of the firm. Once output is determined, the optimal price is then set according to the demand curve. Because aggregate demand slopes downward, the optimal price, p^m, is greater than marginal cost, c, as we have seen many times before.

The monopoly price p^m and no right-to-purchase fee ($A = 0$) means that the cost to consumers from purchasing the good, whether rich or poor, is $T = p^m q$. Figure 4.9, shows the purchasing decision of consumers with the price p^m. Because there is no right-to-purchase fee and both rich and poor consumers pay the same price, the tariff schedule is a straight line through the origin with a slope of p^m. As Figure 4.9 shows, both types of consumer buy the amount of the good where their indifference curves are tangent to the tariff schedule $T = p^m q$.

We know that the price p^m maximizes the profit of the monopoly when a uniform price is charged to consumers. But the firm can get higher profits by using a two-part tariff. Notice in Figure 4.9 that neither the rich

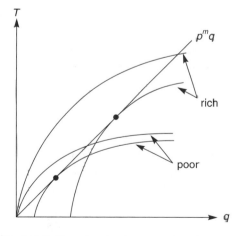

Figure 4.9 The standard monopoly price

nor the poor consumer are indifferent between buying the good and not buying it. The indifference curves through the origin represent lower levels of utility for both consumer types compared with the utility they get when the price is p^m. In other words, the firm's customers are left with some consumer surplus under the price p^m. This consumer surplus represents potential revenue for the monopoly.

4.4.3 The optimal two-part tariff

Consider what would happen if, starting with the price p^m, the monopolist were to charge a right-to-purchase fee. In terms of Figure 4.9, this would represent a parallel upward shift in the tariff schedule, from $T = p^m q$ to $T = A + p^m q$ where $A > 0$. The higher is A, the lower is the utility level for a consumer, so the monopolist must be careful not to set A too high and force some consumers not to buy the good. Clearly, it is the poor consumers who are most likely not to buy the good as A is raised. The monopolist can raise A until the poor consumers are just indifferent between buying and not buying the good, as shown in Figure 4.10.

In Figure 4.10, the poor consumer maximizes utility where her indifference curve that passes through the origin is tangent to the tariff schedule $A + pq$. Thus, poor consumers are indifferent between buying and not buying the good. The rich consumer also maximizes utility at a tangency between an indifference curve and the tariff schedule. But rich consumers are not indifferent between buying and not buying the good. Given the tariff schedule $A + pq$, a rich consumer is on a higher indifference curve than the one through the origin. A two-part tariff, therefore, extracts all the consumer surplus from the poor consumer and leaves the rich

consumer with a positive amount of consumer surplus.

Notice that the price in Figure 4.10 is not the price p^m. It turns out that the optimal price using the two-part tariff is less than the standard monopoly price p^m, i.e. $p < p^m$ where p is shown in Figure 4.10. Why is this? Suppose we start at the price p^m, this price maximizes profit when $A = 0$. Thus, a small decrease in price from p^m will have only a second-order effect on profits. But consumer surplus increases in direct proportion to the price reduction, which is a first-order effect. The monopolist can take away all this extra consumer surplus by increasing A. Since the first-order effect on profit (from increasing A) outweighs the second-order effect on profit (from reducing the price), overall profits must increase when the price is reduced from p^m. Profit is maximized, therefore, with $A > 0$ and $p < p^m$, as shown in Figure 4.10.

There is another way to see that the firm's profit is greater with the two-part tariff than the standard monopoly price p^m. The standard monopoly price is really just a special case of the two-part tariff $T = A + pq$. Set $A = 0$ and the tariff schedule is just $T = pq$,

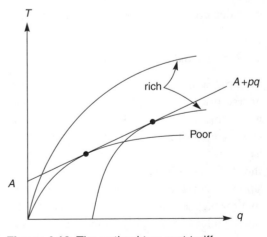

Figure 4.10 The optimal two-part tariff

which corresponds to the standard monopoly price with a zero right-to-purchase fee. Because the no-fee price is a special case of the two-part tariff, profit can be no higher with a no-fee price.

The two-part tariff implies that the per unit tariff to the rich consumers is lower than the poor consumers. The per unit tariff is just T/q, thus:

$$\text{per unit tariff} = \frac{A}{q + p}$$

Clearly, this is a decreasing function of q: the more a consumer buys, the lower is the per unit tariff. Put another way, consumers that buy more are given essentially a *quantity discount*. Quantity discounts, of course, are a widely used retail practice. Seen in this light, therefore, quantity discounts are seen as a way of extracting more revenue from richer consumers.

4.4.4 Non-linear tariffs

Careful consideration of Figure 4.10 shows that the monopoly can increase profit even more by considering a more general pricing scheme than the two-part tariff. As we noted above, the two-part tariff leaves the rich consumer with extra consumer surplus. By using a more sophisticated pricing scheme, the monopoly will be able to extract some of this consumer surplus. Suppose the monopolist, rather than offering a common fee A and common per unit price p, offers distinct T and q bundles to the consumers. This is referred to as a *non-linear tariff*. Basically, the monopolist just raises T charged to the rich consumer. It can't be raised too much, however, otherwise it will create an incentive for the rich consumer to choose the bundle offered to the poor consumer. Consider Figure 4.11.

Figure 4.11 reproduces consumer choices under the two-part tariff. The poor consumer is just indifferent between buying and not buying the good, so the firm can't possibly increase its profit from the poor consumers – any increase in price and they will all drop out of the market. But notice that the rich consumers strictly prefer the bundle they choose to the bundle the poor consumers choose. This means that the firm can increase the amount of revenue it takes from the rich consumer. It can't raise the tariff too much, of course, otherwise the rich consumer will choose the same bundle as the poor consumer.

As you can see from Figure 4.11, the firm raises T to the rich consumer until her indifference curve passes through the bundle chosen by the poor consumer. Profit from the rich consumers is, thereby, increased. This means that the rich consumer is just indifferent between purchasing the bundle the firm wants it to purchase (T_R, q_R) and purchasing the bundle intended for the poor consumer (T_P, q_P).

The firm, therefore, can increase profit by using different price-quantity bundles to discriminate among consumers above the profit from the two-part tariff. This suggests that firms will use non-linear tariffs whenever possible.

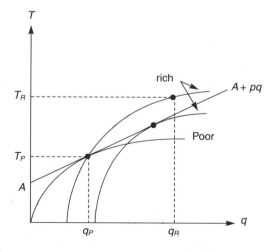

Figure 4.11 The optimal non-linear tariff

Choosing a Mobile Phone Plan

Non-linear tariffs may seem quite exotic at first, but they are quite commonplace in the real world. One application of the two-part tariff, practiced almost everywhere in the world, is in the market for mobile or cellular telephone services. Consider, for example, the services offered by the Australian telephone company Telstra in August 2001. As you can see from the table, Telstra offers no fewer than 13 different plans to prospective (non-business) customers (all figures are in Australian dollars).

Plan	Monthly access fee ($)	Included calls ($)	Call rate (per minute) ($)
10	10	0	1.32
15	15	10	1.20
20	20	15	1.00
30	30	30	0.88
40	40	40	0.72
60	60	60	0.52
80	80	80	0.48
100	100	100	0.42
150	150	150	0.40
250	250	250	0.38
500	500	500	0.36

For each plan, there is a fixed access fee and a per-unit charge represented by the call rate, corresponding exactly to the way we have represented two-part tariffs in this chapter. The price-quantity bundles offered to the consumer for plans 10–40 are shown in Figure 4.12.

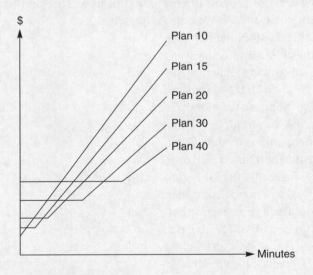

Figure 4.12 Telstra mobile phone plans 10–40

The puzzle for the consumer, of course, is to figure out which plan is right for their individual needs, which essentially boils down to choosing the least expensive way to purchase the required minutes of calls. In terms of the Figure 4.12, this means looking for the required minutes on the horizontal axis, looking for the lowest line exactly above this point, and choosing the plan accordingly. For example, if you expect to spend an hour on the phone per month, plan 40 is the cheapest option for you at $43.20 per month (not including taxes). Choosing the wrong plan can be quite costly. For example, if you chose plan 30 and spent an hour on the phone, the cost would be $52.80. Have you chosen the right plan with your phone company?

4.4.5 Quality discrimination

So far, q on the horizontal axis has referred to quantity. It could just as well refer to *quality*. In terms of the theoretical model, more q increases the consumer's utility, which is true for quantity or quality. More q also increases cost to the firm, which is also true for quantity or quality. Thus, one could re-interpret the preceding as a discussion of why monopoly firms offer consumers different price-quality bundles as opposed to different price-quantity bundles.

In the context of Figure 4.11, the quality interpretation means that the monopoly offers low-quality goods to poor consumers and high-quality goods to rich consumers. The combination of price-quality bundles leads consumers to choose the bundle the monopolist intends them to choose. We have already mentioned that airlines and rail companies offer different classes of service to passengers. Different quality services are just another way for the firm to discriminate among consumers and derive more revenue from the market.

4.4.6 Discounts and premiums

In our discussion of second-degree price discrimination so far, we have used the example of a market with rich and poor consumers. The important thing in this analysis is not the difference in income *per se*, but the impact different incomes has on the shape of the consumers' indifference curves. As seen in Figure 4.6, the income difference results in indifference curves that are steeper for the rich consumers than for the poor consumers. And, as we have seen, preferences shaped this way give rise to quantity discounts.

Indifference curves that are steeper for rich consumers are based on very plausible assumptions about consumer preferences. But, while plausible, they are not necessarily the case. In fact, the optimal tariff may involve quantity premiums rather than quantity discounts. The point is that the shape and distribution of consumer preferences determine the optimal pricing strategy for the firm. In some cases quantity (or quality) discounts will be appropriate; in other cases quantity (or quality) premiums will be appropriate. Only careful research into consumer preferences will inform the firm whether discounts or quantity premiums are optimal.

Consider the following example. Again suppose there are two types of consumer: a low-demand consumer who wants to consume only one unit of a good, and a high-demand consumer who wants to consume two units of the good. Assume that the total surplus of the low-demand consumer is zero if she doesn't consume the good and one if she consumes one or more units of the good. Assume that the total surplus of the high-demand consumer is zero if she doesn't consume the good and four if she consumes two or more units of the good. In other words, the low-demand consumer receives no additional surplus beyond the first unit consumed, while the high-demand consumer receives no additional benefit beyond the second. The optimal tariff for the monopolist is clearly $T = 1$ for $q = 1$ and $T = 4$ for $q = 2$. The per unit cost is 1 for one unit and 2 for two units, so the consumer buying more pays more per unit. What's important here is not that the monopolist practices first-degree price discrimination (which it clearly does), but that there is a quantity premium rather than a quantity discount.

If we use the quality rather than the quantity interpretation of the model, the example suggests that higher quality goods are provided to the consumer at a premium. Examples of quality premiums are found in first-class air travel and automobiles. Evidence indicates that airlines and car makers make a higher profit per unit, respectively, on first-class tickets and luxury cars. This suggests that firms are successful in extracting additional consumer surplus from customers who value luxury and prestige very highly. For example, the list price of a V-6 Toyota Camry with all the optional extras is almost $15,000 less than a similarly equipped Lexus ES-300 even though the two cars share almost all of their components. The profit per unit, therefore, is almost certainly higher for the ES-300 than for the Camry. In other words, customers buying the ES-300 model are willing to pay a quality premium for the more-prestigious Lexus name.

Summary

- Price discrimination occurs when the same good or service is sold to different consumers for different prices.
- Compared with charging a uniform price, price discrimination is a way for firms to get more revenue from a given level of output and, therefore, higher profits.
- Firms can only practice price discrimination when transactions costs are such that arbitrage is not possible. Arbitrage may occur between consumers (i.e. one consumer selling to another) or between types of good or service offered to a consumer (i.e. the consumer chooses one quality of good over another).
- First-degree price discrimination occurs when each consumer is charged a different price; second-degree price discrimination occurs when different prices are charged even though the characteristics of consumers are unknown; and, third-degree price discrimination occurs when different prices are charged on the basis of observable characteristics of the consumer.
- First-degree price discrimination is rare because it requires that the firm has information on all of its customers.
- Second-degree price discrimination is more common. It requires that the firm design pricing schemes to get consumers to self-select among different price-quality or price-quantity bundles.
- Third-degree price discrimination is also common. The firm uses observable characteristics about the consumers to charge higher prices to those with less elastic demand functions, according to the inverse-elasticity rule.

Notes

1 To avoid a hostile response, it might help to explain that you are a student of economics!

2 All these examples are related to travel. We will find out later in the chapter why this is so.

3 Recall that the area of the rectangle under the demand curve represents total revenue to the firm.

4 Recall that the area of a right-angled triangle is $1/2 \times$ base $\times$ height.

5 Source: J. Cigliano: "Price and income elasticities for airline travel: the North Atlantic market." *Business Economics* (September 1980).

6 A more advanced discussion of the material in this section can be found in Tirole (1988), pp. 142–8.

7 Although the price is fixed, it is still the profit-maximizing price when used in conjunction with the right-to-purchase fee. See the discussion in Section 4.2.

Exercises

1 Suppose there are 100 consumers in a small town, each with an identical demand curve, given by:

$$q = 10 - 2p$$

where q is the amount an individual buys and p is the price they pay. Suppose that a monopoly firm facing this market has a total cost function given by $TC = 2Q$, where Q is the total output of the firm. Assume that the firm knows the equation of the identical demand curves, so that it is able to price the good according to a two-part tariff scheme.

(a) Determine the equation of the market demand curve.

(b) Determine the per unit price that the firm will charge.

(c) Determine the total consumers' surplus and, hence, the fixed fee each consumer pays the firm for the right to purchase the good.

(d) Calculate the firm's total revenue, total cost, and profit.

(e) Is it possible for the firm to get any more revenue from this market? Explain.

2 Suppose there are only two consumers in a remote community and one dentist. The demand for dental services from the "poor" consumer is given by:

$$q_P = 10 - 2p$$

and the demand for dental services from the "rich" consumer is given by:

$$q_R = 10 - p$$

Assume that the dentist's total cost function is given by $TC = 2q$, where q is the number of visits she receives. The dentist is well aware of the possibility of using a two-part tariff scheme to charge the rich and poor consumers different prices.

(a) Determine the per unit price the dentist will charge.

(b) Find the fixed fee the dentist will charge the poor consumer and determine how many visits the individual will make to the dentist.

(c) Find the fixed fee the dentist will charge the rich consumer and determine how many visits the individual will make to the dentist.

(d) Calculate the dentist's profits.

3 The cost function for a monopoly is given by $C = 5Q$. The firm sells its output in two distinct markets with (inverse) demand functions given by:

$$P_1 = 55 - Q_1$$
$$P_2 = 35 - Q_2$$

(a) Under what conditions can the monopolist successfully practice price discrimination in these two markets?

(b) Determine the profit-maximizing amounts sold in each market and, hence, the firm's total output.

(c) Determine the price charged by the monopoly in each market.

(d) Calculate the total profit for the firm.

4 The cost function for a monopoly is given by $C = 100 + 8Q$. The firm sells its output in two distinct markets between which price discrimination is possible. The (inverse) demand curves in the two markets are given by:

$$P_1 = 20 - 2Q_1$$
$$P_2 = 40 - Q_2$$

(a) Determine the profit-maximizing amounts sold in each market and, hence, the firm's total output.

(b) Determine the price charged by the monopoly in each market and calculate the total profits of the firm.

(c) Show that the higher price is charged in the market with the lower elasticity of demand.

(d) What is the intuition behind this result?

5 The cost function for a monopoly is given by $C = Q^2 + 10Q$. The firm sells its output in two distinct markets with (inverse) demand functions given by:

$$P_1 = 80 - 2.5Q_1$$
$$P_2 = 180 - 10Q_2$$

(a) Assuming that price discrimination between the two markets is possible, determine the profit-maximizing amounts sold in each market and, hence, the firm's total output.

(b) Determine the price charged by the monopoly in each market and calculate the total profits of the firm.

(c) Now suppose that price discrimination between the two markets is prohibited. Assuming that the firm charges the same price in each market, determine the profit-maximizing amounts sold in each market.

(d) Determine the firm's total profits in this case.

6 Suppose there is a monopoly firm using a two-part tariff scheme such that, for q units purchased by a consumer $T = A + pq$ is the total amount the consumer pays to consume the good, made up of a fixed fee to purchase the good (A) and a constant per unit price (p). Let the total cost function of the monopoly be given by $TC = q$. In addition, suppose that there are two consumers in the market: one is rich, the other is poor, let the utility function of the rich consumer be given by:

$$U^R(T, q) = 4q^{1/2} - T$$

and let the utility function of the poor consumer be given by:

$$U^P(T, q) = 2q^{1/2} - T$$

(a) With T on the vertical axis and q on the horizontal axis, graph the indifference curves through the origin for the rich and poor consumers. [Hint: for the rich consumer, graph the curve which shows all the combinations of T and q that give rise to $U^R = 0$. Do a similar thing for the poor consumer.]

(b) Determine the optimal price charged by the monopoly.

(c) Suppose that the monopoly is able to observe who is the rich and who is the poor consumer. Determine the optimal purchase fee charged to the rich consumer (A^R) and the optimal purchase fee charged to the poor consumer (A^P).

(d) Calculate the total revenue, total cost, and the total profit of the monopoly.

Reference

Tirole, Jean. *The Theory of Industrial Organization* (Cambridge, MA: MIT Press, 1988).

Part II

Strategic Interaction between Firms

....

Chapter 5

Game theory

∙∙

When you are finished with this chapter, you should understand:

- That a manager's choice of a strategy (like market price, advertising expenditure, or research and development spending) will generally affect a competitor's choice of a strategy, and that this strategic interaction can be represented using game theory
- How a game is characterized by a description of players, strategies, payoffs, and rules
- What a player's best-response strategy is, and how to tell whether a player has a dominant strategy
- How to find the Nash equilibrium of a game
- How to represent best-response strategies using reaction functions, and how to use reaction functions to characterize a Nash equilibrium
- That reaction functions are downward-sloping (upward-sloping) when actions are strategic substitutes (strategic complements)

5.1 Introduction

Wasaga Beach, Ontario:[1] the longest freshwater beach in the world. It's the end of a clear day in June, and our young entrepreneur strolls off the pavement to feel the sand. Looking to the west, he sees the sun still high enough to sting his eyes. A short distance to the east, he sees the object of his journey: a single hot-dog stand servicing the entire beach. He compliments himself on

Plate 1 Wasaga Beach, Ontario, Canada

doing his homework. He has found a location where only one potential competitor existed. He can expand his network of carts to this beach and be only the second cart along the whole beach. While he manages seven hot-dog vending carts in Toronto, this will be his first venture out of the big city.[2]

The setting is perfect. Miles of beach stretch in each direction, and his competition will be limited to the single vendor currently serving refreshments to a couple of sun-worshipers. He wanders over to the vendor and buys a soft-drink, but his objective is to survey the list of items for sale. Hot dogs and pretzels, peanuts and chips, soft-drinks and assorted bottled water: pretty basic stuff. He sips his drink and starts to walk east along the beach.

Now the real work begins. He'll need to work quickly to be ready for the Canada Day long weekend. Where should he set up his cart? How much should he charge for hot dogs? Should he branch out and add burgers to his menu? Maybe he should have a chat with the young lady he just bought his drink from. "Well, that's the problem right there, isn't it," he thinks to himself. How will she respond to his presence? This wasn't a problem in Toronto. The license from the city government gave him the right to put his seven carts in a well-defined area, so he didn't have to worry about someone muscling in on his turf. He just spaced his carts evenly throughout his territory.

What if they just split the difference? He could see the end of the beach now. He could set his cart midway between the cart already on the beach and the eastern end. "But that would give the whole rest of the beach to her, wouldn't it?" he thought to himself. Maybe she would just move her cart farther off to the west. But if she was an aggressive competitor, she might just try to squeeze him right off of the beach. 'I could lower my price. I have a pretty good deal with my hot-dog supplier in Toronto. I wonder how much she pays for her hot dogs.' But how will she respond? 'What if she matches my lower price? We'd both be worse off in a price war.'

5.2 *The need for game theory*

There is not a lot in the discussion of the previous chapter that can help our young entrepreneur in his dilemma. And as simplistic as this example seems, it highlights complicated problems faced by decision-makers in firms every day. How will the competition respond if we increase our prices? If we drop prices to attract more demand, will that start a price war? If we introduce a new product, will the competition respond by letting us compete in our own captive share of the market, or will they want to compete with us directly? If we spend more on advertising to increase market share, will the competition do the same?

Answers to these questions will affect the prices of goods and services sold, the market share of firms competing with each other, and the types of goods and services available to consumers, among many other economic variables. The situations we've described with any of these questions all have one important feature in common:

> An action taken by a manager triggers a response by a manager in a competing firm.

Why is this so important? Why can't we just use our model of perfect competition to deal with this problem? In a perfectly competitive market, any single economic agent is very small relative to the size of the market. In such a market, an action taken by a manager causes such a small change in the behavior of the market that the equilibrium in the market is unaffected. No other managers will respond to the change. On the other hand, a monopolist does not need to anticipate the reactions of other managers in the market, since other firms do not pose a competitive threat to the monopolist. There are no other firms which compete with the monopolist.

These two extreme examples of market structure are very rare, and most decisions or actions taken by managers will typically result in a change in market equilibrium which will affect other managers in that market. We need to go beyond the previous chapter's discussion of perfect competition and monopoly, to ensure that we capture the strategic nature of the decision-making environment in which managers operate. The tool that we use to capture the strategic interactions between decision-makers is called *game theory*.

5.3 *Definition of a game*

To use *game theory* to analyze the behavior of a market, we describe the market as a game. The game is completely characterized by four elements:

1 a list of players
2 a list of strategies or actions available to each player
3 a description of the payoff received by each player for each strategy profile
4 the rules of the game

To understand each of these elements of a game, think of modeling the *game* played between our two hot-dog vendors on the beach. The players in the game are the two hot-dog vendors. A list of strategies or actions would include the items that each vendor could choose to sell (hot dogs, hamburgers, pretzels), the price at which output is

sold, and the location of the cart on the beach. We could define payoffs for each player in terms of total profits. But profits or payoffs need to be specified for each strategy profile, which we will define as follows:

> **Definition**
>
> A *strategy profile* is a set of strategies, one for each player in the game.

So one strategy profile might be that both hot-dog vendors set up their carts at opposite ends of the beach, selling only hot dogs, with each charging $1.50 per hot dog. Another strategy profile might be that both vendors set up their carts right next to each other, selling hot dogs at $0.75 a piece. In general, each different strategy profile or choice of strategies by each player will have associated with it a different payoff or level of profits earned by each player. Finally, the rules of the game might be that the vendors cannot change the location of their cart, or must sell hot dogs at a price regulated by the government.

Games can be very simple or very complicated, in the same sense that the behavior of an economic market can be very simple or very complicated. But we can break all games down into some basic groups, depending upon the factors that are most important to the market which they represent.

5.3.1 Time

Games can be either *static* or *dynamic*. In a static game, all players choose their strategies or actions at the same time, and the game is resolved. For example, by the beginning of every major league baseball game, the manager of each team must supply the umpires with lineups and batting orders. A static game would be appropriate to represent this characteristic of a baseball game. But in a dynamic game, one player chooses an action, and then another player responds after having seen the strategic choice made by the first player. For example, the home team in a professional hockey game is always allowed to make the last change in players before play is resumed after a whistle. This gives the home team a strategic advantage since the coach of the home team can play his strongest defensive players when he sees that the visitors play their strongest offense. A dynamic game would be appropriate to represent this characteristic of the hockey game.

In fact, we will see that having the ability to be the follower in a dynamic game (as is the case for the home team in the hockey game) is not always an advantage. For example, a firm which is first to introduce a new product to the market may have an advantage if it can attract a captive share of the market before other firms can respond.

5.3.2 Cooperation

In any particular market, managers may choose their strategies cooperatively or non-cooperatively. A *non-cooperative* game is appropriate to represent behavior in a market where managers do not or cannot cooperate with each other in choosing their strategies. If managers can cooperate with each other and can coordinate their decision-making, then a *cooperative* game is appropriate. We will concern ourselves only with non-cooperative games, for a number of reasons. First of all, cooperative decision-making between firms is often illegal. For example, firms are prohibited by law from cooperating with each other in setting or fixing prices. Second,

cooperative decision-making generally requires additional description of a mechanism to enforce cooperative behavior. If two firms cooperate with each other to limit supply of a good, in an effort to keep up its price, how is this cooperation enforced? In particular, if one firm tries to cheat on the other by selling more to the market to obtain higher profits, how is this firm penalized for cheating? Finally, there are many cases where we can use non-cooperative game theory to generate predictions which have firms behaving as if they were cooperating with each other, so non-cooperative game theory will be sufficient for our purposes.

5.3.3 Information

Depending upon the market situation, we can represent behavior in that market with a game of *complete information* or *incomplete information*. For example, our hot-dog vendor knows the cost of his own hot dogs, but is unaware of how much his competitor pays for her hot dogs. Players in this game have incomplete information. A game of complete information would be appropriate if both the hot-dog vendors knew their own costs and their competitors' costs.

Another important distinction is whether both players have the same information, or whether one player has some important and relevant information which is unavailable to the other player. For example, if each vendor knew their own costs but did not know how much the competition was paying for their hot dogs, then we would want to model this market as a game with *symmetric information*. However, if the vendor from Toronto knew his costs and also the costs of the vendor already on the beach, while the vendor on the beach knew only her own costs, then we would be dealing with a game with *asymmetric information*.

We will find the role of information to be particularly important if one player has an informational advantage over his or her opponent. For example, we could imagine that the outcome of the game played between our hot-dog vendors would be very different if the vendor from Toronto knew his own costs and his competitor's costs. Informational advantages may be very powerful tools in setting business policy.

5.4 Nash equilibrium

What we are ultimately interested in is the outcome of a game which represents behavior in a market. That is, we want to solve for the *equilibrium* of the game. The equilibrium of the game will describe the market outcome of the interaction of the players. In the previous chapter, we described an equilibrium as a situation where the market price resulted in supply being equal to demand. But now we need a different description of equilibrium, one which captures the fact that managers make decisions while taking into account how other managers might respond. If a manager can predict or anticipate how the competition will respond to a decision, we want to be sure that this response is incorporated in the equilibrium market outcome.

For example, if the hot-dog vendor knows that the vendor on the beach will lower her price if he enters the market (the beach) with a lower-priced hot dog, this information will affect his pricing strategy.

So before we define an equilibrium, we need to know how players choose strategies. To do so, we will use the notion of a best-response strategy, defined as follows:

Definition

For any one player, a *best-response strategy* to any particular strategy chosen by all other players is that strategy which has the highest payoff, given the strategy chosen by all other players.

For example, a particular strategy chosen by the vendor already on the beach might be to situate her cart at one end of the beach. The vendor from Toronto can choose to set up his cart anywhere on the beach, given this strategy by his competitor. His *best-response strategy* will be the location which yields the highest profits, given that his competitor has set up her cart at one end of the beach.

Of course, the vendor already on the beach might not set her cart up at one end of the beach. If she sets up her cart in the middle of the beach, the other vendor's best-response strategy would probably be different.

John Nash: 1928–

The term "Nash equilibrium" is named after the American economist and mathematician John Nash, who was awarded the 1994 Nobel Prize in Economic Science. The prize was awarded for his 27-page PhD thesis done more than 45 years earlier at the age of 21. The Nobel prize is usually given for work long since completed, but what sets Nash's case apart is that he suffered through more than three decades of a debilitating mental illness and recovered to receive the Nobel Prize.

John Nash was born on June 13, 1928. He began his stellar academic career with enrollment at Carnegie-Mellon University in 1945. He obtained a Bachelor of Science degree in two years, and completed his doctorate from Princeton on his 22nd birthday. Many of his professors at the time recognized his exceptional talent. One professor's letter recommending Nash for graduate studies at Princeton contained a single line: "This man is a genius." Nash started teaching at MIT in 1951.

Tragedy struck in 1958. By the age of 30, Nash was committed to a psychiatric institution suffering from paranoid schizophrenia. This disease causes its victims to be delusional, hear voices, and leaves the sufferer unable to sort and interpret sensations or reason. Nash had to stop working, gave up publishing scientific papers, and resigned his academic post at MIT.

But in the early 1980s a miraculous remission took place, allowing Nash to do mathematics once again. On December 10, 1994, he was awarded the Nobel Price for Economics.

Source: For more information, see the book by Sylvia Nasar, *A Beautiful Mind*.

The equilibrium concept we will employ is called a *Nash equilibrium*, defined as follows:

Definition

A *Nash equilibrium* is a strategy profile where each player's strategy is a best-response strategy to the strategies chosen by all other players.

Suppose the first hot-dog vendor has her cart set up in the middle of the beach. The vendor from Toronto has a best-response strategy to this location. But given this location by the vendor from Toronto, it might be that staying in the middle of the beach is no longer a best-response strategy by the first vendor. The equilibrium will only be reached once both vendors are playing their best-response strategy to each other. This is the important aspect of the Nash equilibrium: Any player's payoff depends not only on that player's own strategy, but also on the strategy chosen by all other players.

Now we will consider a number of examples of simple games between two players, to demonstrate some of the potential characteristics

of a Nash equilibrium. These examples are intended to show you how to solve for a Nash equilibrium of a game.

5.4.1 Prisoner's dilemma

Two bank robbers have been apprehended by the police. Before they were caught, they stashed their loot in a secret location known only to themselves. But the police have only circumstantial evidence against the two felons. Each thief is interrogated in a separate room. On his own, neither thief knows how the other will respond to the interrogation. If the thieves cooperate with each other, they will each tell a story such that neither is implicated in the crime, and the police will have to let them both go free. In this case, each felon receives a payoff of 2. On the other hand, each thief can implicate the other. In this case, the police officer has enough information to lock both of them up, so each receives a payoff -2.[3]

What if the first thief does not implicate his partner, but the other thief does implicate his partner in the crime? Then the second thief goes free, and gets a payoff of 4. He doesn't have to split the loot, so his payoff is twice the payoff when both thieves go free. His partner goes to jail, and gets a payoff of −4. He is worse off than when both thieves go to jail, because he has to live with the knowledge that his partner is free and spending all of their loot. The opposite outcome is obtained if the first thief implicates the second thief while his partner cooperates.

The only players of any consequence in this game are the two thieves. Each thief can either implicate his partner, or cooperate and not implicate his partner, so there are only two strategies available to each player. All elements of this game are summarized in Figure 5.1. We can identify four potential strategy profiles in this game: (Implicate, Implicate), (Implicate, Cooperate), (Cooperate, Implicate), and (Cooperate, Cooperate). For example, (Implicate, Cooperate) is the strategy profile when the first thief (player 1) implicates his partner and the second thief (player 2) cooperates.

Suppose you were player 1, the first thief. How would you figure out which strategy to play? You need to solve for your best-response strategy to each strategy chosen by your accomplice. Suppose your partner implicated you. The two strategy profiles you want to compare are (Cooperate, Implicate) and (Implicate, Implicate). Your payoff would be −4 if you cooperate, or −2 if you implicate your partner. Your payoff is higher if you implicate your partner, so *Implicate* is the best-response strategy when your partner implicates you.

What if your partner cooperated and did not implicate you in the crime? If you also cooperate, your payoff is 2. But if you implicate your partner, your payoff is 4. Your best-response strategy is *Implicate* if your partner cooperates.

In fact, in this game, the strategy *Implicate* is a *dominant strategy*. Your best-response strategy is independent of the strategy played by your partner.

What about your partner? You should be able to solve for player 2's best-response strategy, for each strategy chosen by player 1, and convince yourself that *Implicate* is also a dominant strategy for player 2. The Nash equilibrium to this game is the strategy profile (Implicate, Implicate), and players will receive payoffs (−2, −2), where the first number is the payoff to the first player.

In the Nash equilibrium to this game, each player plays a dominant strategy. We say that (Implicate, Implicate) is a *dominant-strategy equilibrium*. For each player, the strategy *cooperate* is dominated by the strategy *implicate*, since each player's best response to either strategy chosen by the other player is *implicate*. Any dominant-strategy equilibrium must also be a Nash equilibrium. But as we will see in some of the following examples, it is not necessarily the case that each player plays a dominant strategy in a Nash equilibrium.

An important characteristic of a Nash equilibrium is that it is mutually consistent. At the Nash equilibrium, neither player has an incentive to deviate and choose a different strategy. Given the strategy chosen by your accomplice, you can only make yourself

Player 1 \ Player 2	I (implicate)	C (cooperate)
I	−2, −2	4, −4
C	−4, 4	2, 2

Figure 5.1 Payoffs in the prisoner's dilemma game (player 1, player 2)

worse off by choosing *cooperate* instead of *implicate*.

Finally, we come to the reason that this game is called the prisoner's dilemma. If we looked in on this game from the outside, we cannot help noticing that this Nash equilibrium, as consistent as the outcome happens to be, involves the lowest aggregate payoff for the two players combined. If only the two thieves could get their story straight before being interrogated. They could cooperate with each other, and both would go free. But now we've changed the rules of the game. We were playing a non-cooperative game. If the thieves could cooperate, they could achieve a mutually beneficial outcome. But how could they enforce this cooperative behavior? If each thief played the strategy *cooperate* (a payoff of 2), then each could be made better off by implicating his partner (a payoff of 4). The cooperative outcome is not mutually consistent.

5.4.2 Matching pennies

This game will be familiar to anyone who played *evens-and-odds* in grade school when choosing sides in softball or soccer. Player 1 is nominated to be *evens* and player 2 is *odds*. Each player is given a penny, and has to choose heads or tails. Then the pennies are revealed. If both players choose heads, or both players choose tails, then player 1 wins both pennies. If one player chooses heads while the other chooses tails, then player 2 wins both pennies.

To solve this game, consider the payoffs summarized in Figure 5.2. Suppose we try to solve for the Nash equilibrium in this game. If player 2 plays heads, then player 1's best response is to play heads. If player 2 plays tails, player 1 is best off playing tails. Player 1 does not have a dominant strategy, since

Player 1 \ Player 2	Heads	Tails
Heads	1, −1	−1, 1
Tails	−1, 1	1, −1

Figure 5.2 Matching pennies game

player 1's best-response strategy depends upon the strategy played by player 2.

Player 2 is in a similar predicament. If player 1 plays heads, player 2 wants to play tails. But if player 1 plays tails, player 2's best response is to play heads. Neither player has a dominant strategy in this game.[4]

In fact, we can say a little bit more about each player's optimal strategy in this game. The best that a player can do is to randomize between strategies. That is, player 1 is best off playing heads half the time and tails the other half. But heads and tails must be chosen randomly. What would be player 2's best strategy if player 1 just alternated between heads and tails?

5.4.3 Boxed pigs[5]

One large pig and one small pig are placed in a box. At one end is a lever which when pressed causes a dispenser at the other end of the box to release ten units of food. The effort expended in pressing the lever costs each pig two units. If the small pig presses the lever, the big pig eats nine units of food and only one unit is left for the small pig, so the small pig receives a payoff of −1 units. If the big pig presses the lever, the small pig can consume four units of food by the time the big pig has crossed the box. If both pigs press the lever, the small pig can get to the food first, but can only consume three units of food by the time the big pig arrives. If neither pig presses the lever, each gets 0.

There are two players in this game: the big pig and the small pig. The strategies available to each are either to press the lever or to wait by the food dispenser. The game can be summarized by Figure 5.3. What are the best-response strategies of the big pig? If the small pig presses the lever, then the two relevant strategy profiles are (Press, Press) and (Wait, Press), where the first strategy in either strategy profile is the strategy played by the big pig. The big pig's payoff to (Press, Press) is 5, while its payoff to (Wait, Press) is 9, so the best-response strategy when the small pig plays Press is for the big pig to Wait.

If the small pig waits by the food dispenser, then the two relevant strategy profiles are (Press, Wait), and (Wait, Wait). The big pig's payoff to (Press, Wait) is 4, while its payoff to (Wait, Wait) is 0, so the big pigs best-response strategy when the small pig plays Wait is to play Press. The big pig does not have a dominant strategy. Its best-response strategy is not independent of the strategy played by the small pig.

Now let's look at the behavior of the small pig. If the big pig presses the lever, the small pig is better off waiting (payoff of 4) rather than also pressing the lever (payoff of 1). If instead the big pig waits and does not press the lever, the small pig is still better off waiting and getting a payoff of 0, since the alter-

native is pressing the lever and getting a payoff of −1. Waiting is a *dominant strategy* for the small pig.

Pigs are smart animals, and the big pig has enough information to know that the small pig will always play this dominant strategy. The Nash equilibrium to this game has the big pig pressing the lever and the small pig waiting by the food dispenser. At this point, neither player (pig) can be made better-off by adopting a different strategy, given the strategy chosen by the other player. Note that in this game, one player (the small pig) has a dominant strategy but the other player (the big pig) does not have a dominant strategy.

An important observation which we should make about this game is that the two players are very different: One pig is much larger than the other. But there is still a role for the small pig to choose its action or strategy to great effect, even though it is playing against a larger rival. Just because one player might be seen to be smaller or weaker than its rival does not mean that there is no strategic role which can be played by this smaller player. A relevant example from the business world would be the role played by small regional airlines which service only a small number of commuter routes with inexpensive, "no frills" flights. These airlines are very much smaller than competing national carriers which service many different routes and offer economy class, business class and first-class flights. But these smaller commuter airlines still have the ability to play a significant role in the market for air travel.

5.4.4 Battle of the sexes

A man and woman love each other dearly, and enjoy evenings out together. The man's favorite activity is going out to the neighborhood arena to see a boxing match. The woman's

Big Pig \ Small Pig	Press	Wait
Press	5, 1	**4, 4**
Wait	9, −1	0, 0

Figure 5.3 Boxed pigs game

Game Theory and Auctions

Auctions have been around for hundreds of years, and have been used to sell all sorts of items, from livestock to collectibles to tulips to houses. Governments use auctions to sell assets to private firms, and recently a number of auction sites have emerged on the Internet.* But there are many different types of auctions. Why are different types of auctions used for different goods?

Auctions make a fascinating place to apply some game theory. If we think of an auction as a game, then the players would be all people interested in bidding on an item for sale. Each player's strategy would be to try to buy the item at the lowest possible price p. To describe payoffs, note that there will be two types of players: The person who buys the item, and everyone else. Every bidder has some maximum amount he would be willing to pay for the item being auctioned, which we call $\bar{s}$. Then the person who buys the item (the ith bidder) will receive a payoff of $\bar{s}_i - p$, and all of the other bidders receive a payoff of 0. Of course, $\bar{s}_i - p$ must be positive, or else the winner of the auction would never have bid as high as p!

Finally, we need to describe the rules of the game. Different auctions will have different rules, so let's pick a couple of examples: The English auction and the Dutch auction. In an English auction, the bidders call out successively higher bids, raising the bid until all players except one have dropped out of the auction. The last player (the ith bidder) wins the auction. A Dutch auction works the opposite way. The auctioneer calls out prices in descending order, until a bidder accepts the item at the current price.

To understand the difference between these auctions, suppose you are the bidder with the highest willingness to pay, $\bar{s}_i = \$15$, and suppose the bidder with the next-highest valuation is $\bar{s}_j = \$10$. If bids are raised in \$1 increments, in an English auction, you would pay \$11 for the item, since the last bidder would drop out at \$10. But nobody ever need find out how high you would have been willing to bid, since there's no one left to bid against.

In the Dutch auction, the price would drop from \$17 to \$16, and then to \$15. If you bid now, you pay \$15, but your net surplus would be \$0, so you wait. The price drops to \$14. Now what do you do? You don't know the other bidder's valuations. You'd rather let the price drop further, but someone else might have a valuation of \$14 and you could lose out. So your optimal strategy is to bid and buy the item as soon as the price falls just below your true valuation. You buy at \$14.

Now think of one last player who we haven't considered yet: the seller. If you were the person selling the item being auctioned, which type of auction would you prefer? If the government sells public assets through auction, which type of auction should it use?

*See Lucking-Reiley, David (2000), and the references therein for some excellent examples of recent and historic auctions. For the economic theory of different auction mechanisms, see Milgrom (1989).

favorite pastime is an evening at the ballet. Unfortunately, the woman does not like boxing, and the man is not very keen on the ballet. But the couple are so in love that they would rather be together than apart, even if it means an evening at the fights for the woman or an evening at the ballet for the man.

The two players in this game are the man and the woman. Each can choose to go to the ballet or to the fights. If the couple go to an event together, each receives a positive payoff, since they are happiest when they are together. But at the fights the man receives a payoff of 2, while the woman receives a payoff of 1. At the ballet, the woman receives a payoff of 2 and the man a payoff of 1.

If the couple end up at different events, they receive a negative payoff. Each receives a payoff of -1 if they go to their preferred event. But if the man goes to the ballet and the woman to the fights, not only do they miss each other, but they see their less-preferred event. Each receives a payoff of -5.

We can use Figure 5.4 to represent the possible outcomes of this game. If the woman chooses to go to the ballet, the best response of the man is to go to the ballet (payoff of 1 instead of -1 at the fights). At this point, neither player can make himself or herself better off by switching, so (Ballet, Ballet) is a Nash equilibrium.

However, (Fight, Fight) is also a Nash equilibrium. If both the man and the woman are going to the boxing match, the woman would be worse off going to the ballet on her own (payoff of -1 instead of a payoff of 1 at the fights). Here, we have a game where there exist *multiple equilibria*. And without any more information, we can't tell whether we'll find this couple at the ballet or at the boxing match. Neither player in this game has a dominant strategy.

But if we change the game a bit, we can illustrate a concept which will be very important in the decision-making problem of a manager in a firm. If the woman can buy tickets to the ballet before the man can make up his mind, then the woman has the power to *commit* to a particular strategy. Now the best response of the man is to go to the ballet, since the woman has pre-committed to this strategy. The ability of a player to commit to a strategy will have very important implications for the outcome of a game.

We see many examples of firms which commit to business strategies. The car company which builds a new car plant or the airline which buys new airplanes is committing itself to significant investments, signaling to its competitors that it intends to stay in the market and compete. If a retailer who adopts a *price protection policy* drops his price, he is committed to rebating the difference to any consumer who has already bought at the higher protected price. Restaurants which honor competitor's coupons commit themselves to matching competitor's prices.

5.5 *The strategy space for a firm*

In any one of the games described in Section 5.4, there were only two discrete strategies available to the players. Of course, the decision-making environment of a manager is not quite so simple. Depending upon the market we are dealing with, we will need to be very careful to accurately describe the strategies available to the manager of a firm. These strategies will generally depend upon the time frame or planning horizon which faces the manager. Some of these strategies are listed in Figure 5.5. While the strategy space in every example in Section 5.4 was discrete, the strategy space available to the manager of a firm is typically continuous. A continuum of prices or advertising expenditures are available as possible choices for a manager. A product can be designed as a low- or a high-quality product, or anywhere in between.

Man \ Woman	Fight	Ballet
Fight	**2, 1**	$-1, -1$
Ballet	$-5, -5$	**1, 2**

Figure 5.4 Battle of the sexes game

Short-run	Long-run
• Prices	• Product quality
• Advertising expenditure	• Product design
• Coupons or other promotions	• Investment in R&D
	• Enter a new market
	• Exit the market

Figure 5.5 The strategy space of a manager

Let's formalize the manager's decision-making problem. Suppose that the manager's firm operates in an industry where there are n firms, where $n \geq 2$. If there are only two firms in the market, then $n = 2$. This type of market is called a *duopoly*. In the previous chapter, we looked at firm behavior in markets which were either monopolistic ($n = 1$) or perfectly competitive ($n \to \infty$).

Now consider the manager who is responsible for making decisions at firm i, where $1 \leq i \leq n$. The manager makes decisions by choosing a strategy, which we will represent by s_i. For example, if the strategic variable in question is the price at which to sell output, then s_i will be the price charged by firm i. We say that the *strategy space* for the manager's decision-making problem is the set S_i, consisting of all real numbers greater than zero. (Negative prices don't make sense in economics, so we restrict the strategy space for the manager to be all non-negative numbers). The manager's problem is to choose some price $s_i \in S_i$. In general, the strategy space S_i for firm i can represent any of the strategies listed in Figure 5.5.

If we represent the decision-making environment in this market using a static game, then the manager at firm i chooses the strategy s_i at the same time that managers at all other firms $j \neq i$ choose their strategies s_j. For example, at the beginning of each day, the two hot-dog vendors on the beach choose the price at which to sell hot dogs.

The final element we need to represent is the payoff that each firm receives. We're trying to be as general as possible at this point, so we'll represent the payoff of firm i with the *payoff function π^i*, where:

$$\pi^i = \pi^i(s_1, s_2, \ldots, s_i, \ldots, s_n)$$

Usually the payoff received by any firm will be profits, so the payoff function π^i will just represent profits earned by firm i. Notice that the payoff which firm i receives depends not only on its own strategy s_i, but on the strategy chosen by all firms in the market in which the firm operates. For example, our two hot-dog vendors on the beach will each have a payoff function depending on their own strategy and the strategy chosen by the other vendor:

$$\pi^1 = \pi^1(s_1, s_2)$$
$$\pi^2 = \pi^2(s_1, s_2)$$

So if the hot-dog vendors are choosing prices, the payoff received by the first vendor π^1 will be different if he charges a price $s_1 = \$1.00$ or $s_1 = \$1.25$. But this payoff will also depend upon the price charged by the second vendor. If she charges price $s_2 = \$1.10$ or price $s_2 = \$1.20$, the first vendor's payoff will be different even if he doesn't change his price:

$$\pi^1(s_1 = \$1.00, s_2 = \$1.10) \neq$$
$$\pi^1(s_1 = \$1.00, \quad s_2 = \$1.20)$$

We can also represent the strategy space for the hot-dog vendors graphically. Each vendor can choose any price at which to sell his or her hot dogs, as long as the price is greater than zero. Since there are only two players in this game, we can represent the strategy space for this game using a two-dimensional graph like that in Figure 5.6. If both vendors choose to sell their hot dogs at $1.00, then we can represent this choice of strategies by point A in Figure 5.6. If vendor 1 sells his hot dogs at $1.25 while vendor 2 sets her price at $1.10 per hot dog, we can represent this pair of strategies by point B. In this way, Figure 5.6 represents the entire strategy space for the market.

How can we use this description of strategies and payoffs to represent a Nash equilibrium? The Nash equilibrium uses the strategy by player i which is a best response given the strategy chosen by any other player. If a strategy s_i is player i's best response, we will denote it s_i^*. Of course, this best response depends upon the strategy played by manager i's opponents. For example, suppose that the best response by hot-dog vendor 1 is to match the price charged by vendor 2.

Then if $s_2 = \$1.00$, $s_1^* = \$1.00$. But if $s_2 = \$1.10$, the best response for vendor 1 changes to $s_1^* = \$1.10$.

In a Nash equilibrium, all players must be playing their optimal strategy, so we can represent the Nash equilibrium with the following equation:

$$\pi^i(s_1^*, s_2^*, \ldots, s_{i-1}^*, s_i^*, s_{i+1}^*, \ldots, s_n^*)$$
$$\geq \pi^i(s_1^*, s_2^*, \ldots, s_{i-1}^*, s_i, s_{i+1}^*, \ldots, s_n^*)$$

This equation must hold for all players $i = 1, \ldots, n$, and we interpret it as follows. The left-hand side is the payoff to player i when he plays his best-response strategy s_i^*. On the right-hand side is the payoff to player i for playing any other strategy s_i. In each case, all other players are playing their best-response strategy, s_j^* for all $j \neq i$. This equation says that player i's payoff is highest when he plays strategy s_i^*, since the left-hand side is greater than the right-hand side. If this equation holds for all players, then if any manager i plays a strategy other than s_i^*, the payoff of manager i must fall.

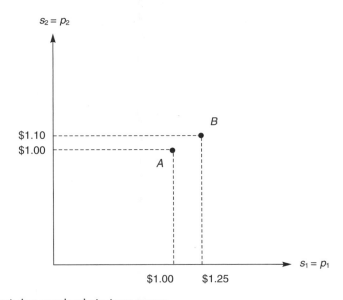

Figure 5.6 The hot-dog vendors' strategy space

5.5.1 Reaction functions

This is a very abstract way of representing a Nash equilibrium. It has the advantage of being very general, since we can have any number of managers, and the strategy s_i is just whatever the appropriate strategy should be. However, it does not allow for a very intuitive description of a Nash equilibrium. To make things a bit more clear, we'll also describe a Nash equilibrium using the graphical representation of the game's strategy space which we drew in Figure 5.6. We need one more tool to complete this task: the manager's *reaction function*.

The reaction function of the manager in firm i will be denoted R^i, and it will summarize the best response of this manager to any strategy chosen by the other managers in the market. As such, the reaction function R^i will have to depend upon the strategies chosen by all other managers, so we will write the reaction function for firm i as:

$$R^i = R^i(s_{-i}) = R^i(s_1, s_2, \ldots, s_{i-1}, s_{i+1}, \ldots, n)$$

The right-hand side of this equation has the strategy of every manager in the market *except* that of manager i.

What would the reaction function of the first hot-dog vendor look like? The reaction function would be:

$$s_1^* = R^1 = R^1(s_2)$$

Whatever the strategy chosen by the second hot-dog vendor, this reaction function gives the best-response for the first hot-dog vendor. If we solved for the first hot-dog vendor's reaction function, we could graph it as shown in Figure 5.7. The reaction function tells us that if the second hot-dog vendor chooses strategy s_2, the best response strategy for the first hot-dog vendor will be s_1^*. Of course, without more information, we cannot tell what the reaction function for the first hot-dog vendor will look like. It may be positively or negatively sloped.

If we solved for the reaction function of both hot-dog vendors, we could graph them as shown in Figure 5.8. The Nash equilibrium will be the pair of strategies (s_1^*, s_2^*) such that each hot-dog vendor is playing his or her best-response strategy: each vendor is on his or her reaction function. The Nash equilibrium in Figure 5.8 is shown as point N.

The shape of the reaction functions will depend completely upon the strategy space

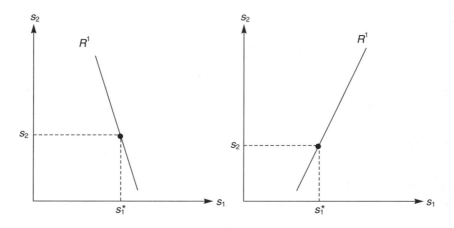

Figure 5.7 Reaction functions

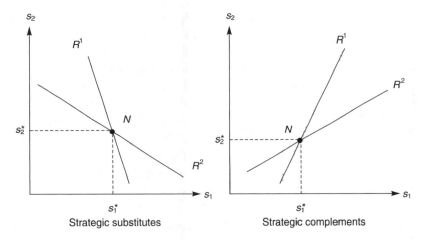

Figure 5.8 Hot-dog vendor's reaction functions

of the firm. That is, depending upon whether managers are competing by choosing prices, advertising expenditures, the characteristics of a product to offer for sale to consumers, or any other variable, the reaction function may be upward- or downward-sloping. We will define strategies or actions to be *strategic complements* if reaction functions are upward-sloping. If reaction functions are downward-sloping, actions are defined to be *strategic substitutes*.[6]

Summary

- We can use game theory to represent and solve problems where a firm's profit-maximizing choice of a strategy depends on the strategy it chooses and strategies chosen by its competitors.
- A *game* comprises a description of players, strategies, payoffs, and rules.
- For any player, a best-response strategy is that strategy which yields the highest payoff for that player, given the strategy chosen by all other players.
- The *Nash equilibrium* of a game is a strategy profile where each player in the game is playing a best-response strategy.
- A player has a *dominant strategy* when his or her best-response strategy is the same for all strategies chosen by the other players.
- Depending upon its characteristics, a game may or may not have a Nash equilibrium. If it exists, the Nash equilibrium may or may not be unique. A Nash equilibrium may or may not be a dominant strategy equilibrium.
- Reaction functions summarize a player's best-response strategies. Reaction functions can slope downwards if actions are strategic substitutes, or slope upwards if actions are strategic complements.

Notes

1 Thanks to the Wasaga Beach Corvette Club, http://www.wasaga.com/corvetteclub/welcome.html for allowing us to use their photo.

2 As we will see in Chapter 7 when we discuss product differentiation, this example is inspired by what has become know as the Hotelling model, based on Hotelling (1929). Another excellent reference for this model is Tirole (1988), pp. 279–87.

3 An excellent example of the Prisoner's Dilemma game can be found in Dixit and Nalebuff (1991), pp. 11–14. This text also has numerous excellent examples of game theory applied to many everyday settings.

4 Technically, we say that there is no *pure-strategy equilibrium* to this game. If we allowed players to choose *mixed strategies*, where each player attaches a probability to each strategy, then we would be able to solve for the *mixed-strategy equilibrium* to this game. But to keep things simple, we will confine our illustrations to pure-strategy equilibria, where players will choose a strategy in equilibrium with probability 1.

5 The boxed pigs game and the battle of the sexes game in the next subsection are due to Rasmusen (1989), pp. 32–5.

6 The terms strategic substitutes and strategic complements are due to Bulow *et al.* (1985).

Exercises

1 Representatives from the eleven member countries of the Organization of Petroleum Exporting Countries (OPEC) meet regularly to set production limits on the number of barrels of oil per day which each member country can produce.

   (a) Imagine characterizing the relationship between OPEC members as a game. Identify the four elements of this game. You can find information to answer this question at http://www.opec.org/.

   (b) Would this be most appropriately characterized as a non-cooperative game or a cooperative game?

2 Suppose there are two firms, called *A* and *B*, which compete with each other in the market for a unique product. Each firm can charge one of two prices for this product: a high price $\bar{p}$ or a low price p. If both firms charge the high price, $\bar{p}$, they split total market profits of 1000. If they both charge the low price p, total market profits fall to 400. If firm *A* charges the high price $\bar{p}$ but firm *B* undercuts its rival by charging the low price p, total market profits fall to 750, but more people buy from firm *B* because it has a lower price, so it gains 80 percent of total market profits. The outcome where firm *A* undercuts firm *B* is symmetric, with firm *A* gaining 80 percent of market profits.

   (a) Describe the four elements of this game.

   (b) Set up a payoff table like those in Section 5.4, and use it to solve for the Nash equilibrium.

   (c) Does either firm have a dominant strategy?

   (d) Is this game similar to any of the examples of Section 5.4?

3 Consider the following game describing the *agency problem* between a supervisor and a laborer. Each player has two strategies. The laborer can either work or shirk, and the supervisor can either monitor the laborer or not monitor. If the laborer works, he produces output valued by the supervisor at v, but if he shirks, the value to the supervisor of the laborer's output is 0. The laborer earns a wage w unless he is caught shirking, in which case the laborer earns 0. Of course, this wage is a cost $-w$ to the supervisor. The laborer experiences disutility from working which reduces his wage by g. Whenever the supervisor monitors the laborer, she incurs a cost h.

(a) Write out a payoff matrix which summarizes the strategies and payoffs for each player in this game.

(b) Find each player's best-response strategy, given the strategy played by his/her opponent. Does either player have a dominant strategy?

(c) Is there a Nash equilibrium (in pure strategies) in this game? Is this game similar to any of the examples of Section 5.4?

4 Use a diagram with reaction functions as in Figure 5.8 when actions are strategic substitutes. Notice that when firm 1's strategy s_1 is on the horizontal axis, its reaction function R^1 is steeper than firm 2's reaction function R^2. Identify the Nash equilibrium and label it N, and label firm 1's (firm 2's) Nash equilibrium strategy as s_1^* (s_2^*).

(a) Suppose firm 2 adopts a strategy $\bar{s}_2 > s_2^*$. Identify firm 1's best response to $\bar{s}_2$ and label it $\bar{s}_1$.

(b) Is $\bar{s}_2$ firm 2's best response to $\bar{s}_1$? Why or why not? If not, would firm 2 rather increase or decrease $\bar{s}_2$?

5 Repeat Question 4 when actions are strategic complements.

6 Consider the reaction functions as displayed in Figure 5.8. What happens to each player's Nash equilibrium strategy if player 1's reaction function shifts to the right? How does this depend upon whether actions are strategic substitutes or strategic complements?

References

Bulow, J., Geanakopolis, J. and Klemperer, P. "Multimarket oligopoly: strategic substitutes and complements." *Journal of Political Economy*, 93 (1985), pp. 488–511.

Dixit, Avinash K. and Barry J. Nalebuff. *Thinking Strategically: The Competitive Edge in Business, Politics, and Everyday Life* (New York: W.W. Norton & Co., 1991).

Hotelling, H. "Stability in competition." *Economic Journal*, 39 (1929), pp. 41–57.

Milgrom, Paul. "Auctions and bidding: a primer." *Journal of Economic Perspectives*, 3:3 (1989), pp. 3–22.

Lucking-Reiley, David. "Vickrey auctions in practice: from nineteenth-century philately to twenty-first-century e-commerce." *Journal of Economic Perspectives*, 14:3 (2000), pp. 183–92.

Rasmusen, Eric. *Games and Information* (Oxford: Basil Blackwell, 1989).

Tirole, Jean. *The Theory of Industrial Organization* (Cambridge, MA: The MIT Press, 1988), pp. 279–87.

Chapter 6

Strategy in a market with two firms

• •

When you are finished with this chapter you should understand:

- The basic models we use to describe behavior in a duopoly market where two firms compete by choosing either price or quantity
- That in the Cournot model of quantity competition, when two firms compete by choosing quantity of output, the equilibrium market price is lower, individual firm profits are lower, and total market output is higher relative to the monopoly equilibrium
- That in the Bertrand model of price competition, adding just one more firm to a market which was initially monopolized drives the market to the perfectly competitive equilibrium, where both firms earn zero profits
- How the simple Bertrand model can be extended to allow for product differentiation or capacity constraints
- How the Stackelberg model describes a market where one firm can commit to the choice of a strategy before its competitor, and that when firms compete in quantities, the Stackelberg leader has a first-mover advantage and is able to increase profits and market share at the expense of its competitor

If the discussion in the previous chapter has shown us anything, it is that the manager's decision-making problem is potentially very complicated when the manager takes into account all of the strategic effects and responses in the marketplace. In order to shed some light on how strategic interactions affect the manager's decision-making problem, we will begin in this chapter by considering the simplest of the manager's problems. As such, some of the analysis of this chapter may seem overly simplistic and restrictive. What we are really doing in this chapter is describing some basic models which we will be able to refine throughout the remainder of the text to consider more complicated aspects of the manager's decision-making problem.

Before we begin, it's worth pointing out that this chapter marks a significant departure from the types of problems which we dealt with in Chapters 3 and 4. In those earlier chapters, a manager worked in a firm which operated in a market that was either perfectly competitive or completely monopolized. Starting now, and for the remainder of the text, we will concentrate on markets which are *oligopolistic*. In general, there will be $n > 1$ firms in the market. As opposed to a firm which is a monopolist, an oligopolist does not have complete market power, since there are some other firms in the market. But as opposed to a firm in a perfectly competitive market, an oligopolist does have some market power.

The general oligopoly model with n firms turns out to be rather complicated to deal with. We will usually consider markets where there are two firms, so that the market can be characterized as a *duopoly*. This simplification is useful because results will be easier to interpret, and we will often be able to plot the strategies of two firms using a simple two-dimensional graph. (Drawing graphs in $n > 2$ dimensions gets very tricky.) But even this simple model with two firms will allow us to capture the important strategic interactions between firms which we are interested in modeling.

In its simplest form, we describe the manager's problem as follows:

$$\max \pi = TR - TC$$
$$= p \cdot q - C(q)$$

That is, the manager wants to choose a strategy or strategies to maximize profit, denoted π, which is defined as the difference between total revenue (TR) and total cost (TC). Total revenue is simply the total quantity sold q multiplied by the market price p, while total cost is some function of total quantity sold, $C(q)$. For now, all we really know about the total cost function $C(q)$ is that it is increasing in q. That is, as the total quantity produced q increases, total cost $C(q)$ increases.

The manager will begin with two important pieces of information: the structure of demand, and the strategic structure of competition in the market. The demand function summarizes the behavior of the consumption sector, and gives the manager the relationship between market price and quantity demanded. We have already described how this relationship is summarized by the demand function $q = D(p)$ or the inverse demand function $p = P(q)$:

$$\text{demand function} \leftrightarrow q = D(p)$$
$$\text{inverse demand function} \leftrightarrow p = P(q)$$

where q stands for the amount of the good or service that consumers demand and p stands for the market price. In its simplest form, this description of the market shows the only two strategic choice variables available to the manager: price and quantity. It is the structure of competition in the market which determines whether competition is taking place in prices or quantities. For example, at the beginning of Chapter 1, we described an example of price competition between Northwest Airlines and its competitors, American Airlines, United Airlines, and Delta Air Lines. The structure of competition in the market for air travel has so evolved that firms in that market compete in prices. But in many markets prices are regulated in some way by governments, so the scope for competition in prices is limited. In many countries, the prices of some alcoholic beverages are either heavily taxed or controlled by the government, and in some cities, governments control the prices of rental housing. In these types of markets, firms respond by finding other ways to compete. For example, beer producers compete in quantities by introducing light beers, premium beers, draft beers, and lower-quality beers which are less costly to produce, and retailers decide which of these products to distribute. When governments control the price of rental housing, building owners respond by changing the level of maintenance of their property, and compete not on the price of rental accommodation but the quality of apartments being leased.

The next two sections describe factors which influence the manager's optimal choice of either price or quantity, depending upon the structure of competition in the market, and demonstrate how to solve the manager's profit-maximization problem in each case.

6.1 Quantity competition

Before we describe the outcome of quantity competition, it is appropriate to describe some examples of what we mean by quantity competition. In general, quantity competition can cover a considerable number of market situations, where a manager can choose from a broad set of choice variables. Quantity competition can refer to the problem where a manager must decide upon the capacity of a new plant. Should the firm invest in capacity to be able to potentially supply to the entire market, or is it best to limit capacity to effectively supply only to a limited and well-defined market segment?

Alternatively, we could think of quantity competition as representing competition over the type of good to be produced. Should the firm design and sell a very high-quality good, or will the firm be better off mass-producing a relatively low-quality product?

We will see that our simple model of quantity competition can be adapted to describe many varied types of competition, and in later chapters, we will examine a number of special cases. For now, we will describe the *basic model of quantity competition* or *Cournot competition.*[1] Suppose we consider a market consisting of two firms producing an identical commodity. The structure of demand for this commodity is summarized by the inverse demand function:

$$p = P(q_1 + q_2)$$

where q_1 is the quantity of the commodity q sold by firm 1, and q_2 the quantity sold by firm 2. The structure of competition between these two firms can be summarized by the following assumptions:

1 the model is inherently static in nature, so that both firms choose outputs at the same time;
2 both firms have full information about market demand, about their own costs of production, and about the structure of the other firms' costs;
3 there is neither entry of new firms nor exit of existing firms;
4 consumers incur no transport costs in buying from either firm 1 or firm 2, so a consumer will always buy from the firm selling at the lowest price.

Let's look at each of these assumptions in turn, since they are very important in defining the outcome of competition in this market. To begin with, the model is static. Both firms will choose quantities q_1 and q_2 at the same time. This means that neither firm has the ability to *go first* and commit to a strategy before the other firm. Of course, it may be important to include some sort of dynamic element to the model, if it is important to represent the fact that one firm can choose a strategy before the other. But this would be a model which is fundamentally different from the Cournot model, and as such is described in Section 6.3.

The second assumption implies that all firms have full information. Of course, it may be that firms do not have complete information about either the structure of demand or of the other firm's costs. The manager may not know the preferences of each consumer who walks into the store. The hot-dog vendor from Toronto may not know whether his competitor buys her hot dogs at a relatively high cost or a relatively low cost. These types of information problems are very important in affecting the manager's decision-making problem. But they make the model more complicated. For now, we will deal with the simple model, and introduce information problems in Chapter 9.

The structure of competition between the two firms in this model would be very different if new firms could enter the market or if one firm could leave the market. For now, we will solve this model when there are only two firms. We will consider the effects of entry and exit in Chapter 10.

We can describe one very important implication of the final assumption without any further analysis at all. Since firms produce exactly the same commodity, any consumer can just as easily buy this commodity from either firm 1 or firm 2. In this case, the consumer will always buy from the firm selling at the lowest price. And this means that in equilibrium, both firms must sell their output *at exactly the same price*. To see why this is so, we need only think of what would happen if firm 1 sold its output at a price higher than that of firm 2: $p_1 > p_2$. No one would buy from firm 1, since the output of firm 2 is the same and costs less. Firm 2 would capture the entire market, and the demand for output from firm 1 would be $q_1 = 0$. We say that *there is no price competition in this model*.

If there is no price competition in this market, then we say that *firms compete in quantities*. The decision-making problem facing the manager of firm 1 is to choose a quantity of output q_1 so as to maximize profits for firm 1, π^1, given that the competition, firm 2, is choosing quantity q_2 to maximize profits for firm 2, π^2. Suppose that demand

for output in this market can be summarized by the following *inverse demand function*:

$$p = P(q_1 + q_2) = a - b \cdot (q_1 + q_2)$$

This demand function is illustrated in Figure 6.1. The intercept is a and the slope is $-b$. For example, if each firm produces output $(\tilde{q}_1, \tilde{q}_2)$, then total output in this market is $\tilde{q}_1 + \tilde{q}_2 = \tilde{q}$, and the market price will be $\tilde{p}$. This is represented by point A in Figure 6.1.

Suppose the cost function facing each firm is given by:

$$C^1(q_1) = f_1 + c_1 \cdot q_1$$
$$C^2(q_2) = f_2 + c_2 \cdot q_2$$

Notice that each firm's cost function is increasing in the quantity produced. For each unit increase in production by firm 1, total cost increases by c_1. Firm 1 has a constant marginal cost c_1. There is also a fixed component to total cost. No matter how large or small is total production q_1, firm 1 will have to incur the fixed cost f_1.

Now we can write out the profit-maximization problem facing the manager of each firm,

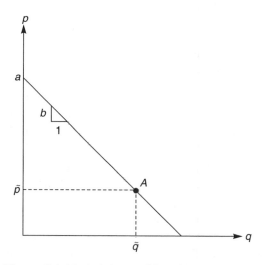

Figure 6.1 Market demand function

using the information given by the demand function and each firm's cost function:

$$\max_{q_1} \pi^1 = p \cdot q_1 - C^1(q_1)$$
$$= [a - b \cdot (q_1 + q_2)] \cdot q_1 - f_1 - c_1 \cdot q_1$$
$$= a \cdot q_1 - b \cdot q_1^2 - b \cdot q_1 \cdot q_2 - f_1 - c_1 \cdot q_1$$

and likewise for firm 2:

$$\max_{q_2} \pi^2 = a \cdot q_2 - b \cdot q_1 \cdot q_2 - b \cdot q_2^2 - f_2 - c_2 \cdot q_2$$

For any given output of firm 2, the manager of firm 1 maximizes profits by choosing q_1 so that the change in profits π^1 is equal to zero. To explain this condition, note that when firm 1 increases output q_1, there are three separate effects on profits π^1:

1 for a given market price, the firm sells more output, so profits increase;
2 as output increases, the market price falls as equilibrium moves down the demand curve in Figure 6.1. As the market price falls, firm 1 receives less revenue for each unit of output sold, so profits fall;
3 as output increases, costs increase, so profits fall.

6.1.1 Cournot equilibrium and reaction functions

Suppose the manager of firm 1 considers increasing production so that q_1 increases. If the first effect dominates effects 2 and 3, then overall profits π^1 will increase. If effects 2 and 3 together outweigh the positive first effect, then the manager is better off decreasing quantity q_1. The best that the manager can do is to change quantity to the point $\tilde{q}_1$ where the first effect is just equal to the sum of effects 2 and 3. We can solve for this condition by taking the derivative of the

profit function with respect to q_1, and setting the resulting equation equal to zero:

$$\frac{\partial \pi^1}{\partial q_1} = a - 2b \cdot q_1 - b \cdot q_2 - c_1 = 0$$

This is the *first-order condition* for profit-maximization for firm 1, given the level of output of firm 2. Of course, the manager of firm 2 is faced with the same symmetric profit-maximization problem, so we would find a similar first-order condition for firm 2:

$$\frac{\partial \pi^2}{\partial q_2} = a - b \cdot q_1 - 2b \cdot q_2 - c_2 = 0$$

These two first-order conditions, one for each firm, are two linear equations in two variables, q_1 and q_2. We can solve these two equations for the *Cournot equilibrium* quantities for each firm, which we'll label (q_1^c, q_2^c). First, solve firm 1's first-order condition for q_1:

$$2b \cdot q_1 = a - b \cdot q_2 - c_1$$
$$q_1 = \frac{a - c_1}{2b} - \frac{q_2}{2}$$

Now substitute this equation into firm 2's first-order condition to eliminate the variable q_1:

$$2b \cdot q_2 = a - b \cdot q_1 - c_2$$
$$2b \cdot q_2 = a - b \cdot \left[\frac{a - c_1}{2b} - \frac{q_2}{2} \right] - c_2$$
$$\left(2b - \frac{b}{2} \right) \cdot q_2 = a - c_2 - \frac{a - c_1}{2}$$
$$\frac{3b}{2} \cdot q_2 = a - c_2 - \frac{a - c_1}{2}$$
$$q_2 = \frac{2}{3b} \cdot \left(a - c_2 - \frac{a - c_1}{2} \right)$$
$$q_2 = \frac{a + c_1 - 2c_2}{3b}$$

If we solved for q_1 instead of q_2, we would find that the solutions were symmetric, so the *Cournot equilibrium in quantities* is given by:

$$(q_1^c, q_2^c) = \left(\frac{a - 2c_1 + c_2}{3b}, \frac{a + c_1 - 2c_2}{3b} \right)$$

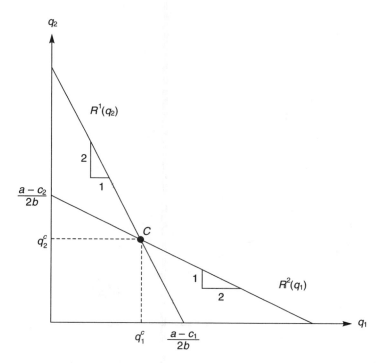

Figure 6.2 Cournot equilibrium and reaction functions

We can solve for this equilibrium graphically by using the concept of *reaction functions* introduced in the previous chapter. Recall that the reaction function for firm 1 gives the strategy which is the best response that firm 1 can adopt given the behavior of firm 2. The reaction function for firm 1 is found by solving firm 1's first-order condition for its strategic choice q_1 as a function of firm 2's strategic choice variable q_2. In fact, we solved for this function when we solved for firm 2's Cournot equilibrium quantity above:

$$q_1 = R^1(q_2) = \frac{a - c_1}{2b} - \frac{q_2}{2}$$

Likewise, we could re-arrange firm 2's first-order condition to solve for its reaction function:

$$q_2 = R^2(q_1) = \frac{a - c_2}{2b} - \frac{q_1}{2}$$

These two reaction functions are graphed in Figure 6.2. The Cournot equilibrium (q_1^c, q_2^c) is labeled as point C. Note that each firm's reaction function is downward-sloping. Given our discussion of reaction functions in the previous chapter, this means that *actions are strategic substitutes*.

Notice as well that the Cournot equilibrium is a *Nash equilibrium*. At point C, each firm is on its reaction function, so it must be the case that each firm's strategic choice of quantity produced is a best-response given the choice made by the competition. When firm 2 chooses q_2^c as its strategic choice of quantity produced, firm 1's best response is q_1^c, so firm 1 has no incentive to deviate from the Cournot equilibrium at point C. And firm 2 cannot do any better than producing q_2^c at point C when firm 1 chooses to produce q_1^c. Note as well that when reaction functions

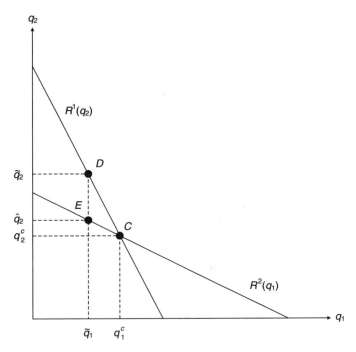

Figure 6.3 Mutual consistency of Cournot equilibrium

are linear (as they are in this example), the Cournot equilibrium must be unique.

We can make this point another way, by showing that any strategic choice of quantity other than (q_1^c, q_2^c) is *not* a Nash equilibrium. Suppose firm 2 chooses some quantity $\tilde{q}_2 \neq q_2^c$. Then the best that firm 1 can do is to choose the quantity $\tilde{q}_1$ so that firm 1 is on its reaction function, since the reaction function $R^1(q_2)$ gives firm 1's best response to any strategy chosen by firm 2. This situation is illustrated in Figure 6.3. The best that firm 1 can do is choose the quantity at point D. But now firm 2 is not on its reaction function. That is, $\tilde{q}_2$ is not firm 2's best response when firm 1 chooses quantity $\tilde{q}_1$. Firm 2 would rather produce $\hat{q}_2$ at point E. Of course, $\tilde{q}_1$ is not firm 1's best response to $\hat{q}_2$. The only pair of quantities where each firm is choosing its best-response strategy given the strategy

played by the other firm is at the Cournot equilibrium at point C.

We are now in a position to describe the effects of changes in market conditions on each firm's strategic choice of quantity. For example, suppose that firm 2 discovers some cost-reducing technological improvement, whereby firm 2 can produce the same quantity at a lower cost. We can model this change by supposing that firm 2's marginal cost of production falls from c_2 to $\tilde{c}_2$. If we look back to Figure 6.2, we see that this change will have no effect on firm 1's reaction function. The slope remains 2, and the intercept remains $(a - c_1/2b)$. But the vertical intercept of firm 2's reaction function will change. Since $\tilde{c}_2 < c_2$, it must be the case that:

$$\frac{a - \tilde{c}_2}{2b} > \frac{a - c_2}{2b}$$

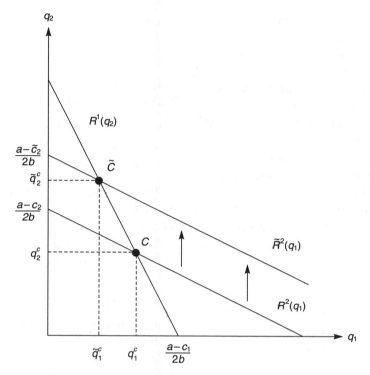

Figure 6.4 Cournot equilibrium when firm 2's costs fall

As such, firm 2's reaction function shifts upwards, from $R^2(q_1)$ to $\tilde{R}^2(q_1)$, as demonstrated in Figure 6.4. Given this change in firm 2's reaction function, the Cournot equilibrium changes from C to $\tilde{C}$. The technological improvement results in an increase in firm 2's quantity and a reduction in firm 1's quantity:

$$\tilde{q}_1^c < q_1^c \quad \tilde{q}_2^c > q_2^c$$

Result

All other things being equal, a cost-reducing technological improvement by firm 2 will increase the market share of firm 2 and decrease the market share of firm 1.

What happens to the overall market equilibrium due to this cost-reducing technological improvement by firm 2? Total market output before the change in costs was given by:

$$q^c = q_1^c + q_2^c$$

$$q^c = \frac{a - 2c_1 + c_2}{3b} + \frac{a + c_1 - 2c_2}{3b}$$

$$q^c = \frac{2a}{3b} - \frac{c_1}{3b} - \frac{c_2}{3b}$$

$$\frac{\partial q^c}{\partial c_i} = -\frac{1}{3b} < 0, \ i = 1, 2$$

So we see that a technological improvement by firm 2 which reduces c_2 will increase total market output q_c. This will move the market equilibrium down the demand curve, so we get the following result:

Result

A cost-reducing technological improvement by firm 2 will increase equilibrium market output and decrease equilibrium market price.

Notice that firm 1 is unambiguously worse off as a result of the technological improvement discovered by firm 2. The market price went down, firm 1's market share went down, and costs of firm 1 did not change, so firm 1's profits must have fallen. It has become more difficult for firm 1 to compete in this market against firm 2.

Of course, there are other interesting market changes which we could analyze with this simple model. For example, suppose that the technological improvement was not proprietary to firm 2. What would happen if both firms benefited from a discovery which reduced marginal production costs? On the other hand, what would happen to the market equilibrium if there was an exogenous increase in demand? This could be reflected in our model by a rightward shift in the market demand function, or an increase in the demand parameter a. Either way, you should be able to analyze the effects of either of these changes by examining their effect on each firm's reaction function. For example, see Question 4 at the end of this chapter.

6.1.2 Cournot versus monopoly and competitive equilibria

In Chapter 3, we described the solution to the firm's problem and the market equilibrium when a single firm operated as a monopolist, and when a firm operated in a perfectly competitive market. We can now compare these equilibrium market outcomes to one where two firms compete as duopolists in a market where firms compete in quantities. To keep this example as simple as possible, we will simplify the cost side of the firm's problem so that fixed costs are zero and both firms face the same constant marginal cost c. On the demand side, we suppose that the market demand function is given by the following equation:

$$p = 120 - (q_1 + q_2 + \cdots + q_n)$$

$$p = 120 - \sum_{i=1}^{n} q_i,$$

where n is the number of firms in the market. We want to consider three different examples:

$$n \to \infty \quad \text{perfect competition}$$
$$n = 1 \quad \text{monopoly}$$
$$n = 2 \quad \text{duopoly}$$

Perfect competition: In Chapter 3, we showed that a firm in a perfectly competitive market must operate in equilibrium where price equals marginal cost, so in a perfectly competitive equilibrium,[2]

$$p^{pc} = c$$
$$q^{pc} = 120 - c$$

This equilibrium is illustrated at point PC in Figure 6.5.

Monopoly: The monopoly equilibrium has the single firm setting marginal revenue equal to marginal cost. In this example, total revenue and marginal revenue are given by:

$$TR = p \cdot q = (120 - q) \cdot q$$
$$p \cdot q = 120q - q^2$$
$$MR = \frac{\partial TR}{\partial q} = 120 - 2q$$

When the monopolist sets marginal revenue equal to marginal cost, we get the monopoly equilibrium in this market:

$$q^m = 60 - \frac{c}{2}$$
$$p^m = 60 + \frac{c}{2}$$

This equilibrium is illustrated at point M in Figure 6.5.

Cournot duopoly: If there are two firms in this market, then each firm's profit function can be written as:

$$\pi^1 = (120 - q_1 - q_2) \cdot q_1 - cq_1$$
$$\pi^2 = (120 - q_1 - q_2) \cdot q_2 - cq_2$$

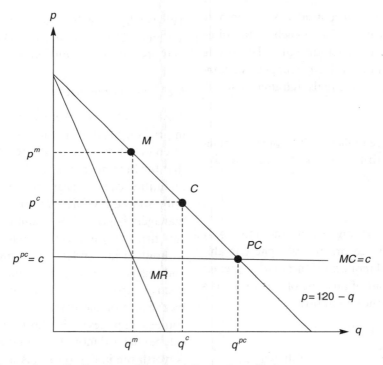

Figure 6.5 Monopoly, perfectly competitive, and Cournot equilibria

To solve each firm's problem, we solve for each firm's first-order condition:

$$\frac{\partial \pi^1}{q_1} = 120 - 2q_1 - q_2 - c = 0$$

$$\frac{\partial \pi^2}{q_2} = 120 - q_1 - 2q_2 - c = 0$$

We can solve these two equations for the Cournot equilibrium q_1 and q_2:

$$q_1 = q_2 = \frac{120 - c}{3}$$

Therefore, the market price and output in the duopoly market are given by:

$$q^c = 80 - \frac{2c}{3}$$

$$p^c = 40 + \frac{2c}{3}$$

We can compare all three of these by examining Figure 6.5.[3] The market price is lowest in the perfectly competitive equilib-

rium; $p^{pc} = c$ at point PC. The price is highest at the monopoly equilibrium; $p = p^m$ at point M. The Cournot equilibrium at point C lies between the perfectly competitive equilibrium and the monopoly equilibrium.

As we saw in Chapter 3, the socially efficient outcome in this market is the perfectly competitive equilibrium. If we think of starting off this market with only one firm, then adding another firm to this market (moving from a monopoly to a Cournot duopoly) will cause the equilibrium market price to fall, and will move this market closer to the perfectly competitive equilibrium by increasing the equilibrium quantity demanded to $q^c > q^m$. In fact, we would find that if we added more firms to this market, the equilibrium would continue to move closer and closer to the perfectly competitive equilibrium at PC.

The final point to consider is to compare equilibrium firm profits in each of the three market scenarios. Each firm must be earning zero profits in the perfectly competitive equilibrium, since price equals marginal cost:

$$\pi^{pc} = 0$$

Since prices are higher in the Cournot equilibrium, each firm must be earning positive profits, equal to:

$$\pi_i^c = (p^c - c) \cdot q_i^c$$

Profits must be highest in the monopoly equilibrium, since prices are highest in this case, and total monopoly output q^m is greater than the output of any one of the duopolists q_i^c in the Cournot equilibrium:

$$\pi^m = (p^m - c) \cdot q^m$$

This allows us to state the following:

Result

All other things being equal, adding more symmetric firms to the same market will reduce the equilibrium market price, reduce profits earned by firms, and increase the equilibrium market quantity demanded.

This is why we will sometimes say that adding more firms to a given market will make that market *more competitive*.

6.2 Price competition

Now consider a market where firms compete in prices instead of quantities. This structure of competition may be the result of the fact that for the time period under consideration, quantities cannot easily be changed, so the only strategic choice variable available to managers is price. For example, in the short run, firms may not be able to increase output without hiring and training more workers, and this is costly and takes time. Or the productive capacity of the firm may be limited by the size of the plant. In short, firms will compete in prices in the short run, since prices can be changed more easily in the short run. It is worth reminding ourselves of the structure of the market in which firms operate. We will suppose that we are still dealing with a market consisting of two firms producing an identical product. Just as under quantity competition, this will imply that consumers are completely indifferent between the output of firm 1 and firm 2 when both firms charge the same price.

Quantity Competition and OPEC

It's not too difficult to come up with examples of markets where firms compete in prices. Commercials and flyers which announce changes in market prices and calls of "We will not be undersold!" all attest to the fact that firms in many markets compete with each other by choosing price as a strategic choice variable. But at first thought, it might seem difficult to come up with examples of markets where firms compete in quantities.

We mentioned a couple of examples of quantity competition at the beginning of Section 6.1. These included markets where firms chose the capacity of a production facility. Of course, the production capacity of a firm directly affects its ability to provide output to a market: A larger production capacity implies that the quantity of output which a firm can sell is higher. In general, firms compete in quantities whenever they choose a variable which directly affects the quantity of output sold. For example, by doubling the size of its sales staff, the firm increases its ability to sell output. Whenever firms choose how much to spend on sales and promotion, they are competing in quantities.

The world market for crude oil provides an interesting example of a market where firms (in this case, countries) compete by directly choosing the quantity of output. Countries which sell crude oil on world markets do not choose the price at which their oil is sold. Instead, they choose the quantity of crude oil to pump out of the ground and sell on world markets. Consider the behavior of OPEC.* Formed in September 1960, OPEC currently consists of 11 member countries that set oil production quotas for each of its members. For example, at an OPEC Conference in Vienna, Austria, on July 25, 2001, OPEC members agreed to limit total production to 23,201,000 barrels of oil per day.**

In a market where firms compete in quantities, like the market for crude oil, firms choose the quantity of output, and the output price is determined by the market. In OPEC's case, member countries are assigned a production quota, with the objective of maintaining stable oil prices.

*See Chapter 3 of Scherer, F. M. (1996), *Industry Structure, Strategy, and Public Policy* for an excellent history of the crude oil industry.

**Individual member country quotas are available from the OPEC website at http://www.opec.org/

In order to be able to compare and contrast the results of price competition to those under quantity competition, suppose that the demand function faced by the two firms in this market is the same as that used in the example in Section 6.1.2:

$$q = D(p) = 120 - p$$

As before, to keep things simple, we'll suppose that both firms have the same constant marginal cost of production c, and that fixed costs for each firm are zero.

6.2.1 Price competition and Bertrand equilibrium

The Nash equilibrium we want to find will now be an equilibrium in prices, as opposed to the Cournot equilibrium we solved for when firms were competing in quantities. Now we are looking for a *Bertrand equilibrium*,[4] which we will label (p_1^b, p_2^b). Of course, this must still be a Nash equilibrium, so it must be the case that given p_2^b, the price charged by firm 1, p_1^b, must be firm 1's best response to firm 2's strategic choice of p_2^b.

That is, at the Bertrand equilibrium (p_1^b, p_2^b), neither firm can have an incentive to change its price.

How do we solve for the Bertrand equilibrium? We could write out each firm's profit function, and use this to solve for each firm's optimal pricing strategy. However, when firms are competing in prices, it will be easier just to examine each firm's demand function under alternative pricing strategies. We begin by recalling that, in a market where two firms sell identical products, consumers will buy from the firm selling at the lower price. So if firm 1's price is lower than firm 2's price, so that $p_1 < p_2$, firm 1 will supply the entire market, $q_1 = D(p_1)$, and firm 2 will not have any sales, $q_2 = 0$.

What happens if both firms charge the same price? We will suppose that in this case, the two firms simply split the market, so that when $p_1 = p_2 = p$, $q_1 = q_2 = D(p)/2$.

The simplest way to solve for the Bertrand equilibrium is to suppose that each manager's strategy space is discrete, so the manager can charge one of only three prices. Of course, this is very restrictive, but it will be

Firm 1 \ Firm 2	$p_2 = \$60$	$p_2 = \$42$	$p_2 = \$36$
$p_1 = \$60$	$900, \$900	0, \$936	0, \$504
$p_1 = \$42$	$936, 0	$468, \$468	0, \$504
$p_1 = \$36$	$504, 0	$504, 0	$252, \$252

Figure 6.6 Payoff matrix with price competition

sufficient to allow us to solve this model. Let's suppose that the only three prices that the manager can choose are $p = \$60, \$42$, or $36. Total market demand will be given by the demand function $q = 120 - p$. If the constant marginal cost is $c = 30$, then industry profits will be $\pi = (p - c)q$. The market data for these three alternative market prices are:

Price	Quantity	Profits
$p = \$60$	$q = 60$	$\pi = \$1800$
$p = \$42$	$q = 78$	$\pi = \$936$
$p = \$36$	$q = 84$	$\pi = \$504$

Suppose both firms charge $p = \$60$. Then the two firms would split industry profits of $1800, so each firm would receive a payoff of $900. If both firms charge $p = \$42$, then they split industry profits of $936, so each firm would earn a payoff of $468. If each firm charges $p = \$36$, then each firm earns $252.

If the two firms charge different prices, then consumers will buy from the firm selling at the lowest price. That means that if $p_1 = \$60$ and $p_2 = \$42$, then firm 1 will not have any sales, and firm 2 will capture the entire market. Firm 1 will earn a payoff of 0, while firm 2 gets a payoff of $936.

We can summarize all of the possible outcomes of this pricing game between the two firms in the payoff matrix in Figure 6.6, and use this table to solve for the Bertrand equilibrium. Suppose we start off with each firm charging the equilibrium price from Section 6.1.2: $p = \$60$. Payoffs from this scenario are listed in the top left corner of the payoff matrix, showing that each firm earns $900. But if firms compete in prices, this cannot be an equilibrium. At this point, the manager at firm 1 recognizes that by reducing price to $p_1 = \$42$, firm 1 will undercut its competitor, capturing the entire market and increasing profits to $936, at the expense of firm 2 whose profits fall to 0.

Of course, the manager at firm 2 can follow the same strategy of undercutting the competition. In response to firm 1's strategy, firm 2 could reduce its price to $42 and split the industry profits to earn a payoff of $468. But firm 2 can do even better, by dropping its price to $36 and undercutting firm 1. This way, firm 2 captures the entire market, earns a payoff of $504, and firm 1 earns 0.

At this point, we can see that firm 1 would be better off dropping its price to $36, but now we've run out of space on our payoff matrix. In fact, if firm 1 could continue to undercut firm 2, it would do so, capturing the entire market and earning all industry profits. This process would continue until both firms charged $p = c = \$30$. Beyond this, neither firm could profit from a price reduction. Certainly, if firm 1 drops its price below $p = \$30$, it would capture the entire market. But now price is less than marginal cost, so profits are negative. Once firms undercut each other to the point where both firms earn zero profits, neither firm has an incentive to change its price. So we get the following result:

Result

When firms are competing in prices, the Bertrand equilibrium is characterized by both firms charging the same price, that price being equal to marginal cost: $p_1^b = p_2^b = c$.

Now that we've solved for the Bertrand equilibrium when firms are competing in prices, we can solve for the characteristics of the market equilibrium. If both firms charge the same market price $p_1^b = p_2^b$ equal to marginal cost c in equilibrium, then we know that the market equilibrium must be the same as the perfectly competitive equilibrium we solved for in Chapter 3. We illustrate this Bertrand equilibrium at point B in Figure 6.7, where we have also included the perfectly competitive equilibrium (labeled PC) and the monopoly equilibrium (labeled M). At the perfectly competitive equilibrium PC, firms were earning zero profits, since revenue earned per unit of output p^{pc} was just sufficient to cover the cost of producing one unit of output c. Thus it must be the case that at the Bertrand equilibrium B, the two firms are also earning zero profits. This result is often referred to as the *Bertrand paradox*:

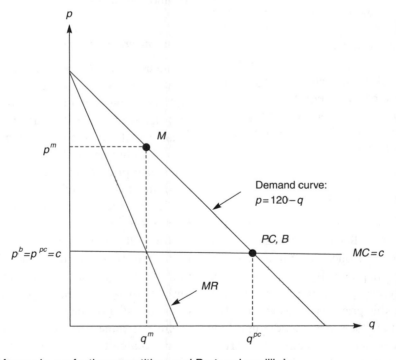

Figure 6.7 Monopoly, perfectly competitive, and Bertrand equilibria

> **Result**
>
> Adding just one more firm to the monopoly equilibrium drives this market to the perfectly competitive equilibrium, where both firms set price equal to marginal cost. Both firms earn zero profits and the equilibrium is socially efficient.

6.2.2 Solutions to the Bertrand paradox

How much sense can we make of the result implied by the Bertrand paradox? It seems very extreme that the price competition implied by adding just one more firm to an initial monopoly equilibrium would cause prices to fall all the way to the socially efficient level where price equals marginal cost. Put another way, the Bertrand paradox implies that adding just one firm to an initial monopoly equilibrium results in complete elimination of all monopoly profits. There are a number of reasons why we might expect that this result would *not* obtain, so that each firm will be earning positive profits in the Bertrand equilibrium. We'll briefly outline some of these reasons here, though some of these reasons will be important enough to be dealt with in greater detail in separate chapters later in the text.

Retaliation and collusion

Upon reflection, we can see that the result implied by the Bertrand paradox is an example of the prisoner's dilemma which we described in Chapter 5. Both firms would be better off by charging $p = \$60$, but if both firms charge this price, each has an incentive to undercut the other. When we discussed the prisoner's dilemma, we noted that if the rules of the game could be changed, we could sus-

tain the outcome where each agent receives the highest payoff. In the example from Chapter 5, the two criminals needed to come up with some mechanism which removed the incentive to implicate the other. In the Bertrand paradox, the two firms could increase profits if they could cooperate and maintain a higher price.

We will not discuss this example any further, except to note that if the firms could collude, an equilibrium where both firms earn positive profits would be sustainable. There are two important reasons for leaving this example at this point. First, we would need to introduce a mechanism whereby the two firms could cooperate, which means we would need to use *cooperative game theory*, which is beyond the scope of this text. But perhaps more importantly, collusion between firms to fix prices or to maintain high prices is illegal in many countries around the world.

Different production costs

In the model from which we derived the Bertrand paradox, we assumed that both firms had the same cost of production. Suppose that this is not the case, but rather that firm 1 has a cost advantage over firm 2: $c_1 < c_2$. Firm 2 would never charge a price below c_2, since then price would be less than marginal cost, and firm 2 would be earning negative profits. So the lowest price that firm 2 can charge is $p_2 = c_2$.

How will the manager of firm 1 set firm 1's price? The manager knows that the competition at firm 2 cannot match a price which is lower than $p_2 = c_2$. So firm 1 can charge a price just slightly below $p_2 = c_2$, say $c_2 - \epsilon$, where ϵ is some very small number. Firm 2 cannot match this lower price, since its profits would be negative. But now firm 1's price is less than firm 2's price, so all consumers would buy from firm 1 at the lower price. And as long as $p_1 = c_2 - \epsilon > c_1$, firm 1 will be earning positive profits. In general, when the costs of firms producing the same good are not the same, then we can expect that some firm(s) will earn positive profits in equilibrium.

Differentiated products

Throughout our discussion of Bertrand (price) competition, we assumed that both firms were producing exactly the same product. The result of this assumption was that consumers would always purchase from the firm selling at the lowest price. There are many circumstances where this assumption is valid. A consumer buying sugar at the grocery store will generally be completely indifferent between a 2 kg package of granulated sugar sold for the same price by two different firms.

But we can easily think of many examples where a consumer is not indifferent between two identical products selling for the same price. Think of our two hot-dog vendors selling hot dogs on the beach. We can imagine a situation where both vendors sell exactly the same hot dog at exactly the same price. But a consumer who is closer to vendor 1 would rather buy a hot dog from vendor 1 than from vendor 2, since the consumer would have to walk farther along the beach to get to vendor 2. This consumer is *not* indifferent to the product sold by the two vendors (firms), even though the same hot dog is being sold at exactly the same price. In fact, this consumer may even be willing to pay a bit more for a hot dog from vendor 1, to substitute for not having to walk all the way to the other vendor.

What this simple example illustrates is a case where our definition of the product being sold is too strict to properly characterize this market. A more careful description of the product being sold lets us describe a situation where a consumer is not indifferent to the output of both firms at the same price. This means that one firm could increase its price and not lose its entire share of the market, so we could expect to see firms earning positive profits in equilibrium.

There are all sorts of ways in which seemingly similar products can be differentiated in the eyes of consumers. Suppose we consider an individual consumer who is purchasing a car. All cars have the same basic characteristic to satisfy the demand of this consumer: they get the consumer from point *A* to point *B*. But this consumer will certainly not be indifferent to all cars at the same price. While a minivan selling for $25,000 and a small sports car selling for $25,000 will get the consumer from *A* to *B*, the consumer will certainly not view these two cars as identical products.

Firms can differentiate their products in a number of dimensions. Depending upon the type of product being sold, producers can sell a product of high or low quality, or can differentiate their product on the basis of size or location. We have already given a simple example where product differentiation can lead to an equilibrium where firms earn positive profits. So it seems important to ask how managers can strategically choose how to differentiate their products in order to maximize profits. This will be the subject of Chapter 7.

Capacity constraints and rationing

Another potential resolution to the Bertrand paradox has to do with an implicit assumption which we've been making in our model of Bertrand competition. To illustrate, we'll use the same example which we used to derive the Bertrand paradox. Suppose two firms sell exactly the same product, face a market demand curve given by:

$$q = 120 - p$$

and have the same constant marginal cost $c = \$30$. The result of Bertrand competition had both firms earning zero profits in equilibrium, selling output at $p = c = \$30$. If either firm raised its price even slightly, the other firm would capture the entire market.

Now suppose that firm 2 raises its price slightly, to $31. Total market demand for firm 1 will be:

$$q_1 = 120 - c = 90$$

since firm 1 is selling output at $p_1 = c = \$30$, and no consumer wants to buy from firm 2 since firm 2 is charging a higher price. But what if firm 1 cannot meet total market demand $q_1 = 90$? What if the capacity of production of firm 1 is less than total market demand? Then there will be some portion of the market left over for firm 2. Some consumers will be unable to buy from firm 1 at firm 1's lower price. Firm 2 will face a *residual demand curve*: that portion of the market left over after firm 1 has sold out all of its output.

Now firm 2 can act as a monopolist over the remainder of the market, and will be able to earn positive profits. Notice that this cannot be an equilibrium. Firm 2 is earning positive profits while firm 1 earns zero profits, so firm 1 has an incentive to raise its price. But the point is that when firms face capacity constraints, firms will generally earn positive profits in equilibrium.

This example brings up another important point. How do firms choose capacity of production? This question is certainly important,

since we just showed that a capacity constraint can imply the existence of profits in equilibrium. We will address the question of how firms choose capacity in Chapter 10.

6.3 Stackelberg equilibrium

The final model to present in this chapter describes the outcome of competition between two firms when one firm has a *first-mover advantage*. Because of the evolution of competition in the industry, the firm which we will call the *Stackelberg leader* has the ability to choose and commit to a strategy before the other firm, which we will call the *Stackelberg follower*. This type of game is often called a Stackelberg game, because it is based on the pioneering work of Heinrich von Stackelberg in 1939. It is also referred to as a leader–follower game.

Suppose two firms are competing in quantities. Both firms produce identical outputs and have the same production technology. To keep things simple, suppose fixed costs are zero and constant marginal cost of production is c. We want to be able to relate and contrast our results from this Stackelberg game to those derived from Cournot quantity competition, so suppose that the market demand function faced by these two firms is given by:

$$p = 120 - (q_1 + q_2)$$

We showed in Section 6.1 that the outcome of Cournot competition in such a model where both firms choose strategies (quantities) at the same time was:

$$q_1 = q_2 = \frac{120 - c}{3}$$

$$q_1 + q_2 = q^c = 80 - \frac{2c}{3}$$

$$p^c = 40 + \frac{2c}{3}$$

Now suppose that firm 1 has established a dominant position in this market, and has the ability to commit to a strategic choice of q_1 before firm 2. Alternatively, we could re-interpret this game as one where firm 1 actively pursues a strategy to commit to q_1 before firm 2 can respond, so firm 1 is trying to make itself the Stackelberg leader. Whatever the case, we already know how firm 2 will respond to any strategy chosen by firm 1. This is given by firm 2's reaction function, which we derived in Section 6.1:

$$q_2 = R^2(q_1) = \frac{120 - q_1 - c}{2}$$

The manager of firm 1 knows that this is firm 2's best response to any strategy chosen by firm 1, so the manager uses this information to solve firm 1's profit-maximization problem, which now becomes:

$$\max \pi^1 = [120 - q_1 - q_2] \cdot q_1 - c \cdot q_1$$

$$= \left[120 - q_1 - \left(\frac{120 - q_1 - c}{2} \right) \right]$$

$$\cdot q_1 - c \cdot q_1$$

The manager at firm 1 just substitutes firm 2's reaction function into firm 1's profit function. Solving for firm 1's first-order condition and re-arranging for q_1 yields the following solution:

$$q_1^s = \frac{120 - c}{2}$$

Firm 2's best response is given by its reaction function:

$$q_2 = \frac{120 - c}{2} - \frac{q_1}{2}$$

$$= \frac{120 - c}{2} - \frac{120 - c}{4}$$

$$= \frac{120 - c}{4}$$

Relative to the Cournot equilibrium, firm 1 has increased output and firm 2 has decreased output.

Total market output in the Stackelberg equilibrium is:

$$q^s = q_1^s + q_2^s$$

$$= \frac{120 - c}{2} + \frac{120 - c}{4}$$

$$= 90 - \frac{3c}{4}$$

The Canadian Beer Wars

Sometimes a firm can gain a Stackelberg leader advantage in a market by being the first of its competitors to introduce a new type of product. In March 1993, Labatt Breweries and Molson Breweries of Canada introduced Ice Beer to the Canadian beer market. Each company claimed that theirs was the first ice-filtered beer in the world, even though Molson introduced its Ice Beer one day before Labatt. In fact, there was evidence that both firms rushed to get their new products to the market first. Labatt accused Molson of launching a pre-emptive strike after learning of Labatt's plans to brew and market Ice Beer. Labatt responded by bringing its planned "launch date" forward from May to March.

Ice Beer is brewed by chilling the beer and then removing the ice crystals that form. The brewers claim that this produces a beer with a taste which is distinctively different from that of regular beer. Ice Beer also has a higher alcohol content than regular beer.

Why would both firms place so much emphasis on getting their new product to the market first? Recent history in the Canadian beer market supports the argument that there exists a significant Stackelberg leader advantage. In 1989, Molson introduced its Dry Beer two months ahead of the launch of Labatt Dry. This head-start caused Labatt Dry to do so poorly relative to Molson Dry that Labatt eventually re-introduced its new product as Labatt Extra Dry. Three years later, Labatt gained a similar advantage by introducing Labatt Genuine Draft before Molson could get Miller Genuine Draft (brewed by Molson under license) to the market. Labatt Genuine Draft remains the dominant bottled draft beer in the Canadian beer market.

So what was the result of the Ice Beer Battle? In 1993, Labatt Ice had a market share of 5 percent of the Canadian beer market (865 million hectoliters), ranking fifth in brands sold in Canada, while Molson Canadian Ice ranked ninth, with a market share of 3 percent (519 million hectoliters). Of course, a number of factors may well have influenced the relative competitive positions of firms in the Ice Beer market. Labatt made significant efforts to patent its process for producing Labatt Ice Beer, to try to convince consumers that Labatt Ice was the only true Ice Beer. Advertising has also figured prominently in each producer's efforts to gain market share. We will return to these important issues in Chapter 9 when we discuss advertising strategies and Chapter 10 when we discuss entry deterrence and accommodation strategies.

Source: Data for this case are from the March 26, 1993 and June 9, 1994 issues of the Toronto *Globe and Mail* newspaper.

So total market output is higher in the Stackelberg equilibrium than in the Cournot equilibrium. Market equilibrium must be at a point farther down the demand curve, so the equilibrium market price must be lower in the Stackelberg equilibrium than in the corresponding Cournot equilibrium.

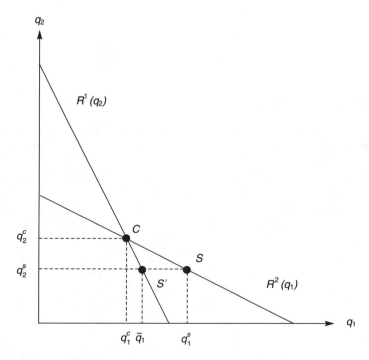

Figure 6.8 Stackelberg equilibrium

Result

Relative to the Cournot equilibrium, the firm which can generate a Stackelberg leader advantage increases market share, and the follower firm loses market share. The market equilibrium moves closer to the perfectly competitive equilibrium, as total market output rises and market price falls.

We illustrate this equilibrium graphically in Figure 6.8. The Stackelberg equilibrium is labeled S, and for comparison, we've included the Cournot equilibrium at point C. It is clear that the Stackelberg leader (firm 1) has increased market share at the expense of the follower (firm 2). But firm 1 is not on its reaction function at the Stackelberg equilibrium. At point S, firm 2 is on its reaction function, so q_2^s is a best-response to q_1^s. But firm 1 would actually be better off producing $\tilde{q}_1$ at point S', since that is its best-response to firm 2's choice of q_2^s.

Why might firm 1 want to stay at S, even though it is better off on its reaction function at S'? To answer this question, we need to consider the behavior of firm 2. If firm 1 moves from S to S', then firm 2 will no longer be on its reaction function. Firm 2 would want to increase q_2. This process would continue until firms found their way back to the Cournot equilibrium at C. The manager at firm 1 knows that if output is reduced from S to S', the market equilibrium will ultimately move back to point C. Firm 1 is better off being the Stackelberg leader at point S than playing to a Cournot equilibrium at point C, so the Stackelberg equilibrium at S is sustainable, even though firm 1 is not on its reaction function.

Summary

- The basic models introduced in this chapter consider behavior in a duopoly market where two firms compete in price or quantity. The strategic choice variable for the manager is either price or quantity.
- The strategic choice variable in the Cournot model of quantity competition can be interpreted very broadly, and can represent a level of investment in capacity or a level of product quality.
- Relative to the monopoly equilibrium, in the Cournot model of quantity competition, when two firms compete by choosing quantity of output, the equilibrium market price is lower, individual firm profits are lower, and total market output is higher in the Cournot equilibrium.
- A cost-reducing technological improvement by one firm in a model where firms compete in quantities will increase the market share of that firm, decrease the market share of its competitor, increase equilibrium market output and decrease equilibrium market price.
- Adding more firms to a market where firms compete in quantities will make that market more competitive, increasing equilibrium market output, decreasing market price, and reducing profits earned by any individual firm.
- In the Bertrand model of price competition, if firms sell the same product and have the same production costs, they will all charge the same price in equilibrium.

> ### *Summary contd*
>
> - When firms compete in prices, adding just one more firm to a market which was initially monopolized drives the market equilibrium to the perfectly competitive equilibrium, where both firms earn zero profits. This extreme result is known as the Bertrand paradox.
> - If the simple Bertrand model of price competition is extended to allow for product differentiation or capacity constraints, duopolists will generally earn positive profits in equilibrium when competing in prices.
> - The Stackelberg model describes a market where one firm can commit to the choice of a strategy before its competitor. When firms compete in quantities, the Stackelberg leader has a first-mover advantage and is able to increase profits and market share at the expense of its competitor.
> - Relative to the Cournot equilibrium when firms choose quantities simultaneously, the Stackelberg equilibrium is characterized by a lower equilibrium market price and a higher level of total market output.

Notes

1 This is often referred to as the *Cournot model*, after the pioneering work of the French economist Augustin Cournot from his 1838 text *Researches into the Mathematical Principles of the Theory of Wealth*.

2 We want to restrict marginal cost c to lie between 0 and 120, else the equilibrium quantity could be negative.

3 Notice that this graph shows the market equilibrium, so that the level of output q on the horizontal axis measures total output in the market, which is the sum of output of each firm. This is not the same as the information in Figures 6.2–6.4, which showed each firm's reaction function and allowed us to solve for each individual firm's level of output.

4 The label Bertrand equilibrium, and the concept of the Bertrand paradox, described later in this section, refer to the work of the French economist Joseph Bertrand. A more advanced treatment of this material can be found in Tirole (1988), pp. 209–18.

Exercises

1 Consider a market where two firms are competing in quantities. Suppose that the market inverse demand function is given by:

$$p = 750 - 15 (q_1 + q_2)$$

Each firm has zero fixed costs and constant marginal cost of production c.

(a) Write out each firm's profit function, and solve for the two first-order profit-maximization conditions.

(b) Use the two first-order conditions to solve for each firm's reaction function, and plot these two reaction functions.

(c) Solve for the Cournot equilibrium (q_1^c, q_2^c).

(d) Use the demand function to solve for the equilibrium market price, and then solve for the level of profits earned by each firm in equilibrium.

2 Suppose instead that firm 1 was the Stackelberg leader in this market. Re-write firm 1's profit function, using firm 2's reaction function, and solve for the Stackelberg equilibrium. Once you've solved for the equilibrium market price and total market demand, you should be able to tell whether consumer surplus has increased or decreased.

3 Using the same demand and cost functions, suppose that firms competed in prices instead of quantities. Solve for the Bertrand equilibrium, including market demand, market price, and profits earned by each firm. Contrast your answers to those in the previous questions.

4 Suppose that the market demand function is given by:

$$p = a - b\,(q_1 + q_2)$$

as in Section 6.1.1. Each firm has zero fixed costs and constant marginal cost of production c. An increase in demand causes the demand function to shift upwards, reflected by an increase in the parameter a to $\tilde{a} > a$. What effect does this have on each firm's reaction function, and the Cournot equilibrium?

5 Refer to Figure 6.3. What would happen if firm 2's reaction function were steeper than firm 1's reaction function? Can you relate your answer to stability of the Cournot equilibrium?

References

Bertrand, Joseph. "Théorie mathématique de la richesse sociale." *Journal des Savants* (1883), pp. 499–508.

Tirole, Jean. *The Theory of Industrial Organization* (Cambridge, MA: The MIT Press, 1988) pp. 218–21.

Von Stackelberg, Heinrich. *Marktform und Gleichgewicht* (Market Structure and Equilibrium) (Vienna: Julius Springer, 1939).

Chapter 7

Product differentiation

•••

When you are finished with this chapter you should understand:

- How goods can be differentiated on the basis of physical location, quality, size, appearance, or many other characteristics, and how the notion of *product space* can be defined to accommodate these product characteristics
- That product differentiation can resolve the Bertrand paradox because consumers will not be indifferent to the same good produced by different firms at the same price
- That with differentiated products, firms can compete over prices in the short-run, with product location taken as fixed, but in the longer run, firms can vary both their market price and the location of their product in product space
- How the effect of a change in product location can be broken down into a *market-share effect* and a *strategic effect*
- That competition between firms over product location can result in *minimum product differentiation* or *maximum product differentiation*

It's time to head back to the beach, to see whether we can say anything more about the problem facing our hot-dog vendors. You'll recall that when we last left the beach, there was one established hot-dog vendor who had already set up her cart and had been in business for some time. The newcomer to the beach was trying to decide where to set up his hot-dog cart. How can these two vendors benefit from our discussion of competition between two firms from Chapters 5 and 6? Is there anything that we've learned from the models of competition between two firms which we can use to figure out what the outcome of competition between these two vendors will be?

To proceed, we need to figure out which of the models of competition we've developed is most relevant to this market situation. One way to do this is to consider this market as a game being played between the two hot-dog vendors. In Chapter 5, we said that we could completely characterize a game by the following elements:

1 a list of players
2 a list of strategies or actions available to each player
3 a description of the payoff to each player for each possible outcome
4 the rules of the game

The first element is straightforward: The players of the game are the two hot-dog

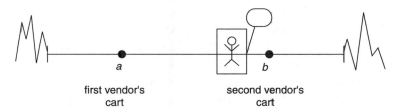

Figure 7.1 Hot-dog carts on the beach

vendors. The second element is already a bit more complicated, so we'll make some assumptions about the strategies available to each hot-dog vendor. We'll suppose that they sell only hot dogs, and that they sell the same type of hot dog. The only strategies available to the hot-dog vendors are:

- the price at which to sell a hot dog
- where to set up the cart

Payoffs to each vendor will be total profits from selling hot dogs. To keep the problem simple, we'll suppose that the rules of the game are that each vendor sets up his or her cart first thing in the morning, and cannot move the cart until the end of the day. The game is played once a day.

By now, you should see that the most appropriate model we have to deal with this market is our Bertrand model of price competition. To see how well the Bertrand model described the competition between our hot-dog vendors, let's draw a simple picture of what the beach may look like, illustrated in Figure 7.1. In this description of the beach, the first vendor's cart is parked at *a*, to the west of the second vendor's cart which is located at *b*. Of course, the two carts could be closer together, or farther apart. For now, let's suppose that this is where they've set up their carts for the day.

We haven't said anything about the consumers in this market yet. The whole length of the beach will be populated by swimmers

and sunbathers. We've included one sunbather in Figure 7.1. When she gets hungry and wants a hot dog, where will she go? To keep things simple, suppose she knows that each vendor is selling the same type of hot dog at exactly the same price. She's obviously set up her towel, umbrella, and other sunbathing gear closer to the second vendor at *b*, so she would rather buy her hot dog from the second vendor than walk all the way back and forth to the first vendor.

Now recall the characteristics of our Bertrand model of price competition. In Chapter 5, we showed that consumers were completely indifferent between the output of two different firms when firms charged the same price for the same product. This is certainly not the case on the beach. The sunbather is clearly not indifferent between the same hot dog at the same price from the two vendors. So we need to expand our Bertrand model, to accommodate the fact that consumers are not indifferent between the same product at the same price.

7.1 The characteristics approach

We've described a situation where the output of two firms (the hot dogs sold by the two vendors) are completely identical from the point of view of the producers, yet consumers are not indifferent between the two goods at the same price. Of course, this problem can be significantly more complicated. All automobiles provide the same basic service of transportation to consumers, yet there are many different types of automobiles. Radios all serve the same basic purpose, which is to receive signals broadcast over the airwaves, yet radios come in many different shapes and sizes. These are all goods which are exactly the same in some dimension (transportation for cars, local reception for radios) yet very different in some other dimensions. The same is true of the hot dogs sold by the two vendors: they are exactly the same, except for the place where they are sold.

One way of modeling this type of product differentiation is the *characteristics approach*, pioneered by the economist Kelvin Lancaster in 1966. The consumer is described by preferences over not the consumption goods themselves, but over the characteristics of the goods consumed. For any particular consumption good, the consumer has some optimal bundle of characteristics. Think of two types of automobiles, a family car and a pick-up truck, both of which are being sold for $20,000. The family car will be closer to the optimal bundle of characteristics of an automobile for a family of four, while the pick-up truck will be better suited to a building contractor. In a similar way, the hot dog sold by the second vendor is closer to the *optimal bundle of characteristics* of the sunbather in Figure 7.1 than a hot dog sold by the first vendor.

7.2 The notion of product space

We will expand our models of competition between two firms to incorporate the effects of product differentiation by supposing that as far as consumers are concerned, the goods produced by firm 1 and firm 2 are generally the same. However, there are some particular characteristics which differentiate the output of the two firms. In general, there could be very many differences between these two goods. If the two firms are producing radios, we would observe any two firms selling radios of different colors, different sizes, different weights, etc. For simplicity, we will proceed by supposing that there is only one characteristic for which consumers can differentiate between the goods produced by the two firms. Of course, this assumption is restrictive, but it keeps our model relatively simple.[1]

To completely formulate our model, we will make four additional assumptions:

1 Product space can be represented by a horizontal line of length equal to one.
2 There are a finite number of consumers uniformly distributed along this line.
3 Except for the one characteristic for which consumers can differentiate between the goods produced by each firm, all consumers have identical preferences, and will buy either zero units or one unit of output. Every consumer derives a level of utility or *gross surplus* equal to $\bar{s}$ from consumption of one unit of this good.
4 Total cost of consumption for any consumer will be the market price of the good p_i plus the *transport cost* incurred by consuming a good which is some distance away from the consumer's optimal bundle of characteristics.

Of course, each of these assumptions is very important, so we'll consider each in turn.

As long as products are differentiated in only one dimension (consumers can tell apart the output of firms 1 and 2 because only one thing is different between each firm's output), the first assumption is completely innocuous. We set the length of the line equal to 1 because 1 is an easy number to multiply and divide by.

We assume that the number of consumers is finite so that our problem is well-defined.

The assumption that consumers are evenly distributed along the unit interval (the market) is made for convenience more than anything else. We could just as easily assume that consumers are clustered at various points along the unit interval. For example, it might be interesting to see how our analysis of competition between the hot-dog vendors changes if sunbathers congregate around two of three points along the beach. There are many reasons why this might happen. For example, there may be two or three parking lots opposite the beach, so swimmers and sunbathers may set up their blankets and umbrellas as close as possible to the spots where their cars are parked. But for simplicity, we will begin by assuming that sunbathers are uniformly distributed along the beach.

The third assumption is certainly restrictive, but is made to keep our model sufficiently simple. We interpret this assumption as follows: the consumer's location along the unit interval is dictated by his or her optimal choice of the characteristics. If each consumer was able to consume his or her optimal bundle of characteristics, then each consumer would derive the same surplus $\bar{s}$ from consumption of one unit of output. This implies that each consumer has the same *reservation price* of $\bar{s}$, so that no consumer will pay more than $\bar{s}$ dollars to buy one unit of output. We also assume that each consumer buys at most one unit of output for simplicity. We could suppose that consumers have different preferences, or that some consumers would buy more than one unit of output. But this would make the model more complicated than is necessary to derive the results in which we are interested, which are the outcome of competition between two firms selling differentiated products.[2]

The final assumption implies that we can break the cost of consuming one unit of output into two distinct parts. The first part of this total consumption cost is just the market price p_i which must be paid to buy one unit of output from firm i. The second part of the total consumption cost reflects the fact that the good sold by firm i may not be having exactly the best characteristics which the consumer wants. This second part of the total consumption cost will be called the *transportation cost*.

We're now in a position to illustrate this market using a simple graph. We'll use the horizontal axis to represent product space. Let the extreme left or west end of the market (the beach) be at 0, and the extreme right or east end will be 1. On the vertical axis, we'll record the total surplus received by a consumer who buys one unit of output. The highest surplus must be received by the consumer who is located at the same spot on the unit interval as the firm. So if firm 1 is located at point a and firm 2 is located at point b, with $0 \le a, b \le 1$, the surplus received by the consumer located at a will be $\bar{s}$ minus the price charged by firm 1, p_1. Likewise, the consumer located at b will receive an overall surplus of $\bar{s} - p_2$ when buying one unit of output from firm 2. This situation is illustrated in Figure 7.2.

This product space can represent any single dimension in which products are differentiated. It is easy to see how physical location can be represented in this way, by noting that the extreme west end of the beach can be point 0 and the extreme east end can be point 1. But we could also use this simple model to represent quality space. The extreme left of the interval could represent the lowest-quality car, and the extreme right end could represent the highest-quality car. Or the unit interval could represent the size or weight of a product. The smallest or lightest radio would be at point 0, while the largest or heaviest radio could be at point 1.

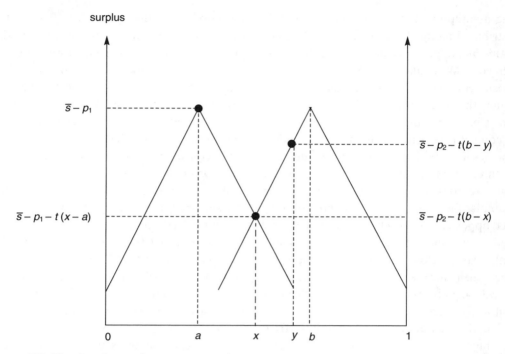

Figure 7.2 Firm location and consumer surplus

What would be the surplus received by a consumer who must travel to the location of the store at a or b? Consider the consumer located at point y. When she buys one unit of output from firm 2, this consumer will receive total surplus $\bar{s}$, and will pay p_2. But this consumer must also incur a transport cost for traveling to firm 2. We will suppose that the transport cost increases the farther that the consumer has to travel to buy 1 unit of output. The distance that the consumer must travel to get to firm 2 is $b - y$, so the transport cost incurred by this consumer will be represented by $b - y$ times the cost $t > 0$ per unit traveled. As a result, the total transport cost will be $t(b - y)$, and the net surplus received by this consumer will be $\bar{s} - p_2 - t(b - y)$.

Would this consumer buy from firm 1 or firm 2? This consumer must travel farther to get to firm 1. To put it another way, the characteristics of the output of firm 2 are more like the set of characteristics which this consumer would prefer. The output of firm 1 is farther from her optimal consumption bundle, since the distance from her location at y to firm 1, $y - a$, is greater than the distance she must travel to get to firm 2. So the consumer located at point y would buy from firm 2, and would not buy from firm 1.

If we look at Figure 7.2, we see that there is one particular consumer, located at point x, who is just indifferent between buying from firm 1 or from firm 2. For our purposes, this will be the most important consumer in the market. All consumers located to the west of the consumer at x are closer to firm 1, and will buy from firm 1. All consumers to the east of the consumer at x will buy from firm 2. So we can use the location of consumer x to derive information about the demand for each firm's output.

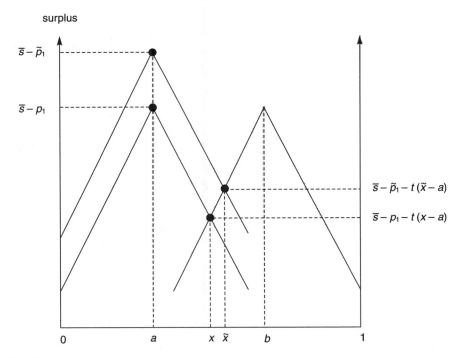

surplus

$\overline{s} - \tilde{p}_1$

$\overline{s} - p_1$

$\overline{s} - \tilde{p}_1 - t(\tilde{x} - a)$

$\overline{s} - p_1 - t(x - a)$

0   a   x $\tilde{x}$ b   1

Figure 7.3 Firm 1 drops its price

What happens if something in the market changes? Each firm has two strategic variables to choose: price and location. Suppose that firm 1 drops its price from p_1 to $\tilde{p}_1$. Then for any consumer buying from store 1, total surplus will increase. We can illustrate this effect in Figure 7.3: note that the consumer who is indifferent between buying from firm 1 or 2 is now farther to the right, at $\tilde{x}$ instead of x. Also note that the net surplus received by the indifferent consumer increases. This shows how firm 1 can use a strategy of dropping its price to increase market share.

Now consider another example where firm 1 is located at a, firm 2 is located at b, but firm 1 has a much lower price than firm 2. This example is described in Figure 7.4.

As in the previous example, the consumer who is located exactly at the same spot as firm 2 at point b derives a net surplus of $\overline{s} - p_2$. If this consumer wants to buy from firm 1,

she derives the same gross surplus $\overline{s}$, and pays firm 1's market price p_1, but must also pay the transport cost $t(b - a)$. However, in this example, the difference between firm 1's price p_1 and firm 2's price p_2 is so large that even when paying the transport cost $t(b - a)$, the consumer located at point b would rather buy from firm 1. In this example, firm 1 has a price so low that firm 2 is priced out of the market, and firm 1 has a complete monopoly.[3]

The final market situation we want to describe before solving for equilibrium is one where there are some consumers who do not want to buy from either firm. As before, the consumer located at point a, the location of firm 1, will receive a net surplus of $\overline{s} - p_1$. The consumer located at b buys from firm 2 and receives surplus $\overline{s} - p_2$. This situation is illustrated in Figure 7.5.

Consumers who must travel to either store still incur a transport cost t. But in this

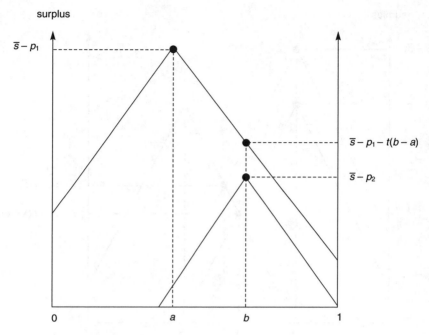

Figure 7.4 Firm 1 has a monopoly

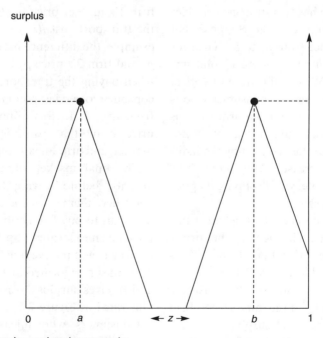

Figure 7.5 Each firm has a local monopoly

example, all of those consumers in the area labelled z in Figure 7.5 are so far away from either firm that the transport cost $t(z - a)$ or $t(b - z)$ makes the net surplus of buying from either store negative. For example, to buy from firm 1, a consumer located in the area z must pay market price p_1 and the transport cost $t(z - a)$. These two costs together are greater in absolute value than the total surplus $\bar{s}$ derived from consuming the output of firm 1. This consumer would rather not buy from either firm. In this situation, we say that each firm has a *local monopoly*. Each firm has a captive part of the market, and some portion of the market between the two firms is not served.

But what will the market equilibrium between these two firms actually look like? To solve for the market equilibrium, we need to describe each firm's profit maximization problem, as a function of the two choice variables price and location. To proceed, we must first solve for each firm's demand function. Of the three market situations which we described in Figures 7.2–7.5, we are most interested in the case where two firms are both competing over the market represented by the unit interval, so we will only consider the example where the entire market is served, neither firm has a local monopoly, and both firms have positive demand. This was the example described in Figure 7.2. In either of the other examples, one or both firms have a monopoly, and we've already described the characteristics of a monopoly equilibrium in Chapters 3 and 4.

As we noted earlier in our discussion of Figure 7.2, when firm 1 is located at a and firm 2 located at b, there is some consumer located at x who is just indifferent between buying from firm 1 or firm 2. All consumers to the left of x will buy from firm 1, so x represents the demand function for firm 1. Firm 2 gets all consumers to the right of x, so since the market is one unit

long, firm 2's demand function is represented by $1 - x$. So to find each firm's demand function, all we have to do is solve for x.

Since the consumer located at x is just indifferent between buying from firm 1 or firm 2, it must be the case that the cost of buying from firm 1, including the transport cost, is exactly equal to the cost of buying from firm 2. A consumer located at x is $x - a$ distance away from firm 1, so to buy from firm 1, the consumer must incur the transport cost $t(x - a)$. This makes the total cost of buying one unit of output from firm 1 equal to the market price p_1 plus the transport cost $t(x - a)$. Likewise the cost of buying one unit of output from firm 2 will be the market price p_2 plus the transport cost $t(b - x)$, since the consumer is $b - x$ distance away from firm 2. If the total cost of buying from firm 1 is the same as the cost of buying from firm 2, the following condition must hold:

$$p_1 + t(x - a) = p_2 + t(b - x)$$

We can solve this condition for x as follows:

$$p_1 + tx - ta = p_2 + tb - tx$$
$$2tx = (p_2 - p_1) + t(a + b)$$
$$x = \frac{a + b}{2} + \frac{p_2 - p_1}{2t}$$

If we add and subtract $2a/2$ from the right-hand side, we get:

$$x = \frac{2a}{2} + \frac{a + b - 2a}{2} + \frac{p_2 - p_1}{2t}$$
$$= a + \frac{b - a}{2} + \frac{p_2 - p_1}{2t}$$

Now that we have written firm 1's demand function in this form, we see that we can break firm 1's demand function down into three components. We can give an intuiti~ description of these three compone~ supposing first that $p_1 = p_2$. ~ third component will be equ~ can interpret the first ter~

All consumers to the left of firm 1's location will make up firm 1's captive market. None of these consumers would buy from firm 2.

The second part of firm 1's demand function is represented by the term $(b - a)/2$. If we note that $b - a$ is the area between firm 1 and firm 2, we see that firm 1 gets half of the consumers between a and b. So if both firms sell the same good at the same price, all consumers to the left of the point midway between firms 1 and 2 will buy from firm 1, and all consumers to the right of this point will buy from firm 2.

The final part of firm 1's demand function is the term $(p_2 - p_1)/2t$. This term captures the effects of price competition between the two firms. If firm 1 lowers its price, so that p_1 falls, then the term $(p_2 - p_1)/2t$ increases, so demand for firm 1 will rise. We've already illustrated this effect in Figure 7.3. As p_1 falls, the surplus received by anyone purchasing firm 1's output will rise, so the location of the indifferent consumer x moves to the right, away from firm 1's location at a. This causes demand for firm 1's output to rise.

Since firm 2 gets all of the market to the right of the indifferent consumer located at x, firm 2's demand function will be given by $1 - x$, which we can solve for as follows:

$$1 - x = 1 - a - \frac{b - a}{2} - \frac{p_2 - p_1}{2t}$$
$$= 1 - a + \frac{a - b}{2} + \frac{p_1 - p_2}{2t}$$

If we add and subtract $(2a - 2b)/2$ to the right-hand side, we get:

$$1 - x = \frac{2a - 2b}{2} + 1 - a - \frac{2a - 2b}{2} + \frac{a - b}{2}$$
$$+ \frac{p_1 - p_2}{2t}$$
$$= 1 - b + \frac{a - 2a + 2b - b}{2} + \frac{p_1 - p_2}{2t}$$
$$= 1 - b + \frac{b - a}{2} + \frac{p_1 - p_2}{2t}$$

So firm 2's demand function can be broken down in the same way as firm 1's demand function. Firm 2 gets its *turf* $(1 - b)$, half of the market between the two firms, $(b - a)/2$, and the final term capturing the effect of price competition between the two firms.

The last step before moving on to each firm's profit-maximization problem is to relate market share to actual market demand. We need one more bit of information: the size of the market. Since consumers are uniformly distributed along the unit interval which we're using to represent the market, we can find each firm's total market demand by multiplying its market share by the size of the market. For example, if we knew that there were 1,000 sunbathers on the beach, then the size of the market would be 1,000. Total demand for firm 1's product would be $x \cdot 1,000$ and demand for firm 2's output would be $(1 - x) \cdot 1,000$. So if we had found that $x = 0.4$, then demand for firm 1's product would be 400 units, while demand for firm 2's output would be 600 units.

We're now in a position to solve for each firm's profit function. Recall that there are no fixed costs in this market, and firms 1 and 2 face constant marginal cost c_1 and c_2, respectively. Profits for each firm are the difference between total revenue and total cost. If p_1 is the price at which firm 1 sells its output, then total revenue is just p_1 times firm 1's demand x. With constant marginal cost, total cost for firm 1 is just $c_1 x$. Firm 1's profits can be written as:

$$\pi^1 = p_1 x - c_1 x$$
$$\pi^1 = (p_1 - c_1) \cdot x$$

We just solved for total demand for firm 1's output x, as a function of each firm's price p_1 and p_2, and each firm's location a and b. Using this information, we can substitute for x in firm 1's profit function to get:

$$\pi^1 = (p_1 - c_1) \cdot \left[a + \frac{b-a}{2} + \frac{p_2 - p_1}{2t} \right]$$

We can repeat this process to solve for firm 2's profit function π^2, using firm 2's demand function $1 - x$ which we derived earlier:

$$\pi^2 = (p_2 - c_2) \cdot \left[1 - b + \frac{b-a}{2} + \frac{p_1 - p_2}{2t} \right]$$

The manager of each firm has two problems to solve, corresponding to the two choice variables in each firm's profit function. The manager of firm 1 needs to solve for the price p_1 which maximizes profits, and the location a which maximizes profits. We will solve the manager's problems in two stages, which we can think of as two separate problems: a short-run problem and a long-run problem. In the short-run, we solve for the Nash equilibrium in prices, since the manager of each firm will take location as given in the short-run. Solving this short-run problem will give us the outcome of price competition in this model. Then we'll move on to the second stage of the manager's problem. This will allow us to solve for the Nash equilibrium in locations, by solving the long-run problem when the manager can choose location, given the outcome of price competition.

7.3 Equilibrium in prices

To solve for the Nash equilibrium in prices, the first step is to solve for each firm's first-order condition. Recall that this condition implies that the change in profits for any marginal change in the firm's price be equal to zero. We solve for this condition by setting the price derivative of each firm's profit function equal to zero, as follows:

$$\frac{\partial \pi^1}{\partial p_1} = a + \frac{b-a}{2} + \frac{p_2 - p_1}{2t}$$
$$- \frac{1}{2t} \cdot (p_1 - c_1) = 0$$
$$\frac{\partial \pi^2}{\partial p_2} = 1 - b + \frac{b-a}{2} + \frac{p_1 - p_2}{2t}$$
$$- \frac{1}{2t} \cdot (p_2 - c_2) = 0$$

These are the two first-order conditions, one for each firm, which we can solve for the two unknown variables: the market prices p_1 and p_2. To proceed, re-write each first-order condition to isolate each firm's market price:

$$\frac{p_1}{t} = a + \frac{b-a}{2} + \frac{p_2 + c_1}{2t}$$
$$\frac{p_2}{t} = 1 - b + \frac{b-a}{2} + \frac{p_1 + c_2}{2t}$$

If we multiply both sides of each equation by the transport cost t, we get:

$$p_1 = t \cdot \left(\frac{a+b}{2} \right) + \frac{c_1}{2} + \frac{p_2}{2}$$
$$p_2 = t \cdot \left(1 - \frac{a+b}{2} \right) + \frac{c_2}{2} + \frac{p_1}{2}$$

Recall that we want to solve for each firm's price, p_1 and p_2, taking all other variables as given. So costs c_1 and c_2, the transport cost t, and locations a and b are all treated as fixed for the time being. But then these two equations are just each firm's reaction function. Given costs and locations, the last equation gives firm 2's best response price p_2 for any price p_1 charged by the other firm. Notice that these reaction functions are linear, and are upward-sloping. This implies that the choice variables (prices) are strategic complements.

Each firm's reaction function is graphed : Figure 7.6. The Nash equilibrium in pr illustrated at (p_1^n, p_2^n), where e⁻ choice of price is the best r⁻ other firm's price. We c⁻

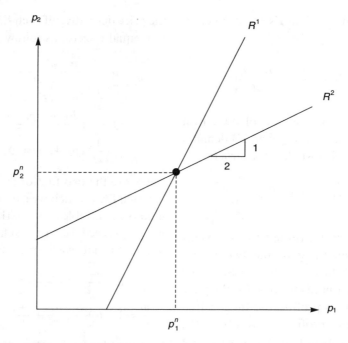

Figure 7.6 Reaction functions when firms choose prices

firm's Nash equilibrium in prices, by substituting firm 1's reaction function into firm 2's reaction function, as follows:

$$p_2 = t \cdot \left(1 - \frac{a+b}{2}\right) + \frac{c_2}{2}$$

$$+ \frac{1}{2} \cdot \left[t \cdot \left(\frac{a+b}{2}\right) + \frac{c_1}{2} + \frac{p_2}{2}\right]$$

$$p_2 - \frac{1}{4}p_2 = t - t \cdot \left(\frac{a+b}{2}\right) + \frac{t}{2} \cdot \left(\frac{a+b}{2}\right)$$

$$+ \frac{c_2}{2} + \frac{c_1}{4}$$

$$\frac{3}{4}p_2 = t - \frac{t}{2} \cdot \left(\frac{a+b}{2}\right) + \frac{c_1 + 2c_2}{4}$$

$$p_2^n = \frac{4t}{3} - \frac{t(a+b)}{3} + \frac{c_1 + 2c_2}{3}$$

Likewise, we would be able to solve for firm 1's Nash equilibrium price:

$$p_1^n = \frac{2t}{3} + \frac{t(a+b)}{3} + \frac{2c_1 + c_2}{3}$$

This is the Nash equilibrium in prices, (p_1^n, p_2^n). At this point, neither firm has an incentive to change its price, since the Nash equilibrium price is the best-response price. Firm 1 would only make itself worse off (in the sense that profits would fall) if it charged a price other that p_1^n, given that firm 2 is charging the equilibrium price p_2^n.

We can now derive a number of interesting results regarding the outcome of price competition between these two firms, given that neither firm is changing its location. We can think of these as short-run results, since it's generally easier for firms to change prices than to change locations. This is clear when we are describing the physical location of the firm, but is also relevant when we use location to describe the location of each firm's product in characteristics space. For example, if we re-interpret the location space to reflect the location of each firm's product in quality space, then the extreme left end of the unit interval can represent low quality and the extreme right end could represent high quality. It is easier for any firm to change the price at which it sells its output, than to re-design its product to represent a higher or lower level of quality.

The first result we note is that, since $a + b < 2$,[4] price must be greater than marginal cost, so firms earn positive profits in equilibrium. As we noted in Chapter 6, one solution to the Bertrand paradox is to incorporate product differentiation into a model of Bertrand price competition, so we have shown that:

Result

When duopolists sell differentiated products, price competition will yield an equilibrium where both firms earn positive profits.

Now suppose that firm 1 has a lower marginal cost of production than firm 2, so that $c_1 < c_2$. Then firm 1's equilibrium market price will be lower than that of firm 2. But notice that firm 2 will not necessarily be shut out of the market. This is an important result, since in our discussion of Bertrand competition in Chapter 6, when firm 1 had a cost advantage, this was enough to give firm 1 complete monopoly power. Firm 1 only needed to set the market price slightly below the marginal cost of firm 2. Then firm 2 could never earn positive profits, so firm 2 was shut out of the market.

Why doesn't this happen in this model with product differentiation? To illustrate, suppose both firms start off with the same marginal cost, and firm 2 discovers a cost-reducing technological improvement, so that its marginal cost c_2 falls to $\tilde{c}_2$. In terms of our hot-dog vendors example, we could suppose that both vendors initially buy their hot dogs from the same manufacturer at the same

price. Then at some time, vendor 2 discovers another hot-dog manufacturer from whom he can buy hot dogs at a lower price. To find out what happens to the equilibrium, look at each firm's reaction function. Note that firm 1's reaction function is independent of firm 2's marginal cost c_2, so when c_2 falls to $\tilde{c}_2$, nothing happens to firm 1's reaction function. But firm 2's reaction function will shift when c_2 falls. Since $\partial p_2 / \partial c_2 = 1/2$, a decrease in c_2 to $\tilde{c}_2$ will cause firm 2's reaction function to shift downwards, from R^2 to $\tilde{R}^2$. This is illustrated in Figure 7.7. The Nash equilibrium in prices will move from point A to point B. Note that *both* firms will reduce their price. But firm 2 will drop its price by more than firm 1. It can afford to do so, since its costs have fallen. But in order to remain competitive, firm 1 must also drop its price, even though its costs are unchanged. We can see this result by looking at the change in the Nash equilibrium prices of each firm when c_2 changes:

$$\frac{\partial p_1^n}{\partial c_2} = \frac{1}{3} < \frac{2}{3} = \frac{\partial p_2^n}{\partial c_2}$$

We can demonstrate this result in another way, using our illustration of the linear product market space in Figure 7.8. Recall that neither firm changes location, so a and b will stay the same. When firm 1 drops its price, the consumer located at a will be made better off by exactly the amount of the decrease in firm 1's price, since this consumer does not need to incur any transport cost to buy from firm 1. So the distance marked m represents the increase in surplus to the consumer located at a due to firm 1's price reduction. Likewise, the distance n represents the drop in firm 2's price and the increase in surplus c^c the consumer at firm 2's location at $po^\cdot$

But firm 2 drops its price by more t^h so $n > m$. As we can see in Figure surplus functions implies tha$^\cdot$

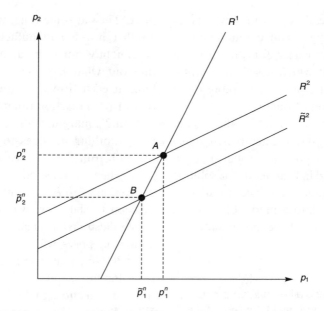

Figure 7.7 Firm 2 discovers a cost-reducing technological improvement

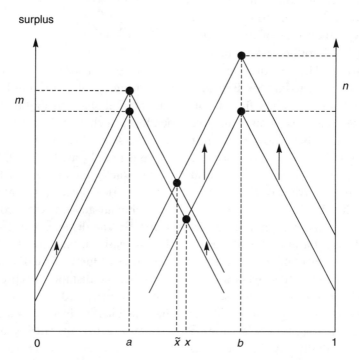

Figure 7.8 Effect of price change on indifferent consumer

was initially indifferent between buying from firm 1 or firm 2, located at point x, would now rather buy from firm 2, since firm 2 has dropped its price by more than firm 1. In fact, the indifferent consumer is now located at $\tilde{x}$, so firm 2's market share has increased. Thus we find that:

> ## Result
>
> In a duopoly when two firms sell differentiated products and one firm has a cost advantage, it may still be possible for both firms to earn positive profits in equilibrium.

7.4 Equilibrium in locations

Now let's move on to the second stage of the manager's problem: the choice of location in the long run. We've figured out how our hot-dog vendors will determine the equilibrium price to charge per hot dog on any given day. How will the vendors choose the location at which to set up their carts in equilibrium? This problem is a bit more complicated, since in the longer run, a change in location must be made with the knowledge that prices may also change. So we'll proceed by supposing that only firm 2 is considering how to change its location, given the behavior of firm 1. To keep things as simple as possible, suppose that the new hot-dog vendor is firm 2, and he's deciding where to move his cart to, given the behavior of the first hot-dog vendor,

firm 1, who has already set up her cart at point a on the beach. The first hot-dog vendor cannot move her cart right away, but may well change her price when firm 2 changes his location.

In terms of the pictures we've been using so far, we want to figure out what happens when b moves, given that a is fixed. But we must allow firms to change prices, so p_1 and p_2 must be allowed to respond to the change in location b. Recall firm 2's profit function:

$$\pi^2 = (p_2 - c_2) \cdot \left[1 - b + \frac{b-a}{2} + \frac{p_1 - p_2}{2t} \right]$$

From this profit function, we see that a change in location by firm 2 will have three effects on profits:

1 $\partial \pi^2 / \partial b$, the direct effect of a change in location on profits;
2 $\partial \pi^2 / \partial p_1$, the indirect effect of a change in firm 1's price on profits, since firm 1 will change its price when firm 2 changes its location;
3 $\partial \pi^2 / \partial p_2$, the indirect effect of a change in firm 2's price on profits, since firm 2 will change its own price when it changes its location.

Let's begin by looking at the third effect. As long as both firms end up charging Nash equilibrium prices, this effect will be equal to zero, since firm 2 will always charge price p_2 such that the marginal effect on profits is exactly equal to zero. This is just firm 2's

> ## Product Differentiation in the Canadian Mattress Market
>
> According to a retail industry analyst, the retail mattress business is one of the most profitable in Canada. We can use some of the results from our analysis of product differentiation models t⊢ explain why this industry might be so profitable.
>
> There are four major brands of mattresses available in Canada: Sealy, Simmons, S⊢ Marshall. But any one of these producers will offer a large variety of mattresses. Th⊢

are typically differentiated on the basis of quality. The major factors affecting the quality of a mattress are the number of coils in a mattress (coil count), the filling used on the outside of the coils, and the warranty.

While there are only four major mattress producers in Canada, there are a great many more retail mattress stores, including large chains like Eatons and Sears and specialty mattress stores across the country. With so many competitors in the retail mattress industry, we might expect that this industry would be relatively competitive. Why is it that profitability in the retail mattress industry is so high?

Often a producer will distribute a mattress with a particular set of characteristics through only one retailer in an area. So a consumer in Vancouver may walk into Sears and see a particular model of Sealy mattress. This consumer may comparison shop at Eatons, but will not be able to find the same model of Sealy mattress, since Sealy has produced and labeled this particular model only for Sears. Eatons may have a Sealy mattress with the same coil count and similar features, but the fact that the mattress bears a different label makes it difficult for consumers to compare, and as a result, retailers are able to differentiate their products, even when they are very similar. This allows retailers to maintain relatively high prices and earn relatively high profit margins.

Source: Facts for this case were taken from an episode of the CBC-TV show Marketplace, aired on January 21, 1997.

first-order condition for profit maximization: $\partial\pi^2/\partial p_2 = 0$. So we only need to solve for the first two effects: $\partial\pi^2/\partial b$ and $\partial\pi^2/\partial p_1$.

The first effect is given by the derivative of firm 2's profit function with respect to its location b. This is equal to:

$$\frac{\partial\pi^2}{\partial b} = (-1 + 1/2) \cdot (p_2 - c_2)$$

$$\frac{\partial\pi^2}{\partial b} = \frac{-(p_2 - c_2)}{2} < 0$$

This is the *market-share effect* of a change in location, and is interpreted as follows: if b is increased, so that firm 2 moves farther away from firm 1, then firm 2's market share will fall, and profits will fall. If firm 2 decreases b by moving closer to firm 1, its market share will increase, and profits will rise.

Now let's look at the second effect, which takes into account the fact that when firm 2 changes location, firm 1 will respond in equilibrium by changing its market price p_1. This is the *strategic effect* of a change in firm 2's

location, and it is made up of two parts: the effect of a change in location on firm 1's price, given by the term $\partial p_1/\partial b$, and the effect of a change in firm 1's price on firm 2's profits, given by the term $\partial\pi^2/\partial p_1$. We can solve for each of these as follows:

$$\frac{\partial\pi^2}{\partial p_1} = \frac{p_2 - c_2}{2t}$$

$$\frac{\partial p_1}{\partial b} = \frac{t}{3}$$

The strategic effect will be the product of these two effects, given by:

$$\frac{\partial\pi^2}{\partial p_1} \cdot \frac{\partial p_1}{\partial b} = \frac{p_2 - c_2}{2t} \cdot \frac{t}{3}$$

$$\frac{\partial\pi^2}{\partial p_1} \cdot \frac{\partial p_1}{\partial b} = \frac{p_2 - c_2}{6} > 0$$

So the strategic effect of a change in location for firm 2 is always positive. When firm 2 increases b and moves away from firm 1, firm 1 will respond by increasing its price ($\partial p_1/\partial b > 0$). This will increase profits of firm 2, since $\partial \pi^2 / \partial p_1 > 0$. We say that when firm 2 changes its location and moves away from firm 1, this *softens price competition*. Both firms will have the ability to increase their market price, leading to an increase in profits. If firm 2 changes its location and moves closer to firm 1, firm 1 will see this as a move to increase competition. Firm 1 will respond by dropping its price, and this *increases price competition*. So if firm 2 decreases b and moves closer to firm 1, the result of the strategic effect of this change in location will be an increase in price competition and a decrease in profits for firm 2. If firm 2 increases b and moves away from firm 1, the result will be softened price competition and an increase in profits for firm 2.

What will be the outcome of competition in location in this model? The market share effect of a change in location will have firms moving closer together in product location space, as firms try to capture more market share to increase profits. But the strategic effect has firms moving farther apart, as firms try to soften price competition to increase profits. So if the market share effect dominates, we'll see firms locating as close to each other as possible. We call this outcome the case of *minimal product differentiation*. If the strategic effect dominates, we'll see firms locating as far apart as possible. This outcome represents the case of *maximal product differentiation*.

There is one simple example we can consider first. Suppose that firms always charge the same price. It might be the case that some government regulation prohibits firms from charging a price greater than $\bar{p}$, and if neither firm wants to drop its price, both firms will charge the same price $\bar{p}$. Now the strategic effect of a change in location will always be zero. If firm 2 changes its location, firm 1 does not change its price in response. The only effect left is the market share effect.

This is always negative for firm 2, so firm 2 will always move as close as possible to firm 1. Suppose firm 1 is located at $a = 1/4$. Then the best that firm 2 can do is to locate at $b = 1/4$, right next to firm 1. But firm 2 wants to be just to the right of firm 1, since $3/4$ of the market is to the right of firm 1.

But this cannot be an equilibrium in the long run, since firm 1 now has an incentive to change its location. If firm 1 could change its location, it would want to leapfrog over firm 2 and locate just to the right of firm 2, thereby capturing the larger share of the market. This process will continue until neither firm has an incentive to change its location. This will only happen when both firm are located right next to each other in the middle of the market, with $a = b = 1/2$.

In our model with linear transport costs, we showed that the market-share and strategic effects of a change in location are given by:

$$\text{market-share effect:} \quad \frac{-(p_2 - c_2)}{2}$$
$$\text{strategic effect:} \quad \frac{p_2 - c_2}{6}$$

The market-share effect is three times as large as the strategic effect. Clearly the market-share effect will dominate in this model, so we'd predict that the outcome of competition in locations between two firms would be minimal product differentiation.

Does this happen? Will this happen? Let's think of some examples of firms competing in location. To apply our model, we need to think of some examples where competing firms offer products for sale which are completely the same except for one feature of the product.[5] A good example is gasoline. For many car drivers, gas sold by one servi~ station or another is effectively the ~ except for the location of the servi~ How many times have you ~ through town, looking f~

when you come upon an intersection where two gas stations are located right across the street from each other?

Another good example is the location of chartered banks. Many of the services offered by chartered banks are the same in the eyes of consumers. A savings or checking account from one bank or another will offer very similar rates of return and service charges. But any consumer would find it less costly to frequent a bank located closer to home or closer to work than one which is farther away. How many times have you noticed two or even three branches of different banks located at the same intersection?[6]

In fact, it is not unusual to see particular types of stores locating very close together. In many large cities with large shopping areas, furniture stores are located very close together in a small area of the downtown core, instead of being spread throughout the city. If you want to buy camera equipment in New York city, you will find a large collection of camera stores on 42nd Street at Times Square. If we define a product called *fast*

food, the minimal product differentiation result could be used to explain why we often see fast food restaurants located very close together, often right across the street from each other.

Of course, we won't see minimal product differentiation in all markets where firms compete in locations. In the model we worked through, when consumers incurred linear transport costs, the market share effect dominated the strategic effect. But what would happen if transport costs were not linear? What if the rate at which consumers were worse off actually increased as they had to travel farther from their most preferred set of characteristics?

In the appendix, we work through the same model of product differentiation when transport costs are *quadratic*. The algebra for this example is more complicated, so let's just work through an intuitive example. Suppose you're on the beach, and you want a hot dog. You're quite hungry, and would be willing to buy a hot dog for $5 from a vendor if the cart was right next to your towel and umbrella. If

Product Differentiation in UK Politics

An interesting extension of this product differentiation model beyond cases where goods or services are differentiated in physical space can be seen by considering competition between political parties. We could define the "political" unit interval as follows: the more conservative right-wing parties would be located farther to the right along the unit interval, while the more socialist left-wing parties would be located closer to the left end of the unit interval.

In the United Kingdom, parties competing for representation in the House of Commons choose a location along the unit interval to compete for votes. The Labor Party, the Conservative Party, the Liberal Democratic Party, and a number of smaller parties each choose a platform which is made up of a position on a number of political and social issues that defines each party's position along the political spectrum. Voters will vote for the party whose position is closest to the voter's own position.

The minimal product differentiation result could explain why some parties have adopted similar platforms on many issues. As an example, consider the election of May 1997, when the Labor Party defeated the Conservative Party, ending 18 consecutive years of rule by the Conservatives in the House of Commons. An important policy issue during the 1997 election campaign was entry of the United Kingdom into the European Monetary Union. The minimal product differentiation result is evidenced in the fact that both the Labor Party under Tony Blair and the Conservatives under John Major each took a hard line representing Britain's interests in Europe. In the run-up to the June 2001 UK election, both Labor and the Conservatives displayed similar policies on health, education, and crime.

Of course, the product differentiation model needs to be modified for this example, since the assumption that consumers (voters) are uniformly distributed along the political spectrum is most likely inappropriate. In fact, a larger share of voters in the United Kingdom may be clustered around the centre of the political spectrum. This could explain why the Liberal Democrats have recently fared poorly in Federal elections, since the Liberal Democrats now seem to be positioned farther to the left along the political spectrum than the other major political parties.

the vendor was 1 km away, you'd be willing to pay $4. But if the cart was 2 km away (twice as far away), you'd only be willing to pay $2. You incur a transport cost of $1 ($5 − $4) to travel the first kilometer. But the transport cost for traveling the second kilometer is $2 ($4 − $2), so your transport cost is increasing the farther you have to travel to get your hot dog. This is different from the model we described earlier, since if transport costs were linear, each kilometer you walked would cost you $1.

As we show in the appendix, in a game where firms compete in locations when transport costs are quadratic, the negative strategic effect of a change in location will dominate the positive market share effect. The outcome of this game will be *maximal product differentiation*! Firms will locate as far apart from each other as possible, in order to soften price competition as much as possible.

Suppose we want to explain the marketing and pricing behavior of a health food store. This store competes against other stores selling food products, so we could use our unit interval to model the different types of food sold at food stores. At the far right end of the unit interval would be our health food store, selling the most healthy foods,

while a variety store selling chocolate bars and ice cream would be *located* at the far left end of this unit interval. The health food store could choose to sell ice cream, but then it would be increasing competition with the variety store. By concentrating on selling only health foods, the health food store is engaging in maximal product differentiation, and at the same time restricting price competition.

There's a very important lesson to learn here, and it's one we'll come back to over and over again throughout the remainder of the text.

The results of any modeling experiment depend completely upon the specification of the model.

This may seem like a trivially simple statement, but it's the most important notion to keep in mind when setting up any model. It implies that when examining behavior in any particular market, the model must be chosen *very carefully*, to most accurately represent the characteristics of the market being considered.

We've just seen one implication of lesson. The outcome of competitio tions between two firms will *different* depending on transport costs. With linear transport costs, our model predicts *minimal* product differentiation. With quadratic transport costs, we'd expect to see *maximal* product differentiation. At the heart of this result is the role played by the strategic effect in competition over location. For the health food store, this strategic effect is very important, so the health food store will locate as far away from other food stores as possible, selling only health foods, and thereby minimizing price competition. For camera stores in New York city, this strategic effect is not as important as the market share effect, so we see minimal product differentiation.

What does this tell us about our two hot-dog vendors? If we think that consumers on the beach incur constant (linear) transport costs, then the outcome of competition between the two hot-dog vendors will see both vendors setting up their carts in the middle of the beach. If consumers incur increasing (quadratic) transport costs, we should see the two hot-dog carts as far away from each other as possible, located at the extreme ends of the beach.

Does the Characteristics Approach Work?

A study by Peter Burton[*] has proposed an ingenious way to test some predictions of the characteristics theory of product differentiation. The author examines pricing behavior in the market for insecticides, to see whether producers of insecticides set prices to be consistent with the fact that insecticides are purchased not for the products themselves, but for the characteristics which they provide to consumers.

Insecticides are used by farmers who spray their fields to control insect populations. Insecticides were described in terms of three different characteristics which they provided: They were harmful to insects, they persisted in environment, and they were harmful to mammals. The first two characteristics were positive. An insecticide was more efficient if the same amount was more harmful to insects, and if the same amount persisted or lasted longer. The third characteristic was negative. A more efficient insecticide was less harmful to mammals. Different insecticides embodied different levels of these three characteristics. Furthermore, users of insecticides could combine two insecticides to produce a mixture which had a different set of characteristics from either of the initial two insecticides.

For example, suppose insecticide *A* was very efficient at controlling insects but was relatively harmful to humans, while insecticide *B* was not as efficient at controlling insects but was less harmful to humans. A farmer could mix these *A* and *B* together, and this mixture would have a combination of the characteristics of each.

Now suppose an insecticide firm marketed a new insecticide, called *C*, which had the exact characteristics of this mixture of *A* and *B*. Characteristics theory predicts that the firm would not price the new product *C* to be more expensive than the cost of the mixture of *A* and *B* which had the same characteristics.

Burton checks the pricing of 15 different insecticides over the period 1944–87, and quantifies the characteristics of each different product. His results show that in the market for insecticides, the predictions of the characteristics theory are supported.

*See Peter Burton's article in the February, 1994 issue of the *Canadian Journal of Economics*.

Let's consider one final example. So far, we haven't paid any attention at all to the well-being of the consumers on the beach. Suppose the government had the ability to give permits to the hot-dog vendors, restricting them to set up their carts at specific places on the beach. If both vendors located in the middle of the beach, then sunbathers at the extreme ends of the beach would have to travel half the length of the beach to get a hot dog. On the other hand, if the vendors located at the ends of the beach, the consumer in the middle of the beach would have to travel half the length of the beach to get a hot dog.

The best that the government could do in this example would be to issue permits restricting one vendor to locate at 1/4 and the other to locate at 3/4, if the length of the whole beach was 1. Then the farthest that any consumer would have to travel to get a hot dog would be 1/4. This would be the solution to the government's problem if the objective of the government was to minimize transport costs on the beach.

Summary

- Consumers may not be indifferent between the same good produced by different firms at the same price, if the characteristics of the output of one firm are closer to the consumer's most-preferred set of characteristics.
- Goods can be differentiated on the basis of physical location, quality, size, appearance, or many other characteristics, so the notion of *product space* needs to be carefully defined.
- If consumers are not indifferent between the same good produced by different firms at the same price, then price competition between firms will generally not result in the complete elimination of firm profits, so product differentiation is an important market feature to resolve the Bertrand paradox.
- With differentiated products, firms can compete over prices in the short-run, with product location taken as fixed.
- In the longer run, firms can vary both their market price and the location of their product in product space.
- The choice of product location can be broken down into a *market-share effect* and a *strategic effect*.
- How consumers respond to product differentiation will determine whether the market-share effect or the strategic effect is dominant. If the market-share effect is greater, then firms will locate as close to each other as possible in product space, resulting in minimal product differentiation.
- If the strategic effect is dominant, then firms will want to locate as far from each other as possible in product space, to reduce the negative effects of price competition on their profits.

Notes

1 This treatment of product differentitation is due to Hotelling (1929). See also Tirole (1988), pp. 97 and 279. A practical example of *attribute analysis*, which can be used to model situations where consumers choose goods with more

than one characteristic or attribute, is given in Chapter 14 of Rowcroft (1994), pp. 337–66. This chapter includes a number of examples which are solved using matrix algebra.

2 Some examples where consumers have different preferences can be found in Anderson *et al.* (1992) and Yu (1996), and the references therein, though the material is somewhat more advanced.

3 It is worth nothing at this point that these are only examples of market situations. We do not know what the actual market equilibrium will look like yet. But this example illustrates a problem with linear transport costs. At any point in time, each firm has an incentive to drop its price to gain market power and attempt to monopolize the market. The problem is that the firm's demand function is discontinous, and as a result, no unique pure strategy equilibrium exists in this game. We won't go into this problem in any detail here, because it requires a more advanced theoretical treatment of market equilibrium. However, the problem can be resolved by assuming that consumers incur *quadratic transport costs*. Since this example is more advanced, it is solved in the appendix to this chapter, for the interested reader.

4 Since firms are locating along the unit interval, the largest that a or b can be is 1, so $a + b$ must be smaller than 2.

5 Some of these examples are taken from Tirole (1988), pp. 286–7.

6 At the corner of Sherbrooke St. W. and Victoria in Montreal, there is a branch of the Royal Bank, the Canadian Imperial Bank of Commerce, and Laurentienne Bank.

Exercises

1 Can you use the model of product differentiation to explain the fact that all major brewers introduced a type of ice beer within a very short period of each other? Is this an example of maximal or minimal product differentiation?

2 Suppose two firms sell products in a particular market, but consumers do not regard the output of each firm as perfectly identical. The two firms face the following demand curves:

$$q_1 = 30 - 4p_1 + 2p_2$$
$$q_2 = 60 + 2p_1 - 4p_2$$

Each firm has the same constant marginal cost of production, so that $c_1 = c_2 = \$15$. Fixed costs are zero.

(a) Write out each firm's profit function, of the form $\pi^i = (p_i - c_i) \cdot q_i$, for $i = 1, 2$.

(b) Solve for each firm's first-order condition, $\partial \pi^i / \partial p_i = 0$, for $i = 1, 2$, and use it to solve for each firm's reaction function.

(c) On a graph with p_1 on the horizontal axis and p_2 on the vertical axis, graph each firm's reaction function.

(d) Use the equations of each firm's reaction function from part (b) to solve for each firm's equilibrium price p_i, level of output q_i, and profits π^i.

(e) Do firms earn positive profits in equilibrium? Does this result confirm or contradict the Bertrand paradox? Explain your answer.

3 Using the information in the previous question, suppose that workers at firm 1 go on strike and demand a higher wage. To settle the dispute, managers at firm 1 increase wages paid to workers, so that the marginal cost of production at firm 1, c_1 increases.

(a) What happens to firm 1's reaction function? What happens to firm 2's reaction function?

(b) What happens to each firm's price as a result of the increase in costs at firm 1?

(c) What happens to market share and profits for each firm as a result of the increase in costs at firm 1?

4 Firm 1 and firm 2 sell a similar but differentiated product, charging market price p_1 and p_2, respectively. Suppose fixed costs are equal to

zero, and each firm has the same constant marginal cost c, so that in equilibrium, each firm charges the Nash equilibrium price given by:

$$p_1^n = \frac{2t}{3} + \frac{t(a+b)}{3} + c$$

$$p_2^n = \frac{4t}{3} - \frac{t(a+b)}{3} + c$$

where a (b) is the location of firm 1's (2's) product, $0 < a < b < 1$. Suppose firm 1 changes its location and moves closer to firm b (i.e. a increases).

(a) Will firm 2 respond by increasing or decreasing its price? Does the change in firm 1's location result in increased or softened price competition?

(b) Suppose instead that Nash equilibrium prices were given by:

$$p_1^n = c + t(1 - a - b) \cdot \left[1 + \frac{a-b}{3}\right]$$

$$p_2^n = c + t(1 - a - b)\left[1 + \frac{b-a}{3}\right]$$

where $1 - a - b < 1$. Would an increase in a result in an increase or softening of price competition? Would firm 2's response be more or less aggressive than in part (4a)?

Appendix

Suppose firm 1 is located at a, firm 2 is located at $1 - b$, and transport costs incurred by consumers are quadratic, so that a consumer located at x will incur travel costs $t(x - a)^2$ to buy from firm 1 and $t(1 - b - x)^2$ to buy from firm 2. If consumers are uniformly distributed along this unit interval, there will exist a consumer who is indifferent between buying at firm 1 or 2 for whom:

$$p_1 + t(x - a)^2 = p_2 + t((1-b) - x)^2$$

$$p_2 - p_1 = t(x^2 - 2ax + a^2)$$
$$- t((1-b)^2 - 2x(1-b) + x^2)$$

$$\frac{p_2 - p_1}{t} = a^2 - 2ax - (1-b)^2$$
$$+ (1-b)(2x)$$

$$\frac{p_2 - p_1}{t} = a^2 - 1 + 2b - b^2$$
$$+ 2x(1 - a - b)$$

$$x = \frac{-a^2 + 1 - 2b + b^2}{2(1 - a - b)}$$
$$+ \frac{p_2 - p_1}{2t(1 - a - b)}$$

If we note that:

$$((1-b) - a)^2 = (1-b)^2 + a^2 - 2a(1-b)$$

$$((1-b) - a)^2 = 1 - 2b + b^2 + a^2$$
$$- 2a + 2ab$$

$$((1-b) - a)^2 = (1 + b^2 - 2b - a^2)$$
$$+ 2a^2 - 2a + 2ab$$

so that $1 + b^2 - 2b - a^2$
$$= ((1-b) - a)^2 + 2a - 2a^2 - 2ab$$

then we can rewrite the above demand function x for firm 1 using:

$$\frac{1 + b^2 - 2b - a^2}{2(1 - a - b)} = \frac{((1-b) - a)^2}{2(1 - a - b)}$$
$$+ \frac{2a(1 - a - b)}{2(1 - a - b)}$$

$$\frac{1 + b^2 - 2b - a^2}{2(1 - a - b)} = \frac{1 - a - b}{2} + a$$

so that $x = a + \frac{1 - a - b}{2}$
$$+ \frac{p_2 - p_1}{2t(1 - a - b)}$$

and $1 - x = 1 - a - \frac{1 - a - b}{2}$
$$+ \frac{p_1 - p_2}{2t(1 - a - b)}$$

or $1 - x = \dfrac{2 - 2a - 1 + a + b}{2}$

$+ \dfrac{p_1 - p_2}{2t(1 - a - b)}$

so that $1 - x = b + \dfrac{1 - a - b}{2}$

$+ \dfrac{p_1 - p_2}{2t(1 - a - b)}$

We can interpret these demand functions as follows: for equal prices, firm 1 sells to its *turf* a and half of the customers between it and firm 2. The final term on the difference between prices p_1 and p_2 reflects the sensitivity of demand to the price differential.

To solve for the Nash equilibrium in prices, given locations a and $1 - b$, write out each firm's profit function:

$$\pi^1 = (p_1 - c) \cdot \left[a + \dfrac{1 - a - b}{2} + \dfrac{p_2 - p_1}{2t(1 - a - b)}\right]$$

$$\pi^2 = (p_2 - c) \cdot \left[b + \dfrac{1 - a - b}{2} + \dfrac{p_1 - p_2}{2t(1 - a - b)}\right]$$

Solve for each firm's first-order condition by taking the output price derivative of each profit function and set equal to zero:

$$\pi_1^1 = a + \dfrac{1 - a - b}{2} + \dfrac{p_2 - p_1}{2t(1 - a - b)}$$

$$- \dfrac{p_1 - c}{2t(1 - a - b)} = 0$$

$$\pi_2^2 = b + \dfrac{1 - a - b}{2} + \dfrac{p_1 - p_2}{2t(1 - a - b)}$$

$$- \dfrac{p_2 - c}{2t(1 - a - b)} = 0$$

Write this system of two linear equations in the two unknowns (p_1, p_2) in matrix form as follows:

$$\begin{pmatrix} \dfrac{1}{t(1 - a - b)} & \dfrac{-1}{2t(1 - a - b)} \\ \dfrac{-1}{2t(1 - a - b)} & \dfrac{1}{t(1 - a - b)} \end{pmatrix} \begin{pmatrix} p_1 \\ p_2 \end{pmatrix}$$

$$= \begin{pmatrix} a + \dfrac{1 - a - b}{2} + \dfrac{c}{2t(1 - a - b)} \\ b + \dfrac{1 - a - b}{2} + \dfrac{c}{2t(1 - a - b)} \end{pmatrix}$$

A unique solution will always exist as long as the determinant of the coefficient matrix is non-zero, given by:

$$|A| = \dfrac{1}{t^2(1 - a - b)^2} - \dfrac{1}{4t^2(1 - a - b)^2}$$

$$|A| = \dfrac{3}{4t^2(1 - a - b)^2}$$

Solve for p_1^n using Cramer's rule as follows:

$$p_1^n = \dfrac{\begin{vmatrix} a + \dfrac{1 - a - b}{2} + \dfrac{c}{2t(1 - a - b)} & \dfrac{-1}{2t(1 - a - b)} \\ b + \dfrac{1 - a - b}{2} + \dfrac{c}{2t(1 - a - b)} & \dfrac{1}{t(1 - a - b)} \end{vmatrix}}{\dfrac{3}{4t^2(1 - a - b)^2}}$$

$$p_1^n = \dfrac{4t^2(1 - a - b)^2}{3} \cdot \left[\dfrac{a}{t(1 - a - b)}\right.$$

$$+ \dfrac{1 - a - b}{2t(1 - a - b)} + \dfrac{c}{2t^2(1 - a - b)^2}$$

$$\dfrac{b}{t(1 - a - b)} + \dfrac{1 - a - b}{4t(1 - a - b)}$$

$$\left. + \dfrac{c}{4t^2(1 - a - b)^2}\right]$$

$$p_1^n = \dfrac{4ta(1 - a - b)}{3} + \dfrac{2t(1 - a - b)^2}{3} + \dfrac{2c}{3}$$

$$+ \dfrac{2t(1 - a - b)}{3} + \dfrac{t(1 - a - b)^2}{3} + \dfrac{c}{3}$$

$$p_1^n = c + t(1 - a - b)$$

$$\cdot \left[\dfrac{4a + 2b}{3} + \dfrac{3(1 - a - b)}{3}\right]$$

$$p_1^n = c + t(1 - a - b) \cdot \left[1 + \dfrac{a - b}{3}\right]$$

Likewise we could solve for firm 2's Nash equilibrium price p_2^n:

$$p_2^n = c + t(1 - a - b)\left[1 + \frac{b - a}{3}\right]$$

Now suppose firm 1 chooses its location. We need to solve for the effect on firm 1's profits of a change in its location, $\partial\pi^1/\partial a$. We know that $\partial\pi^1/\partial p_1 = 0$ from firm 1's first-order condition, so we get:

$$\frac{\partial\pi^1}{\partial a} = [p_1 - c] \cdot \left[\frac{\partial D^1}{\partial a} + \frac{\partial D^1}{\partial p_2}\frac{\partial p_2}{\partial a}\right]$$

For simplicity, suppose that marginal cost is equal to zero. From firm 1's demand function, we get:

$$D^1 = a + \frac{1 - a - b}{2} + \frac{p_2 - p_1}{2t(1 - a - b)}$$

$$\frac{\partial D^1}{\partial a} = 1 - \frac{1}{2} + \frac{(p_2 - p_1)2t}{(2t)^2(1 - a - b)^2}$$

$$\frac{\partial D^1}{\partial a} = \frac{1}{2} + \frac{p_2 - p_1}{2t(1 - a - b)^2}$$

We know that:

$$p_2 - p_1 = t(1 - a - b)\frac{b - a - a + b}{3}$$

$$p_2 - p_1 = t(1 - a - b)\frac{2b - 2a}{3}$$

$$p_2 - p_1 = 2t(1 - a - b)\frac{b - a}{3}$$

so that:

$$\frac{\partial D^1}{\partial a} = \frac{1}{2} + \frac{b - a}{3(1 - a - b)}$$

$$\frac{\partial D^1}{\partial a} = \frac{3 - 3a - 3b + (b - a)2}{6(1 - a - b)}$$

$$\frac{\partial D^1}{\partial a} = \frac{3 - 5a - b}{6(1 - a - b)}$$

Now we need to solve for $(\partial D^1/\partial p_2)$ $(\partial p_2/\partial a)$:

$$\frac{\partial D^1}{\partial p_2} = \frac{1}{2t(1 - a - b)}$$

$$\frac{\partial p_2}{\partial a} = -t \cdot \left(1 + \frac{b - a}{3}\right)$$

$$+ t(1 - a - b)\left(\frac{-1}{3}\right)$$

$$\frac{\partial p_2}{\partial a} = -t \cdot \left(\frac{3 + b - a + 1 - a - b}{3}\right)$$

$$\frac{\partial p_2}{\partial a} = t \cdot \left(\frac{-4 + 2a}{3}\right)$$

so that:

$$\frac{\partial D^1}{\partial p_2} \cdot \frac{\partial p_2}{\partial a} = \frac{1}{2t(1 - a - b)} \cdot \frac{t(-4 + 2a)}{3}$$

$$\frac{\partial D^1}{\partial p_2} \cdot \frac{\partial p_2}{\partial a} = \frac{-2 + a}{3(1 - a - b)}$$

Putting these two terms together, we can solve for the effect of a change in firm 1's location on its profits. Since $p_1 - c$ must be positive, $\partial\pi^1/\partial a$ must have the same sign as:

$$\frac{\partial D^1}{\partial a} + \frac{\partial D^1}{\partial p_2} \cdot \frac{\partial p_2}{\partial a} = \frac{3 - 5a - b}{6(1 - a - b)}$$

$$+ \frac{-2 + a}{3(1 - a - b)}$$

$$\frac{\partial D^1}{\partial a} + \frac{\partial D^1}{\partial p_2} \cdot \frac{\partial p_2}{\partial a} = \frac{3 - 5a - b - 4 + 2a}{6(1 - a - b)}$$

$$\frac{\partial D^1}{\partial a} + \frac{\partial D^1}{\partial p_2} \cdot \frac{\partial p_2}{\partial a} = \frac{-1 - 3a - b}{6(1 - a - b)} < 0$$

since $1 - a - b > 0$. Since profits are decreasing in location a, firm 1 will want to make a as small as possible. We'd get the same result for firm 2 regarding its location b, so that the optimal locations for each firm would be $a = b = 0$, implying maximal product differentiation. Firms would locate at opposite ends of the unit interval.

We can decompose this result as follows:

market-share effect:

$$\frac{\partial D^1}{\partial a} = \frac{1}{2} + \frac{3 - 5a - b}{6(1 - a - b)}$$

strategic effect:

$$\frac{\partial D^1}{\partial p_2} \cdot \frac{\partial p_2}{\partial a} = \frac{-2 + a}{3(1 - a - b)}$$

If the location of firm 1 is not too big ($a \leq 1/2$, noting that $(1 - b) > a$), then the market share effect tends to $1/2$, implying that the firm would want to locate at the center. However, the strategic effect is larger (in absolute value) than the market-share effect, so since the strategic effect is negative, firms will locate at the endpoints of the product spectrum. This shows firm 1's acknowledgement of the fact that a decrease in product differentiation (moving toward $a = 1/2$) triggers a strategic response whereby firm 2 lowers its price.

References

Anderson, S. P., de Palma, A. and Thisse, J.-F. *Discrete Choice Theory of Product Differentiation* (Cambridge: MIT Press, 1992).

Burton, Peter. "Support for a characteristics approach: evidence from the market for insecticides." *Canadian Journal of Economics* (1994), 27:1, pp. 1–19.

Hotelling, H. "Stability in Competition." *Economic Journal*, 39 (1929), pp. 41–57.

Lancaster, K. "A new approach to consumer theory." *Journal of Political Economy*, 74 (1966), pp. 132–57.

Rowcroft, John E. *Mathematical Economics: An Integrated Approach* (Scarborough: Prentice-Hall Canada Inc., 1994), pp. 337–66.

Tirole, Jean. *The Theory of Industrial Organization* (Cambridge, MA: The MIT Press, 1988), pp. 279–87.

Yu, Weiqiu. "Estimating demand for differentiated products." *Canadian Journal of Economics* 29: Special Issue Part II (1996), pp. S490–3.

Chapter 8

Advertising

•••

When you are finished with this chapter you should understand:

- That advertising expenditures by the firm include any expenditures aimed at increasing sales or protecting market share
- How goods can be classified as *search goods, experience goods*, or *credence goods*, depending upon whether consumers have information about their surplus derived from consumption before or after purchasing the good
- How a monopolist can use a *rule of thumb* for optimally setting advertising expenditures as a share of total revenue
- How optimal advertising expenditures can depend upon factors such as the effectiveness of advertising and persistence effects if advertising could affect a firm's stock of goodwill
- That in a market with more than one firm, changes in advertising expenditures by one firm have a *market-share effect* and a *strategic effect*, and that more advertising makes a market more competitive

The boards and ice surfaces of most professional hockey arenas, and the grass of many cricket and football pitches are all festooned with information about local and national producers of many different sorts of commodities. Many professional athletes can regularly be seen on television using consumer products ranging from soft drinks to court shoes. Approximately 25 percent of every hour of prime time network television programming consists of advertisements paid for by firms attempting to convince consumers to buy more of their products. Consumers find flyers, coupons, and trial samples of products stuffed in their mailboxes on a regular basis, often many times a week.

What is advertising? Why do firms find it necessary to expend resources on advertising? Why are some types of goods very heavily advertised, while other goods are hardly advertised at all? Why do some firms advertise more than others, even though they produce similar products? How do firms decide how much to spend on advertising?

To answer these questions, we must first determine the role that advertising plays in the economy. It turns out that there is one characteristic which is common to all types of advertising, whether it be television or radio advertising, billboards or newspaper advertisements, logos and labels signaling endorsement of a product by an individual or group, or any other type of advertising. To identify this characteristic, we need to go back to our initial description of consumer behavior.

In Chapter 3, we made a number of assumptions about the role played by consumers in the economy. In particular, we assumed that every consumer knew everything there was to know about the product in question, including the price of that product, the prices of substitutes and complements, and all of the characteristics of that product.

That's a lot of information. At the simplest level, prices of many goods change quite frequently, and it's a bit of a stretch to think that a consumer is aware of the price at which a particular good is sold at every point in time. And the products themselves can change, or new goods are introduced into the market. Whenever we described consumers, we assumed that they knew about all characteristics of all products. This is clearly a lot of information, particularly when we're dealing with new products which a consumer may not even know exist.

8.1 Issues in advertising

Advertising is all about information. In the simplest description of consumer behavior, every consumer knows everything that there is to know about all products, so there is no role for advertising. The gas station doesn't need to post the price per liter of gasoline, and the car company doesn't need to advertise the features of a new model or employ salespeople to assist car consumers in selecting the appropriate vehicle, since the consumer already knows everything about all products. Any resources spent on advertising to give the consumer more information are wasted.

In reality, consumers lack information about many goods, for many different reasons.

Consumers will generally not be aware of new goods introduced to the market, or of significant price changes of goods which arise due to significant technological change. Try to imagine how many times over the last six months that the price of a particular computer hardware package (processor including memory and hard drive, monitor, keyboard, and accessories) has changed.

But advertising plays another role, besides giving information about products to consumers. Advertising can also be intended to change a consumer's preferences. In all of our models so far, we've assumed that a consumer's preferences or tastes are fixed. But as far as a manager is concerned, this assumption is not relevant. The manager must also consider that a consumer who is computer-illiterate today might take computer classes in the future, or have to learn about computers for work. A student may not be able to afford a car today, but may want to buy a car some time in the future. By that point in the future when the consumer enters the computer market or the car market, her preferences over cars will have been affected by commercials on television and newspaper and magazine ads for different models of computers and cars. The manager spends money on advertising today, even though the consumer being reached by the ad may not be in the market for a computer or a car, because the ad may well change the consumer's preferences in the future.

For the remainder of this chapter, we'll relax the assumption that consumers are completely informed, so we can deal with markets where the consumer may not know all that the consumer needs to know in order to decide whether or not to buy a product, or how much of a product to buy.

In order to focus our discussion, let's start off with a definition of advertising.

Definition

Advertising is defined as all expenditures incurred by the firm aimed at increasing sales or protecting market share, by either conveying information to consumers or by attempting to influence their preferences.

This definition implies that advertising by a firm must include all amounts spent on media, including television and radio, newspapers and magazines, and flyers and coupons. But because of the role played by advertising, we must also include all payments to a sales force and publicity department, product and packaging design departments, and so on. The efforts of all of these areas are all aimed at giving the consumer information about the product being advertised.

8.1.1 Types of goods

The role played by advertising will not be the same for all types of goods, because the way that consumers derive information about different types of consumption goods is not always the same. Instead, it depends upon the type of consumption good in question. We've said that the ultimate role of advertising is to convince consumers to purchase a good. In our simple partial equilibrium model, we've typically assumed that a consumer will purchase a good when total surplus $\bar{s}$ derived from consumption is greater than the price of the good p. We may expect that a reasonably well-informed consumer will have good information about the prices of different types of goods. But how does the consumer know what the surplus $\bar{s}$ will be before the good is even consumed? To answer this question, it's useful to classify goods into the following three different types:[1]

1 *Search goods*: these are goods where the consumer has good information about surplus from consumption even before the good is purchased;
2 *Experience goods*: these are goods where the consumer cannot determine the surplus from consumption until after the good has been consumed;
3 *Credence goods*: these are goods where the consumer may never be able to determine the surplus from consumption.

It's not too difficult to think of examples of search goods. A pair of jeans, an apple, photocopier paper, and a new CD player are all search goods, and any consumer would know beforehand the surplus derived from consumption of any of these goods.

On the other hand, a consumer has no idea of the surplus derived from a can of tuna or beef stew, or of a new novel or new CD, before actually consuming these goods. These are examples of experience goods. The consumer can only ascertain total surplus from consumption after actually reading the novel, listening to the CD, or eating the tuna or stew.

A consumer may not determine the total surplus from consumption of a particular type of toothpaste until his next visit to the dentist, if he ever determines total surplus at all. This is an example of a credence good.

Think of the different roles to be played by advertising for the different types of goods listed above. The consumer already knows about search goods, so advertising might be limited to providing information about price and availability. But for experience goods and credence goods, advertising can also inform the consumer about characteristics of the product which will affect total consumer surplus, since without advertising, the consumer would only learn all of the

131

characteristics of these types of products after having consumed them.

8.1.2 Types of advertising

We can also describe different types of advertising, depending on the type of information being conveyed. We can describe the following two different types of advertising.

Hard or informative advertising

Hard advertising conveys information about a product's price, availability, or quality. This type of advertising will generally reduce any product differentiation between the same types of goods which would result from a lack of information about products. Hard advertising will generally lead to an increase in competition, and can encourage the production of high-quality goods, since firms have an incentive to reveal the type of their product through hard advertising. This type of advertising may be most representative of newspaper advertising.

Soft or persuasive advertising

Different professional athletes drinking different types of colas or using different running shoes are examples of soft advertising. This type of advertising does not give the consumer any concrete information about the price or existence of a product, but rather tries to associate the product with a particular image or personality. From the manager's point of view, soft advertising will still be effective if it affects the consumer's preferences and increases demand for the firm's product. For example, a consumer's surplus from consumption of a can of cola will ultimately depend upon how well the consumer's thirst is sated by consuming that particular can of cola. Whether or not the picture of some famous sports celebrity is painted on the outside of the can of cola will not affect the extent to which that cola satisfies the consumer's thirst. But the consumer may derive utility from drinking a cola which is associated with a particular image, in which case the consumer's surplus will depend not only on how well a cola quenches thirst, but also on the perceived image of the personality associated with the cola through advertising. Either way, if sales increase because positive brand association causes consumers to perceive a higher surplus because a particular soda is associated with a particular sports celebrity, then that advertising must be viewed as effective by the firm. Television advertising can often be characterized as soft advertising.

8.1.3 Other issues in advertising

Before we explicitly incorporate advertising into our economic model of the firm's decision-making problem, we'll quickly describe two more aspects of advertising which may become important. We introduce these aspects of advertising at this point in order to complete our introduction to the various important aspects of advertising. We will describe how many of these aspects fit into our economic model of the behavior of the firm in Sections 8.2 and 8.3.

Interfirm effects

From the point of view of the firm, the objective of any increase in advertising expenditures must be to increase demand for the firm's product. But this same change in advertising expenditures may have very different effects on other firms in the market, depending upon the type of good being

Firm 1 \ Firm 2	Not advertise	Advertise
Not advertise	10, 10	5, 12
Advertise	12, 5	**7, 7**

Figure 8.1 Payoffs to cigarette firms

advertised. For example, suppose there are two cigarette firms, each with 50 percent of the total cigarette market. In an initial equilibrium where neither firm advertises, each firm receives profits of $10.

Now suppose firm 1 advertises, at a cost of $3. If non-smokers are not induced to start smoking, then the whole size of the cigarette market does not change. But firm 1 attracts a larger share of the market, so firm 1's revenues rise by $5, and firm 2's revenues fall by $5. In this case, we say that advertising is *predatory*, since an increase in advertising by firm 1 increases firm 1's market share, at the expense of firm 2. We can represent these payoffs in Figure 8.1.

If both firms end up advertising, then the two firms end up back where they started, each with 50 percent of the market. But now each firm spends $3 on advertising, so each firm receives profits of $7.

The Nash equilibrium to this advertising game has both firms advertising. You probably recognize the outcome of this simple game from the prisoner's dilemma example from Chapter 5. Industry profits can be increased if neither firm advertises, but neither firm has an incentive to unilaterally reduce advertising, for fear of losing market share. We say that firms are *over-advertising*, since if both firms reduced advertising expenditures, both firms could see increased profits.

Advertising Competition in the US Beer Industry*

The evolution of market structure in the US beer industry since 1950 provides a remarkable illustration of the potential for competition in advertising to affect a firm's market share and profitability. In 1950, Anheuser-Busch was the largest US brewer, with a national market share of 4.1 percent. By 1990, this figure had risen to over 40 percent, with the four largest US brewers (Anheuser-Busch, Miller, Coors, and Stroh) controlling up to 86 percent of the national beer market.

While a number of factors affected the evolution of the US beer industry, advertising played a significant role. In 1947, average advertising-to-sales ratios of US brewers were just over three percent. By the early 1960s this figure had climbed to almost seven percent.

But the real explosion in advertising expenditures occurred in the 1970s. Real industry advertising more than doubled over the period 1970–88. Miller's advertising expenditures were estimated to have risen by over 320 percent from 1970 to 78, while Coors increased advertising expenditures by over 660 percent between 1975 and 1980.

Evidence from this industry suggests a considerable increase in price competition, while the three firms which engaged in this significant increase in competition through advertising all experienced increases in market share. These results are consistent with the predictions of our duopoly model with competition in advertising. But it is possible to take this argument a step further, and argue that there now exists *over-advertising* in the US beer industry. If firms are *over-advertising*, then profitability could be increased by a reduction in advertising expenditures.

This result would be consistent if competition in advertising corresponded to a prisoner's dilemma game. If US brewers could cooperate so that each producer reduced advertising expenditures, each would see an increase in profitability, as advertising costs fall. But no individual brewer has an incentive to unilaterally reduce advertising expenditures, for fear of losing market share.

*Data for this case are from Greer (1993).

But what if we think of a different market? Consider two firms, one which grows and sells apples and another which sells oranges. In an initial equilibrium where neither firm advertises, each firm receives profits of $10.

Now suppose that the apple grower tries to stimulate demand for apples by advertising the fact that fresh fruit in general, and apples in particular, are very healthy. Consumers may respond by buying more apples, but may also recognize that oranges are also very healthy fruits. In this case, advertising by apple growers is *cooperative*, since it results in an increase in demand for both apples and oranges. Producers of other fresh fruits benefit from the advertising expenditures undertaken by the apple growers. The positive effects on demand of advertising expenditures by one producer (apple growers) spill over into increased demand for the products of other producers (orange growers) who did not necessarily spend any resources on advertising.

To illustrate, suppose advertising costs $3. If any one firm advertises, each firm experiences an increase in demand and as a result gets an increase in revenue of $2. If both firms advertise, each gets an increase

Apple grower \ Orange grower	Not advertise	Advertise
Not advertise	**10, 10**	12, 9
Advertise	9, 12	11, 11

Figure 8.2 Payoffs to fruit growers

in revenue of $4. Payoffs in this simple game are represented in Figure 8.2. You should be able to verify that the Nash equilibrium in this game will have no advertising. While each firm benefits from advertising, neither wants to be the first to advertise. Each firm would rather benefit from advertising expenditures incurred by the other firm.

Of course, these examples are overly simplistic, but they do illustrate that whether advertising is cooperative or predatory can affect the manager's decision when planning whether to advertise and how much to advertise. In a market where advertising is cooperative, no producer has the incentive to be the first to advertise, since competitors can then *free ride* as the cooperative benefits of advertising by the first producer spill over into increased demand for their product.

Intertemporal effects

We have already noted that the firm may incur advertising expenditures today to affect or change the preferences of consumers in the future. In general, advertising can have an immediate effect on consumption, and may also have intertemporal effects. At issue here is the relationship between advertising and the reputation of the firm or the product which the firm sells. For example, advertising may be particularly aimed at convincing the consumer that the firm sells a high-quality product or offers very high-quality service and support. We could say that in this case, advertising contributes to the firm's *stock of goodwill*. IBM has consistently sought to differentiate its computer equipment products from those of the competition by providing a high degree of post-purchase support, and one means of reinforcing this reputation is through advertising. By the same token, this stock of goodwill can depreciate. That is, if

IBM stops advertising that it is a producer of relatively high-quality products who provides very strong support, consumer perception of IBM's reputation may deteriorate, leading to a drop in demand.

8.2 Advertising in a monopoly

We'll begin our discussion of the effects of advertising using an economic model where a monopolist produces a single output q. This good q may be a search good, in which case the monopolist could use advertising to inform consumers about the price and availability of the good. Or q could be an experience good, and the monopolist's advertising effort could include other specific characteristics about the product about which the consumer may not be aware. Either way, we're starting off with the monopolist's problem since it's simpler to deal with only one producer at a time. Once we have a better idea of how advertising works in this model, we'll move on in Section 8.3 to a description of equilibrium in a duopoly market with advertising.

We'll denote the market price for the monopolist's output as p. An increase in the market price p will lead to a decrease in demand for the monopolist's output q, so the monopolist faces a downward-sloping demand curve. Suppose that the level of advertising expenditures incurred by the monopolist is represented by a. We'll assume that for any given market price, as the monopolist increases spending on advertising, so that a increases, the quantity demanded for the monopolist's output will increase. We summarize the effect of changes in the market price p and the level of spending on advertising a have on demand for the monopolist's output q with the market demand function:

$$q = q(p, a)$$

If the market demand curve which the monopolist faces is downward-sloping, then $q_p = \partial q / \partial p < 0$. We have also assumed that an increase in advertising by the monopolist leads to an increase in demand, so that $q_a = \partial q / \partial a > 0$. But we make no assumption about the *size* of the effect of a change in advertising on demand, only its *sign*. As we will see below, the size of this term will be of crucial importance to the monopolist's problem of choosing the optimal level of advertising.

The monopolist's cost of production will be an increasing function of the level of output:

$$C(q) = C[q(p, a)]$$

The monopolist's problem is to choose a market price p and a level of spending on advertising a in order to maximize profits. We can write the monopolist's profit maximization problem by noting that total profits will be the difference between total revenue $p \cdot q$ and total cost, where total cost is the sum of production costs $C(q)$ and advertising expenditures a:

$$\max_{p, a} \pi^m = p \cdot q(p, a) - C[q(p, a)] - a$$

Notice that advertising has two separate effects on the monopolist's total cost. Of course, there is the direct effect of a change in advertising expenditures on costs, represented by the final term $-a$ in the monopolist's profit function. But advertising also has an indirect effect on costs, since an increase in advertising causes an increase in market demand through the demand function $q = q(p, a)$. An increase in advertising will increase market demand, causing an increase in the monopolist's production cost.

To solve the monopolist's problem, we need to solve for two first-order conditions, one for each choice variable (price p and

advertising a). The first-order condition on prices is found by setting the price derivative of the profit function equal to zero:

$$\partial \pi^m / \partial p = q + (p - c) \cdot \frac{\partial q}{\partial p} = 0$$

$$p - c = -q \cdot \frac{\partial p}{\partial q}$$

where $c = \partial C(q) / \partial q$ is the monopolist's marginal cost of production.[2] We solve for the first-order condition on advertising by setting the derivative of the profit function with respect to advertising equal to zero:

$$\partial \pi^m / \partial a = (p - c) \cdot \frac{\partial q}{\partial a} - 1 = 0$$

$$p - c = \frac{\partial a}{\partial q}$$

Note that the left-hand side of each first-order condition is the same, so we can combine these two first-order conditions to get:

$$\frac{\partial a}{\partial q} = -q \cdot \frac{\partial p}{\partial q}$$

To make sense of this expression, multiply both sides by $q / a \cdot p$:

$$\frac{q}{a \cdot p} \cdot \frac{\partial a}{\partial q} = -\frac{q^2}{a \cdot p} \cdot \frac{\partial p}{\partial q}$$

$$\frac{1}{p} \cdot \frac{q}{a} \cdot \frac{\partial a}{\partial q} = -\frac{q}{a} \cdot \frac{q}{p} \cdot \frac{\partial p}{\partial q}$$

We use the definitions of the price elasticity of demand:[3]

$$\epsilon_p = \left| \frac{\partial q}{\partial p} \cdot \frac{p}{q} \right|$$

and the advertising elasticity of demand:

$$\epsilon_a = \frac{\partial q}{\partial a} \cdot \frac{a}{q}$$

Substituting these definitions into the equation above gives:

$$\frac{1}{p} \cdot \frac{1}{\epsilon_a} = \frac{q}{a} \cdot \frac{1}{\epsilon_p}$$

$$\frac{\epsilon_a}{\epsilon_p} = \frac{a}{p \cdot q}$$

The right-hand side of this expression is the ratio of advertising expenditures a to total revenue $p \cdot q$. The monopolist will never choose an equilibrium where profits are zero, so total revenue must be greater than total cost, and advertising expenditures a make up only a part of total cost. This means that the expression $\epsilon_a/\epsilon_p = a/p \cdot q$ must be some fraction between zero and one. This simple rule for profit maximization says that the monopolist should choose a level of spending on advertising in such a way that the share of advertising expenditures out of total revenue is equal to the ratio of the advertising elasticity of demand to the price elasticity of demand. For example, if the price elasticity of demand is ten times as large as the advertising elasticity of demand (so that $\epsilon_a/\epsilon_p = 0.10$), the monopolist should spend 10 percent of total revenue on advertising. In the literature on economics and advertising,[4] this is referred to as the monopolist's *rule of thumb* for choosing a level of advertising expenditures to maximize profits. If the ratio of demand elasticities is constant, then this *rule of thumb* gives the monopolist a very convenient rule for determining how much to spend on advertising.

We noted earlier that the effect of a change in advertising on demand for the monopolist's output was of crucial importance in solving the monopolist's problem. We can get further intuition from the monopolist's *rule of thumb* for advertising expenditures by looking a bit more closely at the definition of the advertising elasticity of demand, the term which summarizes the effect of a change in advertising expenditures on demand. More specifically, for a one percent increase in spending on advertising, ϵ_a gives the percentage increase in demand for the monopolist's product. If the monopolist is in an industry

How Do Managers Choose Advertising Budgets

The monopolist's *rule of thumb* for choosing the level of advertising expenditures implies that advertising budgets should be chosen as a particular percentage of total sales revenue. This percentage should depend upon demand elasticities, which will generally be different between different industries, so that the advertising-to-sales ratio a/pq should vary between industries. To give you an idea of how different these values can be, we've listed the advertising-to-sales ratios for selected industries in 1994:*

Industry	a/pq%
Beverages	7.5
Cigarettes	4.4
Stuffed toys	15.1
Games and toys	16.4
Grocery stores	1.1
Hhld. audio & video equip.	3.6
Management services	1.5
Records and CD's	11.7
Prepackaged software	3.8
Videotape rental	2.0

But do managers actually use such a *rule of thumb* in choosing the size of advertising budgets? Of course, applying our theory in any of the industries listed above would be inappropriate, for a number of reasons. In deriving our *rule of thumb*, we assumed that we were dealing with a monopolist, and it is difficult to argue that any of the above industries are monopolized. Also, the size of advertising budgets is most likely affected by many factors which we have not incorporated into our simple model, such as persistence effects of advertising (see Section 8.2.1), and competition over advertising (see Section 8.3).

A number of researchers have surveyed managers to determine the method used to determine expenditures on advertising by firms with significant advertising budgets. A survey of the 100 leading advertisers in the US in 1980 found that well over 50 percent of respondents used some form of *percent of sales* method for setting advertising budgets. A similar survey of 92 British firms in 1975 found that 76 percent of respondents used the percentage approach.

Why would such a significant share of managers use a simple *rule of thumb* approach to setting advertising budgets, when so many other factors may affect optimal advertising expenditures? While budgeting practices may have become more sophisticated since these surveys were taken, it is still the case that the *rule of thumb* approach is very simple, and may provide managers with a practical and cost-effective mechanism for budgeting.

*Selected industries from Table 16–1 in Batra *et al.* (1996), pp. 542–7.

**Patti and Blasko (1981) and Gilligan (1977).

where consumers can be expected to respond very little to changes in advertising expenditures, then the advertising elasticity of demand will be relatively small. In this case, the *rule of thumb* would instruct the monopolist in this market to spend a smaller share of total revenue on advertising.

The extreme example would be the case where consumers are all fully informed about the monopolist's product. In this case, the effect of advertising on demand will be exactly zero, since consumers already have all of the information that they want and need about the monopolist's product. The advertising *rule of thumb* shows that there is no role for advertising in this kind of market, so the monopolist should set $a = 0$.

On the other hand, if the monopolist is producing output in a market where consumers are less aware of the characteristics of the good produced by the monopolist, we would expect a 1 percent increase in spending on advertising to have a much greater effect on market demand. All other things being equal, the larger is the advertising elasticity of demand, the larger should be the share of advertising expenditures out of total revenue.

8.2.1 Advertising and goodwill[5]

Earlier in this chapter, we noted that it was likely that advertising could affect future sales as well as current sales, since advertising could affect the reputation of the firm in the marketplace. In order to model this aspect of advertising, we will suppose that the monopolist has a stock of *goodwill*, denoted G, which affects market demand. This stock of goodwill can change over time, so we will need to write goodwill at any point in time t as G_t. A higher stock of goodwill at any point in time will lead to a higher level of demand for the monopolist's output, thereby leading to increased profit, *cet par*.

The monopolist can increase the stock of goodwill by advertising. However, if the monopolist does not spend any effort on advertising, the stock of goodwill will depreciate. We'll suppose that the stock of goodwill depreciates at rate $(1 - \delta)$, where $0 < \delta < 1$. Then we can write the relationship between goodwill at time t and advertising at time t as follows:

$$G_t = \delta G_{t-1} + a_t$$

Note that if the monopolist does not spend any effort on advertising in period t ($a_t = 0$), then goodwill in period t will be given by the goodwill left over from the previous period G_{t-1} after depreciation. We can rewrite this equation so that advertising in period t is a function of the current and past stock of goodwill:

$$a_t = G_t - \delta G_{t-1}$$

Now advertising only affects market demand indirectly, by changing the stock of goodwill. So we need to amend the market demand function of the previous section:

$$q_t = q(p_t, G_t)$$

Total cost will again be given by the sum of total production costs $C(q_t)$ and advertising expenditures a_t. Thus we can write the monopolist's profit function at time t as follows:

$$\pi_t = p_t \cdot q(p_t, G_t) - C(q(p_t, G_t)) - (G_t - \delta G_{t-1})$$

As in the previous model, the monopolist has two choice variables at any time t: the market price p_t and the level of advertising expenditures a_t. But this model is more complicated, because advertising at time t will affect the stock of goodwill not only in time t, but also into the future. To illustrate, let's write out the monopolist's profits in the next period, at time $t + 1$. To get this expression, we just

increase the time counter in the profit function above from t to $t + 1$, and from $t - 1$ to t:

$$\pi_{t+1} = p_{t+1} \cdot q(p_{t+1}, G_{t+1}) - C(q(p_{t+1}, G_{t+1}))$$
$$- (G_{t+1} - \delta G_t)$$

These are the monopolist's profits in time period $t + 1$. Notice that they are directly affected by the stock of goodwill at time t, G_t. Of course, G_t depends directly upon advertising at time t, so we see that the effects of advertising at time t will affect profits in time period $t + 1$. If the monopolist advertises more today, then the stock of goodwill tomorrow will be higher, affecting tomorrow's profits.

But the monopolist needs to pick a_t today, at time period t. At time period t, profits which the monopolist expects only in period $t + 1$ are not as valuable, since the monopolist must wait until period $t + 1$ to receive future profits. So at time period t, the monopolist will discount profits from period $t + 1$, at some rate which we will write as $\alpha > 0$.

In the appendix, we solve the monopolist's discounted profit maximization problem. As a result, we derive the *modified rule of thumb*:

$$\frac{\epsilon_G}{\epsilon_p} = (1 - \alpha\delta) \cdot \frac{G_t}{q_t \cdot p_t} \quad \forall\, t$$

This expression is the same as the original rule of thumb result we derived earlier, except for two items:

- The result depends upon the elasticity of demand with respect to goodwill (instead of advertising) and the ratio of goodwill (instead of advertising) to total sales at time t;
- The numerator of the right-hand side is multiplied by the term $1 - \alpha\delta$.

How do we interpret this result? The simplest way to illustrate is to consider a special case: what happens if goodwill depreciates at a rate of 100 percent? This would mean that $\delta = 0$, so the expression for goodwill would become:

$$G_t = a_t$$

There is no persistence to advertising, and we just get our original rule of thumb result. The initial model with no goodwill was just a special case of this model when goodwill depreciates completely in each period.

This means that the same results which we derived in our simple model will apply here, except that the vital information which the monopolist now needs in order to apply the modified rule of thumb is the way in which the stock of goodwill affects demand. This information is reflected in the elasticity of demand with respect to goodwill, ϵ_G. In the simple rule of thumb result, the monopolist needed to know about the elasticity of demand with respect to advertising, ϵ_a, which described the way that advertising expenditures affected market demand.

But what is the real difference between these two models of advertising? Essentially the difference comes down to the type of information being conveyed by any particular type of advertising. If a car company or local computer store advertises today for a sale which lasts for the next week, then any goodwill generated by this advertising may well depreciate completely by the time the week is over and the sale has expired. On the other hand, advertising today for a 5-year warranty on an automobile or a free lifetime service contract on a new computer can be expected to have effects on goodwill which will last far into the future. The most important element to keep in mind about these models is to carefully consider the type of good (search good or experience good) being advertised and the characteris-

tics of the particular form of advertising, and then to apply the appropriate rule of thumb result.

How can we amend this model to incorporate the effectiveness of advertising? In the introduction to this chapter, we noted that advertising could be predatory or cooperative. It is difficult to deal with this aspect of advertising at this point, if for no other reason than we are currently working with a model with only one firm.[6] But we can get an idea of how this might work by supposing that there was some other firm which could spend resources on advertising which directly affected the monopolist's stock of goodwill. If we call the monopolist firm i, and the other firm j, then a change in advertising by firm j (a_j) could affect the monopolist's stock of goodwill (G_i). Then depending upon whether advertising is cooperative or predatory, we would get the following:

$$\text{cooperative} \leftrightarrow \partial G_i / \partial a_j > 0$$
$$\text{predatory} \leftrightarrow \partial G_i / \partial a_j < 0$$

If advertising is cooperative, then an increase in advertising by the apple grower (firm j) will lead to an increase in the stock of goodwill of the orange grower (firm i). But if advertising is predatory, an increase in advertising by cigarette company j (a_j) leads to a drop in the stock of goodwill of cigarette company i (G_i).

In fact, we could even think of our modified rule of thumb result as a special case of this much more complicated model, where advertising by any other firm has no effect at all on the monopolist's stock of goodwill. But now our model is getting overly complicated, so we will leave this topic for the interested reader to pursue independently.

8.3 Advertising in a duopoly market

We now proceed to describe the outcome of competition between two firms who compete by choosing a level of advertising in order to affect consumer demand for their product. We proceed by adapting the model of product differentiation which we described in Chapter 7. You'll recall that this model was characterized by the following assumptions:

- there are two firms in the market, with firm 1 located at a and firm 2 located at b;
- firms sell the same output at constant marginal cost c;
- consumers are uniformly distributed along the unit interval;
- all consumers derive surplus $\bar{s}$ from consumption of one unit of output;
- consumers incur transport cost t (or quadratic transport costs tx^2 and $t(1 - x)^2$).

To keep things simple, we continue to deal with a market where there are only two firms. As was the case in Chapter 7, we assume that both firms produce and sell the same good with the same production technology, so they both have the same constant marginal cost c. There is only one characteristic which differentiates the output of each firm, represented by the firm's location along the unit interval. Consumers have different preferences for this product, summarized by their location along the unit interval. As we noted in Chapter 7, this unit interval representing product differentiation can represent any single characteristic by which the products of the two firms can be differentiated. This could be physical location, but could also be any other characteristic such as color, size, quality, etc.

We're primarily interested in competition over advertising, so we will assume that the goods produced by the two firms are max-imally differentiated. This means that firm 1 will be located at $a = 0$ and firm 2 will be located at $b = 1$. We can justify this assumption based on the outcome of competition in locations between these two firms when consumers incur quadratic transport costs, since we showed in Chapter 7 that firms would choose to locate as far away from each other as possible in such a model. We'll denote the price that each firm charges per unit of output as p_i, for $i = 1, 2$.

In order to establish a role for advertising in this model, we suppose that consumers are initially unaware of the existence of either firm's product. The only way that consumers can learn about the existence of either firm's product is if the consumer receives an ad from the firm. Suppose that ψ_1 and ψ_2 are the fraction of consumers receiving an ad from firm 1 and 2, respectively, so that $0 \leq \psi_1 + \psi_2 \leq 2$. We denote the cost to firm i of sending ads which inform ψ_i consumers as $A(\psi_i)$. Suppose that this cost function over advertising is given by:[7]

$$A(\psi_i) = \frac{a \cdot \psi_i^2}{2}$$

This implies that the most that a firm will ever spend on advertising is $a/2$, the cost of informing all consumers ($\psi_i = 1$).

From the point of view of firm 1, there will be two types of consumers:

1 $1 - \psi_2$: share of consumers not receiving an ad from firm 2. This is firm 1's *turf*.
2 ψ_2: consumers who receive at least one ad from firm 2. This is the more competitive portion of firm 1's demand function.

We can already get an idea of the role played by advertising in this model. From the point of view of firm 1, the more ads sent out by firm 2, the greater will be the number of consumers ψ_2 who are aware of firm 2's product. The larger is ψ_2, the *more competitive* is the market for firm 1's output.

Given prices p_1 and p_2, we showed in Chapter 7 that there was a consumer located at x along the unit interval who was just indifferent between the output of firm 1 and 2. For this consumer, the following condition holds:[8]

$$p_1 + tx^2 = p_2 + t(1-x)^2$$

As was the case in Chapter 7, we don't want to worry about special cases where some consumers are not served in equilibrium and each firm has a local monopoly, since we are most interested in the outcome of competition between the two firms. So we suppose that even for the consumer located at x, total surplus received from consumption of this good $\bar{s}$ is at least as large as the price plus the transport cost for consuming one unit of output:

$$\bar{s} > p_1 + tx^2 = p_2 + t(1-x)^2$$

In Chapter 7, we solved for the demand function for firm 1's output:

$$D^1(p_1, p_2) = \frac{p_2 - p_1 + t}{2t}$$

Of course, this demand function becomes a bit more complicated, since we have to incorporate the fact that some consumers receive ads and some do not. Firm 1 will compete with firm 2 only over those consumers who receive an ad from firm 2. For the other $1 - \psi_2$ consumers who do not receive an ad from firm 2, firm 1 only needs to send an ad to capture their business. So the demand function for firm 1 becomes:

$$D^1 = \psi_1 \left\{ (1 - \psi_2) + \psi_2 \left(\frac{p_2 - p_1 + t}{2t} \right) \right\}$$

One way of measuring the effect of changes in advertising on competitiveness in the market is to look at how changes in advertising affect the elasticity of demand. The demand elasticity for firm 1's output ϵ_1 is defined as the percentage change in firm 1's output derived from a given percentage change in firm 1's market price:

$$\epsilon_1 = \frac{-\partial D_1}{D_1} \bigg/ \frac{\partial p_1}{p_1}$$

$$\epsilon_1 = \frac{-\partial D_1}{\partial p_1} \frac{p_1}{D_1}$$

This demand elasticity tells us the percentage reduction in demand for firm 1's output when firm 1 raises its price by one percent. If the market is very competitive, then a one percent increase in the price will cause a relatively large reduction in demand (ϵ_1 is relatively large), but if the market is not very competitive, then the reduction in demand from a one percent increase in the price will be relatively small (ϵ_1 is small).

Both firms have the same technology and sell the same product in the same market, so in equilibrium, both will charge the same price ($p_1 = p_2 = p$) and incur the same amount of advertising $\psi_1 = \psi_2 = \psi$. So we can solve for firm 1's demand elasticity as follows:

$$\epsilon_1 = \frac{-\partial D_1}{\partial p_1} \frac{p_1}{D_1}$$

$$\epsilon_1 = \frac{\psi^2}{2t} \frac{p}{\{\psi \cdot [(1 - \psi) + \psi(1/2)]\}}$$

$$\epsilon_1 = \frac{\psi p}{t(2 - \psi)}$$

So the larger the amount of advertising ψ, the greater will be the demand elasticity ϵ_1, so more advertising makes the market more competitive.

To find out how much firms will advertise in equilibrium, we need to solve each firm's profit maximization problem for the equilibrium level of prices and advertising. Recall that both firms face the same constant marginal cost of production c. So if $a\psi_1^2/2$ is the cost of advertising, we can write firm 1's profit maximization problem as follows:

$$\max_{p_1, \psi_1} \pi^1 = \psi_1 \cdot \left[(1 - \psi_2) + \psi_2 \left(\frac{p_2 - p_1 + t}{2t} \right) \right]$$
$$\cdot (p_1 - c) - \frac{a\psi_1^2}{2}$$

To solve this problem, we need to derive firm 1's two first-order conditions. The firm chooses the level of advertising ψ_1 and price p_1 such that the marginal change in profits due to a change in either prices or advertising is equal to zero. The solution to this problem is completely written out in the appendix to this chapter. In equilibrium, both firms charge the same price p^a and inform the same number of consumers ψ^a.

$$p^a = c + \sqrt{2ta} \quad \text{assuming} \quad a \geq \frac{t}{2}$$

$$\psi^a = \frac{2}{1 + \sqrt{\frac{2a}{t}}}$$

If we substitute these back into the firm's profit function, we get the following expression for equilibrium profits:

$$\pi^1 = \pi^2 = \frac{2a}{\left(1 + \sqrt{\frac{2a}{t}}\right)^2}$$

Now that we've solved the firm's problem in this duopoly model of product differentiation with advertising, we are in a position to interpret the results. The best way to do this is to compare the results in this model to those we found in Chapter 7, since the model used in both chapters is essentially the same. Recall that in Chapter 7, we solved for the firm's equilibrium market price as:

$$p_1^n = p_2^n = p^{fi} = \frac{4t - t(a + b)}{3} + c$$

This is the equilibrium market price that each firm would charge when consumers have full information about the products which each

firm is selling, so we label the equilibrium price p^{fi} since it's the full-information equilibrium price.

So far in this chapter, we've supposed that firms are located at opposite ends of the unit interval, so $a = 0$ and $b = 1$. If we substitute these values into the full-information price above, we get:

$$p^{fi} = c + t$$
$$p^a = c + \sqrt{2at}$$

As long as $2a > t$, then $\sqrt{2at} > t$, in which case the equilibrium price in the model with advertising p^a will be higher than the equilibrium price under full information p^{fi}. When consumers do not have full information about the products available for consumption in the market, firms see a lower demand elasticity, so the equilibrium market price will be higher. Prices will be increasing with transport costs t, and with the cost of advertising a.

It might help to think of this result in another way. We can re-interpret the full-information product differentiation model as one where both firms advertise to every consumer. If each firm advertised up to the point where $\psi = 1$ for each firm, then the market outcome is the same as in Chapter 7, where consumers had full information. But firms do not want to advertise that much, since doing so makes the market too competitive.

Result

Relative to a market with full information, prices are higher in a market where firms advertise.

How much will firms advertise in equilibrium? By looking at the expression for ψ^a, we see that firms will advertise more the lower is the cost of advertising a, and the

Advertising in the Optometric Services Industry

How can we check whether advertising really does increase competition, resulting in lower market prices? If we plot advertising expenditures against the market price in some industry, we won't necessarily get an answer to our question, since market prices are affected by many different factors.

In separate studies, Lee Benham and John Kwoka Jr.* found an ideal environment in which to solve this problem, by examining advertising and pricing strategies in the market for optometric services in the United States At any given point in time, some states in the United States allowed advertising for eye examinations, while in other states, advertising of optometric services was prohibited. Using data from 1963, Benham found that the prices of optometric services were 18–22 percent higher in those states where advertising was prohibited.

While this result supports the conclusion that advertising increases competition and lowers market prices, there is a potential problem which Benham did not account for. As we will see in the next chapter, when products are differentiated on the basis of quality, producers may end up charging higher prices for higher-quality goods. The idea here is that not all eye exams are equal. Prices may be higher in states which prohibit advertising because optometrists in those states spend more time with their patients, providing a higher-quality service.

Kwoka accounted for differences in quality of optometric services by including data on the amount of time optometrists spent per patient. He found that stores which advertised charged prices which were 9–11 percent lower than those which did not advertise, supporting the conclusion that advertising increases competition. But he also found that optometrists who advertised spent 3–5 fewer minutes with their patients, thereby offering a lower-quality service. This is an important issue which we will address in the next chapter. When dealing with experience goods which are differentiated on the basis of quality, a consumer will not know the quality of the good before purchase, and may try to deduce quality from some observable signal-like advertising or the market price.

*This case draws on material in Benham (1972) and Kwoka (1984).

higher is the transport cost t. But of course, the firm would be most interested in the effect of advertising on profits.

From the expression for equilibrium profits, we see that higher transport costs t lead to more advertising, a higher equilibrium market price p^a, and higher profits. But the most interesting result we get is that profits are increasing in the cost of advertising. That is, an increase in the cost of advertising to the firm will lead to an *increase in profits*.

How can a higher advertising cost allow the firm to earn higher profits? The technical answer to this question is a bit complicated, so we'll relegate it to the appendix. Instead we'll provide an intuitive answer to this question, by considering the effect of a change in the cost of advertising on the equilibrium amount of advertising by the firm. We saw earlier that as the cost of advertising a increases, the equilibrium amount of advertising will fall. Thus a change in the cost of advertising will have two effects on profits:

1 *Direct effect*: an increase in a will decrease profits;

2 *Strategic effect*: an increase in a will decrease advertising, increasing the informational distortion, so that firms can charge higher prices, leading to higher profits.

The direct effect is simple to understand: as *a* increases, *cet par.*, the firm's costs will rise, so profits will fall. But it is the strategic effect which is most interesting. As the cost of advertising rises, the firm will advertise less. This increases the informational distortion in the market, since now fewer consumers will be aware of the differences between each firm's product, since firms are advertising less. As such, the market becomes *less competitive*, and firms can respond by increasing the equilibrium market price (recall that as *a* increased, the equilibrium market price p^a increased). This is the strategic effect of a change in the cost of advertising. It is in each firm's interest to advertise *less*, since in doing so, the market becomes less competitive, and each firm can charge a higher market price and thereby earn higher profits. As it turns out in this example, this strategic effect dominates the direct effect of a change in advertising costs, so the firm's profits will be increasing in the cost of advertising.

This is a very important result, since it once again highlights the importance of the strategic interaction between the two firms in the market. If we didn't consider this strategic effect of a change in advertising, we would have come to the wrong conclusion: Advertising costs go up so profits must go down (the direct effect). Once we include the strategic effect, we realize that the indirect effect of a change in the cost of advertising works in the opposite direction of the direct effect, by changing the amount of competition in the market.

Summary

- Advertising includes all expenditures incurred by the firm aimed at increasing sales or protecting market share, by either conveying information to consumers or by attempting to influence their preferences.
- Advertising can be *informative* if it gives hard information about the price or existence of a good, or it can be *persuasive* if it tries to affect consumers' perceptions of a product by associating the product with a particular image or personality.
- Goods can be classified as *search goods, experience goods*, or *credence goods*, depending upon whether consumers have information about their surplus derived from consumption before or after purchasing the good.
- Advertising can be *cooperative* or *predatory* depending upon how advertising by one firm affects a competitor's demand.
- A monopolist's optimal *rule of thumb* for advertising expenditures implies that, all other things being equal, advertising as a share of total revenue should be higher in industries where the price elasticity of demand was lower or the advertising elasticity of demand was higher.
- Optimal advertising expenditures could also depend upon factors such as persistence effects if advertising could affect a firm's stock of good-will.
- In a market with more than one firm, changes in advertising expenditures by one firm have a *market-share effect* and a *strategic effect*.
- The *strategic effect* implies that more advertising makes a market more competitive, resulting in lower prices and lower profitability.

Notes

1 These classifications are used in Tirole (1988), p. 106, and are taken from Nelson (1970) and Darby and Karni (1973).

2 Note that we need to apply the chain rule to solve for the change in production costs due to a change in the output price p, since a change in p affects production costs indirectly through the change in quantity demanded q. That is:

$$\frac{\partial C}{\partial p} = \frac{\partial C(q)}{\partial p} \quad \frac{\partial C}{\partial p} = \frac{\partial C[q(p, a)]}{\partial p}$$

$$\frac{\partial C}{\partial p} = \frac{\partial C(q)}{\partial q} \cdot \frac{\partial q}{\partial p} \quad \frac{\partial C}{\partial p} = c \cdot \frac{\partial q}{\partial p}$$

We also use the chain rule to solve for the change in cost of production due to a change in advertising a.

3 Note that we're writing the price elasticity of demand as the absolute value of the percentage change in quantity over the percentage change in the market price. As long as the demand curve is always downward-sloping, $\partial q/\partial p$ will always be negative, so writing the price elasticity of demand using absolute values ensures that this term is always positive.

4 The principal reference for this model and the *rule of thumb* result is Dorfman and Steiner (1954). See also Schmalensee (1972), and the references in Tirole (1988).

5 Material in this subsection is more advanced, since it requires knowledge of discounting behavior by the firm. As such, most of the results are derived in the appendix, and are only indirectly referred to here. The principal references for this material, though they are somewhat advanced, are Nerlove and Arrow (1962) and Friedman (1983).

6 A more advanced treatment of this problem can be found in Friedman (1983), pp. 152–60.

7 This model is presented in Grossman and Shapiro (1984).

8 Note that we're assuming that consumers incur quadratic transport costs. A consumer located at x who wishes to buy from the firm located at the extreme left end of the unit interval ($a = 0$) must travel a distance given by x, and as such will incur a transport cost tx^2 to buy from this store.

Exercises

1 In the example in Figure 8.2, what would the payoff matrix look like if advertising by both firms increased each firms revenues by $6 instead of $4? Does this change the Nash equilibrium? Can you relate your answer to the elasticity of demand with respect to advertising and the effectiveness of advertising?

2 A monopolist produces a single output q with constant marginal cost c and zero fixed costs. He faces the following demand function:

$$q = b_0 - b_1 p + b_2 a \qquad b_0, b_1, b_2 > 0$$

where p is the market price per unit of output and a is advertising expenditures.

(a) Write out the monopolist's profit function, as a function of the market price p and advertising expenditures a.

(b) Solve for the two first-order maximization conditions, and use them to solve for the monopolist's optimal market price p^* and level of advertising expenditures a^*.

(c) Use the demand function to solve for the elasticity of demand with respect to the market price ϵ_p and with respect to advertising expenditures ϵ_a.

(d) Use your answers to parts 2b and 2c to verify the optimal share of advertising expenditures out of total revenue according to the monopolist's *rule of thumb*: $\epsilon_a/\epsilon_p = a/(p \cdot q)$.

3 In many countries, associations of professionals (dentists, for example) argue that advertising should not be allowed in their industry because it increases competition, creating incentives for professionals to cut costs and reduce quality of service.

Suppose you were a government official in charge of regulating advertising by dentists.

Would you want to allow advertising by dentists, or would you rather ban advertising by dentists? What effect would your recommendation have on:

- price of dentist's services

- quality of dentist's services

- profitability in the dentist industry

When making your recommendation, what account would you take of:

- the effectiveness of advertising by dentists

- whether advertising by dentists would be predatory or cooperative

- whether dentist's services are search goods, experience goods, or credence goods

4 Consider an industry where two producers sell a product which is differentiated only by quality, in a market where a share $0 < \psi < 1$ of consumers are aware of the quality of the product being sold, but the other $1 - \psi$ consumers are unaware of the quality of each producer's output. Producer H sells the highest-quality good, while producer L sells the lowest-quality good. The two producers compete in prices.

   (a) Suppose producers cannot advertise. Of all the models we have discussed so far, which is most appropriate for this market? Is one model more appropriate for the ψ informed consumers? Would you use a different model for the $1 - \psi$ uninformed consumers? Why?

   (b) Now suppose the producers can advertise the quality of their product. If $\psi = 0$ initially, does increased advertising make the market more or less competitive? Can you relate your answer to the Bertrand paradox?

   (c) Now suppose $\psi = 1$, so all consumers know that L sells the lowest-quality good, and H sells the highest-quality good. If

producer L can advertise to make consumers believe he is producing a higher-quality good, discuss his incentive to advertise. Would this increase or decrease price competition? How would you expect producer H to respond?

Appendix

Modified rule of thumb with goodwill

Denote the monopolist's stock of goodwill and advertising at time t as G_t and a_t, respectively. If goodwill depreciates at rate $1 - \delta$, we get:

$$G_t = \delta G_{t-1} + a_t$$
$$a_t = G_t - \delta G_{t-1}$$

If the monopolist discounts next period profits at rate α, then total profits at time $t = 0$ can be written as:

$$\sum_{t=1}^{\infty} \alpha^{t-1} \begin{bmatrix} p_t \cdot q(p_t, G_t) \\ - C(q(p_t, G_t)) - (G_t - \delta G_{t-1}) \end{bmatrix}$$

Maximization yields a pair of first-order conditions for all time periods t:

$$\frac{\partial}{\partial p_t} = 0 = \alpha^{t-1} \left[q_t + (p_t - C_t') \cdot \frac{\partial q_t}{\partial p_t} \right]$$

$$\frac{\partial}{\partial G_t} = 0 = \alpha^{t-1} \left[(p_t - C_t') \cdot \frac{\partial q_t}{\partial G_t} - 1 + \alpha \delta \right]$$

$$p_t - C_t' = \frac{q_t}{\frac{\partial q_t}{\partial p_t}}$$

$$p_t - C_t' = \frac{1 - \alpha \delta}{\frac{\partial q_t}{\partial G_t}} \qquad \forall \, t$$

$$\frac{q_t}{G_t \cdot p_t} \cdot \frac{q_t}{\frac{\partial q_t}{\partial p_t}} = \frac{1 - \alpha \delta}{\frac{\partial q_t}{\partial G_t}} \cdot \frac{q_t}{G_t \cdot p_t}$$

$$\frac{q_t}{G_t} \cdot \frac{1}{\epsilon_p} = \frac{1 - \alpha \delta}{p_t} \cdot \frac{1}{\epsilon_a}$$

$$\frac{\epsilon_G}{\epsilon_p} = (1 - \alpha \delta) \cdot \frac{G_t}{q_t \cdot p_t} \qquad \forall \, t$$

Solution to duopoly profit-maximization problem with advertising

When firm 1 faces the demand function:

$$D^1 = \psi_1 \left\{ (1 - \psi_2) + \psi_2 \left(\frac{p_2 - p_1 + t}{2t} \right) \right\}$$

we can write out firm 1's profit-maximization problem as follows:

$$\max_{p_1, \psi_1} \pi^1 = \psi_1 \cdot \left[(1 - \psi_2) + \psi_2 \left(\frac{p_2 - p_1 + t}{2t} \right) \right]$$

$$\cdot (p_1 - c) - \frac{a \psi_1^2}{2}$$

Optimal choice of advertising ψ_1 and price p_1 implies the following two first-order conditions:

first-order condition on advertising:

$$\frac{\partial \pi^1}{\partial \psi_1} = 0$$

$$(p_1 - c) \cdot \left[(1 - \psi_2) + \psi_2 \left(\frac{p_2 - p_1 + t}{2t} \right) \right] = a \cdot \psi_1$$

$$\frac{p_1 - c}{a} \cdot \left[(1 - \psi_2) + \psi_2 \left(\frac{p_2 - p_1 + t}{2t} \right) \right] = \psi_1$$

first-order condition on price:

$$\frac{\partial \pi^1}{\partial p_1} = 0$$

$$\psi_1 \cdot \left[(1 - \psi_2) + \psi_2 \left(\frac{p_2 - p_1 + t}{2t} \right) \right] = (p_1 - c) \frac{\psi_1 \psi_2}{2t}$$

$$1 - \psi_2 + \psi_2 \left(\frac{p_2 - p_1 + t}{2t} \right) = (p_1 - c) \frac{\psi_2}{2t}$$

$$1 - \psi_2 + \frac{\psi_2}{2t} \cdot (p_2 + t) + \frac{\psi_2}{2t} \cdot c = p_1 \cdot \left(\frac{\psi_2}{2t} + \frac{\psi_2}{2t} \right)$$

$$1 - \psi_2 + \frac{\psi_2}{2t} \cdot (p_2 + t + c) = p_1 \cdot \frac{\psi_2}{t}$$

$$\left(\frac{1 - \psi_2}{\psi_2} \right) \cdot t + \frac{p_2 + t + c}{2} = p_1$$

We know that the equilibrium will be symmetric since both firms are the same. So to solve for the equilibrium price p^a and level of advertising ψ^a, we substitute $p_1 = p_2 = p$ and $\psi_1 = \psi_2 = \psi$ into the first-order conditions:

$$\psi = \left(\frac{p - c}{a} \right) \cdot \left(1 - \psi + \frac{\psi}{2} \right)$$

$$\psi = \left(\frac{p - c}{a} \right) \cdot \left(1 - \frac{\psi}{2} \right)$$

$$\psi = \frac{p - c}{a} - \psi \cdot \left(\frac{p - c}{2a} \right)$$

$$\psi \cdot \left[1 + \left(\frac{p - c}{2a} \right) \right] = \frac{p - c}{a}$$

$$\psi = \frac{2(p - c)}{2a + p - c}$$

$$1 - \psi = \frac{2a + p - c - 2p + 2c}{2a + p - c}$$

$$1 - \psi = \frac{2a - p + c}{2a + p - c}$$

$$\frac{1 - \psi}{\psi} = \frac{2a - p + c}{2(p - c)}$$

$$p = \frac{p}{2} + \frac{t + c}{2} + \frac{1 - \psi}{\psi} \cdot t$$

$$\frac{p}{2} = \frac{t + c}{2} + \frac{2a - p + c}{2(p - c)} \cdot t$$

$$p \cdot (p - c) = (p - c) \cdot (t + c) + t(2a - p + c)$$

$$0 = p^2 - cp - tp - cp + ct + c^2$$

$$+ tp - ct - 2ta$$

$$0 = p^2 - 2cp + c^2 - 2ta$$

$$p = \frac{2c \pm \sqrt{4c^2 - 4(c^2 - 2ta)}}{2}$$

$$p = \frac{2c \pm \sqrt{8ta}}{2}$$

$$p^a = c + \sqrt{2ta} \quad \text{assuming} \quad a \geq t/2$$

$$\psi = \frac{2(p - c)}{2a + p - c}$$

$$\psi = \frac{2(c + \sqrt{2ta} - c)}{2a + c + \sqrt{2ta} - c}$$

$$\psi = \frac{2\sqrt{2ta}}{2a + \sqrt{2ta}}$$

$$\psi^a = \frac{2}{1 + \sqrt{\frac{2a}{t}}}$$

$$\pi^1 = \pi^2 = \frac{2a}{\left(1 + \sqrt{\frac{2a}{t}} \right)^2}$$

Effect of a change in cost of advertising *a* on profits

We find the effect of a change in the cost of advertising on profits by solving for the derivative of profits π^a with respect to the cost of advertising *a* as follows:

$$\pi^a = \frac{2a}{\left(1 + \sqrt{\frac{2a}{t}}\right)^2} = 2a \cdot x(a)^{-2}$$

where: $x(a) = 1 + \sqrt{\frac{2a}{t}}$

Applying the chain rule of differentiation we get:

$$\frac{\partial \pi^a}{\partial a} = 2x(a)^{-2} - 4ax(a)^{-3} \cdot \frac{\partial x(a)}{\partial a}$$

where: $\frac{\partial x(a)}{\partial a} = \frac{1}{2}\left(\frac{2a}{t}\right)^{-1/2}\frac{2}{t}$

$$= \left(\frac{2a}{t}\right)^{-1/2}\frac{1}{t}$$

so that: $\frac{\partial \pi^a}{\partial a} = 2x(a)^{-2} - \frac{4a}{t}x(a)^{-3}\left(\frac{2a}{t}\right)^{-1/2}$

$$= 2x(a)^{-3} \cdot \left[x(a) - \frac{2a}{t} \cdot \left(\frac{2a}{t}\right)^{-1/2}\right]$$

$$= 2x(a)^{-3} \cdot \left[x(a) - \sqrt{\frac{2a}{t}}\right]$$

where: $x(a) = 1 + \sqrt{\frac{2a}{t}}$

$$= 2x(a)^{-3} > 0$$

This derivative is positive, so an increase in *a* leads to an increase in profits.

References

Batra, Rajeev, John G. Myers and David A. Aaker. *Advertising Management*, 5th Edition, Upper Saddle River (New Jersey: Prentice Hall, 1996), pp. 542–7.

Benham, Lee. "The effect of advertising on the price of eyeglasses." *Journal of Law and Economics*, 15 (1972), pp. 337–52.

Darby, M. and Karni, E. "Free competition and the optimal amount of fraud." *Journal of Law and Economics*, 16 (1973), pp. 67–88.

Dorfman and Steiner. "Optimal advertising and optimal quality." *American Economic Review*, 44 (1954), pp. 826–36.

Friedman, James. *Oligopoly Theory* (Cambridge: Cambridge University Press, 1983), pp. 136–42.

Gilligan, Colin. "How British advertisers set budgets." *Journal of Advertising Research*, 17 (1977), pp. 47–9.

Greer, Douglas F. "The beer industry." In *Industry Studies*, edited by Duetsch, Larry L. (Englewood Cliffs, NJ: Prentice-Hall, 1993).

Grossman, G. and Shapiro, C. "Informative advertising with differentiated products." *Review of Economic Studies*, 51 (1984), pp. 63–82.

Kwoka Jr., John E. "Advertising and the price and quality of optometric services." *American Economic Review*, 74 (1984), pp. 211–16.

Nelson, P. "Advertising as information." *Journal of Political Economy*, 81 (1970), pp. 729–54.

Nerlove, M. and Arrow, K. "Optimal advertising policy under dynamic conditions." *Economica*, 29 (1962), pp. 129–42.

Patti, Charles H. and Vincent Blasko. "Budgeting practices of big advertisers." *Journal of Advertising Research*, 21 (1981), pp. 23–9.

Schmalensee, R. *The Economics of Advertising* (Amsterdam: North-Holland, 1972).

Tirole, Jean. *The Theory of Industrial Organization* (Cambridge, MA: The MIT Press, 1988), pp. 106, 115, 289–95.

Chapter 9

The role of information

•••

When you are finished with this chapter you should understand:

- How models of *asymmetric information* can be used to describe situations where an economic agent has some information which other economic agents do not have
- The difference between *adverse selection* problems and *moral hazard* problems
- How contracts and warranties can be used to mitigate adverse selection or moral hazard problems
- That consumers will use price as a signal of quality when they cannot directly observe the quality of a good
- How a producer's strategy regarding the optimal provision of quality depends upon how quickly consumers learned about quality, the number of informed consumers, and the ease with which the producer can vary the provision of quality
- That when a producer's reputation can affect a consumer's perception of quality, higher prices can serve as compensation to the producer for provision of higher quality

One of the most common assumptions made in economic modeling is that all economic agents have complete information. We've just spent the last chapter describing different factors affecting the producer's motivation to give information to consumers in the form of advertising. We're now going to take a somewhat broader look at the problem of information (or the lack thereof) between consumers and producers. In fact, we're going to assume that the producer does *not* advertise at all. Instead, if it is the case that the producer has some information about the product being sold which the consumer doesn't have, how does this affect the *type* of good which the producer sells, and the price at which that good is sold?

Let's focus our introduction with some examples. Suppose a single producer is selling some particular product: A baker selling a loaf of bread or a used car salesman selling a 1998 minivan. The baker can produce a simple loaf of white bread, or can bake the finest loaf of bread, using only the most expensive flour and the freshest ingredients. Of course, the baker would know which loaf of bread was which. But to any consumer walking into the bakery, the two loaves of bread would look the same. Which should the baker produce? How should they be priced?

The minivan salesman has a slightly different problem. The 1998 minivan may have been well-serviced or not serviced at all. In fact, independent of how well its previous owner had taken care of the minivan, the machine itself could be a well-made minivan or a lemon. Either way the salesman can do very little to affect the quality of the good being sold. The salesman is good enough to know whether the minivan is a lemon or not, but any prospective customer cannot tell. How should the minivan salesman price the product being sold?

It turns out that these types of problems and others which we'll deal with in this chapter to turn up in various forms in many different modeling applications. For that reason, we'll start off in Section 9.1 with a general description of models which incorporate the information problems we'll be dealing with. Then in Section 9.2 we'll apply these models to the case where a monopolist must choose the type of product to sell to consumers.

9.1 Adverse selection and moral hazard

The problems which we are interested in exploring in this section come under the broad heading of *asymmetric information models*. These models describe economic interactions between two economic agents, or two players in a game. In some games with asymmetric information, one player will be a seller or producer, and the other player will be a buyer or consumer, though the exact characteristics of either player will typically depend upon the particular example in question. In general, in games with asymmetric information, the information set available to the two players at any point in time is not necessarily the same. One player knows something that the other does not know. Using the examples from the Introduction above, the baker knows the quality of the loaf of bread being sold, but the customer in the bakery does not. The minivan sales-

man knows whether the 1998 minivan is a lemon or not, but the potential minivan buyer cannot tell.

These asymmetric information models are broken down into two general categories, depending on the particular form of the informational asymmetry between the two players. In either case, one player knows something that the other does not, and we say that the informational asymmetry is caused by one of two problems:

1 In a model with an *adverse selection problem*, one player knows some piece of information or *type*, but the other player does not. This *type* is determined by nature, and cannot be affected by either player. Adverse selection problems involve a *hidden type*.
2 In a model with a *moral hazard problem*, one player can take an *action* which is not observed by the other player. Moral hazard problems involve a *hidden action*.[1]

To continue with the examples we've been using so far, the baker has the ability to choose the level of quality of the loaf of bread. This is an example of a moral hazard problem. The baker knows the quality of loaf of bread being sold, but the consumer does not. Furthermore, by taking an action, the baker can decide whether the loaf is a high-quality loaf of bread or just another regular loaf of bread. The baker takes an action which is hidden from the other player.

There is also an informational asymmetry between the minivan salesman and the minivan buyer. The salesman knows whether the 1998 minivan is a high- or a low-quality vehicle. But whether the minivan is a lemon or not was decided by nature, not by the salesman. The *type* of the minivan is known by the salesman but is not known by the consumer. This is an adverse selection problem,[2] since it involves a hidden type.

The distinction between adverse selection and moral hazard problems is a fine one, so it is probably best that we illustrate this distinction with some more examples. A classic moral hazard problem exists between a landlord and a tenant. Before she moves into the apartment, a tenant knows whether she is a *good tenant* or *bad tenant*. She may be a *good tenant*, in the sense that she takes very good care of the apartment and does not have loud parties until 4 am which disturb other tenants. Or she may be a *bad tenant*, who vacuums only once a year, and plays her stereo very loud at all hours of the night.

The tenant can take an action which determines whether she is a good tenant or bad tenant, but this action is hidden from the landlord. The tenant can decide how often to vacuum her apartment, and when and how loud to play her stereo. The informational asymmetry between the two players involves a hidden action. This is a moral hazard problem.

In fact, there may be another moral hazard problem affecting the outcome of the game between the landlord and the tenant. The landlord may be a very good landlord, who can easily be reached if there is ever a problem with the apartment, and will fix any plumbing or electrical problems very quickly. Or he may be a bad landlord, who never seems to be in and will repair a damaged light switch only after considerable time and effort. The landlord has control over whether he is a good landlord or a bad landlord, but before she moves into the apartment, the tenant does not know whether the landlord is good or bad. In this case, the hidden action is taken by the landlord.

The fact that a well-defined moral hazard problem exists in this situation has direct and predictable implications for the outcome of the game which is played between the tenant and the landlord. If the tenant moves in and the landlord accepts the tenant, *a contract* is signed between the two parties, which takes the form of a rental agreement. The rental agreement is made up of various clauses which are designed to protect both tenant and landlord from the negative effects of any moral hazard problem.

Now let's give an example of another adverse selection problem. Consider the manager of a machine shop (the employer) who has to decide whether or not to hire a new welder (the employee). The potential employee may be the best welder available, or may be barely capable of welding together two pieces of copper tubing. The employee knows his type, but whether he is a good welder or a bad welder is beyond his control. Nature has decided whether he is a gifted welder, or is merely capable. The employer has no way of telling whether the employee is skilled or not. She is missing some information which the welder knows. This informational asymmetry is caused by an adverse selection problem between the employer and the employee.

The outcome of this game between employer and employee may also be affected by the fact that the employer can anticipate the adverse selection problem, just as the rental agreement in the moral hazard game took into account the informational asymmetry between the landlord and the tenant. For example, the employer may decide to hire the employee on a temporary basis at first, for some limited period of time, and then evaluate the employee's performance. If after two months the employer is satisfied with the employee's work, she can decide to hire the welder on a permanent basis.

Of course, this problem could be much more complicated than we have just described. For example, suppose that the adverse selection problem given above exists, and suppose for argument's sake that the welder is the best welder in town. He's hired by the manager for 2 months, but while in the manager's employ, he doesn't apply himself to his work. He is a lazy and sloppy worker. This characteristic of the employee is directly under his control, so this is a moral hazard problem. The manager may be so busy that she doesn't have time to observe the performance of the welder. After two months, she may decide to fire the welder because his work was sloppy, but she has misinterpreted the welder's type as being due to a lack of skill.[3]

Adverse Selection and Health Insurance

What level of health insurance should a government provide for its citizens? Should the government provide complete coverage for all, or should public health insurance only cover basic medical expenses like annual checkups?*

Different countries have responded to these questions by adopting public health insurance plans with different characteristics. Many countries in Europe have public health care programs which cover a significantly greater share of an individual's cost of health care than, for example, the United States. Some public health insurance programs cover spending on prescription drugs, while many public health insurance programs do not cover spending on dental services. One reason for these differences is to take account of an adverse selection problem.

To describe this adverse selection problem, we identify the two players in this game: the individual and the insurer. The individual knows her own type (whether she is healthy or sick, has diabetes or a heart condition), but the insurer does not. Furthermore, whether the individual is sick or healthy is determined (for the most part) by nature. Suppose the insurer provides complete insurance, so that all health care expenditures by the individual are covered by a public health insurance program.

A common problem which exists when complete insurance is available when an adverse selection problem is present is that the individuals will have above-average utilization rates for the insured service. For example, if public health insurance covers every visit to the doctor, then on average, people will go to the doctor more often. Someone who is feeling a bit run-down and feels a cold coming on might go to the doctor instead of just staying in bed and getting some rest. If prescription drugs are covered by public health care, then the doctor might be more inclined to prescribe antibiotics, and the patient will not be as concerned about the cost of filling the prescription, since this cost is covered by public health insurance.

Of course, this makes the cost of government health insurance higher than it would otherwise be. People make claims on health insurance when they should be resting at home and taking a couple of aspirin instead of going to the doctor and taking antibiotics. To resolve this problem, we could make individuals responsible for some of their own health care expenditures. But then the lucky people who are always healthy spend very little on health care, while individuals who are unlucky and get sick have to spend a much larger share of their income on health care. How can we come up with a health insurance system which is efficient, resolves this adverse selection problem, and is also *fair*? This is a very complicated problem, and a complete understanding all of these issues constitute the better part of a full-semester course in Health Economics at many universities.

* Many interesting aspects of health care reform are discussed in a series of articles on "The Future of Medicare" in the Spring 2000 issue of the *Journal of Economic Perspectives*.

In fact, this is a common problem, particularly in large organizations with many employees.[4] There exist mechanisms which managers can use to mitigate these problems. Employees can be paid depending upon their performance, or the manager can hire a supervisor to manage the employees and report more accurately on their skill and effort level. Such solutions may be costly. How much do we pay a supervisor, and how many supervisors do we need? But at the very least, these models identify potential problems for the firm, due to different types of informational asymmetries. Once these problems are understood, the manager is better able to lessen the negative effects of these informational asymmetries on the performance and profitability of the firm.

9.2 Quality and information with a single producer

To keep our discussion relatively straightforward, we will restrict our analysis to the case where a monopolist produces a single good. This will allow us to concentrate on the role played by the informational asymmetry between the two players in the game, the monopolist and the consumer.

Recall that in the previous chapter, we described the following classification of goods produced by the firms:

1 *Search goods*: those goods where the consumer has good information about surplus from consumption even before the good is purchased.
2 *Experience goods*: those goods where the consumer cannot determine the surplus from consumption until after the good has been consumed.
3 *Credence goods*: those goods where the consumer may never be able to determine the surplus from consumption.

In this section, we will be concerned primarily with *experience goods*. The monopolist will produce either a high-quality good or a low-quality good. Since this is an experience good, the consumer will not know the quality of the good before consumption. If this were a *search good*, the consumer would already know all of the relevant characteristics of the good before consumption, so there would be no informational asymmetry between the producer and the consumer. This is why we want to concentrate on experience goods, since then the monopolist will have information of which the consumer is unaware. This will allow us to model the effects of the informational asymmetry on the monopolist's decision about the level of provision of quality.

There are a number of characteristics of the good being produced and sold by the monopolist which will alter the way that the informational asymmetry between monopolist and consumer affects the outcome in the market. We'll begin with the simplest example: The case where the good is only purchased once by any one consumer.

9.2.1 One-time purchases

To keep our model as simple as possible, suppose that the monopolist produces a single good at constant marginal cost. The monopolist can choose to produce a high-quality good at cost c_h, or a low-quality good at cost c_l, with $c_h > c_l$ (we're implicitly assuming that producing higher quality is more costly to the monopolist). The market price of the good is p, independent of the quality of the good. The consumer cannot observe quality before purchase, so the consumer knows only that she will earn some surplus $\bar{s} - p$ from consumption of this good. This is a moral hazard problem. The monopolist can vary the quality of the good being produced, but the consumer does not know the quality of the good for sale.

In this example, the monopolist will never produce a high-quality good. Notice that demand is independent of the quality of the good being sold. The consumer will always purchase as long as $\bar{s} - p$ is positive. The monopolist will earn strictly higher profits when producing a low-quality good, since costs are lower when the monopolist produces a low-quality good.

Obviously this is a very special result, derived from a very special case. What are some of the things which we've implicitly assumed which generate this result? We've assumed that there is a complete lack of information on the consumer's side about the quality of the monopolist's product. Suppose we relax this assumption, so that there exist some consumers who know about the quality of the good which the monopolist sells, and some other consumers who do not.[5] Those consumers who know the quality of the monopolist's output may have spoken with someone who already consumed 1 unit of the monopolist's output, or they may have read a trade magazine[6] which contains this sort of information. We'll suppose that ψ is the fraction of informed consumers, with $0 < \psi < 1$.

There are three types of economic agents in this model: The uninformed consumers, the informed consumers, and the monopolist. We'll start with the two types of consumers. Suppose that both types of consumers will pay up to $\bar{s}$ for a high-quality product, but neither consumer will buy the product sold by the monopolist if it is a low-quality product. Then either consumer will buy a high-quality product as long as $\bar{s} - p > 0$ (i.e. as long as the total surplus from buying one unit of the high-quality product is higher than the price that the consumer must pay).

The informed consumers know whether the monopolist's output is high quality or low quality, so their problem is straight forward. If the monopolist produces a high-quality good, they buy. If not, they don't. So let's consider the $1 - \psi$ uninformed consumers. These consumers do not know whether the monopolist is selling a high- or low-quality good. One of two cases can obtain: Either these $1 - \psi$ consumers buy the monopolist's output, or not. We're going to show that these consumers will purchase the monopolist's output. To do so, we'll suppose that they *don't* purchase the monopolist's output, and then show that this leads to a contradiction.

If the $1 - \psi$ consumers do not purchase the monopolist's output, then the monopolist has two choices: provide high quality or low quality. If the monopolist provides low quality, then the ψ informed consumers will not purchase, since no consumer will purchase a low-quality good. The monopolist's profits will be zero if he provides a low-quality good. If he provides a high-quality good, the monopolist will earn profits of $\psi(p - c_h)$, so as long as $p > c_h$, the monopolist will always provide a high-quality good.

But the uninformed consumers can work through this problem too, so even though they are uninformed, they can anticipate that the monopolist will always provide a high-quality good. So the uninformed consumers will buy the high-quality good produced by the monopolist. But we started-off with the $1 - \psi$ uninformed consumers *not* purchasing the monopolist's output. This is the contradiction, so it must be the case that the uninformed consumers always buy the monopolist's output.

Now consider the monopolist's problem. If he provides low quality, then cost c_l will be low, and the $(1 - \psi)$ uninformed consumers will buy. If he provides high quality, then cost $c_h > c_l$ will be high, so that the $(1 - \psi)$ uninformed consumers and the ψ informed consumers all buy. Since each consumer will only ever buy one unit of output from the monopolist, we can write the monopolist's profits as follows:

profits under high-quality	profits under low-quality
$(p - c_h) \cdot [\psi + (1 - \psi)]$	$(p - c_l) \cdot (1 - \psi)$

The monopolist will provide high quality as long as profits from doing so are higher than those from providing low quality. This will happen when:

$$p - c_h \geq (1 - \psi)(p - c_l)$$
$$(1 - (1 - \psi))p \geq c_h - (1 - \psi)c_l$$
$$\psi p \geq c_h - (1 - \psi)c_l$$

In this example, the fact that there exist some ψ informed consumers is useful information for the $1 - \psi$ uninformed consumers. Suppose that you are an uninformed consumer. You witness someone walking into the monopolist's store and buying one unit of the monopolist's output. You don't know whether the monopolist has produced a high- or low-quality good. But you know that there is a chance that the person who just bought one unit of output from the monopolist is an informed consumer. You also know that this person would not buy a low-quality good. If this was an informed consumer, you know that the monopolist is selling a high-quality good. We say that the informed consumers exert a *positive externality* on the uninformed consumers. Just by buying a high-quality good, the informed consumers are giving useful information to the uninformed consumers.

The higher is the market price p, the better the chance that this condition will be satis-fied, in which case the monopolist would produce high quality. If there are enough informed consumers in the market, then this condition will be satisfied, and we would be able to conclude that:

> **Result**
>
> Uninformed consumers can use the market price as a signal of quality, and higher prices will signal higher quality.

Also notice that the higher is the fraction of informed consumers ψ, the more likely it is that the monopolist will provide high quality.[7]

The case we've just analyzed is one where a moral hazard problem exists with the monopolist. He can decide whether to produce a high- or low-quality good. What would happen if instead we dealt with an adverse selection problem? That is, suppose that the monopolist is selling either a high- or low-quality good. He knows the type of the good being sold, but cannot alter the quality of the good. This is the problem we encountered earlier where the used car salesman was selling a 1998 minivan. The minivan could be a high-quality vehicle or a *lemon*. The problem on the consumer's side is the same. There may exist some consumers who are informed. These may be consumers who are more mechanically inclined, who change their own oil and spark plugs regularly, and have some interest and understanding in the functioning of motor vehicles. Then there are uninformed consumers, the extent of whose knowledge about cars is how to change a tire. How does this latter group of consumers determine whether a used minivan at a particular price is a good buy (because it is a high-quality vehicle) or a bad buy (because it is a lemon)? What are the implications of their decision-making process for the used car salesman's profit maximization problem?

We can use one result from the previous example to describe what happens in this used car market: The uninformed consumers will use prices as a signal of quality when they cannot directly observe quality. All other things being equal, higher prices are interpreted as signals of higher quality. This will be true whether the informational asymmetry is due to a moral hazard problem or an adverse selection problem. An uninformed consumer will perceive that a more expensive bottle of wine or higher-priced premium beer is of higher quality than a lower-price bottle of wine or beer, even though the consumer hasn't tried either before. Likewise, the uninformed car buyer will believe that a higher price for the used minivan signals higher quality.

What does this mean for the used car salesman? The existence of the informational asymmetry means that the price mechanism in the used car market does not work the way that it would in a market with full information. To illustrate, suppose a condition of excess supply existed in a market where consumers had complete information. At some particular market price, quantity demanded was less than quantity supplied. The appropriate strategy in this market would be for the manager to reduce the market price.

Moral Hazard and Automobile Insurance

A quiet drive down the highway on a clear sunny day, relatively little traffic, and all of a sudden you are cut off by a driver talking on a cellular phone. He clips your front bumper and the two cars spin onto the shoulder. No one is hurt, but both cars are damaged.

This is one of the reasons why we buy automobile insurance. A moral hazard problem exists between you and any other driver on the road. Another driver may be a very careful and safety-conscious driver, or an accident-waiting-to-happen. You never know who you're sharing the road with, so you buy insurance to protect yourself in the case of an accident.

This problem is far more complicated than it may seem, since there are many different types of insurance. Consider two types of insurance used in different regions around the world: *liability* insurance versus *no-fault* insurance. Under *liability* insurance, a share of the blame for an accident is assigned to each party. The man on the cellular phone may be responsible for 80 percent of the accident, while you are assigned blame for the remaining 20 percent. Under *no-fault* insurance, no assessment of blame needs to be made before either party is compensated for damages. Which type of insurance exists depends upon where you live. For example, in Canada, some provinces have a system of *liability* insurance while other provinces use *no-fault* insurance.*

There are two significant differences between *liability* and *no-fault* insurance systems. One is a simple benefit of the *no-fault* system: since responsibility does not need to be assessed, a *no-fault* system is less costly to administer.

But another important difference between the two systems is the way in which they affect the moral hazard problem inherent in driving. Under a *liability* insurance system, a driver who causes an accident due to carelessness will be found at fault, and will bear the costs of the accident. We can say that the *liability* system may mitigate some of the moral hazard problem associated with careless driving, since drivers end up assuming some of the responsibility for their driving behavior.

Critics of the *no-fault* system claim that this factor is significant, since the *no-fault* system does not impose this penalty on careless drivers. A number of studies (see Devlin 1993) indicate that fatal driving accidents increased by 9–16 percent when automobile insurance switched from a *liability* system to a *no-fault* system.

Of course, whether the auto insurance industry is characterized by a *liability* or a *no-fault* system has important implications for insurance companies as well. But the public policy issues when there exist such moral hazard problems can clearly be very important.

*For a more complete and detailed description of liability and no-fault insurance systems, see Devlin (1993).

What would happen if the used car salesman tried this strategy? If the used car salesman has too many 1998 minivans which he cannot sell at a given price, a reduction in the market price could bias consumer's perception of quality downwards. This would make the problem even worse, because of the way that consumers use the market price as a signal for quality. A seller who knows the quality of the good for sale will generally find that demand for the good is lower when the buyer does not know the quality than when the buyer is perfectly informed.

9.2.2 Warranties

Even when there exist informational asymmetries which affect the behavior of the market mechanism, there are other strategies available to the manager which can be used to mitigate the effects of a moral hazard or an adverse selection problem. A good example can be illustrated by looking at the options available to the used minivan salesman. If he has an excess supply of used minivans, we've already seen that dropping the price might not be the best strategy, since doing so can indicate a lower level of quality to consumers who use the market price as a signal for quality. Instead, the minivan salesman can offer a warranty which covers some or all repairs for some period of time.

The consumer does not know whether the used minivan is a lemon or not. But if the minivan salesman offers the consumer a warranty, then the consumer is more likely to believe that the used minivan is a high-quality product. Even if the minivan turns out to be a lemon, the consumer is protected by the warranty, which offers the consumer some form of insurance against buying a potentially low-quality product.

In general, warranties are a common strategic-choice variable used by producers of many different kinds of products, including cars, televisions, camcorders, computers, skates and skis, and many other consumer products. The warranty is a signal to the consumer who cannot directly observe the quality of the product. But even for any one particular type of consumer good, many different types of warranties exist. For example, different car producers offer different types of warranties. Some producers offer warranties on the entire drive train of the automobile, while others only warranty the frame of the car. Some warranties run for 48 months, others for 60 months. Some producers offer extended warranties, which a car buyer can purchase for some price in order to extend the warranty coverage for a longer period of time. Warranties on used cars generally protect the consumer for a shorter period of time than new car warranties. Warranties never cover the exhaust system of the car. Tires usually have separate warranties, depending upon the quality of the tire.

Why do producers use different warranties? Why not offer a complete warranty, covering all parts of the used minivan for some period of time? Again, the problem is due to an information problem. The used minivan salesman does not know what kind of driver is buying the vehicle. If I am considering buying the used minivan, the salesman does not know if I will drive cautiously and always bring the vehicle into the garage for scheduled maintenance, or if I'm a bad driver who never changes the oil and never has the vehicle serviced. There is a moral hazard problem since I may be a good driver or a bad driver. If something goes wrong with the minivan after I've bought it, it might be due to the fact that I'm a bad driver who didn't take care of the vehicle, in which case a full warranty would allow me to take advantage of the minivan salesman. The minivan salesman is better off offering a partial warranty.

9.2.3 The role of repeat purchases and reputation

When the consumer cannot directly observe the quality of a good because it is an experience good, there are a number of variables which affect the consumer's perception of quality. We've already seen that the consumer can use price as a signal for quality, and that warranties can affect the consumer's beliefs. The producer may also have a reputation for providing products of a particular quality. The issue of reputation is particularly important when the producer is introducing a new product to the market.

When a producer's reputation affects the consumer's perception of quality, a number of factors are important:

- How easily can the producer change quality?
- How quickly does the consumer learn about quality?
- How often does the consumer purchase the good?

We'll briefly discuss each of these factors.

Producer chooses quality once

The simplest example to consider is the one where the producer cannot vary the level of quality. Suppose that a major car producer is planning to market a new brand of minivan. The car producer can produce a high- or low-quality minivan, but once the vehicle has been designed, the assembly line and complete production facility has been built, and the marketing strategy has been put together, the producer can no longer change the quality of the minivan. Producing a higher-quality vehicle is more costly to the producer. The car manufacturer would rather sell a low-quality vehicle at a high price, since that strategy yields the highest profits. This is an appropriate strategy if consumers never repeat purchase (consumers buy a new minivan only once every 10 years, by which time the car maker has switched to producing subcompacts) and if consumers only learn about the quality of the minivan over a long period of time.

But suppose that consumers learn about quality very quickly, and can then tell their friends about the true quality of the new brand of minivan. A producer of a low-quality vehicle will lose sales very quickly since his reputation will deteriorate very quickly. He may earn high profits at first, but the reputation effects will cause a large drop in sales once consumers learn of the producer's true reputation.

This also holds if consumers purchase the good frequently. A producer of photographic equipment who is deciding whether to introduce a high- or a low-quality 35 mm film must recognize that consumers will repeat their purchase of this product frequently. A consumer who learns that the producer has introduced a low-quality film onto the market will quickly switch to a different type of film, so the producer is penalized when introducing a low-quality product when consumers repeat purchase. In general, when the producer chooses the quality of the good once and cannot change the quality after the good has been introduced to the market, the following result will hold:

> **Result**
>
> The more rapidly the consumers learn about quality, or the more often the consumers repeat purchase, the more likely a producer will introduce a high-quality good.

We can tie these results together, by recalling the model from the previous chapter on advertising where the producer accumulated a stock of goodwill. This concept of goodwill works the same way as the reputation effects work in this model where the producer must decide on the provision of a level of quality. Consider the problem of the German car producer BMW in deciding the level of quality to provide when producing the Z3 roadster, introduced to the car market in 1996. The consumer's perception of the quality of the new Z3 is affected by a number of variables, including the price at which the car is offered for sale, and the reputation of the producer BMW. This reputation itself is affected by the quality of cars which BMW has produced and sold over the years, and by the level of advertising undertaken by BMW,

since advertising will affect the stock of goodwill or reputation.

BMW has a reputation for producing a high-quality product, and has reinforced this reputation through advertising. At the same time, BMWs typically sell for a higher price than cars in the same class produced by the competition. In particular, the suggested retail price of the Z3 roadster is significantly higher than the suggested retail price of the Mazda Miata. Producing a higher-quality car is more costly, and maintaining the reputation of producing a higher-quality car is also costly. In this way, the price premium on the Z3 may well serve as compensation to BMW for the costs of providing a high-quality product. These costs would include the higher production costs associated with a higher-quality car, as well as the advertising costs necessary to maintain the reputation of being a producer of a high-quality product.

Producer can change quality every period

Now suppose that the producer is introducing a new product to the market, and the product can be a high- or low-quality good. But the producer has the ability to change the quality of the good after some period of time. Suppose a pizza franchise opens in the neighborhood. The producer can start-off by producing a high-quality pizza, but after some time might switch to a lower-quality cheese or use less pepperoni, thereby reducing the quality of the product. How will repeat purchases and the speed with which consumers learn about quality affect the producer's decision to produce a high- or low-quality pizza at any point in time?

It turns out that the result we illustrated in the previous case where the producer cannot change quality will also hold when the producer can change the quality of the good produced after some period of time. That is, the more that consumers repeat purchase and the more quickly that consumers learn about the quality of the good, the greater the incentive for the producer to produce a high-quality good, or not to switch to a lower-quality good. For example, if the pizza producer switched to a lower-quality cheese, then repeat consumers would buy their pizza elsewhere, thereby penalizing the pizza producer.

What happens to the pizza producer's problem when his lease is up? Suppose that when the pizza producer started production, he signed a 3-year lease. When the lease is up the producer can change locations or re-open under another name. In this case the producer has an incentive to reduce the quality of his pizzas in the few months before his lease is up, since consumers can no longer penalize him by switching brands.

Before we finish this section, it might be worth thinking about another extreme example. Suppose that the producer can produce a product of such high quality that the product will never break down, so that consumers will never repeat purchase. In this case, the producer may not want to produce a high-quality product. If the producer makes a lower-quality product, consumers will repeat purchase, and this may increase sales sufficiently to warrant not producing the highest-quality product possible.

Summary

- Models of *asymmetric information* are used to describe situations where an economic agent has some information which other economic agents do not have.
- An *adverse selection* problem exists when the informational asymmetry involves knowledge about a hidden type, while a *moral hazard* problem involves knowledge about a hidden action.
- Contracts and warranties can be used to mitigate adverse selection or moral hazard problems.
- Asymmetric information problems are most relevant to markets for experience goods.
- Consumers will use price as a signal of quality when they cannot directly observe the quality of a good.
- When a moral hazard problem exists on the part of a producer deciding on the provision of a level of quality, the level of quality will be higher when consumers repeat purchase.
- The producer's strategy regarding the optimal provision of quality depends upon how quickly consumers learned about quality, the number of informed consumers, and the ease with which the producer can vary the provision of quality.
- When a producer's reputation can affect a consumer's perception of quality, higher prices can serve as compensation to the producer for provision of higher quality.

Notes

1 Here's a simple trick to remember the difference between adverse selection and moral hazard problems. The first two letters of "hazard" stand for "hidden action."

2 The classic reference which discusses this particular adverse selection problem is Akerlof, G.

"The market for 'Lemons': qualitative uncertainty and the market mechanism." *Quarterly Journal of Economics*, 84 (1970), pp. 488–500.

3 These issues of hiring, compensation, and motivation are very important, and we return to a more thorough treatment of these topics in Chapters 14 and 15.

4 You should recognize this as an *agency problem*, which was discussed in Chapter 2.

5 A number of the results and examples in the remainder of this Section were derived in Klein and Leffler (1981).

6 There exist many magazines which test products like cars, bicycles, skis, photographic equipment, computer hardware and software, and many others. For example, a computer magazine will test different types of printers and rank them on the basis of price, quality, and performance. So a consumer can inform himself/herself about the different printers in the market by reading the computer magazine to research the different prices and qualities of different printers in the market.

7 The change in the left-hand side of this expression for a given change in ψ is p, while the change in the right-hand side is c_l. If the monopolist earns positive profits in equilibrium (this problem would not exist if profits were negative, since the monopolist would not produce output to earn negative profits), then $p > c_l$, so as ψ increases, the left-hand side increases faster than the right-hand side, making it more likely that this condition is satisfied.

Exercises

1 University Law Schools typically require applicants to their programs to write a uniform Law School Admissions Test (LSAT).

   (a) What sort of information could a Law School deduce from an applicant's LSAT score? What sort of information problem could this correct?

   (b) There exist many LSAT Preparation Classes in which applicants can enroll to prepare for the LSAT, but these Classes are costly. Some applicants incur this cost to take a Preparation Class, but other students do not. Suppose that Law Schools cannot tell whether an applicant took a Preparation Class before writing the LSAT. How does this affect the information which a Law School can deduce from an LSAT score?

   (c) Short of asking an applicant whether they took a Preparation Class, can you think of anything that a Law School can do to resolve the information problem in question 1b?

   (d) Would you expect a Law School which did not require an LSAT score as an admission requirement to be a higher- or lower-quality School?

2 What would happen to the consumer's perception of quality if BMW started producing a pick-up truck which sold for the same price as comparable trucks produced by Ford, General Motors, or Chrysler? What might you expect to happen to sales of BMW's sedans and sports cars, if BMW did not change its pricing strategy on these cars? Compare the effects of this strategy of introducing an inexpensive competitive pick-up truck to the alternative of introducing an expensive high-quality truck.

3 Suppose a consumer is initially unaware of the quality of wine. As we discussed in this chapter, the consumer could use price as a signal of the quality of wine. But another option would be to do some research into different types of wine, by reading magazines about wine, or taking a wine appreciation course.

   (a) Does an informational asymmetry exist between wine producers and this wine consumer? What type of information problem exists?

   (b) Discuss the wine producer's incentive to produce a high-quality wine as a function of the number of wine experts in the economy.

(c) Would a producer want to produce a higher-quality wine if more wine magazines were published or more wine appreciation courses were offered.

(d) How important is the cost of wine magazines or wine appreciation courses? Would you change your answers to parts 3b and 3c if the government subsidized wine appreciation courses?

(e) Suppose a group of local wine producers formed a Wine Growers Association which published a monthly wine magazine which was distributed to consumers free-of-charge. If you were a wine producer, would you want to be a member of this Association? Would the existence of this Association and its magazine make the wine industry more or less competitive?

4 Many retailers offer warranties on the goods they sell, whether they be electronic products (computers, stereo components), white goods (washing machines and fridges), or cars.

(a) What sorts of informational asymmetries exist between buyers and sellers which

would motivate retailers to offer warranties? Are these moral hazard or adverse selection problems?

(b) If a consumer would never buy a retailer's product more than once, what would happen to the retailer's incentive to offer a warranty? Would your answer change if consumers could find out about the quality of a retailer's product before purchase?

(c) Many retailers who include warranties with the products they sell also offer *extended warranties* which consumers can purchase at an extra cost. What type of information problem would an extended warranty be designed to correct?

References

Akerlof, George. "The market for 'lemons': qualitative uncertainty and the market mechanism." *Quarterly Journal of Economics*, 84 (1970), pp. 488–500.

Devlin, Rose Anne. "Automobile insurance in Ontario: public policy and private interests." *Canadian Public Policy*, 19:3 (1993), pp. 298–310.

Klein, Benjamin and Keith Leffler. "The role of market forces in assuring contractual performance." *Journal of Political Economy*, 89:4 (1981), pp. 615–41.

Chapter 10

Entry deterrence and accommodation

When you are finished with this chapter you should understand:

- That when firms can enter or exit a market in the longer run, an incumbent firm can strategically choose its scale of production or *capacity* to affect the behavior of potential entrants into its market
- That an incumbent firm can adopt a strategy to *accommodate entry* or to *deter entry* by a potential competitor
- Why an incumbent may decide to *overinvest* in capacity to deter entry, and the role played by fixed costs in determining the incumbent's optimal investment strategy
- How the concept of a limit price can be used to describe conditions under which it would be more profitable to deter entry or accommodate entry of a new firm
- How the effect of an investment in capacity by an incumbent can be broken down into a *direct effect* and a *strategic effect*, and how the strategic effect will depend upon whether the incumbent wants to deter or accommodate entry, and whether firms compete in prices or quantities

In 1981, DeLorean Motorcars Ltd. began production of the DeLorean DMC-12 in Dunmurry near the city of Belfast in Northern Ireland. Over a period of three years from 1981 to 1983, 8,583 cars were produced and sold. In 1983, production of the DeLorean ceased. Most cars were sold in the United States.[1]

In 1980, the total share of Japanese cars sold in Canada was 14.8 percent, while the share of Japanese cars produced in Canada was 0 percent. By 1995, the share of Japanese cars sold in Canada had risen to 25.4 percent, and the share of Japanese cars produced in Canada had risen to 15.1 percent. In 1995, 362,314 Honda Accords and 322,371 Honda Civics were sold in Canada and the United States. Of all of these Accords and Civics, 96.3 percent were produced in plants in Alliston, Ontario, and Marysville and East Liberty, Ohio.

At any point in time, the global automobile market can be viewed as a relatively static market in terms of the number of producers. From one year to the next, market forces cause changes in the market share of the different producers. But in the long run, the North American car market can be characterized by significant entry and exit of firms. The data on production and sale of Japanese cars in North America is evidence of a long-run strategy on the part of Japanese

Plate 2 The DeLorean DMC-12

auto firms to enter the North American automobile market. The DeLorean example is a case where a new firm entered the market and then later exited the market.

Up to this point, our discussion of strategic decision-making has focused on shorter-run problems: how do managers choose market prices, the level of advertising, and so on. But in the long run, managers must also pay attention to entry and exit problems, since in the long run, new firms can enter an industry and incumbent firms (those already producing in a market) can grow by increasing capacity or can exit an industry. How does an incumbent firm react to the threat posed by a potential entrant? How does an incumbent firm decide whether or not to exit an industry in the long run? What factors affect the decision of a potential entrant to begin production and sales of a new product in a new market?

The answers to these questions will ultimately give an indication as to why some industries are dominated by a small number of firms while others are characterized by competition between very many firms. We will see that an important determinant of market structure is the structure of costs in an industry. In particular, fixed costs will play a central role in affecting the outcome of the entry deterrence and accommodation game played between an incumbent firm already in the market and a potential entrant. Because an incumbent is already in the market, it has already invested in any fixed costs necessary to produce output, so the incumbent may be able to treat these as *sunk costs*: costs which cannot be recovered upon exiting an industry. An incumbent who has invested in sunk costs has committed to production in an industry, since those costs cannot be recovered. As we will see, this commitment can give the incumbent significant power in affecting whether another firm can profitably enter the market as a competitor.

10.1 Strategic choice of capacity

In this section, we'll describe the interaction between firms which are already in the market (incumbent firms) and firms which are considering entering the market (potential entrants). To keep the model as simple as possible, we will suppose that there is only one incumbent firm, so that the market is initially monopolized. This incumbent monopolist faces the threat of entry by a single potential entrant. In this way we can model the interaction between incumbent firms and potential entrants as a game between two players: Firm 1, the incumbent, and firm 2, the potential entrant.

It will be important to be able to model not only the decision of whether on not firm 2 enters the market, but also the decision of how large or small a firm should be, whether it be the incumbent firm or the entrant. For this reason, we will need to discuss the *capacity* of production of the incumbent firm and the potential entrant. We will label capacity as K: The level of production beyond which the marginal cost of production rises to infinity in the short run. In order to produce a level of output greater than K, the firm must invest in additional plant and equipment, something which can only be done in the longer run.

The game between the two firms will be one where the incumbent chooses a capacity of production, and the potential entrant chooses whether or not to enter. If the entrant decides to enter the market, the outcome of the game will also imply a choice of capacity for the entrant, so we will be able to tell whether the entrant comes into the market as a relatively large firm or a relatively small firm.

The model we will use to represent the interaction between the incumbent and the entrant is very similar to the Cournot duopoly model introduced in Chapter 6, where two firms competed over quantities. In one example in Chapter 6, we supposed that

demand for the output of firms in this market was summarized by the following inverse demand function:

$$p = 120 - (q_1 + q_2)$$

This demand function expressed the market price p as a function of the sum of the level of output of the two firms, $q_1 + q_2$. In this section, we will use a demand function which expresses the market price p as a function of the level of capacity of each firm. If we write the capacity of firm i as K_i, for $i = 1, 2$, then the demand function becomes:

$$p = 120 - (K_1 + K_2)$$

To give an intuitive interpretation of this demand function, note that as either firm increases its capacity of production K_i, it has the ability to increase total production and total quantity sold to the market, and this will put downward pressure on the market price p. Or to put it another way, in order to increase production, firms must increase capacity, so there is an implicit relationship between a firm's capacity K_i and its level of production q_i.

Suppose that the incumbent monopolist produces output with some technology such that fixed costs are equal to F and marginal costs are constant and equal to c. Suppose as well that the cost structure of the potential entrant would be the same as that of the monopolist. The simplest version of this game has fixed costs equal to zero, so for the time being, we'll suppose that $F = 0$. We'll incorporate the effects of positive fixed costs a bit later on.

10.1.1 Accommodated entry

The game between firm 1 and firm 2 will be structured as a Stackelberg leader-follower game. The incumbent firm starts the game already in the market so that firm 1 has a first-mover advantage. The potential entrant must choose whether or not to enter the market, and if so must choose a level of capacity. So we're dealing with a two-stage game. In the second stage of the game, the entrant chooses whether or not to enter and chooses a level of capacity if it enters. In the first stage of the game, the incumbent firm chooses a level of capacity.

If the entrant decides to enter the market in stage 2, it takes the incumbent's capacity as given and maximizes its profits, which will be given by:

$$\pi^2 = (120 - K_1 - K_2) \cdot K_2 - cK_2$$

The first-order profit-maximization condition for the entrant is found by setting the derivative of firm 2's profit function with respect to capacity choice K_2 equal to zero:

$$\partial \frac{\partial \pi^2}{K_2} = 120 - K_1 - 2K_2 - c = 0$$

This first-order condition can be re-arranged to solve for the entrant's reaction function:

$$K_2 = \frac{120 - K_1 - c}{2}$$

The incumbent firm knows that a profit-maximizing entrant will choose its capacity according to this reaction function, so the incumbent's profit-maximization problem takes into account the entrant's capacity response:

$$\pi^1 = K_1 \cdot (120 - K_1 - K_2) - cK_1$$
$$\pi^1 = K_1 \cdot \left(120 - K_1 - \frac{120 - K_1 - c}{2}\right) - cK_1$$
$$\pi^1 = K_1 \cdot \left(\frac{120}{2} - \frac{K_1}{2} - \frac{c}{2}\right)$$

Firm 1's profit-maximizing first-order condition is found by setting the derivative of π^1 with respect to K_1 equal to zero:

$$\pi_1^1 = \frac{120}{2} - \frac{K_1}{2} - \frac{c}{2} - \frac{K_1}{2} = 0$$

So the incumbent firm is best off investing in capacity $K_1^s = (120 - c)/2$, and the incumbent's best response (given by firm 2's reaction function) is $K_2^s = (120 - c)/4$. In this equilibrium, the market price is $p^s = 120 - K_1^s - K_2^s = (120 + 3c)/4$, so that each firm earns profits $\pi^1 = (60 - c)/2 \cdot (30 - c)/4$ and $\pi^2 = [(30 - c)/4]^2$.

In this example, we say that firm 1 has *accommodated entry* by firm 2, since both firms earn positive profits in the Stackelberg equilibrium after firm 2 has entered the market. In particular, the incumbent firm has maximized profits π^1 by incorporating the entrant's reaction function. Firm 1 played this game with the presumption that firm 2 was going to enter the market. Of course, firm 1 could have played an entirely different game: choose capacity K_1 to keep firm 2 out of the market. This is the next game we'll look at. But first we want to point out a couple of interesting features of the outcome of the accommodated entry game.

First of all, note that firm 1 earns higher profits than firm 2. This is the first-mover advantage of firm 1 since it is the incumbent firm and was in the market first.

Another noteworthy feature of the accommodated entry game is illustrated by comparing the outcome of this game to the game in which neither firm has a first-mover advantage. That is, suppose both firm 1 and firm 2 choose capacity K_1 and K_2 at the same time. This is exactly like the game of Cournot quantity competition in Chapter 6. Now both firms face the same profit function and will have the same reaction function:

$$K_1 = \frac{120 - K_2 - c}{2}$$
$$K_2 = \frac{120 - K_1 - c}{2}$$

167

Solving by substitution we get:

$$K_1 = \frac{120 - \frac{120 - K_1 - c}{2} - c}{2}$$

$$K_1 = \frac{120 - c}{2} - \frac{120 - c}{4} + \frac{K_1}{4}$$

$$\frac{3}{4} K_1 = \frac{120 - c}{4}$$

$$K_1 = \frac{120 - c}{3}$$

So in the game where each firm chooses capacity simultaneously, each firm invests in capacity $K_1^c = K_2^c = 40 - c/3$. In this game, the equilibrium market price is $p^c = 1 - K_1^c - K_2^c = 40 + 2c/3$, so each firm earns total profits $\pi^1 = \pi^2 = (40 - c/3)^2$.

Both of these equilibria are illustrated in Figure 10.1, by plotting each firm's reaction function. The Stackelberg equilibrium where the incumbent firm accommodates the potential entrant is labeled S, while the Cournot equilibrium where both firms choose capacities simultaneously is labeled C.

Total output under the Stackelberg equilibrium with sequential entry is $K_1^s + K_2^s = 90 - 3c/4$, while under the Cournot equilibrium with simultaneous choice of capacity, total output is $K_1^c + K_2^c = 80 - 2c/3$. So total output is higher when an incumbent firm accommodates entry by the potential entrant.[2] If total market output is higher in the Stackelberg sequential entry game, then the market price must be lower at point S, so consumers must be better off in the sequential entry game than in the simultaneous entry game.

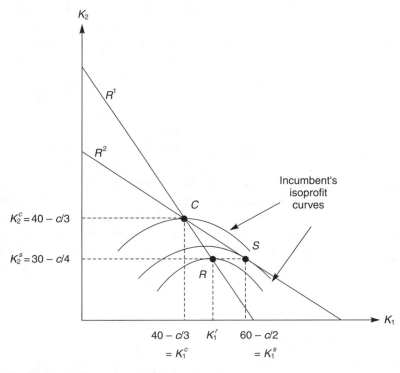

Figure 10.1 Equilibrium with accommodated entry

Another important characteristic of the Stackelberg equilibrium in the sequential entry game is that the incumbent firm is not on its reaction function. This is very important. How can point S represent an equilibrium when firm 1 is not on its reaction function? In particular, when firm 2 plays $K_2^s = 30 - c/4$, the best response by firm 1 is at point R, where firm 1 plays K_1^r which is somewhere between $40 - c/3$ and $60 - c/2$. Why does firm 1 play K_1^s instead of K_1^r?

In fact, we've answered this question in Chapter 6. What happens if firm 1 plays K_1^r? Now firm 2's best response is no longer K_2^s. Firm 2 will respond by increasing capacity. This process will continue until both firms reach the Cournot equilibrium at point C. Of course, the incumbent is worse off at point C than at point S, so the incumbent would rather maintain K_1^s, even though it is not on its reaction function.

We can describe this result in another way, by using the incumbent firm's *isoprofit curves* which are drawn in Figure 10.1. The incumbent must be maximizing profits along the reaction function R^1, so the slope of the incumbent's isoprofit curves must be zero along the reaction function. Profits are increasing on isoprofit curves closer to the horizontal axis, so profits for the incumbent are highest at point R, lower at point S, and lower still at point C. Of course, this is consistent with profits for the incumbent in the Stackelberg equilibrium relative to the Cournot equilibrium. Also, we noted that the incumbent could increase profits by producing on its reaction function at point R, relative to the Stackelberg equilibrium at point S. But at point R, the entrant has an incentive to change capacity, so the best that the incumbent can do is produce at the Stackelberg equilibrium at point S, where its isoprofit curve is just tangent to the entrant's reaction function. In this way,

the incumbent is on an isoprofit curve which is as close as possible to the horizontal axis, representing the highest profits, while at the same time, the entrant is on its reaction function.

Result

The incumbent firm has *overinvested in capacity* since firm 1 is not on its reaction function. The level of capacity K_1^s is greater than the best-response level of capacity given by K_1^r, so firm 1 has overinvested.

The element of this model which is most important in deriving this result is the fact that firm 1's investment in capacity is irreversible. Because the investment in capacity is irreversible, the incumbent firm can credibly commit to capacity K_1^s, even though it is not on its reaction function. Even though firm 1 is not on its reaction function (i.e. K_1^s is not the incumbent firms best response to the strategy played by the entrant), the strategy K_1^s is credible because the investment is irreversible. If this investment in capacity could be changed, then the strategy by the incumbent of playing K_1^s would not be credible.

It might help to explain this point with some examples. The strategy by any major car maker to invest in significant modifications to an assembly line in order to build a new or significantly re-designed automobile implies a credible commitment to a particular capacity of production, because the assembly line cannot be used for some other purpose. Any potential entrant (and in fact any fellow competitor in the industry) must view this type of investment strategy as a commitment to produce a particular number of a particular type of vehicle.

If we think about our hot-dog vendors on the beach, the incumbent firm would be the owner of the first hot-dog cart on the beach, and she may well undertake a particular investment strategy to accommodate the potential entrant from Toronto. For example, she could decide to invest in a permanent facility on the beach. This could be a small hut or a larger type of restaurant. The potential entrant would have to take the existence of this level of capacity as given when deciding to enter this particular market.

Role of fixed costs

This discussion points out a significant limitation of the model we have used. Recall that we assumed earlier that the fixed cost F was equal to zero. In fact, it would make much more sense to suppose that this fixed cost was positive. What would happen to the results of our model if we relaxed this assumption and allowed $F > 0$?

We'll start at the same point where we started earlier, with the potential entrant's profit function. With fixed costs equal to F, the profit function becomes:

$$\pi^2 = (120 - K_1 - K_2) \cdot K_2 - cK_2 - F$$

As before, the entrant's first-order condition is found by setting the derivative of firm 2's profit function with respect to capacity choice K_2 equal to zero:

$$\partial \frac{\partial \pi^2}{K_2} = 120 - K_1 - 2K_2 - c = 0$$

But this is exactly the same as the first-order condition when fixed costs were equal to zero. In fact, the only element of the solution to the Stackelberg sequential entry game which is affected by the presence of positive fixed costs is the equilibrium level of profits earned by each firm. Each firm's reaction function is the same since each firm's first-order profit-maximization condition is the

same. Recall that firm 2 earned profits of $\pi^2 = (30 - c/4)^2$ in the sequential entry game. Now firm 2 will earn profits

$$\pi^2 = (30 - c/4)^2 - F$$

As long as $(30 - c/4)^2 > F$, the entrant will earn positive profits in the sequential entry game when the incumbent firm accommodates entry. But if $(30 - c/4)^2 < F$, firm 2 would never enter this market since firm 2 would earn negative profits in equilibrium.

10.1.2 Deterred or blockaded entry

In the previous example, we solved for the equilibrium in the game where the incumbent firm invested in capacity to maximize profits given that it accommodated entry by firm 2. What would happen if firm 1 tried to deter entry by firm 2? To do so, the incumbent firm would want to choose the level of capacity K_1^d so that firm 2 could never earn positive profits (we use the d superscript to denote the level of capacity which *deters* firm 2 from entering).

We just saw that if $(30 - c/4)^2 < F$, firm 2 would never be able to earn positive profits in this market, so this example would not be very interesting if $(30 - c/4)^2 < F$. So we will suppose that fixed costs F are small enough that the entrant could earn positive profits if the incumbent firm accommodated entry. The potential entrant must still take the level of investment in capacity by the incumbent as given, since the incumbent firm still has the first-mover advantage.

If firm 2 faces the inverse demand function $p = 120 - (K_1 + K_2)$, and faces constant marginal cost c and fixed cost F, then firm 2's profit function can be written as:

$$\pi^2 = K_2 \cdot (p - c) - F$$
$$\pi^2 = K_2 \cdot (120 - K_1 - K_2 - c) - F$$

The first-order profit-maximization condition for firm 2 is found by setting the derivative of π^2 with respect to K_2 equal to zero:

$$120 - K_1 - 2K_2 - c = 0$$

From this first-order condition we can solve for firm 2's reaction function:

$$K_2 = \frac{120 - K_1 - c}{2}$$

$$K_2 = \frac{120 - c}{2} - \frac{K_1}{2}$$

Of course, this is the same as the reaction function that firm 2 had in the accommodated entry problem, since firm 2's problem is the same: if it can enter the market, choose K_2 to maximize profits π_2, given firm 1's capacity K_1. The problem which the incumbent firm solves is to choose it's level of investment in capacity $K_1 = K_1^d$ to deter entry by firm 2, given that firm 2 will invest in capacity K_2 according to it's reaction function above. That is, firm 1 chooses K_1^d such that firm 2's profits are equal to (or less than) zero:

$$\pi^2 = K_2 \cdot (120 - K_1^d - K_2 - c) - F = 0$$

The solution to this problem is derived in the appendix at the end of this chapter. The level of capacity K_1^d which deters entry by firm 2 is given by:

$$K_1^d = 120 - c - 2\sqrt{F}$$

If the incumbent firm invests in capacity K_1^d, then firm 2's best response is given by its reaction function:

$$K_2 = \frac{120 - c}{2} - \frac{K_1^d}{2}$$

$$K_2 = \frac{120 - c}{2} - \frac{120 - c - 2\sqrt{F}}{2}$$

$$K_2 = \sqrt{F}$$

Recall that firm 2's profit function is given by:

$$\pi^2 = K_2 \cdot (120 - K_1 - K_2 - c) - F$$

If we substitute the solution for K_1^d and K_2 above into this expression we get:

$$\pi^2 = \sqrt{F} \cdot (120 - (120 - c - 2\sqrt{F}) - \sqrt{F} - c) - F$$

$$\pi^2 = \sqrt{F} \cdot (\sqrt{F}) - F$$

$$\pi^2 = 0$$

So capacity K_1^d by the incumbent firm deters entry because firm 2 cannot earn positive profits in equilibrium.

How does firm 1 do? If the incumbent firm invests in capacity to deter entry by firm 2, the equilibrium market price is found by substituting K_1^d into the market demand function (we don't need to worry about K_2 since firm 2 will not enter this market):

$$p = 120 - K_1^d$$

$$p = 120 - (120 - c - 2\sqrt{F})$$

$$p = c + 2\sqrt{F}$$

This means that the incumbent firm will earn profits:

$$\pi^1 = (p - c) \cdot K_1^d - F$$

$$\pi^1 = 2\sqrt{F} \cdot \left(120 - c - 2\sqrt{F}\right) - F$$

$$\pi^1 = 2\sqrt{F} \cdot (120 - c) - 2\sqrt{F} \cdot \left(2\sqrt{F}\right) - F$$

$$\pi^{1d} = 2\sqrt{F} \cdot (120 - c) - 5F$$

Recall that when firm 1 was choosing capacity to accommodate entry, it earned profits:

$$\pi^{1s} = (60 - c/2) \cdot (30 - c/4) - F$$

So if $\pi_1^{1s} > \pi_1^{1d}$, the incumbent firm would rather accommodate entry. But if $\pi_1^{1d} > \pi_1^{1s}$, then the incumbent firm earns higher profits by deterring entry.

Notice that the incumbent firm's optimal investment strategy depends upon the structure of costs in the industry. Whether the incumbent wants to deter entry or accommodate entry depends upon whether $\pi_1^{ls} > \pi_1^{ld}$ or not. This condition will depend upon the size of fixed costs F and marginal costs c. In order to understand this point more completely, you should work through Exercise 2 at the end of this chapter.

In order to represent this equilibrium in our graph with reaction functions, we need to pay particular attention to the potential entrant's problem. Recall that firm 2's reaction function summarizes the entrant's best response to any level of investment in capacity by the incumbent firm. In general, this is given by the reaction function which we derived earlier:

$$K_2 = \frac{120 - c}{2} - \frac{K_1}{2}$$

This is the appropriate reaction function whenever the incumbent firm invests in a level of capacity that is smaller than K_1^d. But when firm 1 invests in K_1^d, firm 2 earns profits of zero, so its best response is $K_2 = 0$. In fact, as long as the incumbent firm chooses a level of capacity equal to or greater than K_1^d, the best response by the entrant is to choose $K_2 = 0$. This implies that firm 2's reaction function will be discontinuous at K_1^d, as illustrated in Figure 10.2.

As in the previous example where the incumbent firm accommodated entry by firm 2, the optimal level of capacity which the incumbent chooses to deter entry, K_1^d, is greater than the Cournot equilibrium capacity K_1^c in the simultaneous entry game. As a result, the solution to the entry deterrence

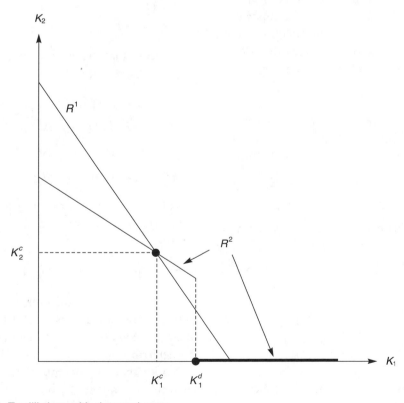

Figure 10.2 Equilibrium with deterred entry

problem for firm 1 is characterized by over-investment in capacity by the incumbent firm to deter entry.

10.1.3 Extensions

Our discussion thus far has been focused on a narrowly defined game between a single incumbent and a single potential entrant, with each firm choosing a single well-defined strategic variable (capacity). We'll finish off this section by considering some simple ways of extending this game to represent different real-world problems.

Multiple incumbents

What would happen to the results of our entry deterrence example if there were more than one incumbent firm in the market? To answer this question, we need to explicitly acknowledge that there exists a cost to the incumbent firm of deterring entry. This is the cost associated with overinvestment, since

the incumbent firm invests beyond the Cournot equilibrium level of capacity to deter entry. Of course, a single incumbent is happy to incur this cost to deter entry, as long as profits from deterring entry outweigh this cost. To use a very simple example, if the cost of deterring entry is $1 and the profits earned by the incumbent are $1.50, then entry deterrence is worthwhile.

But what if there are initially two incumbent firms in the market? Let's use the same simple example described above. Either incumbent firm can deter entry at a cost of $1. The total profits from deterring entry are $1.50, but these must be split between the two incumbents. In this case, neither firm wants to deter entry, because the $1 cost is greater than the $0.75 profits which each firm earns. Notice that a surplus to entry deterrence still exists in this example, since overall profits of $1.50 are greater than the $1 deterrence cost. Neither firm wants to deter entry, but each firm would like the other firm to incur the $1 cost and deter entry.

Competition between Internet Service Providers

What happens when a firm uses an entry deterrence strategy against a competitor who is already in the market? This argument might sound a bit strange, but if we re-label the *entry deterrence* strategy as an *exit inducement* strategy, we see that the objective would be the same: limit competition to gain market share and market power. If we imagine a market with two firms, then firm 1 might employ a strategy to induce firm 2 to exit the market, leaving firm 1 as a monopolist.

To illustrate such a strategy, consider the market for internet services. Firms in this market are called Internet Service Providers, or ISPs. These firms provide consumers with access to the Internet, including software to enable web browsers and e-mail access. Consumers typically pay a monthly fee for some maximum number of hours of access to the Internet.

The dominant ISPs in the United States include America Online (AOL), CompuServe, Microsoft's MSN, and Netcom Online.* Of these, the largest ISP is AOL. In late 1996, AOL adopted a new pricing strategy whereby consumers could gain unlimited Internet access for a $19.95 (€ 21.89) per month flat fee. This strategy had some very predictable effects. Business at AOL rose dramatically, as new members joined to take advantage of the new pricing strategy. But since there were no limits on the number of hours per month that consumers could gain access to the Internet, many consumers would simply log on to the Internet and stay logged on. As a result,

AOL's service became overloaded, and many users could not get through AOL's jammed access lines.

How has competition in the Internet market changed as a result of AOL's new pricing strategy? AOL itself has promised to invest in new infrastructure, to increase its capacity to serve consumers and ensure access. Many competitors followed suit, offering their consumers Internet access for a fixed flat fee. The most dramatic effect has been on ISPs bottom line: while the Internet service industry earned revenues of \$1.4 billion (€1.54 billion) in the US in 1996, the two largest ISPs, AOL and CompuServe, lost more than \$0.5 billion (€0.55 billion). The increase in competition due to AOL's new pricing strategy led to huge losses in the US Internet market.

Of course, firms cannot continue to earn significant losses year after year. Eventually, some firms must either change their pricing strategy or go out of business. This might be AOL's plan: incur short-run losses, drive some of the competition out of business, and gain more market share and market power in the longer run. This is referred to as a *War of Attrition* game.** For it's part, AOL has signaled to the competition that it plans to be around for a while, by committing to a significant investment in capital to enhance access to its consumers. Time (and strategy) will tell who is around in the ISP market 5 years hence.

* Data for this case can be found on p. 75 of the March 8, 1997 issue of *The Economist*.
** For information on war of Attrition games, see Tirole (1988), pp. 311–14.

Strategies to deter entry

There are a number of different strategies which an incumbent can employ in order to deter entry. In the entry deterrence example which we considered earlier, the incumbent firm chose a level of investment in capacity to deter entry. But other strategies can also be employed by an incumbent firm in order to deter entry.

Learning-by-doing

Suppose that an incumbent follows the strategy of overinvesting in capacity by choosing a large K_1 to deter entry. Of course, one principal effect of this strategy is that the incumbent firm will be able to produce more output as a result of greater capacity K_1. But there may be other potential benefits which may be derived from the overinvestment strategy. It may be that the incumbent firm can learn how to produce output more

efficiently when it expands capacity and increases production. For example, the incumbent firm may find better ways to organize production along an assembly line as the assembly line is expanded and workers along the line can work more efficiently. As well as increasing production, the higher investment in capacity may lead to lower production costs, which give a further competitive advantage to the incumbent firm.

Advertising expenditures

As we saw in Chapter 8, an increase in advertising expenditure will generally lead to an increase in demand for a firm's product, especially when consumers do not have full information about the characteristics of the firm's output. This means that an incumbent firm can increase advertising expenditures to increase its captive share of the market, so that there is less of the market left over for any potential entrant. This will make entry more costly for any potential entrant. In this way, an incumbent firm can use a strategy of increasing advertising expenditures to deter entry.

Network of exclusive franchises

Another preemptive strategy to deter entry is to set up a *network of exclusive franchises*. This strategy is often employed by clothing producers, who produce goods to be sold at selected exclusive retail locations. Retail stores are often selected because of the particular image associated with a particular store. For example, a producer of high-quality fashion clothing will typically distribute its product through stores with an image of selling only high-quality clothing, and not sell its fashions through a *bargain basement* distributor. This can make it more difficult for a potential entrant to enter the high fashion clothing market because of the agreement between the incumbent producer and the high-quality retail distributor.

10.2 Limit pricing

Up to this point we have described an incumbent's problem of choosing a strategy to deter or accommodate entry when actions were strategic substitutes. Actions are strategic substitutes as long as the reaction functions of the two players are downward sloping. But we showed in Chapter 5 that actions could be strategic substitutes or strategic complements. In general, when price is the strategic choice variable, reaction functions will be upward sloping and actions will be strategic complements. What happens to the incumbent firm's entry deterrence or accommodation problem when the manager chooses prices?

The concept used to address this problem is the *limit price*. This concept was introduced by Bain (1949), and is easiest to illustrate by considering a monopolist choosing price as strategy. If the incumbent monopolist does not face the threat of entry, the firm will charge the monopoly price p^m, and will earn profits π^m. With the threat of entry, this price is too high to deter entry since an entrant can come into the market and undercut the monopolist's price of p^m and still earn positive profits. In order to deter entry, the incumbent monopolist must charge a price p^e or lower, where p^e is the *limit price*. If the incumbent monopolist chooses a price in excess of p^e, entry will occur, and the incumbent will earn profits π^e. But the incumbent monopolist can deter entry by selecting a sufficiently low price. Suppose the best that the monopolist can do when deterring entry is to charge price $p_d \leq p_e$, and suppose that in this deterrence equilibrium the monopolist earns profits π^d. If profits earned while deterring entry are greater than profits earned when charging the limit price p^e, so that $\pi^d > \pi^e$, the monopolist will deter entry. But if $\pi^d < \pi^e$, the incumbent monopolist will accommodate entry.

These potential outcomes are illustrated in Figure 10.3. With no threat of entry, the monopolist will choose the equilibrium level of output q^m where marginal revenue is equal to marginal cost, and sets price equal to p^m. But when the monopolist faces the threat of entry, the incumbent can deter entry by charging a price $p^d < p^e$, or can accommodate entry by charging a price $p^a > p^e$. The monopolist will choose whichever strategy yields higher profits.

The problem with the limit pricing model is that the behavior of the entrant is not well specified. To illustrate, note that the entrant has only two options: enter the market or

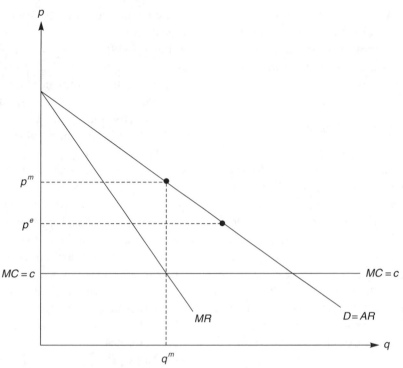

Figure 10.3 Limit pricing by an incumbent monopolist

stay out of the market. If the entrant stays out of the market, then the entrant must earn zero profits. If the entrant decides to enter the market, then suppose that the two firms play to a Bertrand duopoly equilibrium. If this equilibrium is characterized by both firms earning positive profits, then the entrant is better off entering the market than staying out of the market. This is true whether or not the incumbent monopolist tries to deter entry by charging p^d. The threat of deterring entry by charging p^d is not a credible strategy by the incumbent monopolist.

A number of attempts have been made at resolving this problem by giving a more realistic description of the entrant's problem. A very important issue is the information available to the incumbent and the potential entrant. The simple limit pricing model described above implicitly assumes that the incumbent and the entrant both have the same complete information, both about the structure of demand and the structure of costs. But it may be more realistic to assume that the incumbent firm has better knowledge than the entrant. The incumbent may well have better information about the structure of demand since the incumbent might know how demand changes in response to changes in the market price. Also, the incumbent firm may have an informational advantage about costs of production since the incumbent is already producing output. In fact, it may be most appropriate to assume that the entrant does not even know the structure of the incumbent firm's costs. This issue was addressed in a paper by Milgrom

Entrant's costs	market price is low ($\underline{p}$)	market price is high ($\bar{p}$)
$\bar{p} < c^e$	entrant earns zero profits	entrant earns zero profits
$\underline{p} < c^e < \bar{p}$	entrant earns zero profits	entrant earns positive profits
$c^e < \underline{p}$	entrant earns positive profits	entrant earns positive profits

Figure 10.4 Profits earned by the potential entrant

and Roberts (1982). Suppose that the incumbent monopolist has constant marginal cost which is either $\underline{c}$ or $\bar{c}$. That is, the incumbent firm is either a high-cost producer or a low-cost producer. The monopolist knows this cost but the potential entrant does not. The entrant tries to deduce whether the monopolist is high cost or low cost from the price charged by the monopolist.

We can illustrate this example by considering the hot-dog vendor example which we've used in previous chapters. The incumbent monopolist is the vendor whose cart is already on the beach. She may be a high-cost monopolist or a low-cost monopolist, depending upon the arrangement which she has with her hot-dog supplier. The incumbent's strategic choice variable is the market price, p. She can choose to charge either a high price $\bar{p}$ or a low price $\underline{p}$.

The potential entrant from Toronto does not know if the incumbent is high cost or low cost. But he can use the price charged by the incumbent firm as a signal of the incumbent firm's true type. The entrant will use the price charged by the incumbent firm to decide whether or not to enter the market. The entrant's strategic choice variable is whether or not to enter the market. His decision will be based upon the market price charged by the incumbent firm, since he cannot observe

the incumbent vendor's cost. This market price will determine whether the entrant can earn positive profits by entering the market.

Entrant's problem

The entrant's optimal strategy on whether or not to enter this market will depend upon his own costs, c^e. We can think of three possible cases, summarized in Figure 10.4. If the entrant's costs are higher than $\bar{p}$, so that $\bar{p} < c^e$, then the entrant will never be able to earn positive profits, no matter what the price charged by the incumbent. The entrant would never enter the market if $\bar{p} < c^e$. On the other hand, if the entrant's costs are lower than $\underline{p}$, the entrant will be able to earn positive profits no matter which price the incumbent vendor charges, so the entrant will always enter the market if $c^e < \underline{p}$.

Only the intermediate example is non-trivial, since in either of the two cases described above, the entrant's problem does not depend upon the action of the incumbent. So we will focus on the case where the entrant's costs are somewhere between the two possible prices charged by the incumbent: $\underline{p} < c^e < \bar{p}$. Now, if the incumbent hot-dog vendor charges a low price, the entrant must also charge a low price when

Incumbent's costs	Incumbent charges low price ($\underline{p}$)	Incumbent charges high price ($\bar{p}$)
low cost ($\underline{c}$)	$\underline{\pi}^d$	$\underline{\pi}^a$
high cost ($\bar{c}$)	$\bar{\pi}^d$	$\bar{\pi}^a$

Figure 10.5 Profits earned by the incumbent

entering the market (recall that the two firms play to a Bertrand equilibrium when both firms are in the market). This price is low enough so that the entrant cannot earn positive profits, since $\underline{p} < c^e$, so he will not enter the market when the incumbent vendor charges $\underline{p}$. But if the incumbent charges a high price $\bar{p}$, the entrant will be able to enter the market and earn positive profits, since $c^e < \bar{p}$.

Incumbent's problem

Now we can solve the incumbent's problem. If the entrant's costs are so high that he can never earn positive profits, then the incumbent has no problem, since she does not face the threat of entry. If the entrant's costs are lower than $\underline{p}$, then the entrant can earn positive profits no matter what strategy is played by the incumbent vendor. Either way, the incumbent's problem is straightforward.

But if $\underline{p} < c^e < \bar{p}$, the incumbent can deter entry by charging a low price $\underline{p}$, or can accommodate entry by charging a high price $\bar{p}$. Whether the incumbent wants to deter entry or accommodate entry depends upon whether profits are higher when entry is deterred or accommodated, and these profits will depend upon whether the incumbent is a high-cost or a low-cost producer. All alternatives are summarized in Figure 10.5. In fact, even if the incumbent is a high-cost producer, if $\bar{\pi}^d > \bar{\pi}^a$, it pays for the incumbent to engage

in limit pricing by using a low price as a signal to the potential entrant to deter entry.

10.3 A summary of deterrence and accommodation strategies

The objective of this final section is to pull together the entry deterrence and accommodation strategies which we have described so far in this chapter. As we have seen, an incumbent firm's optimal strategy on whether to deter entry or accommodate a potential entrant depends upon a number of factors, including whether firms compete in prices or in quantities, or whether actions are strategic substitutes or strategic complements. But either way, the ultimate objective of the incumbent firm is to choose the strategy which affects the structure of competition in the market so as to yield the highest level of profits. To do this, the incumbent firm must evaluate the following two problems:

1 does the incumbent want to deter entry or accommodate entry?
2 does the incumbent want to be big (i.e. overinvest so that K_1 is large) or small?

In fact, the solutions to each of these two problems are not independent. For example, if the incumbent decides that it is best to deter entry, then that will dictate the appropriate investment strategy (i.e. whether K_1 should be large or small).

The appropriate strategy to deter entry or to accommodate entry will depend upon a number of factors, including:

- how does a change in capacity by the incumbent affect her own profits
- how does a change in capacity by the incumbent firm affect the profits of the potential entrant
- do firms compete in prices or quantities (are actions strategic substitutes or strategic complements)

To analyze any of these situations, we'll need to write out the profit function of the incumbent firm (firm 1) and of the potential entrant (firm 2). If the two firms compete in quantities, then each firm's profit function can be written as follows:

$$\pi^1 = \pi^1(K_1, q_1(K_1, K_2), q_2(K_1, K_2))$$
$$\pi^2 = \pi^2(K_1, q_1(K_1, K_2), q_2(K_1, K_2))$$

If firms compete in prices, then the profit functions become:

$$\pi^1 = \pi^1(K_1, p_1(K_1, K_2), p_2(K_1, K_2))$$
$$\pi^2 = \pi^2(K_1, p_1(K_1, K_2), p_2(K_1, K_2))$$

Note that profits earned by each firm depend upon the capacity K_1 chosen by the incumbent firm, and the strategic choice variables. These strategic choice variables themselves will depend upon the incumbent's choice of capacity, which is why we write q_i and p_i as a function of the incumbent's capacity K_1. For example, if the incumbent chooses a larger capacity K_1, then if firms compete in quantities, firm 1's optimal choice of quantity q_1 might be higher.

Given the investment strategy pursued by the incumbent firm, each of the two firms will then maximize profits by appropriate choice of the strategic variable, depending upon whether the two firms would compete in prices or in quantities. If the two firms would compete in prices, then actions will be strategic complements, implying that reaction functions will be upward sloping. On the other hand, if the two firms would compete in quantities, then actions will be strategic substitutes, and reaction functions will be downward sloping. This description of strategic substitutes and complements was intro-

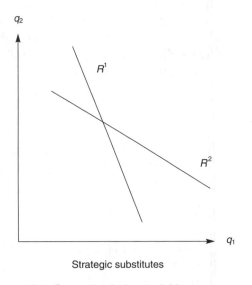

Strategic substitutes

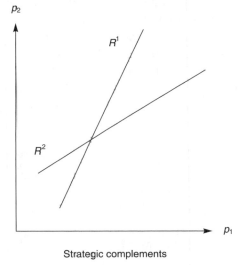

Strategic complements

Figure 10.6 Strategic choice variables

duced in Chapter 5, and is illustrated in Figure 10.6.

Entry deterrence

Suppose that the incumbent firm wants to deter entry by the potential entrant. In this case, the incumbent wants to choose capacity K_1 so that profits earned by the entrant are less than or equal to zero, since if the entrant can never earn positive profits, he will never want to enter the market.[3]

We will use the following definitions to describe the complete set of investment strategies available to the incumbent firm:[4]

- *Top dog*: be big or strong to look tough or aggressive.
- *Puppy dog*: be small or weak to look soft or inoffensive.
- *Lean and hungry look*: be small or weak to look tough or aggressive.
- *Fat cat*: be big or strong to look soft or inoffensive.

These strategies are implemented by an investment in capacity by the incumbent firm. But whether the appropriate strategy to deter entry is to choose a large K_1 or a small K_1 will depend upon how a change in capacity by the incumbent firm affects the profits of the potential entrant. This interaction between the incumbent's investment in capacity K_1 and the effect on the entrant's profits is summarized in Figure 10.7.

In order to solve for the effect of a change in the incumbent firm's capacity K_1 on firm 2's profits, we need to totally differentiate firm 2's profit function. Suppose for example that the two firms would compete in quantities.

$$d\pi^2 = \frac{\partial \pi^2}{\partial K_1} dK_1 + \frac{\partial \pi^2}{\partial q_1} \cdot \frac{\partial q_1}{\partial K_1} dK_1 + \frac{\partial \pi^2}{\partial q_2} \cdot \frac{\partial q_2}{\partial K_1} dK_1$$

Any change in capacity by the incumbent dK_1 will ultimately cause a change in profits earned by the potential entrant, $d\pi^2$. Given an investment in capacity by the incumbent, if the entrant tries to enter the market, his objective would be to choose a quantity q_2 to maximize his profits. His first-order profit-maximization condition would be:

$$\frac{\partial \pi^2}{\partial q_2} = 0$$

Of course, the incumbent knows that the potential entrant would try to maximize profits, so she can incorporate the potential entrant's first-order profit-maximization condition into her problem of choosing the best capacity K_1 to deter entry. This means that the final term in the equation above for π^2 is equal to zero, so the effect of a change in capacity K_1 on the entrant's profits can be rewritten as:

$$d\pi^2 = \frac{\partial \pi^2}{\partial K_1} dK_1 + \frac{\partial \pi^2}{\partial q_1} \cdot \frac{\partial q_1}{\partial K_1} dK_1$$

	Entrant's profits increase	Entrant's profits decrease
Incumbent increases K_1	fat cat	top dog
Incumbent decreases K_1	puppy dog	lean and hungry look

Figure 10.7 Definition of investment strategies available to the incumbent

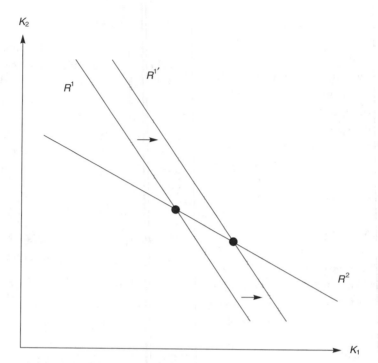

Figure 10.8 Overinvestment makes the incumbent look tough

We have broken down the effect of a change in the incumbent's capacity K_1 on the entrant's profits into two separate effects:

$$\text{Direct effect} \rightarrow \frac{\partial \pi^2}{\partial K_1}$$

$$\text{Strategic effect} \rightarrow \frac{\partial \pi^2}{\partial q_1} \cdot \frac{\partial q_1}{\partial K_1}$$

So how might a change in capacity by the incumbent affect the potential entrant's profits? Suppose that an increase in capacity by the incumbent firm affects the marginal cost of production by the incumbent, because of economies of scale or learning-by-doing effects. As the incumbent gets bigger, any marginal unit of output can be produced at a lower cost. The direct effect of such an investment on the entrant's profits may well be zero, since this benefit accrues only to the incumbent firm. But suppose that the two firms would compete in

quantities. A reduction in marginal cost will shift the incumbent firm's reaction function outwards leading to an increase in output by the incumbent and a decrease in potential output by the entrant, as illustrated in Figure 10.8. This strategic effect of a change in the incumbent's capacity will cause the entrant's profits to fall. If outputs are strategic substitutes and an increase in capacity makes the incumbent firm look tough and aggressive, then the appropriate strategy for firm 1 to deter entry is a *top dog* strategy.

If we re-interpreted the investment in capacity K_1 as an advertising or promotional campaign, then it might be the case that *overinvestment* (which in this case implies overadvertising) will ensure that the incumbent firm gets a larger captive market, leaving a smaller potential market for the entrant. In this case, the direct effect of an increase in *capacity* on the potential entrant's profits will also be negative, and the *top dog* strategy is best to deter entry.

Even if the two firms would compete in prices, so that actions would be strategic complements, the incumbent firm still wants to look tough or aggressive in order to deter entry. So, as long as overinvesting makes the incumbent firm look tough, the incumbent is better off overinvesting. If an increase in capacity makes the incumbent look soft and weak, then the incumbent should underinvest and choose a lower capacity in order to deter entry. For example, if an increase in capacity when the two firms would compete in prices would call for the incumbent to charge a higher market price, this makes it easier for the entrant to enter the market and also charge a higher price. In this case, overinvesting makes the incumbent look soft and inoffensive because price competition would be softer. The best strategy for the incumbent to deter entry would be the *lean and hungry look*.

All of these strategies are summarized in Figure 10.9. In general, the incumbent wants to overinvest if doing so makes it look tough, whether the firms would compete in prices or quantities.

Accommodation of entry

Now suppose that the incumbent firm wants to choose a level of capacity K_1 while accommodating entry. In this case, the incumbent firm is not concerned with the profits earned by the entrant. The incumbent only wants to choose K_1 in order to maximize her own profits. As we saw earlier, when firms compete in quantities, the incumbent's profit function will be given by:

$$\pi^1 = \pi^1(K_1, q_1(K_1, K_2), q_2(K_1, K_2))$$

If firms compete in prices, then the incumbent's profit function becomes:

$$\pi^1 = \pi^1(K_1, p_1(K_1, K_2), p_2(K_1, K_2))$$

Now the incumbent is concerned with the effect of a change in capacity K_1 on her own profits. This effect is found by totally differentiating the incumbent's profits function. To illustrate, suppose that the two firms compete in quantities.

$$d\pi^1 = \frac{\partial \pi^1}{\partial K_1} dK_1 + \frac{\partial \pi^1}{\partial q_1} \cdot \frac{\partial q_1}{\partial K_1} dK_1 + \frac{\partial \pi^1}{\partial q_2} \cdot \frac{\partial q_2}{\partial K_1} dK_1$$

The incumbent will choose the quantity of output q_1 in order to maximize profits. Her first-order profit-maximization condition over quantity q_1 will be:

	Investment makes incumbent look tough	Investment makes incumbent look soft
Actions are strategic substitutes	top dog	lean and hungry look
Actions are strategic complements	top dog	lean and hungry look

Figure 10.9 Investment strategies to deter entry

	Investment makes incumbent look tough	Investment makes incumbent look soft
Actions are strategic substitutes	top dog	lean and hungry look
Actions are strategic complements	puppy dog	fat cat

Figure 10.10 Investment strategies to accommodate entry

$$\frac{\partial \pi^1}{\partial q_1} = 0$$

Using this first-order profit-maximization condition in the incumbent's problem of choosing the best capacity K_1 to accommodate entry, we can show that the effect of a change in capacity K_1 on the incumbent's profits can be rewritten as:

$$d\pi^1 = \frac{\partial \pi^1}{\partial K_1} dK_1 + \frac{\partial \pi^1}{\partial q_2} \cdot \frac{\partial q_2}{\partial K_1} dK_1$$

We have again broken the overall effect of a change in capacity by the incumbent, dK_1, into a direct effect on the incumbent's profits and a strategic effect:

$$\text{Direct effect} \rightarrow \frac{\partial \pi^1}{\partial K_1}$$

$$\text{Strategic effect} \rightarrow \frac{\partial \pi^1}{\partial q_2} \cdot \frac{\partial q_2}{\partial K_1}$$

The most interesting element is the strategic effect. Suppose that the two firms compete in quantities. An increase in capacity by the incumbent which reduces her costs will shift her reaction function outwards, just as in the previous example in Figure 10.8. In this case, overinvestment makes the incumbent look tough, so the *top dog* strategy is appropriate when the incumbent is accommodating entry. On the other hand, if an increase in capacity causes an *increase* in the

incumbent's costs, then overinvesting makes the incumbent look soft, so the appropriate strategy is to underinvest and use the *lean and hungry look* strategy.

What happens if the two firms compete in prices? If an increase in capacity makes the incumbent look tough, then overinvesting will lead the incumbent to charge a lower price as costs fall. Since firms are competing in prices, the entrant will also charge a lower price. This hurts the incumbent, who would earn higher profits if prices were higher. So if the two firms compete in prices, when investment makes the incumbent look tough, the incumbent wants to *underinvest*. This is the *puppy dog* strategy. On the other hand, if investment makes the incumbent look soft, the incumbent should follow the *fat cat* strategy when accommodating entry. When the two firms compete in prices, the incumbent wants to choose the strategy which results in softened price competition, since the equilibrium market price will be higher.

All of these investment strategies when the incumbent accommodates entry are summarized in Figure 10.10.

10.3.1 Applications of investment strategies

The objective of this last subsection is to provide some concrete examples of strategies to accommodate or deter entry. We have already described some examples. For example, when an investment in capacity affects the incumbent's costs because of learning-by-doing effects, then overinvestment makes the incumbent look tough because the potential entrant sees that the incumbent will be able to produce at lower cost. The *top dog* strategy is appropriate to deter entry if the firms compete in quantities or prices. But, if the incumbent wants to accommodate entry and the firms compete in prices, then overinvestment will signal tougher price competition. In this case, the *puppy dog* strategy will result in softer price competition, so this is the best strategy for the incumbent who wants to accommodate entry.

Product differentiation

Let's re-interpret the incumbent firm's investment in capacity K_1 as an investment to differentiate the incumbent's product. In this example, overinvestment will mean that the incumbent makes herself large enough to stock many different brands of products. If we think of the product differentiation model of Chapter 7, where consumers are distributed along a unit interval, then an incumbent who overinvests can stock many different types of goods to serve many different consumers. This *top dog* strategy of overinvesting was followed by warehouse superstores and large electronics and home improvement stores. On the other hand, small specialty electronics stores which specialize in high-end and high-quality products follow a *puppy dog* strategy. These stores underinvest and limit themselves to competition in a small well-defined segment of the product spectrum. For example, a stereo store which specializes in top-quality audio and video equipment signals to the market that it is limiting competition by competing only for consumers who are interested in purchasing the highest quality audio and video components. This *puppy dog* strategy is appropriate when these firms compete in prices, which is typically the case in the retail electronics sector.

Price protection policy

An interesting example of a *puppy dog* strategy which results in softened price competition is the so-called *price protection clause.*[5] This strategy has been adopted by firms in a number of different industries in recent years, especially consumer electronics products. Suppose that a firm sells a product at some price $\bar{p}$. If the firm adopts a price protection policy, then over some well-defined time period, if the firm sells the same product at a price $\tilde{p}$ lower than $\bar{p}$, the firm is committed to rebating the difference $\bar{p} - \tilde{p}$ to any consumer who bought at the higher price. Any consumer who purchases the product is protected from a price decrease by the price protection clause.

Why would any firm want to adopt a price protection clause? How does the price protection clause result in softened price competition? To answer these questions, suppose that an incumbent firm (firm 1) accommodates entry by a potential entrant (firm 2), and suppose that the two firms compete in prices, so that actions are strategic complements. After the entrant begins producing and selling output in this market, the two firms play to a Bertrand equilibrium. This situation is illustrated by point N in Figure 10.11.

Would the incumbent firm prefer to charge a price higher than the Bertrand equilibrium price p_1^{η}? Suppose that the incumbent firm raises its price to $\bar{p}_1$. Now the incumbent is no longer on its reaction function, so this must make the incumbent worse off. However, the entrant responds to the price increase by also

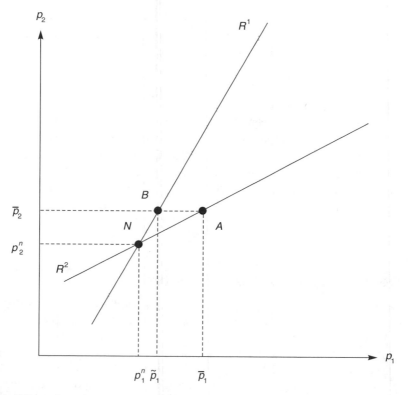

Figure 10.11 Effect of a price protection policy

increasing its price to $\bar{p}_2$, illustrated by point A in Figure 10.11. This softening in price competition leaves both firms better off, so the incumbent has an incentive to raise its price to $\bar{p}_1$ since the entrant will also increase its price. Firm 1 is better off since it has made itself into the Stackelberg leader.

But now the incumbent is not on its reaction function. Does the incumbent firm have an incentive to lower its price? A reduction in price to $\tilde{p}_1$ will move the incumbent back to its reaction function at point B in Figure 10.11. However, because of the price protection clause, the incumbent will have to pay the difference in price, $\bar{p}_1 - \tilde{p}_1$ to all consumers who purchased at the higher price, and this definitely makes the incumbent worse off. The price protection clause is the mechanism by which the incumbent can credibly commit to maintaining the higher price $\bar{p}_1$, which softens price competition and leaves both firms better off.

Coupons

Another mechanism which firms can use to affect price competition is coupons. Of course, coupons can be used as a mechanism to advertise prices, as we saw in Chapter 8. However, firms also issue coupons which consumers can reimburse for discounts or special prices. For example, many pizza restaurants issue coupons which consumers can use to buy two pizzas for the price of one. Other firms advertise in newspapers which consumers can use for a percentage reduction on the price of the advertised good. These are all examples of a *top dog* strategy since these coupons all signal increased price competition.

Another way in which firms can use coupons to affect price competition is by honoring all competitor's coupons. This is another example of a *top dog* strategy, whereby a firm commits to matching any special offers or price discounts advertised by coupons issued by any competitors. For example, a pizza restaurant may respond to coupon competi-

tion by its competitors by announcing that it will honor all special offers advertised by its competitor's coupons.

Limited competition

In an established market which is dominated by one or a few very strong competitors, a potential entrant may decide to enter the market by confining itself to servicing only a very small portion of the market in order to limit competition. This is an example of

US Market for Large Turbine Generators

A classic example of firms using a price protection clause to limit competition is the case of General Electric (GE) versus Westinghouse in the US market for large turbine generators in the early 1960s.* These generators converted steam into electrical power, and were purchased by electric utilities, which used turbine generators to produce electricity. In 1963, GE and Westinghouse had a combined market share of over 98 percent. The production side of the turbine generator market in the United States could be characterized as a duopoly, with the two firms, GE and Westinghouse, competing in prices.

The two competitors provided their salespeople with *price books*, which listed the prices and characteristics of different turbine generators which GE and Westinghouse were capable of producing. Competition in this market included the use of discounts on posted book prices, so that in 1963, actual prices were on average 35 percent below book prices. In fact, this is the sort of result we would expect in a duopoly where firms compete in prices. Bertrand price competition results in an equilibrium where firms have very small profit margins.

In May 1963, GE adopted a new pricing policy, by publishing a new set of book prices, and adopting a price protection clause. If GE ever reduced its prices, customers who had purchased a turbine generator in the previous six months would receive a rebate of the price difference. Westinghouse responded by publishing its own new set of book prices which were virtually identical to GEs, and adopted a price protection clause of its own. This pricing policy continued through the early 1970s.

The most remarkable feature of this case is the fact that the Justice Department of the United States ruled that some elements of the pricing practices in the turbine generator market violated the Sherman Act. Among other things, this Act prohibits collusion between firms for the purpose of fixing prices. The Justice Department ruled that the pricing strategies employed by GE and Westinghouse resulted in collusive pricing behavior, and prohibited GE and Westinghouse from publishing price books and using a price protection clause to retroactively reduce prices.

*The reference for this case is Porter. *General Electric versus Westinghouse in Large Turbine Generators* (1983), pp. 102–18, and the corresponding Harvard Business School case.

a *puppy dog* strategy, and is particularly relevant in markets where firms compete in prices. This may be the strategy which was adopted by DeLorean Motorcars in the early 1980s. Instead of entering the market by offering a very wide range of products, DeLorean concentrated on a very small segment of the market for automobiles, signaling to incumbent automakers that DeLorean would compete for market share in a small portion of the market. The objective of such a strategy is to limit the strategic response by the incumbent firms. If DeLorean threatened to take a large market share, it could have expected a more aggressive strategic response by the incumbent automakers, making it much more difficult for DeLorean to enter the market. Instead, DeLorean chose to compete in a small segment of the car market, increasing the likelihood that incumbent automakers would accommodate entry by DeLorean. Other examples of this *puppy dog* strategy are evidenced by a new restaurant which serves only a particular type of food, or an electronic components distributor who services only the highest end of the market and deals in the highest quality electronics products.

Bundling and tied sales

Consider a producer who produces and sells two different but related goods. A good example to think of here is any good which is a component of a system, like a television and a VCR, or a stereo receiver and a CD player. For example, a single firm might produce both stereo receivers and CD players. A strategy which has been adopted by many producers of component goods in recent years is called *bundling*, where related goods are designed to be sold together as a package or system. For example, you could buy a stereo receiver from firm 1 and a CD player

from firm 2. But firm 1 may design their CD players to have special features which work only when you also use one of their stereo receivers. If you buy the components from separate firms, you may need a separate remote control to operate the receiver and the CD player. But if you buy both components from the same firm, the same remote control may be used for both components.

This is an example of *tied sales*. The two components are designed to be sold together. This strategy may make firm 1 look tough if designing the two products to work together is an investment in cost reduction. For example, when the two goods are designed to work together as a system, some elements of each product (those which affect operation of the remote control) may be the same, and this may reduce firm 1's production costs. In this case, *bundling* the two goods is a *top dog* strategy which is appropriate for entry deterrence. This strategy is also appropriate for accommodation of entry if the firms compete in quantities.

But other types of bundling strategies are available to the firm which produces and sells different but related products as a package. If firm 1 sells a stereo receiver at price p_r and a CD player at price p_c, then if this firms competes with firm 2 in prices, it may adopt a strategy of bundling the two goods together, selling the two components as a package at a price lower than $p_r + p_c$. This price discount would only be available if you bought both components together from firm 1. This is an example of a *top dog* strategy since it results in increased price competition. As we saw earlier, this is an appropriate strategy to deter entry of a competitor, as long as increased price competition makes firm 1 look tough. But this strategy hurts firm 1 if entry is accommodated, since increased price competition results in lower prices which makes firm 1 worse off.

Summary

- In the longer run, we must assume that firms can enter or exit a market.
- An incumbent firm can strategically choose its scale of production or *capacity* to affect the behavior of potential entrants into its market.
- An incumbent firm can adopt a strategy to invest in capacity so as to *accommodate entry* by another firm, or to *deter entry* by a potential competitor.
- An incumbent may decide to *overinvest* in capacity to deter entry, implying that in equilibrium, the incumbent is not on its reaction function.
- An incumbent's fixed costs are important in determining its optimal investment strategy.
- The concept of a limit price can be used to describe conditions under which it would be more profitable to deter entry or accommodate entry of a new firm.
- The effect of an investment in capacity by an incumbent can be broken down into a *direct effect* and a *strategic effect*. The strategic effect will depend upon whether the incumbent wants to deter or accommodate entry, and whether firms compete in prices or quantities.
- When firms compete in prices, an incumbent should follow a *top dog* strategy of overinvestment in capacity to deter entry, but should employ a *puppy dog* strategy of underinvestment to accommodate entry, to avoid excessive price competition, as long as investment made the incumbent look tough.

Notes

1 This photo was obtained under copyright from the "DeLorean Owners Association Collection," www.delorean-owners.org, which is an excellent reference for information about DeLorean Motorcars.
2 It must be the case that $c < 120$, since otherwise the solution to either game would imply negative output. The difference between output in the Stackelberg equilibrium versus the Cournot equilibrium is given by:

$$(K_1^s + K_2^s) - (K_1^c + K_2^c) = \left(90 - \frac{3c}{4}\right) - \left(80 - \frac{2c}{3}\right)$$

$$(K_1^s + K_2^s) - (K_1^c + K_2^c) = 10 - \frac{c}{12}$$

Since $c < 120$, this expression must always be positive, so output in the sequential entry game must be greater than output in the simultaneous entry game.
3 See Dixit (1980) for a more advanced treatment of this problem.

4 These definitions are from Fudenberg and Tirole (1984) and Bulow *et al.* (1985).
5 This policy is also referred to as a *Most-favoured customer clause*. For example, see Cooper (1986), and Salop (1986).

Exercises

1 In Section 10.1, we showed that when the incumbent firm 1 accommodated entry, it earned profits:

$$\pi^{1a} = (60 - c/2) \cdot (30 - c/4) - F$$

When this same firm chose capacity to deter entry, it earned profits:

$$\pi^{1d} = 2\sqrt{F} \cdot (120 - c) - 5F$$

The incumbent will deter entry as long as $\pi^{1d} > \pi^{1s}$, or as long as $\pi^{1d} - \pi^{1s} > 0$. Suppose marginal cost $c = 60$.

(a) Solve for $\pi^{1d} - \pi^{1s}$.

(b) For which values of the fixed cost F will the incumbent deter entry?

(c) Can you interpret the fixed cost F as a *cost of entry deterrence*? Is the incumbent more or less likely to deter entry as F gets larger?

2 In Section 10.1.2, we showed that when the market demand function was given by $p = 120 - (K_1 + K_2)$, the incumbent firm deterred entry by producing the level of output K_1^d and earned profits π^{1d}, given by:

$$\pi^{1d} = 2\sqrt{F} \cdot (120 - c) - 5F$$
$$K_1^d = 120 - c - 2\sqrt{F}$$

If the incumbent accommodated entry, the incumbent earned profits in the Stackelberg equilibrium given by:

$$\pi^{1s} = (60 - c/2) \cdot (30 - c/4) - F$$

The incumbent firm 1 and the entrant firm 2 produced output given by:

$$K_1^s = (120 - c)/2$$
$$K_2^s = (120 - c)/4$$

(a) Suppose marginal cost $c = 5$, and fixed cost $F = 100$. Solve for the equilibrium market price, each firm's level of output, and equilibrium profits for both firms, when the incumbent accommodates entry.

(b) Now suppose the incumbent deters entry. Solve for market price, and output and profits of each firm. Would the incumbent firm rather accommodate or deter entry? Explain your answer.

(c) Now suppose $F = 25$. Repeat parts (a) and (b). Would the incumbent want to follow the same strategy as in part (b)? Relate your answer to the cost of entry deterrence.

3 Consider the following examples:

(a) A maker of ski boots and bindings designs a new ski boot to be used only with its own bindings, with increased safety properties.

(b) A clothing outlet sells only last season's fashions at bargain basement prices.

(c) An optometrist installs an in-house facility to make glasses to fit a prescription *while-you-wait*.

In each case, discuss whether the firm is following a *top dog, puppy dog, lean-and-hungry look*, or *fat cat* investment strategy. Is the strategic effect of the firm's investment strategy likely to increase or soften price competition? Is the firm accommodating entry or deterring entry (or inducing other firms to exit)?

4 Identify the *strategic effect* of an incumbent firm's investment strategy from Section 10.3 when the incumbent:

- deters entry
- accommodates entry

Discuss the differences between these two versions of the *strategic effect* of the incumbent's investment strategy. In each case, whose profits is the incumbent interested in? If firms are competing in prices, is this *strategic effect* positive or negative?

Appendix

If firm 2 faces the inverse demand function $p = 120 - (K_1 + K_2)$, and faces constant marginal cost c and fixed cost F, then firm 2's profit function can be written as:

$$\pi^2 = K_2 \cdot (p - c) - F$$
$$\pi^2 = K_2 \cdot (120 - K_1 - K_2 - c) - F$$

The first-order profit-maximization condition for firm 2 is found by setting the derivative of π^2 with respect to K_2 equal to zero:

$$120 - K_1 - 2K_2 - c = 0$$

From this first-order condition we can solve for firm 2's reaction function:

$$K_2 = \frac{120 - K_1 - c}{2}$$

$$K_2 = \frac{120 - c}{2} - \frac{K_1}{2}$$

The problem which the incumbent firm solves is to choose its level of investment in capacity $K_1 = K_1^d$ to deter entry by firm 2, given that firm 2 will invest in capacity K_2 according to it's reaction function above. That is, firm 1 chooses K_1^d such that firm 2's profits are equal to (or less than) zero:

$$\pi^2 = K_2 \cdot (120 - K_1^d - K_2 - c) - F$$

$$\pi^2 = \left(\frac{120 - c}{2} - \frac{K_1^d}{2}\right)$$
$$\cdot \left[120 - K_1^d - \left(\frac{120 - c}{2} - \frac{K_1^d}{2}\right) - c\right]$$
$$- F = 0$$

$$\pi^2 = \left(\frac{120 - c}{2} - \frac{K_1^d}{2}\right)$$
$$\cdot \left(\frac{120 - c}{2} - \frac{K_1^d}{2}\right) - F = 0$$

$$F = \left(\frac{120 - c}{2} - \frac{K_1^d}{2}\right)^2$$

$$\sqrt{F} = \left(\frac{120 - c}{2} - \frac{K_1^d}{2}\right)$$

$$\frac{K_1^d}{2} = \left(\frac{120 - c}{2}\right) - \sqrt{F}$$

$$K_1^d = 120 - c - 2\sqrt{F}$$

We can solve for the equilibrium market price using the demand function:

$$p = 120 - (K_1 + K_2)$$
$$p = 120 - \left(120 - c - 2\sqrt{F}\right)$$
$$p = c + 2\sqrt{F}$$

References

Bulow, J., Geanakopolis, J. and Klemperer, P. "Multimarket oligopoly: strategic substitutes and complements." *Journal of Political Economy*, 93 (1985), pp. 488–511.

Bulow, J., Geanakopolis, J. and Klemperer, P. "Holding idle capacity to deter entry." *Economic Journal*, 95 (1985), pp. 178–82.

Cooper, T. "Most-favoured customer pricing and tacit collusion." *Rand Journal of Economics*, 17 (1986), pp. 377–88.

Dixit, Avinash. "The role of investment in entry deterrence." *Economic Journal*, 90 (1980), pp. 95–106.

Fudenberg, D. and Tirole, J. "The fat cat effect, the puppy dog ploy, and the lean and hungry look." *American Economic Review: Papers and Proceedings*, 74 (1984), pp. 361–8.

Milgrom, P. and Roberts, J. "Limit pricing and entry under incomplete information." *Econometrica*, 50 (1982), pp. 443–60.

Porter, Michael. *Cases in Competitive Strategy* (New York: Macmillan, 1983), pp. 102–18.

Porter, Michael. *General Electric vs. Westinghouse in Large Turbine Generators* (B) and (C) (Boston, MA: HBS Case Services, 1980).

Salop, S. "Practices that (credibly) facilitate oligopoly coordination." In *New Developments in the Analysis of Market Structure*, edited by J. Stiglitz and F. Mathewson (Cambridge, MA: MIT Press, 1986).

Tirole, Jean. *The Theory of Industrial Organization* (Cambridge, MA: The MIT Press, 1988), pp. 311–14.

Chapter 11

Government regulation of industries

••

When you are finished with this chapter you should understand:

- The "deadweight loss" rationale for government regulation of prices.
- Arguments against government regulation of prices.
- The distinction between natural monopolies and legally created monopolies.
- The two measures of market concentration: the concentration ratio and the Herfindahl–Hirschman Index.
- Government policy toward mergers and acquisitions and the role of anti-trust legislation.
- Government policy to control pollution.

So far in the book we've basically ignored the government and any affect that its actions may have on firms. In reality, however, governments affect many aspects of the firm's behavior. In some industries, like agriculture, governments may control output prices. Many countries have minimum wage laws that control the price of labor. There are regulations about minimum quality standards that products have to meet, particularly in the food industry and air transportation. And almost all industries are subject to environmental regulations and labor laws. At an even more abstract level, governments potentially influence every business decision made in the economy through corporate income taxes, sales taxes, and taxes on property.

The relationship between government and business is by no means one-way either. To be sure, governments try to influence the behavior of firms through regulations and

other policy. But firms also try to influence the government. Firms lobby to have existing laws changed and new laws instated. Firms rely on governments to police various markets and protect them from unfair business practices. At an even wider scope, some firms may lobby for protection from foreign competition, as we will see in Chapter 12.

We can't possibly examine all these aspects of business–government relations in this chapter, so we'll concentrate on a few important elements. The first thing to look at is the classic rationale for government intervention in the market place.

11.1 The basic rationale for regulation

In order to understand how to react to regulation, managers have to understand the rationale for regulation in the first place. The argument in favor of regulation is most clear-cut in the case of a monopoly firm. Basically, the argument goes as follows. Because a monopoly firm has, by definition, no competitors, it will restrict output in order to get a high price from consumers. As a result, some consumers are priced out of the market. Moreover, consumers who do remain are forced to pay a higher price than they would if the industry were more competitive. Of course, the monopoly firm gains because the lack of competition results in higher profits. But the higher profits to the monopoly are more than offset by the losses suffered by consumers, resulting in a net loss to society as a whole. To restore the loss to society, the argument goes, the government must step in to promote competition or, if that isn't possible, to control the price of the monopoly firm.

To see the argument more precisely, consider Figure 11.1. The diagram shows the demand curve D and the supply curve S for a perfectly competitive industry. The supply curve is labeled MC because, in a competitive market, supply is the sum of all the individual firms' marginal cost curves. Market equilibrium occurs at the price p^C and output level q^C. Now suppose that all the competitive firms join together to form a single large monopoly firm. The monopoly maximizes profit at the intersection of the marginal revenue curve MR and the marginal cost curve MC. The resulting equilibrium output q^M is sold at the price p^M. Relative to perfect competition, therefore, price rises from p^C to p^M and output falls from q^C to q^M.

Consumers are willing to pay p^M to purchase the marginal unit at q^M. Put another way, if consumers are willing to pay p^M for the marginal unit at q^M, then p^M is a dollar measure of the marginal benefit to consumers at q^M. Provided that the buyer is the only one who benefits from the good, the price measures the marginal benefit to society from the good. Usually the buyer is the only one who benefits. When someone buys a steak, for example, the benefit to society is the benefit received by the individual because no one else receives a benefit. But this isn't always the case. For example, someone

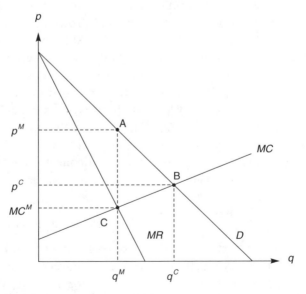

Figure 11.1 The deadweight loss due to monopoly

hiring a gardener receives a benefit but their neighbors also receive a benefit from having more pleasant surroundings. We ignore this complication for now and assume that the marginal benefit to the individual equals the marginal benefit to society.

The marginal cost of producing q^M units is given by MC^M. As long as all the costs of production are borne by the firm, MC measures the marginal cost to society of producing the good. In many cases, the firm's costs reflect society's costs. The cost of making beer, for example, are the costs of water, barley, and hops and so on, as well as the costs of plant, equipment, and labor. But again there are exceptions. The cost to society of nickel smelting may not only include the costs to firms but also the cost to people living downwind who suffer the consequences of acid rain. We'll return to this issue later in the chapter when we look at environmental regulation. For now, we'll assume that the marginal cost to the firm equals the marginal cost to society.

Returning to Figure 11.1, p^M is greater than MC^M at the monopoly output level q^M. The marginal benefit to society, therefore, is greater than the marginal cost to society. This means that if the monopoly were to increase output, the net benefit to society would increase. The marginal cost to society from increasing output would be more than offset by the larger marginal benefit to society. However, even though it is in the interest of society to increase output from q^M, it is not in the interest of the monopoly. At output levels above q^M, the marginal revenue to the monopoly is less than the marginal cost, so the profit of the monopoly would fall if output were increased.[1] Thus, the monopoly will keep output at q^M.

The marginal benefit to society, given by D, is greater than the marginal cost to society, given by the MC, at all the levels of output between q^M and q^C. This means that there is a potential net benefit to society from every output level between q^M and q^C. Because the monopoly won't produce any level of output other than q^M, these net benefits will never be realized. Adding up all the net benefits between q^M and q^C amounts to determining the area of the triangle ABC. This area is a measure of the potential benefits to society from increasing output from the monopoly to the competitive level. Because the benefits are never realized, they can also be interpreted as a cost of the monopoly. This cost, represented by the area ABC, is referred to as the *deadweight loss* from monopoly.

In a nutshell, deadweight loss is a rationale for regulating monopoly firms. At the competitive output level q^C, price equals marginal cost. Consequently, the marginal benefit to society equals the marginal cost to society at q^C. Increasing output beyond q^C would add more to society's marginal cost than to society's marginal benefits, implying a negative net benefit to society. The output level q^C, therefore, maximizes the net benefit to society from the production of a good. The monopoly will not voluntarily produce q^C, because it doesn't maximize profit. Regulation is a way to force the monopoly to produce the output level q^C.

Deadweight loss is not the only problem with a monopoly. *Inefficient management* is also a potential problem. Firms facing competition have an incentive to keep costs as low as possible in order to stay in business. Monopoly firms don't face any competition. Monopolies also make large profits, so there is less incentive to control costs than there is by a firm operating on slimmer margins. As a result, monopolies may waste resources. In the United Kingdom, Railtrack owns and operates all of the country's railway infrastructure – the tracks, signals, tunnels, bridges, viaducts, level crossings, and stations. Even if Railtrack's management claimed its costs were as low as possible, there is almost no way this could be independently verified. Since there are no rival firms that provide railway infrastructure, shareholders have no way to gauge Railtracks' costs. The lack of competition imposes less incentive on Railtracks' managers to control costs tightly. Inflated costs that arise because of monopoly can be added to the deadweight loss as another cost to society from monopoly.

Another potential problem with monopoly is the lack of incentive to invest in *research and development*. Competition encourages firms to develop new products and improve the quality of existing products in order to keep ahead of their rivals. Monopoly firms have no such incentive. Critics of the North American automobile industry argue that a lack of competition after the World War II made domestic manufacturers complacent. When consumers turned to smaller, more fuel-efficient cars, North American firms quickly lost market share to Japanese and European imports. The race for North American producers to catch-up to the quality and technological sophistication of imported cars drove one manufacturer (American Motors) out of business and another (Chrysler) to the verge of bankruptcy.

Lastly, monopoly firms may engage in wasteful *rent seeking* behavior. Owing to the potential for huge profits, firms may devote a great deal of effort toward getting and keeping monopoly power. Because monopoly "profits" are also called monopoly "rents," this sort of behavior is known as rent-seeking. Rent-seeking behavior may take the form of lobbying the government for protection from competition or deterring the entry of potential competitors. Whatever their form, these actions represent a cost to society because they use up scarce resources. The costs of rent seeking are potentially very large indeed. A firm would be willing to spend an amount almost equal to the extra profit derived from monopoly in order to secure a monopoly position. The larger the extra profits at stake, the more the firm would be willing to expend on rent seeking.

Lobbying to Maintain a Monopoly

Digital satellite television was introduced in the United States in 1990 by PrimeStar and followed by DirecTV in 1994. Because the services use a digital signal, as opposed to the analog signal used by cable services, they are able to supply hundreds of channels of television and radio with high-resolution pictures and CD-like sound. After purchasing or leasing a relatively inexpensive pizza-sized satellite dish and decoder, subscribers pay a monthly fee on par with the rates for cable television. The new services were extremely popular, signing millions of new customers in the first year of operation.

In 1994, DirecTV applied to the Canadian Radio and Telecommunications Commission (the government agency that oversees regulation of the television industry in Canada) for a license to offer their service. At the same time, a new Canadian company called ExpressVu aimed to set-up a similar service. ExpressVu argued that DirecTV should be kept out of the Canadian market on the grounds that it could not compete with the larger US firm and that it was important to have a domestic supplier in a "culturally sensitive" industry such as television.

Clearly, ExpressVu's profits would be much higher if DirecTV were prevented from getting a license to operate in Canada. Had ExpressVu been able to get its way they would have been the only firm supplying satellite television in Canada. Thus, although couched in terms of cultural nationalism, ExpressVu's lobbying was also consistent with rent-seeking.

After intense lobbying of the federal government by both sides, the CRTC came up with a compromise that gave ExpressVu a head start: DirecTV was to be granted a license that would come into effect one year after the Canadian service went on the air. As it turned out, technical difficulties with ExpressVu's transmission hardware led to lengthy delays in the start-up of the service. At the end of 1996, DirecTV got fed up with waiting for ExpressVu to start and withdrew their license application. ExpressVu finally went on air in September 1997, but surprisingly not as a monopoly. The delays in the start-up of ExpressVu allowed a rival Canadian company, Star Choice, to start up a competing service within months of ExpressVu. As it turned out, all the lobbying by ExpressVu was a waste of time. All the resources used up by ExpressVu's lobbying – the time of lawyers, experts, government officials, and legislators – went for nothing.

11.2 Regulation of monopolies

Deadweight loss, inefficient management, lack of research and development, and rent-seeking are all costs of monopoly. As such, they provide the rationale for government intervention in the form of regulation. Nonetheless, some economists oppose regulation on several grounds.

For one thing, the deadweight losses are small if demand is inelastic. In fact, if demand is perfectly inelastic, there is no deadweight loss from monopoly at all. Even if the deadweight loss is very small, the gain from eliminating it may not cover the administrative cost of the regulation. In this case, society would actually be worse off imposing regulations rather than leaving the monopoly alone. An American economist, Arnold Harberger, estimated that the deadweight loss in industries even with very limited competition amounted to no more than three percent of the value of output.

The *theory of second-best* provides another argument against regulation. The discussion in the previous section looked at the effect of monopoly in a single market. But the economy is made up of many markets. And the markets are inter-related: what goes on in one market has an impact in what goes on in another market. Looking at one market in isolation is incomplete, therefore, because it ignores the potential links between markets. The theory of second best states that, while it may be true that eliminating monopoly in one market removes the deadweight loss *in that market*, it is not necessarily true that society is better off overall. The links between the monopoly market and other markets may be such that deadweight losses elsewhere actually go up when the monopoly is eliminated. One implication of the theory for public policy is that reforming one market at a time is not guaranteed to increase the well-being of society. Having said that, public policy tends to proceed in exactly this fashion: one industry is tackled at a time.

Another argument against regulation claims that, far from discouraging competition, monopolies actually provide the impetus needed for competition. The idea is that the large profits earned by monopolies provide the incentive to firms to provide competing products. According to this view the very existence of monopoly profits provides the spur to

competition. Therefore, eliminating monopoly profits by regulation will reduce competitive forces in the economy. For example,
when 3M introduced Post-It notes in the
early 1980s the product was so profitable it
spawned a host of imitators that eventually
forced the price of the product down. Had the
monopoly profits available to 3M when the
product was first invented been taken away,
then arguably the competing products would
not have been produced, consumers would
have had less choice, and the price remained
high. A related argument that applies to
inventions is examined later in Section 11.4
on intellectual property rights.

The above arguments are against the regulation of monopoly. On the other side of the
same coin are regulations to promote competition. These are the subject of the section
below on competition policy (or anti-trust
policy as it is known in the United States).
In the next section we look at a kind of
market structure, known as a *natural monopoly*, where it doesn't make any sense to
promote competition.

11.2.1 Natural monopoly

A *natural monopoly* arises when the costs of
production are lower if there is only one firm
in the industry. Figure 11.2 illustrates an
average cost curve for an industry that is
likely to be a natural monopoly. Suppose
that output in the industry is q_1. If there is
only one firm in the industry, the average
cost of producing q_1 is AC_1. If there are two
firms in the industry each producing the same
level of output, output per firm falls to $q_1/2$
and the average cost at each firm rises to
AC_2. Because average cost is declining over
the entire range of output, dividing industry
output among even more firms will only

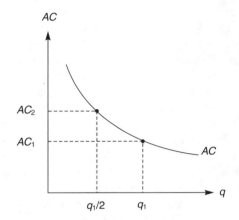

Figure 11.2 A natural monopoly

increase average cost per firm further. Therefore, when the average cost of production
continues to fall when output increases, the
industry is a natural monopoly.

The question is: under what circumstances
does the average cost of production continue
to fall when output increases? Industries
where the fixed costs make up a very large proportion of total cost are likely to have con-
tinuously falling average costs. For example,
the distribution of natural gas requires a very
expensive network of underground pipelines
to bring the gas from remote or offshore
areas where it is produced to consumers in
towns and cities that may be thousands of
kilometres away. Once in place, however, the
system is relatively inexpensive to run,
requiring little more than monitoring and
maintenance. Natural gas distribution is,
therefore, characterized by very high fixed
costs to establish the distribution network
and relatively low variable costs to keep the
system running. As more consumers are
added to the network, the fixed cost of the
system can be spread over more people and
the cost per household, i.e. the average cost,
decreases. Thus, natural gas distribution is a
classic case of a natural monopoly. Another

example of an extensive network that is very expensive to build yet relatively low cost to operate is a railway network. Thus, railtrack in the United Kingdom, mentioned earlier in the chapter is another good example of a natural monopoly.

Natural monopolies raise an interesting problem for public policy. As with any monopoly, an unregulated natural monopoly will charge a price to the consumer that exceeds marginal cost, resulting in a dead-weight loss to society. One option, therefore, is to encourage competition by breaking up the monopoly into smaller firms. However, as we saw in Figure 11.2, the very nature of costs in the natural monopoly implies that the breakup will lead to an increase in average costs. The smaller firms will be unable to reap the cost benefits of large scale production. Hence, public policy toward natural monopoly must weigh the benefits of increased competition against the increased average cost of production.

In the past, policy in many countries has favored preserving the natural monopoly in order to keep average costs down. At the same time, the prices charged by the natural monopoly are regulated in an attempt to reduce the deadweight loss. Another way of controlling monopolies is public ownership. The next section discusses the issues that arise in price regulation of privately owned monopolies. The following section discusses the issues that arise when the monopoly is publicly owned.

11.2.2 Price regulation

As we have seen, a natural monopoly that is allowed to set its own price will not set price equal to marginal cost. The divergence between price and marginal cost results in a deadweight loss. A straightforward way for

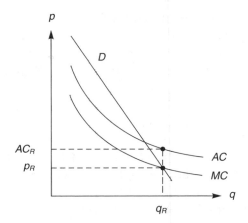

Figure 11.3 Regulated price equal to marginal cost

regulation to eliminate the deadweight loss, therefore, is to require that the monopoly set a price equal to marginal cost. This is shown in Figure 11.3. The deadweight loss is eliminated where the marginal cost curve MC intersects the demand curve D. A regulated price of p_R, therefore, achieves the desired result.

There is a major problem with the regulated price of p_R, however. The price p_R results in output of q_R. The average cost of producing q_R is AC_R. Because AC_R is greater than p_R, the regulated firm is making a net loss of $(AC_R - p_R)$ on every unit produced. Multiplying this per unit loss by the total amount of output gives a total loss to the firm. Clearly, in the long run, the losses of $(AC_R - p_R) \times q_R$ will cause the firm to exit the industry.

The fact that price equal to marginal cost results in a loss to the firm is no accident. Because the industry is a natural monopoly, a regulated price equal to marginal cost will *always* result in losses to the firm. The definition of natural monopoly is that average cost is declining over the entire range of output. But if average cost is declining, marginal cost must lie below average cost. Hence, any price equal to marginal cost will be less than aver-age cost and mean a per unit loss to the firm. The very fact that the firm is a natural mono-poly, therefore, means that a regulated price equal to marginal cost results in a loss to the firm.

Since any output is better than no output at all, the regulator has to think of ways to keep the firm in the industry. There are two options: subsidize the firm's losses, or come up with a pricing rule that avoids losses to the firm. Government subsidies have to be raised through tax revenue. But taxation imposes economic problems of its own. As well, the managers of the firm have an incent-ive to claim that costs are higher than they really are in order to get a larger subsidy from the government. In fact, privately owned monopolies are rarely subsidized by governments. Public monopolies are often subsidized, however, as we shall see below.

An alternative pricing rule that avoids losses to the firm sets the price equal to aver-age cost, as shown in Figure 11.4. Because $p_R = AC_R$, the firm makes zero profit on every unit produced and a total profit of zero. This means that the firm is earning a

rate of return on its capital that is equal to the rate of return it could earn in another industry. As a result, the firm has no incent-ive to leave the industry even in the long run. Of course, setting price equal to average cost results in a deadweight loss, because price is not equal to marginal cost. But an average cost price results in a higher level of output than an unregulated monopoly would pro-duce. A price equal to average cost can be thought of as a way of getting the highest level of output from the firm while allowing the firm to earn a competitive rate of return on its capital at the same time.

In practice, setting a price equal to average cost is not quite as straightforward as deter-mining where the average cost curve inter-sects the demand curve. Regulators may have a rough idea of what the firm's average cost curve looks like, but they are unlikely to have as much information about the average cost curve as the firm. One option, of course, is for the regulators to ask the firm to dis-close cost information so that the average cost, and hence the price, can be computed. But if the firm's managers know that the regulators will base their price on informa-tion supplied by the firm, the managers have an incentive to misrepresent the firm's costs in order to obtain a higher regulated price. For example, if the managers are able to convince regulators that the firm's average cost curve is given by AC', shown in Figure 11.5, regulators will set a price of p'_R. In this case, the regulators unwittingly set a price equal to the profit-maximizing price of the monopoly.

Regulatory bodies that set prices are well aware of the firm's incentive to misreport costs. As a result, in practice, the firm's financial statements are subject to audit by the regulatory authority. This process is fairly time-consuming and costly, but there

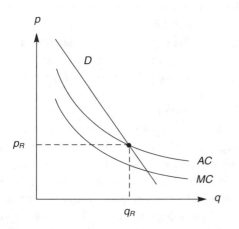

Figure 11.4 Regulated price equal to average cost

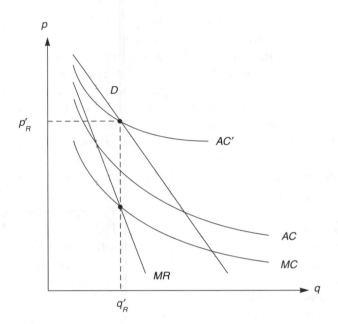

Figure 11.5 The incentive to misreport costs

is a more serious problem with regulation than the administration costs.

Suppose a regulated firm finds, through research and development, a lower cost way to produce its output. In terms of Figure 11.4, the innovation shifts the average cost curve downward. At the next round of price-setting by the regulatory agency, the effect of the reduction in average cost is a reduction in the price the monopoly is allowed to charge. In other words, the firm gets no benefit, or at least only a short-lived benefit between the innovation and the next round of price-setting, from its research and development. The average cost pricing rule, therefore, may actually discourage firms from undertaking research into more efficient production methods.

11.2.3 Public ownership

Another tactic the government may pursue to control a natural monopoly is to take own- ership out of the private sector altogether. This has been used more often in Europe, Canada, and Australia than the United States, but there are examples of publicly owned monopolies in the United States, such as the postal service and most community water utilities. In fact, the postal service and water utilities are publicly owned monopolies in most countries, including most EU countries, Canada, and Australia.[2] Typically, state or publicly owned enterprises are subject to the same kind of pricing regulations that govern private monopolies. Public ownership raises additional problems, however.

For one thing, managers at public corpor- ations may not face the same incentive to control costs that a manager at a private firm faces. This is particularly true if the managers at a state-owned corporation know that the government will subsidize any losses incurred by the corporation. To cover high costs, many national postal services have been recipients of large subsidies from the governments that own them. Shareholders in a private corporation would be very reluctant to put up with losses of such sizes. The view that public funds are unlimited may also lead to inefficient management decisions.

Another concern is that public corporations maybe subject to political pressures. In this case, decisions may be made on the basis of political expediency rather than economic fundamentals. Politicians don't like jobs to be lost in their constituencies, so a state-owned corporation trying to layoff workers in a drive for efficiency may be prevented from so doing. There may also be political pressure to maintain money-losing services to remote communities and make up the losses from more profitable services. This practice, referred to as *cross-subsidization*, is common in postal services. US Mail, for example, charges the same to deliver a letter to an isolated community in Alaska as it does to a major urban area: mail service to out-of-the-way places is subsidized by larger communities.

There has been a recent worldwide trend of selling state-owned companies to private interests, a policy referred to as *privatization*. In the United Kingdom, for example, the state-owned rail and bus services were sold to private corporations, as well as the water utilities. In the United States, Amtrack, which operates passenger rail service, has been partially privatized. In Canada, the state-owned oil company, Petro-Canada, and the main airline, Air Canada, have been sold to private owners. To be fair, privatization isn't all about economic efficiency. Selling of companies is also a way for heavily indebted governments to raise much needed funds.

11.3 Regulation of oligopolies

Recall from Figure 11.1 that deadweight loss arises because output price is not equal to marginal cost. Any firm facing a downward sloping demand curve will set a price that is not equal to marginal cost. Deadweight losses, therefore, arise in many different market structures and not just in a monopoly market. Put another way, firms with even a limited amount of market power keep output below the competitive level of output and, hence, give rise to deadweight losses. For this reason, regulations are applied not only to natural monopolies but also to any industry where firms have significant market power. The basic aim of the regulations is to promote competition. For this reason, the regulations are sometimes referred to collectively as *competition policy*.

11.3.1 Measures of industry concentration

To get an idea of the level of competition in industry, we look at two measures of market concentration. The *concentration ratio* in a particular industry is measured by the proportion of total sales (or revenue) in the industry that is accounted for by the largest firms. Concentration ratios are typically computed for the largest four and the largest eight firms. For example, let r_1 be the revenue of the largest firm, r_2 be the revenue of the second-largest firm, r_3 be the revenue of the third-largest firm, and so on, in an industry of n firms. Then the four-firm concentration ratio is defined as:

$$c_4 = \frac{r_1 + r_2 + r_3 + r_4}{\sum_{i=1}^{n} r_i}$$

In other words, the four-firm concentration ratio is just the combined market share of the largest four firms in an industry.

Table 11.1 shows c_4 for selected US manufacturing industries. By this measure, the degree of competition varies a lot across industries. For example, the household laundry equipment industry (i.e. washing machine and dryer manufacturing) and the battery industry both have concentration ratios of over 90 percent. In these two industries, the largest four firms account for over 90 percent of all the sales in the industry. At the other end of the scale, the ready-mix concrete and retail bakery industries are much more competitive – the largest four firms account for less than 10 percent of total sales in these industries.

Another measure of market concentration is the *Herfindahl–Hirschman index* (HHI). It is calculated by squaring the market share (measured as a percentage) of each firm in the industry and summing the resulting numbers. For example, in an industry consisting of three firms with market shares of 20, 30, and 50 percent, the HHI is 3,800 ($20^2 + 30^2 + 50^2 = 3,800$). The HHI takes into account both the relative size and the distribution of firms in the industry. It approaches zero in an industry with a large number of firms of roughly equal size. It increases as the number of firms in the industry decreases and as the disparity in size between the firms rises.[3] Table 11.1 also shows the HHI for selected US manufacturing industries. It should be apparent from Table 11.1 that the four-firm concentration

Table 11.1 Four-firm concentration ratios and Herfindahl–Hirschman indexes for various US industries, 1997

Industry	Number of firms	Concentration ratio (4 firms)	Herfindahl–Hirschman index
Household laundry equipment	10	90.4	2,870.3
Batteries	35	90.1	2,882.9
Breakfast cereal	48	82.9	2,445.9
Automobiles	173	79.5	2,349.7
Chocolate and confectionery from cacao beans	152	79.5	2,567.1
Tires	110	72.4	1,690.3
Men's and boys' trousers, slacks, and jeans	199	68.9	2,253.8
Distilleries	44	59.8	1,075.7
Coffee and tea	215	52.5	1,028.3
Semiconductors and related devices	993	52.5	1,080.1
Luggage	270	51.9	1,418.6
Bottled water	109	51.7	986.6
Soft drinks	388	47.2	800.4
Electronic computers	531	45.4	727.9
Wineries	637	43.2	837.5
Games, toys, and children's vehicles	756	42.7	564.0
Roasted nuts and peanut butter	128	37.5	551.1
Audio and video equipment	521	29.8	414.7
Petroleum refineries	122	28.5	422.1
Sporting and athletic goods	2,477	21.4	161.1
Fluid milk	402	21.3	204.6
Women's and girls' dresses	747	14.2	111.3
Jewelry (except costume)	2,278	12.5	81.4
Ready-mix concrete	2,888	7.0	29.4
Retail bakeries	6,906	2.5	3.7

ratio and the HHI give roughly similar signals about the degree of competition in an industry. By and large, industries with high four-firm concentration ratios also have high HHI values. However, there are some differences between the two measures. For example, distilleries have a higher concentration ratio than the luggage industry, but the HHI for luggage is greater than the HHI for distilleries. How can they be different? Well, for one thing, the HHI uses the market shares of *all* the firms in the industry, whereas the concentration ratio uses the market shares of only the *largest four* firms in the industry. Also, the HHI is based on the squared market share values; the concentration ratio just uses the market shares values directly. Thus, relative to the concentration ratio, the HHI places a greater weight on firms with larger market shares.

The concentration ratio or the HHI may be used as rough guides to the level of competition in an industry. But in some instances they can be misleading measures of the degree of competition. One thing to remember is that concentration ratios or Herfindahl–Hirschman indexes are typically computed at the national level, which may hide significant market power at a local level. For example, while the concentration ratio in fluid milk is very low, specific regions of the country may have much higher concentration ratios. Some communities may have only two or three producers of milk. So, although the industry appears competitive at the national level, individual firms may have substantial market power in specific regions.

A second problem with the numbers in Table 11.1, is that they are based only on figures for domestic production in the United States. That is, the numbers exclude imports into the United States from other countries.

Take the automobile industry, for example. The concentration ratio indicates that the top four American firms account for 79.5 percent of the automobile industry. But this figure completely ignores sales in the United States of cars imported from Japan, Europe, Korea, and so on. Taking into account sales of cars manufactured outside the United States by Toyota, Honda, BMW, Hyundai, and so on, would significantly lower the four-firm concentration ratio for automobiles reported in Table 11.1

11.3.2 Competition policy

Broadly speaking, competition policy, or anti-trust policy, refers collectively to the set of regulations governments use to promote competitive behavior in markets. When the United States passed the *Sherman Antitrust Act* in 1890, it was unique in the world. Now more than 80 countries have some form of anti-trust legislation enacted as well as national agencies to ensure that the laws are enforced. It is obviously not practicable to discuss separately the competition policy in each country. Instead, we'll focus on the similarities in national competition laws and illustrate the application of the laws with cases drawn from several different countries. Competition policy focuses on three areas that affect the level of competition in a market: *mergers and acquisitions*, *restrictive trade practices*, and *collusion*. We discuss each of these in turn.

Mergers and acquisitions

Roughly speaking, mergers and acquisitions fit into one of three categories. A *horizontal merger* involves two firms competing in the same industry. A *vertical merger* involves a firm and its supplier. A *conglomerate merger* involves two firms in unrelated activities. By definition, horizontal mergers necessarily reduce competition in an industry. The effect that vertical or conglomerate mergers have on competition depends by and large on their specific circumstances. Mergers and acquisitions are scrutinized by the Merger Task Force (MTF) in the European Union, the Department of Justice (DOJ) and the Federal Trade Commission (FTC) in the United States, and the Office of Fair Trading in the United Kingdom. It is the job of these agencies to determine whether mergers are detrimental to the public interest. How can they determine whether a merger is in the public interest? One way is to see how the merger will effect the level of competition in an industry.

Consider the approach taken by the DOJ in the United States. The DOJ classifies industries in which the HHI is less than 1,000 as *unconcentrated*; those with an HHI between 1,000 and 1,800 as *moderately concentrated*; those with an HHI over 1,800 are considered to be *concentrated*. According to DOJ guidelines, a horizontal merger may be challenged if it increases the HHI by more than 100 points in an industry classified as concentrated.[4] This is not to say that all mergers in concentrated industries that raise the HHI by 100 points or more will be challenged. The DOJ uses several additional criteria to evaluate a merger such as the extent of foreign competition, the possible emergence of a new technology, whether one of the firms would go out of business without the merger, and the extent of efficiency gains that may result from the merger. In this way, a merger may be approved even if it reduces competition in the industry either because, say, there is sufficient competition from firms based outside the United States, or because

the efficiency gains from the merger can be passed along to consumers.

In July 2001, following a recommendation from the MTF, the European Commission blocked the proposed $42 billion (€46 billion) merger between General Electric (GE) and Honeywell. The decision was based on the dominant position that GE held in the market for jet engines before the merger was announced, and the fact that the merger would further increase the market power of GE in aircraft manufacturing. Interestingly, much of the information used by the MTF to justify blocking the deal was supplied by two American firms – United Technologies and Rockwell Collins – that are competitors to GE.[5]

Restrictive trade practices

Several kinds of marketing strategies followed by firms are illegal because they are viewed by regulatory agencies as indirect ways of increasing market power. Such marketing strategies are collectively referred to as restrictive trade practices. For example, it is illegal for firms to prevent price competition among retailers selling their product, a practice known as *resale price maintenance*. While suggesting a list price is acceptable, it is not legal for firms to force distributors to charge a specific price, nor is it legal for firms to refuse to supply retailers who sell for less than the suggested price.

In the United Kingdom, for example, makers of over-the-counter remedies are no longer allowed (since May 15, 2001) to set minimum retail prices for their products. To see the implication of outlawing resale price maintenance, consider the price of 200 mg Ibuprofen pills in the United Kingdom before the practice was declared illegal and the prices for equivalent products in the United States

Table 11.2   Cost of 200 mg ibuprofen pills

Store	Brand	Price (£)
Superdrug.com (UK)	Nurofen	9.45 for 96
CVS.com (US)	Advil	5.94 for 100
Drugstore.com (US)	Advil	5.94 for 100
Longs.com (US)	Advil	5.24 for 100
Pharmacy.ca (Canada)	Advil	3.63 for 100

and Canada, where the practice has been illegal for much longer. As Table 11.2 shows, resale price maintenance resulted in prices that were almost 60 percent higher in the United Kingdom. In fact, after the practice was declared illegal, supermarkets in the United Kingdom announced price reductions of up to 50 percent on many popular medicines.[6]

The practice of *tied selling* or *bundling* is another restrictive trade practice that may be against the law. Bundling occurs when two or more products are packaged together and sold for a single price. In 1998, Microsoft was accused by the DOJ (and 20 states) of attempting to increase its monopoly position in operating systems by bundling its browser Internet Explorer with Windows. Nonetheless, bundling is common practice – a car company may offer a financing package with the purchase of a new car, for example, or a hotel may include breakfast with the purchase of a room. In these examples, bundling may be good for the consumer: by saving time in negotiating the purchase of a car, or by guaranteeing the quality of a meal in an unfamiliar location. In such cases, regulating authorities would be unlikely to prosecute the car company or the hotel. This serves to highlight again that regulations governing firms are not necessarily clear-cut. This can be a major headache for managers, who may be wise to consult lawyers and economists

before they embrace a new marketing strategy.

Selling below cost in order to drive weaker competitors out of business, or *predatory pricing,* is also prohibited by law in most countries. Major airlines are often accused of predatory pricing. Faced with a low-cost airline entering a route, an established airline can increase the number of planes on the route and discount fares substantially. When the new firm is eventually driven out of business, the established airline withdraws the excess planes from the route and raises fares back to their original levels. In fact, the DOJ sued American Airlines in May 1999 for doing just this to force a rival, Vanguard Airlines, from routes to and from the Dallas-Fort Worth International Airport (DFW). For example, American's high fares on the Wichita–DFW route attracted Vanguard Airlines, which offered much lower fares and soon picked up about 25 percent of the passengers on the route. American responded by increasing the number of its flights between DFW and Wichita and offering fares to match Vanguard. After less than a year, Vanguard was forced to withdraw from the DFW–Wichita route and American immediately raised fares by more than 50 percent. In its defense, American Airlines says its behavior reflects a standard competitive response to a rival firm. The issue is whether this claim is true or whether American operated at a loss for the purpose of driving Vanguard out of business.

Price discrimination (see Chapter 4), whereby firms charge different prices for the same product, is also illegal unless the price differences result from different costs of serving the consumers, or consumers buy different qualities or quantities of the good. Price discrimination is often used by firms together with bundling, since different bundles of goods at different prices may appeal to different groups of customers. Lastly, *misleading advertising* is another form of restrictive trade practice that is prohibited in most countries.

Collusion

Some forms of collusion between firms are deemed socially beneficial – like product standards, research and development, and limits on promotion and advertising. But collusion between firms to raise prices or to restrict output to raise prices, often referred to as *price fixing*, is strictly illegal in many countries. Firms found guilty of collusion can be fined and, in some countries, their managers can be imprisoned. However, price collusion can be very difficult to prove simply because equal prices alone are not sufficient evidence of collusion. For instance, all the firms in an industry with a dominant large firm will tend to charge the same price, even if there is no conspiracy between the firms to set the same price. Recall that firms in a perfectly competitive industry will all charge the same price. But this is the result of the equilibrium forces of competitive behavior, not collusive behavior. Thus, while illegal, cases of collusion may be difficult to prosecute in practice.

11.4 Intellectual property regulation

All of the legislation we have discussed so far in this chapter is either designed to regulate a monopoly or discourage monopoly through promoting competition. Thus, the basic effect of the legislation is to reduce monopoly power. In the case of *patents*, however, government regulation deliberately creates monopolies. Why is this?

Inventions and innovations bring enormous benefit to our lives. The telephone, automobile, fax machine, jet engine, and countless prescription drugs are just a few of the modern innovations that have improved the quality of life over the last century. The research and development costs behind these products are very large and the payoffs are very risky. Nowhere is this more evident than in the case of prescription medicines. Original research into the causes of diseases involves sophisticated and expensive laboratories and highly-trained medical personnel. There is no guarantee that any particular line of research will result in a useful discovery. Even when a new medicine is discovered, bringing the product to market is a long and costly process. Clinical trials to test that the medicine is effective and safe may take years before it is approved for use. Lastly, after approval, the product must be marketed to patients through their doctors. All the time this has been going on, of course, a rival firm may have been developing a similar drug.

The point is, the research and development of products that are very beneficial to society is also very costly to individual firms. Also, there is no guarantee when the research is started that the exercise will be profitable, and even if it does turn out to make money, the profit is years down the road. Firms may, therefore, be reluctant to engage in this kind of research. More importantly, once the discovery has been made and the drug successfully brought to market as a cure for a particular ailment, it is easy for rival firms to make copies of the medicine. If this happens, of course, the developing firm's profit will be significantly reduced. But this reduces the firm's incentive to undertake research in the first place. Unless there is some way to guarantee the firm a decent level of profit once the drug is approved for use, few new medicines would ever be developed.

This is where patent law comes in, of course. In 1994, countries forming the WTO also agreed to standardize their patent laws under an agreement called Trade Related aspects of International Property (TRIPS).[7] Under TRIPS, a patent holder has the exclusive right to produce and sell an invention or innovation for 20 years. During this period, competitors in any WTO-member country are prohibited from producing a similar product or using the invention in a product of their own without the permission of the patent holder. Patent holders always have the option of allowing other firms to produce the patented product, through a *license* agreement, which usually involves a royalty payment to the holder. For example, Philips NV of the Netherlands has the patent to compact-disc technology and licenses many other manufacturers of stereo equipment to use the technology. Similarly, the Dolby noise-reduction system for audio cassettes is licensed from the Dolby laboratories to tape-deck manufacturers.

The patent system effectively gives the inventor a monopoly for 20 years. The idea is to stimulate research and development and ultimately new products which benefit society that would be too costly for firms to develop without monopoly rights. Therefore, patent law attempts to achieve a compromise between society's benefit from innovations on the one hand and the deadweight loss of monopoly on the other. The argument really boils down to short-run cost for long-term gain. Granting monopoly rights to inventors for a limited time period results in a deadweight loss to society of the sort described in Section 11.1. But this loss is offset by new inventions and innovations which benefit society in the long run that otherwise would not be produced. Like many aspects of legislation, the patent law attempts to achieve a balance between competing ends. Having said that, whether 20 years is too long, or

too short, a period for the granting of monopoly rights is debatable.

There are other issues that arise in patent law besides the length of patent protection. The *breadth* of a patent refers to how broadly defined the invention or innovation is. Obviously, the inventor would like a very broadly defined patent because it would exclude more rival products and increase the inventor's profit. There is also the question of what qualifies as patentable. While the laws governing patents are international, there is no international patent-granting agency. Instead, patents are granted by patent offices in individual countries. In the United States, for example, patents are granted by the Patent and Trademark Office which has a staff of more than 3,000 scientists, engineers, and legal experts to examine claims. Patents are granted if the invention satisfies three conditions: (i) it must be novel; (ii) it must have an industrial application; and (iii) it must be something that wouldn't be obvious to someone working in the field. Ideas are not patentable, whereas inventions generally are. The just-in-time production method developed by Toyota, therefore, was not patentable and has been copied by many firms. Marketing ideas are not patentable either. Ray Kroc, the founder of McDonald's, was able to patent the chain's way of making french fries but he was not able to patent his franchising idea for selling hamburgers.

11.5 Environmental regulation

In the last 20 years or so, concerns about the quality of the environment have moved increasingly to the forefront of public policy. Some environmental problems, like emissions from private automobiles, result from the behavior of individuals, and others result

What is a Patent Worth?

Since it was launched in by Eli Lilly & Co. 1988, Prozac has been one of the biggest-selling drugs in history. More than 38 million patients in over 100 countries have taken the anti-depressant, generating Lilly $21 billion (€23 billion) in total sales. In 2000 alone, sales of Prozac were $2.7 billion. All that came to an end on August 2, 2001, when following a long legal battle with generic drug manufacturer Barr Laboratories Inc., a US Court of Appeals deemed Lilly's patent protection on Prozac would expire.

Lilly was originally granted four patents to protect Prozac, the last of which was to expire in 2003. Barr Laboratories mounted a legal challenge on the grounds that two of Lilly's four patents essentially covered the same claim. The court decided in favor of Barr and in the process cut two years from Lilly's monopoly on Prozac. Barr's reward was a six-month window during which only it (along with Lilly) was allowed to sell 20 mg capsules of fluoxetine, the active ingredient in Prozac. Barr's manufacturing facility worked ten hours a day, six days a week, in the period leading up to the patent expiry date to make 150 million capsules of fluoxetine ready for the market.

As a result of the court's decision, analysts predicted that Barr's sales would increase from $600 million to $1 billion. Earnings per share were predicted to rise from $1.66 for the 2000 fiscal year to $3.84 for 2001, representing an increase in profit of $77 million, easily covering the $12 million in legal fees it cost Barr to mount the patent challenge. Moreover, on the day the court decision was announced, the share market wiped an incredible $38 billion from the value of Lilly. Can a two-year patent really be worth that much? Part of the $38 billion obviously reflected the lost profits to Lilly from the end of the Prozac monopoly. Pharmaceutical companies also use their profits to finance research and development of new drugs which will produce profits in the future. Investors thought that the decline in research and development spending at Lilly resulting from the loss of monopoly profits on Prozac would reduce the number of profitable drugs Lilly would bring to market in the future. Lastly, investors may also have interpreted the court's decision as evidence of weakness in the other patents that Lilly owned, also hurting future profitability at the company.

Sources: "Barr Labs Ships Version of Prozac." *Associated Press*, August 2, 2001. "A Bitter Pill." *Fortune*, August 13, 2001.

from the actions of firms. While regulations to control the polluting activities of private households are important, we focus here on firms that are polluting. Having said that, the economic analysis and the policy recommendations that come from the analysis are similar regardless of the source of the pollution.

To illustrate the basic issues, let's consider a straightforward example. Suppose there is a nickel-smelting industry producing sulfur dioxide as a by-product of its operations. The sulfur dioxide enters the atmosphere through the smoke-stacks at the nickel plants and, downwind from the plants, ultimately results in acid rain. The cumulative effects of the acid rain to lakes and rivers downwind from the plants kill fish, birds, and other wildlife that are part of the food-chain. As a result, it also reduces the attractiveness of the lakes to cottagers who spend their summers there and hurts the tourism industry.

Obviously, there are environmental regulations today that attempt to address problems of this type. But, in order to understand what form this regulation may take, consider what would happen if there were no regulation at all. Figure 11.6 illustrates the nickel market. For simplicity, assume that the firms smelting nickel are in a perfectly competitive industry. Price, therefore, is determined at the intersection of the demand and supply curves, denoted p_C.

Because supply is the sum of the firms' marginal cost curves, you might be tempted to think it measures the marginal cost to society of nickel. But each firm's marginal cost only measures the cost *to the firm* of production. The cost in terms of damage to the environment, decreased property value to cottage owners, and lost tourism revenue is not reflected in the firm's cost. But these costs result from nickel smelting, so they represent a cost to society from nickel production. The marginal cost to society is, therefore, underestimated by the marginal cost of production. In the language of environmental economics, we say that nickel smelting has an *external cost* of production. Only when these external costs are added to the marginal cost of production do we get the true marginal cost to society of nickel production. Thus, in Figure 11.6, the marginal cost to society MC_S lies above the supply curve.

As we discussed for the monopoly at the start of this chapter, p_C is a dollar measure of the marginal benefit to consumers at q_C. Provided that the buyer is the only one who benefits from the good, the price measures the marginal benefit to society from the good. Since p_C is less than MC_S at the output level q_C, the marginal cost to society is greater than the marginal benefit to society. This means that if the nickel industry were to reduce output, the net benefit to society would increase. The reduction in marginal benefit to society from reducing output would be more than offset by the larger saving in marginal cost to society. But because firms in the nickel industry don't take the external cost into account and respond only

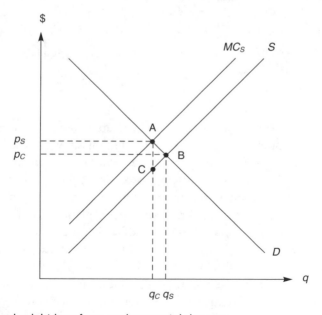

Figure 11.6 The deadweight loss from environmental damage

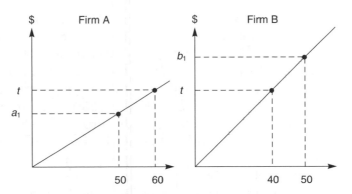

Figure 11.7 Marginal cost of pollution reduction for two firms

to the marginal cost of production, output will stay at q_C.

The marginal cost to society, given by MC_S, is greater than the marginal benefit to society, given by D, at all the levels of output between q_C and q_S. This means that there is a net cost to society from every output level between q_C and q_S. Adding up all the net costs between q_C and q_S amounts to determining the area of the triangle ABC. This area is a measure of the cost to society from the competitive level of output q_C. The cost represented by the area ABC is the deadweight loss from nickel smelting.

Obviously, what's going on here is that the firms are not taking into account the side effect their operation has on the environment, the cottagers, and the tourists. If these external costs were somehow charged to the firms, the marginal cost to the firms would equal the marginal cost to society. In this case, output would fall to q_S in Figure 11.6 and the deadweight loss would be eliminated. Charging the external cost can be done in two ways. But before we describe these schemes, which are not yet widely used, we look at the response to the pollution problem that has typically been followed in the past.

To make things simple, let's assume the nickel smelting industry is made up of two

firms. Figure 11.7 shows the costs associated with pollution reduction at the two firms. The horizontal axis shows the number of units of pollution reduction at the firms, so the origins represent the amount of pollution that the firms emit when there is no control on their pollution. When there are no pollution controls and industry output is q_C, therefore, each firm is at the origin in Figure 11.7. Clearly, the marginal cost of pollution reduction is higher at firm B than at firm A. This could arise, for example, if the smelters at firm A are newer and more efficient than the smelters at firm B.

Suppose, in the absence of any pollution controls that firm A pollutes 60 units and, because it has older equipment, firm B pollutes 140 units. Assume the government has decided it wants to cut pollution by 50 percent to a total of 100 units. A simple way to achieve this target is to get each firm to cut its pollution by 50 units. This is how environmental regulation works in most countries. An overall pollution target is split equally among the firms that cause the pollution. When both firms reduce pollution by 50 units, the marginal cost of pollution reduction is different in the two firms, as shown in Figure 11.7.

This is clearly inefficient: the same amount of pollution reduction could be achieved at a lower total cost. To see this, suppose firm B polluted one more unit, that is, it cut back pollution reduction by one unit. The saving to the firm, and to society, is the amount b_1. At the same time, increase the amount of pollution reduction at firm A by one unit. The cost to the firm, and to society, is a_1. The total amount of pollution reduction is still 100 units – 51 units at firm A and 49 units at firm B – so the pollution target is achieved. But since a_1 is less than b_1, the added cost to society from pollution reduction at firm A is less than the cost saving at firm B. Hence, the total cost to society from reaching the target has fallen. As long as the marginal costs of pollution reduction are different between the two firms, the costs to society of pollution reduction can be reduced by transferring pollution reduction to the firm with the lower marginal cost. This occurs when firm A reduces pollution by 60 units and firm B by 40 units.

The 50–50 split is, therefore, not the least cost way for society to meet the pollution target.[8] Basically, because firm A is "better" at pollution reduction, it makes sense from society's point of view to concentrate pollution reduction at firm A. If the equal pollution target is inefficient, what schemes will work? Remember that the key is to equalize the marginal costs at the two firms.

One way to do this is to impose an *effluent fee* of t dollars on each unit of pollution. Each unit of pollution reduction saves the firm t but imposes on the firm the marginal cost of reducing one unit of pollution. It makes sense, therefore, for the firm to cut back on pollution as long as the effluent fee is greater than or equal to the marginal cost of reduction. As shown in Figure 11.7, the effluent fee of t results in pollution reduction of 60 units at firm A and 40 units at firm B. Firm A reduces its pollution to zero, and firm

B reduces its pollution to 100 units. Because each firm reduces pollution to the point where the marginal cost equals the effluent fee and because the fee is the same for both firms, the marginal cost of pollution reduction is equalized across the firms. The effluent fee, therefore, achieves the desired pollution level at the least cost to society.

Another, more radical, scheme that achieves the same result is to distribute *pollution permits* to the firms and then allow the firms to buy and sell the permits among one another. Possession of a permit entitles the holder to pollute one unit. Because the objective is to reduce the total amount of pollution to 100 units, the government will issue 100 permits, say 50 to each firm. Firm A originally polluted 60 units, so because it now has 50 permits, it will have to reduce pollution by 10 units. Firm B originally polluted 140 units, so because it now has 50 permits, it will have to reduce pollution by 90 units.

As shown in Figure 11.8, the marginal cost to firm B of reducing pollution 90 units is much higher than the marginal cost to firm A of reducing pollution 10 units. Recall also that the firms are allowed to buy and sell the permits. Firm B is willing to pay anything less than b to get an extra permit. If firm B had an extra permit, it would be able to pollute one more unit and save the marginal cost of reducing one unit of pollution. As long as the price of the permit is lower than the marginal cost of pollution reduction, it pays for firm B to buy a permit. Firm A is willing to accept anything more than a to give up a permit. If firm A gives up a permit, it has to pollute one less unit and incur the marginal cost of reducing pollution by one unit. As long as the price it receives for the permit is greater than the marginal cost of reducing pollution by one unit, it pays firm A to sell a permit. Because b is greater than a,

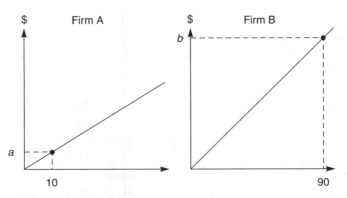

Figure 11.8 Marginal cost of pollution reduction and pollution permits

the price firm B is willing to pay is greater than the price firm A is willing to accept, there is room for a trade in permits to take place.

What will the price of permits be? We won't go into the details here (see Exercise 4), but it turns out that if the market for permits is competitive the equilibrium price of the permits will be t dollars.[9]

Although the effluent fee and tradeable pollution permits to achieve the same result from society's point of view, the schemes are not the same to the individual firms. In the case of the effluent fee, each firm pays t times the number of units of pollution in effluent fees. Thus, firm A pays nothing and firm B pays $100t$ in effluent fees. If the pollution permits are initially distributed to the firms free of charge, firm A ends up making money on the scheme because it sells all 50 units to firm B. Firm B buys 50 permits at a price of t, for a cost of $50t$. Clearly, both firm A and B prefer the tradeable pollution permits scheme.

If the tradeable pollution permits strikes you as the fancy of some economist, it may interest you to know that such a market exists in the United States. In 1993, the Chicago Board of Trade created a market for pollution permits to emit sulfur dioxide

(a substance that causes acid rain) issued by the Environmental Protection Agency to electric utilities. Firms that find it relatively expensive to reduce pollution buy the permits from firms that find it cheaper to cut back sulfur dioxide emissions.

11.6 Government regulation and globalization

It has now become commonplace to see demonstrators and police fighting at international meetings of the WTO, the International Monetary Fund (IMF) and the World Bank, or the G8 countries.[10] Notwithstanding the anarchist element among the protesters, there are many that oppose the global spread of capitalism. Many of the issues these people are concerned about are related to issues we have discussed in this chapter, namely patents and the environment. Both of these areas represent challenges to policy makers the world over and, as new international legislation is introduced, future challenges to managers.

One issue that concerns anti-globalization forces is a perceived link between a policy supported by many governments in the developed world, namely free trade, and environmental degradation. The argument is that free trade will allow polluting multinational firms to move to countries with less environmentally friendly legislation. This way, the relocating firm gains the advantage of lax environmental laws in the new, often poorer country without loosing access to richer markets thanks to free trade.

The counter argument hinges on the observation that environmental quality is what economists call a *normal good*. Loosely speaking, a normal good is something that consumers demand more of as they become richer. History has shown that as countries have become more wealthy, concern for the environment has increased. This explains why environmental issues are at the forefront of policy debate in Europe, for example, while being less of a concern in a poorer region, like India. Given that environmental quality is a normal good then as a country like India becomes richer, the citizens will demand a cleaner environment. Accordingly, what matters in the long term for environmental policy is making poor countries richer. As you will see in the next chapter, trade is one way the countries can get richer. This reasoning calls for more trade, not less. In the long term, free trade is more likely to lead to a cleaner environment than policies that discourage trade. In fact, free trade is neither a cause of environmental problems, nor is it a result of having a weak environmental policy. There are countries with free trade and relatively clean environments – e.g. Canada and the United States – and countries without free trade and a poor environmental record – e.g. Russia.

Another issue that has recently commanded a lot of attention is the question of patent enforcement. Faced by a ravaging epidemic, South Africa proposed in 1997 to import cheap, unlicensed copies of patented drugs to treat HIV and AIDS. A group of 39 European and American pharmaceutical firms sued the South African government on the grounds that this would infringe their patents. South Africa's health ministry argued that millions of people are dying because the drugs sold by the firms are too expensive, so it is bound to seek alternatives in the interests of public health. In the face of mounting public criticism, the drug companies eventually backed down and agreed to pay the South African government's legal costs.

A broader issue, however, pits the access of poor people to potentially life-saving medicine against the need for companies developing such drugs to recoup their development costs. The TRIPS agreement mentioned earlier in the chapter provides a solution. In times of a national health emergency, TRIPS allows countries to set aside patent protection. Why didn't South Africa invoke the TRIPS clause? The reason appears to have been that the rules in TRIPS were not as clear as they might have been. Nonetheless, agreements like TRIPS probably point the way forward to international laws that balance the needs of rich and poor countries alike.

Lastly, while less of a concern to the anti-globalization lobby, coordination of anti-trust policy is clearly an issue that policy-makers will have to address in the near future. An event that brought this to a head is the GE–Honeywell merger discussed earlier in the chapter. It turns out that this merger was actually approved by the US Department of Justice. It was only later that the European body, the Merger Task Force, turned the merger down. GE and Honeywell are multinational corporations that do a lot of business in Europe. Without the approval to operate as a joint entity in Europe, the merger was useless to GE and Honeywell.

Thus, although the merger was between two US firms, it was blocked by the actions of the European agency. As a result, it has been argued that a new agency be created to coord-inate international anti-trust activity. One possibility would be to expand the role of the WTO to act as a global watchdog of competition policy.

Summary

- The existence of a deadweight loss that arises whenever price is not equal to marginal cost gives the basic rationale for regulation.
- Since a monopoly does not set price equal to marginal cost, it results in a deadweight loss to society. Monopolies may also give rise to inefficient management, less research and development, and wasteful lobbying efforts.
- Arguments against regulation are: deadweight losses are small when demand is inelastic; the theory of second best; monopoly profits provide signals to other firms; and, natural monopolies.
- A natural monopoly exists when average costs are lower if the firm is served by one firm rather than by two or more firms. It often arises when there are large fixed costs of production.
- Regulating price equal to marginal cost does not work in the case of a natural monopoly since price will be lower than average cost and the firm will make negative profits. Average cost pricing allows the firm to break even and increases the output beyond the unregulated monopoly level.
- Another public policy response to monopoly is public ownership. Potential disadvant-ages with public ownership are: less incentive to control costs and that management may pursue political, rather than economic, concerns.
- Competitions policy refers broadly to the set rules by which firms must, legally, follow in their business practices.
- In the case of patents, legal monopolies are created in order to encourage research and development.
- Pollution results in an external cost, which means that the cost to society of an activity that results in pollution is underestimated by the cost of production to the firm.
- Effluent fees and tradeable pollution permits are ways of getting polluting firms to take into account the effect their operations have on others.

Notes

1 This should be obvious. Given that q^M maximizes profit, any other level of output gives the monopoly lower profit.
2 The exception is the United Kingdom, where many water utilities are privately owned. They are regulated by the government through the Office of Water Services (Ofwat).
3 The maximum value the HHI can reach is 10,000, corresponding to the case of a monopoly, which by definition has a 100 percent market share.
4 US Department of Justice, *Merger Guidelines*, 1997, Section 1.51.
5 "Engine failure." *The Economist*, July 7, 2001.
6 "Small is vulnerable." *The Economist*, May 17, 2001.

7 As of July 2001, 142 countries have signed on to TRIPS.

8 Of course, if both firms had the same marginal cost of pollution reduction, the 50–50 split would be the least cost way to achieve the target.

9 Of course, there are only two firms in this example, which is hardly a competitive market. Two firms are used only for illustrative purposes. The argument goes through for two firms (or any small number) as long as the price of permits is determined by the intersection of the demand and supply of permits.

10 The G8 group of industrial countries is made up of the United States, Japan, Germany, France, the United Kingdom, Italy, Canada, and Spain.

Exercises

1 Let the inverse demand curve for a monopoly firm be:

$$P = 50 - 0.01\,Q$$

and let the marginal cost curve of the firm be:

$$MC = 10 + 0.02\,Q.$$

(a) Calculate the equilibrium price and output level of the monopolist.

(b) Suppose government regulators decide to use marginal cost pricing to induce the monopolist to produce the socially optimal output level. Calculate the socially optimal output level. Calculate the price that government regulators will have to set under the marginal cost pricing rule in order to induce the monopolist to produce the socially optimal output level.

(c) Make a rough sketch of the demand curve and the marginal cost curve of the monopolist. Indicate on the diagram: (i) the output level produced by the unregulated monopolist; (ii) the socially optimal output level; and (iii) the efficiency loss associated with the output level produced by the unregulated monopolist.

2 Let the inverse demand curve for a monopoly firm be:

$$P = 40 - 0.001\,Q$$

and let the total cost of the firm be:

$$C = 10Q + 0.01Q^2$$

(a) Calculate the equilibrium price and output level of the monopolist.

(b) Determine the average cost curve of the monopoly. Calculate the profit per unit and the total profit for the unregulated monopolist. Calculate the profit per unit and the total profit for the monopolist under the marginal cost pricing rule.

(c) If the marginal cost pricing rule is brought into effect, will the monopolist continue business or will it leave the industry? Explain.

(d) Determine the price if the firm were required by regulation to charge a price equal to average cost. What problems do you think an average cost pricing scheme will encounter?

3 A newsprint company has (private) marginal costs given by:

$$MC_P = 10 + 0.1\,Q$$

Assume that the price of newsprint is determined, in a competitive market, to be $20 per unit. A by-product of the newsprint manufacturing process is sludge, which is dumped into a river. Suppose the costs of the sludge-dumping are estimated to be $4 for every unit of newsprint manufactured.

(a) Determine the output of the newsprint firm.

(b) Determine the marginal social cost of the firm's newsprint manufacturing. Calculate the socially optimal output of newsprint from this firm.

(c) In an attempt to induce the firm to produce the socially optimal output level, the government imposes an effluent fee on the firm of $5 per unit of newsprint produced. Calculate the firm's output after implementation of the scheme.

(d) Does the tax have the desired effect? If not, what change would you suggest? Explain.

4 Suppose a country has two firms, each engaged in different industries. Suppose that the marginal cost of pollution reduction (MC_R) at one firm is given by:

$$MC_R^H = 0.5\, Q_R \qquad (11.1)$$

where Q_R is the amount of reduced pollution, and the marginal cost of pollution reduction at the other firm is given by:

$$MC_R^L = 0.1\, Q_R \qquad (11.2)$$

Note that the firm with MC_R given by (11.1) has a higher level of marginal reduction cost at all levels of pollution than the firm with the MC_R given by (11.2), hence the labels "H," for high-cost, and "L," for low-cost. Assume that, in the absence of laws against pollution in this country, each firm will pollute 100 units.

(a) Suppose the government decides to cut the total amount of pollution by 48 percent. One way to do this is to require each firm to cut pollution by 48 percent. Calculate the amount each firm spends on pollution abatement under this plan. Calculate the total resources spent on pollution abatement, i.e. the sum of the amounts each firm spends.

(b) Suppose the government decides to cut the total amount of pollution by 48 percent using a per-unit tax on pollution output.

What level of the pollution tax will result in a decrease in total emissions by 48 percent?

(c) What are the tax payments of each firm? How much does each firm spend on pollution abatement? What are the total resources spent on pollution abatement? What are the total costs of the tax scheme to each firm?

(d) Another option for the government is to give each firm a number of pollution "permits" such that the total number of permits equals the desired amount of pollution, 104, and then let the two firms trade the permits between one another. Suppose the government allocates each firm 52 pollution permits. Derive the demand, the supply and the equilibrium price of the pollution permits.

(e) How much does each firm spend on pollution abatement? What are the total resources spent on pollution abatement? What are the total costs of the permit mechanism to each firm?

(f) Which scheme will the high-cost firm prefer? Which scheme will the low-cost firm prefer? Which of the above three schemes is most efficient from the point of view of society as a whole? (Remember that the total amount of pollution is the same in all three cases.)

(g) List the key assumptions made in the above analysis.

Reference

Milgrom, Paul and Roberts, John. *Economics, Organization and Management* (Englewood Cliffs, NJ: Prentice Hall, 1992).

Chapter 12

International trade

•••

When you are finished with this chapter you should understand:

- That increased trade can lead to *gains from trade*, which can arise from many sources, including international differences in production technology and relative factor endowments, and increasing returns to scale
- How trade distortions like import tariffs have different effects on different agents within the country applying the distortion and its trading partners
- That trade distortions can make a country better off through a positive terms of trade effect, but the strategic effects of trade distortions take account of retaliation by trading partners which can leave all trading partners worse off
- How application of strategic trade policy can result in a prisoner's dilemma outcome
- How cooperation between trading countries can be encouraged through Preferential Trade Agreements (PTAs) and Multilateral Trade Organizations like the WTO, to avoid the prisoner's dilemma outcome of strategic trade policy

International trade is playing an increasingly important role in the strategic decision-making behavior of managers of all types of firms. The reduction in trade barriers through PTAs like the NAFTA between Canada, the United States and Mexico or the EU, as well as multilateral trade liberalization through the Uruguay Round of trade negotiations and the WTO, increase the extent to which domestic firms are exposed to competitive pressure from competing firms around the world. As a result, a manager who may have had to worry about the behavior of only a few competing domestic firms must now spend more time worrying about the behavior of competitors from around the world.

At the same time, liberalization of global trade and integration of international markets greatly increases the opportunities and options available to managers of domestic firms. If trade barriers are reduced, then foreign markets are more open to domestic exports. Managers must decide on appropriate strategies to take advantage of these opportunities in foreign markets. Is it better to produce at home and export to a foreign country, or should our firm set up an overseas production facility? If we invest overseas, how much should we commit to our investment strategy? Should we advertise our product overseas to increase exposure, or should we form a partnership with a foreign competitor?

To answer these questions, a manager must first understand how and why trade works. How important is international trade for any nation? Why are some goods exported while others are imported? We need to identify reasons why we export some goods and import others, and why we trade more with one country than another.

Why has international trade become more important? Why do nations trade with each other in the first place? With all of the fuss which was made at the end of 1999 at the WTO Ministerial Conference in Seattle in the United States, why would nations want to enter into agreements to liberalize trade and increase the competitive pressures felt by domestic producers? In Section 12.1, we establish reasons which motivate nations to trade with each other.

The way that international trade is conducted between nations is often affected by the behavior of governments. A government can be more aggressive in negotiating trade agreements with its trading partners, and has a number of tools at its disposal to affect trade policy. The trade policy of a government will affect the competitive environment in which a firm operates, so we will need to spend some time examining how the behavior of the government can affect a manager's decision-making problem. The way that trade policy tools like import tariffs, quotas, export subsidies, countervailing duties, and voluntary export restraints are used by governments to affect the international trading environment facing a nation is examined in Section 12.2. In Section 12.3, we'll look at the effects of different mechanisms used to liberalize trade between countries.

12.1 Why do nations trade?

The objective of this section is to provide a very brief description of reasons which moti-

vate international trade between different economies. The examples will all be rather simplistic, to make it easier to understand the process by which nations can gain from trade. But first we'll look at some numbers, to see how important trade might be for some countries.

12.1.1 Trade and growth

To demonstrate the importance of international trade for an economy, we have listed the share of Gross Domestic Product (GDP) which is derived from exports for a number of nations in Table 12.1. Data on imports as a share of GDP would yield similar figures. These data demonstrate the degree of *openness* of an economy. Clearly, international trade makes up a significant component of GDP for all of these countries, though some countries trade more than others. Germany, Canada, and China are all relatively open economies, with exports representing more than 20 percent of the total GDP. On the other hand, the United States and Brazil derive less than 12 percent of GDP from exports.

Table 12.2 reports annual average rates of growth of total production of all goods, and of exports, for the whole world, for different time periods. Two points are evident from Table 12.2. On average, the volume of trade (exports) has been growing faster than total production for all time periods. But more importantly, when trade was growing more quickly, production was growing faster. Table 12.2 provides evidence for the argument that trade stimulates growth, or that nations *gain from trade*.

Exactly how might nations gain by trading with each other? To answer this question, we will describe cases where two economies can make themselves better off by trading with

Table 12.1 Gross national product per capita and exports as share of GDP

Country	GNP per capita 1990 – (US$)	Exports/GDP 1991 (%)
China	370	19.5
Indonesia	570	24.9
Rep. of Korea	5,400	25.3
Singapore	11,160	147.3
Japan	25,430	9.4
EU-12	17,334	22.4
Spain	11,020	11.4
UK	16,100	21.1
Germany	22,320	22.4
Canada	20,470	24.4
United States	21,790	7.1
Mexico	2,490	9.6
World	4,010	15.4

Source: Markusen *et al.* (1995), p. 8.

Table 12.2 Growth in production and exports (Appleyard and Field 2001, p. 3)

	Growth in volume of production (average annual percent change)	Growth in volume of exports (average annual percent change)
1963–73	6.0	9.0
1970–9	4.0	5.0
1980–5	1.7	2.1
1985–90	3.0	5.8
1990–8	2.0	6.5
1998	1.5	4.0
1999	3.0	4.5

Source: Appleyard and Field (2001), p. 3.

each other, relative to a situation where they do not trade with each other. It is very important to note that we are looking for situations where trade makes *both trading partners better off.* If one country is made better off at the expense of its trading partner, that is *not* a situation where there exist gains from trade.

We will describe three reasons why countries might trade with each other:[1]

- international differences in production technology

- international differences in factor endowments
- increasing returns to scale in production

12.1.2 Absolute and comparative advantage

To start our explanation of the existence of *gains from trade*, suppose that two countries, North and South, begin by not trading with each other at all. A country which does not trade at all is said to be in *autarky*. Relative to an initial state of autarky, if both countries can be made better off by trading with each other, then we say that there exist *gains from trade*. We will assume that when the two countries trade with each other, there are no trade distortions like import tariffs, so that we will describe the *gains from free trade*. We will describe the effects of trade distortions like import tariffs in Section 12.2.

Suppose that in North and South, producers can make and sell two goods, cars and trees. All that is needed to produce these goods is labor. In North, a producer needs five units of labor to produce one car or one tree, while in South, 10 units of labor are needed to produce one car but 30 units of labor are needed to produce one tree. This information is summarized in Table 12.3. We say that North has an *absolute advantage* in production of both goods. North has production technology which can produce the same output with fewer units of labor, so it is more efficient at producing both cars and trees. We might think that South now has nothing to gain from trade with North, since North is more efficient at producing both goods. But we can show that both countries can gain from trade.

To illustrate, suppose that North has 80 units of labor, and South has 800 units of labor. To keep things as simple as possible, suppose that consumers in each country like to consume cars and trees in equal proportion, so that production in autarky is given by Table 12.4.[2]

Now suppose that North and South can trade cars for trees, at the rate of one tree for two cars. Before trade, each country changes its production pattern, in anticipation of the trade. North produces one extra tree, which means it can only produce seven cars instead of eight cars. Likewise, South produces one less tree, freeing up labor to produce three extra cars. Now the pattern of production is given by Table 12.5.

If North trades one tree to South for two cars, and South trades two cars to North for

one tree, then each country will end up with goods available for consumption as reported in Table 12.6. In this example, both countries are better off after trade, indicating that even if one country has no *absolute advantage*, there still exist gains from trade. We say that North has a *comparative advantage* in production of trees, while South has a *comparative advantage* in the production of cars. This pattern of comparative advantage exists even though North is more efficient at producing both goods. Even though North has an *absolute*

Table 12.3 Pattern of comparative advantage

	Cars	Trees
North	5	5
South	10	30

Table 12.4 Total production under autarky

	Cars	Trees
North	8	8
South	20	20

Table 12.5 Production before trade

	Cars	Trees
North	7	9
South	23	19

Table 12.6 Goods available for consumption after trade

	Cars	Trees
North	9	8
South	21	20

advantage in both trees and cars, North is *relatively* more efficient in tree production, so North can gain from trade by specializing in trees and exporting these to South in return for cars. Likewise, South has a comparative advantage in cars even though it has an *absolute disadvantage* in production of both goods. If South produced one less tree, this would free up 30 units of labor, which could be used in South to produce three extra cars. If North produced one fewer tree, the extra labor which was freed could be used to produce only one more car. While South requires *absolutely* more labor than North to produce each good, it requires *relatively* less labor than North to produce cars. The pattern of comparative advantage determines the direction or pattern of trade which will make both countries better off, and is determined by differences in production technology between countries.

12.1.3 Other reasons for trade

The gains from trade in the previous example were derived from the fact that one country was relatively more efficient at producing one good. But there are other reasons why nations could benefit from the international exchange of goods.

International differences in factor endowments

Suppose that both countries were exactly the same in every way, except that North had relatively more raw materials required to produce trees, while South had relatively more raw materials needed to produce cars. Again, there will exist *gains from trade*, this time because of international differences in *relative endowments of factors of production*. Both countries would gain from trade if

North produced more trees and exported trees to South, since North has more raw materials needed to produce trees. Likewise, South should produce more cars and export cars to North, since it has a greater availability of the factors of production used in car production.

Increasing returns to scale in production

Another important reason for the existence of gains from trade is the presence of increasing returns to scale in production. For example, suppose that both North and South were exactly the same in every way, and even had the same relative endowments of factors of production. But suppose that in each country, as production of cars or trees increased, the average cost of production fell. That is, to produce 10 cars in North or South, the average cost of production is $12,000. But as production increases to 20 cars, the average cost of production falls to $10,000. Now North and South could each produce 10 cars in autarky. But with trade, South could specialize and produce all 20 cars and then trade cars to North for trees. Now all 20 cars are produced at a lower average cost, which implies that both countries can benefit from trade.

12.2 Strategic trade policy

So far we have described a number of situations which lead to the existence of gains from free trade between economies. But what we have been describing is a convenient fiction, since there exist no economies in the world which are in a state of autarky or a state of free trade. In general, all nations engage in international trade, and trade in all nations is subject to trade distortions. There exist many types of trade distortions,

Table 12.7   Examples of trade distortions

Import tariffs	Export subsidies
Import quotas	Export taxes
Voluntary export restraints (VERs)	Countervailing duties (CVDs)

some of which are listed in Table 12.7. In general, these distortions are applied by domestic governments to affect international trade. The use of these distortions to affect trade is what we call *strategic trade policy*.

We want to describe the effects of trade distortions, so that we can understand some of the motivations behind the application of strategic trade policy, and the implications of such policy decisions. To begin, we'll need to define some terminology. It will be important to distinguish between the *volume of trade* (the physical number of cars imported or exported) and the *value of trade* (how much these imported or exported cars cost). We will let x denote the volume of net exports, so if $x = 10$, we export 10 cars, while if $x = -20$, we import 20 cars. Then if the international or world price of cars is p^*, the value of trade (at world prices) is:

$$p^* \cdot x$$

In general, we'll use a^* to denote international or world prices. Under free trade, domestic prices p and world prices p^* will be the same, but if there is some type of trade distortion, then domestic and world prices will generally not be the same.

$$p \neq p^*$$

One final term we need to define is the *terms of trade*. This is just the ratio of the price of exported goods to the price of imported goods:

$$\text{terms of trade} = \frac{\text{price of exports}}{\text{price of imports}}$$

We say that a country's terms of trade improve if the terms of trade increase. This would imply that, all other things being equal, the relative price of goods which this country exports would rise, making this country better off. Of course, if the country's terms of trade deteriorate, then imports would become relatively more expensive, leaving this country worse off.

Any trade distortion can have many different effects on trade. In order to understand the effects of trade distortions, we will decompose the effects of any trade distortion into two separate effects:

- *Volume of trade effect*: the trade distortion causes a change in the volume of goods which are traded.
- *Terms of trade effect*: the trade distortion can result in a change in the world price of traded goods.

We want to find out whether the volume of trade effect and the terms of trade effect of any trade distortion is either positive or negative.

12.2.1 Effects of an import tariff

We'll illustrate the effects of an import tariff with the following simple example. Suppose some economy (we'll call it "Home") imports tires from some other economy, called "Foreign." The world price per tire is $p^*_{\text{tires}} = \$50$, and the number of tires which Home imports at this price under free trade is x_{tires}. This scenario is illustrated in Figure 12.1, where we plot the demand curve and the supply curve for tires in Home. If the world price per tire is $p^* = \$50$, then tire producers in

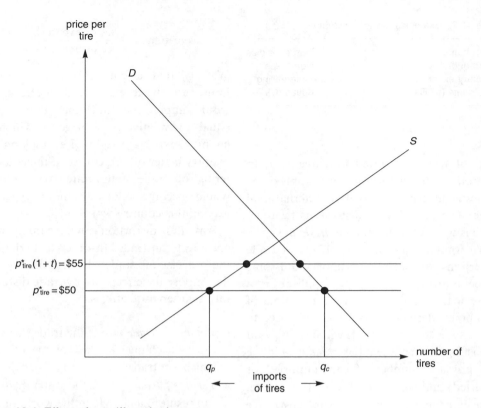

Figure 12.1 Effect of a tariff on tire imports

Home sell q_p tires. Consumers in Home buy q_c domestic and imported tires, so Home as a whole imports $x_{tires} = q_c - q_p$ tires.

Now suppose that the government in Home decides to charge a tariff of $t = 10$ percent on tire imports. The Home (domestic) price per imported tire will now be:

$$p = p^* \cdot (1 + t)$$

That is, if $p^* = \$50$, then $p = \$50 \cdot (1 + 0.10) = \$55$. The immediate effect of this tariff will be that tires in Home will be less expensive (\$50 per tire) than imported tires (\$55 per tire). As a result, Home tire imports will fall as tire consumers in Home substitute less expensive domestically produced tires for more expensive imported tires. This means that any gains from trade

in tires will be reduced, since Home tire imports fall, so the *volume of trade effect* of this import tariff will be negative.

In general, Foreign tire exporters will be worse off since their sales of tires to Home will fall. In fact, this drop in sales may be big enough that Foreign tire producers reduce their price per tire in order to be more competitive. This decrease in the price of a good imported by Home implies an improvement in Home's terms of trade, so the *terms of trade effect* of the import tariff on tires in Home will be positive. But for Foreign, this is a deterioration in their terms of trade, because Foreign exports tires, and the price of a good which they export has fallen.

Suppose that the tariff causes a reduction in Home's demand for imported tires to such an extent that Foreign tire producers drop the price of a tire to $p^* = \$48$ to stimulate demand. In Home, this tire will now cost $p^*(1 + t) = \$48 + \$4.80 = \$52.80$.

How will tire producers in Home respond? At this point, tire producers in Home are still selling tires for \$50 per tire in Home. But they would still be able to sell as many tires as they could at \$52.79 per tire. So the full effect of the tariff will be to lower the world price per tire to \$48, and to raise the price of imported tires in Home *and* of tires produced in Home to \$52.80. Therefore, many things happen as a result of the tariff:

Home

- price of Home tires rises, so tire producers in Home are better off.
- more domestically produced tires are sold in Home, so Home tire producers are better off.
- price of domestic and imported tires in Home is higher, so tire consumers in Home are worse off.
- consumers in Home buy fewer tires in total, so Home consumers are worse off.
- the government in Home collects tariff revenue on tire imports, so the government is better off.

Foreign

- tire exports to Home will fall, so Foreign tire producers are worse off.
- price per tire that Foreign tire exporters receive will fall, so Foreign tire producers are worse off.
- price per tire that consumers have to pay will fall, so Foreign consumers are better off.

To find the overall effect of the import tariff in Home, note that Home receives a positive terms of trade effect (price of an import falls) and a negative volume of trade effect (quantity of imports falls). It may be that the positive terms of trade effect is larger than the (absolute value of the) negative volume of trade effect, in which case the import tariff on tires would leave Home generally better off. However, if Home is a relatively small player in the world tire market, then the terms of trade effect may be very small or zero. In this case, the import tariff makes Home as a whole worse off. But of course, there are some agents in the Home economy (notably, tire producers) who are better off as a result of the tariff. It's not too difficult to imagine tire producers in Home lobbying in favor of such a strategic trade policy.

There is another group which we only indirectly referred to. The group of tire consumers in Home could include producers of automobiles. These producers buy tires as *intermediate inputs* and use them to finish production of automobiles. These agents are worse off due to the import tariff since they must pay more per tire. This directly affects the competitiveness of automobile producers in Home, who are either forced to sell cars at higher prices or must face lower profit margins as their costs increase.

Note that the foreign tire exporters are unambiguously worse off due to Home's import tariff. In response, the foreign government may decide to retaliate by putting their own tariff on imports of cars from Home, which will make Home unambiguously worse off. This point is of critical importance when describing strategic trade policy. Recall that we are interested in incorporating the strategic response of one economic agent to the action played by a rival. This type of tariff game has been described as a *prisoner's dilemma*, a game which we

Home \ Foreign	F (free trade)	T (tariff)
F	10, 10	2, 13
T	13, 2	**5, 5**

Figure 12.2 Tariff war as a prisoner's dilemma game

introduced in Chapter 5. To illustrate, suppose that Home and Foreign experience gains from trade of 10 units each under free trade. To keep the example simple, suppose that Home and Foreign can play one of two strategies: free trade (F) or tariff (T). If Home charges a tariff when Foreign commits to free trade, then relative to Free Trade, Home gets a positive terms of trade effect and a negative volume of trade effect. Suppose the net effect of the tariff in Home is positive, so when playing strategy T, Home gets a payoff of 13. Of course, Foreign must be worse off when Home charges a tariff, since it experiences a negative terms of trade effect and a negative volume of trade effect, so Foreign gets a payoff of 2. These payoffs are reversed if Home commits to free trade while Foreign charges a tariff. If both Home and Foreign charge a tariff, each receives a payoff of 5. These payoffs are summarized in Figure 12.2. You should be able to verify that the unique pure strategy equilibrium to this game has both Home and Foreign charging a tariff. Note that both nations can be made better off by moving to a free-trade equilibrium, but neither has an incentive to deviate from charging a tariff.

We've mentioned the power of commitment as a strategy a number of times already.

If both Home and Foreign could commit to a policy of free trade, they could avoid the low-payoff equilibrium where both countries charge a tariff. This is an important element of trade agreements like those implied by the NAFTA and the WTO, as we will see in Section 12.3.

12.2.2 Other trade distortions

We listed a number of different trade distortions in Table 12.7. These typically work in one of the two ways. Either the distortion directly affects the price of traded goods, and as a result indirectly affects the volume of trade. Or the distortion directly affects the volume of trade, and indirectly affects the price of traded goods. The import tariff we just described directly affects the price of traded goods, making imports more expensive, and indirectly affects the volume of trade. Export subsidies and export taxes have the same sort of effect: They directly affect the price of traded goods. An export subsidy makes exports relatively less expensive, making the domestic exporter more competitive in world markets. This type of trade distortion is used by many countries in agricultural markets to stimulate demand for agricultural exports of the subsidizing country. The indirect volume of trade effect of an export subsidy would be to increase the volume of trade. Export taxes have the opposite effect: they make exports relatively more expensive. The indirect volume of trade effect of an export tax is to decrease the volume of trade.

Quotas and Voluntary Export Restraints are examples of trade distortions which directly affect the volume of trade, and as a result will indirectly affect the prices of traded goods. An example of Import Quotas is the Multi-Fibre Arrangement (MFA) which is a system of restrictions on the volume of imports between individual developing countries textile exporters and individual developing countries textile importers.

Howe Leather and the WTO

Howe Leather* is an Australian company with plants in Victoria, Australia, and Juarez, Mexico, producing leather for the automotive industry. During the 1990s the Australian government afforded assistance to Howe Leather through its Strategic Investment Program and the Automotive Competitiveness and Investment Scheme. In the late 1990s the WTO interpreted this assistance as an export subsidy. Two elements of this case are noteworthy: the technical effects of this assistance program, and the strategic effects.

First of all, we can interpret the effects of an export subsidy. The assistance afforded to Howe Leather would have made it easier for them to compete in the world market for automotive leather. The effect is similar to that of an import tariff. Production of automotive leather for export would increase due to the subsidy, and to the extent that Australia has market power in this market, there would be downward pressure on the world price of automotive leather. This would make it more difficult for other producers of automotive leather to compete with Howe Leather in world markets.

But it is the strategic effects of this case which are interesting. For instance, why was the WTO interested in the Australian government's assistance program? To find out, recall that we just found that the world price of automotive leather would fall due to this assistance program. So producers of automotive leather who are not in Australia and therefore unable to benefit from the assistance program are worse off. No wonder, then, that in 1998, the US launched a dispute against the Australian government through the WTO.

The WTO has a number of rules and regulations to which signatories must adhere if they are to be members of the WTO. One of these regulations prohibits export subsidies because they distort international competition. But the WTO is a voluntary organization. No country is forced to be a member of the WTO. So to ensure that all WTO members *play by the rules* which make up the WTO, there is a Dispute Settlement Mechanism** which is also a part of the WTO.

When the WTO ruled that the Australian assistance program constituted an export subsidy which had to be removed, Australia could have decided to continue the program, and ignore the WTO ruling. But the WTO Dispute Settlement Mechanism would then have given the US permission to retaliate against the Australian export subsidy.

We can interpret the Howe Leather Dispute as a prisoner's dilemma game using Figure 12.2. Suppose Australia is the Home country and the US is Foreign. If the US plays a strategy of Free Trade (F), then Australia can also play F and receive a payoff of 10. But if Australia provides assistance to Howe Leather (equivalent to the tariff strategy in Figure 12.2), it gains a higher payoff of 13. But then the US is worse off, so the US will decide to retaliate by charging a tariff (T) against Australia. As we've already seen, if Australia and the US cannot cooperate, the outcome of this game has Australia retaining its export subsidy, and the US retaliating against Australia. Both countries are worse off, because neither has an incentive *on its own* to pursue a Free Trade strategy (F).

So where does the WTO come in? By interpreting this dispute as a game, the WTO becomes a forum within which Australia and the US can cooperate to ensure that the prisoner's dilemma problem is avoided. If Australia distorts trade to make itself better off, the WTO can rule that Australia should be punished, by allowing the US to retaliate, removing Australia's incentive to make itself better off by distorting trade.

In 2000, Australia reformed its assistance program to remove the export subsidy afforded to Howe Leather.

*Information about Howe Leather can be found at their website: http://www.howe.com.au/

**To learn more about how the Dispute Settlement Mechanism at the WTO works, see http://www.wto.org/english/tratop_e/dispu_e/dispu_e.htm

For example, the MFA quotas between Canada and India restricted the total number of tailored collar shirts which Canada could import from India to 3,532,786 units in 1995.[3] We say that this quota was *binding* if all of the quota was used up. For example, if Canada had only imported three million shirts from India in 1995, then the quota would have no effect in Canada. In fact, this quota was fully utilized in 1995. This means that Canada would most likely have imported more shirts from India. The direct volume of trade effect of this quota is to limit or restrict the physical volume of shirts imported by Canada from India.

This quota will have an indirect effect on the price of Indian shirts in Canada. Since Canadians would rather have imported more shirts from India in 1995, there was an excess demand for Indian shirts in 1995. This would cause the price of shirts imported from India in 1995 to be higher than it would have been without the quota. The indirect effect of the import quota is to raise the price of the imported good. This makes Canadian consumers of Indian shirts worse off, since they must pay a higher price for imported Indian shirts. On the other hand, Canadian producers of shirts which are substitutes for imported Indian shirts are better off. The quota protects Canadian shirt producers from competition in the same way that an import tariff would afford protection to Canadian producers. The price of the competing import should rise and market share of the domestic producer should rise.

A VER has the same sort of effect as an import quota, except that the restriction is applied by the exporting country. The import quota on shirts from India was applied by Canada, the importing country. A corresponding VER would have been applied by India, the exporting country. But as far as Canadian producers and consumers are concerned, the effects of a VER are much the same as the effects of an import quota. A VER would directly limit the volume of exports from India to Canada, and indirectly affect the price of the traded good.

Another potentially important role for strategic trade policy is to take advantage of the gains from trade derived from increasing returns to scale. To illustrate, we will consider a simple example. Suppose that hockey sticks are produced in only two countries in the world, Canada and Russia. To keep things simple, suppose that each country has half of the world market for hockey sticks, and that the average cost of producing a hockey stick in each country is $5. If there are increasing returns to scale, then the average cost of production would decrease if total output in any country increased. This means that if something happened to cause Canada to get a larger share of the world hockey stick market, Canada would be able to produce hockey sticks at a lower average cost. So we could argue that giving Canadian hockey stick producers a subsidy to make them more competitive would allow them to gain a larger market share, produce hockey sticks at a lower average cost, and ultimately be able to supply hockey sticks to the world market at a lower price since their average production costs would fall.

Unfortunately, this motivation for the application of strategic trade policy is much more complicated than appears in this simple example, because of a number of implicit assumptions we have made. First and foremost, the introduction of a distortion like the subsidy described above is a very simple matter, but removing the distortion once its desired effect has been achieved is usually very difficult. For example, once Canadian hockey stick producers have gained a larger market share, the government should remove the subsidy. But this is a politically difficult change to make.

Another important consideration when describing the effects of such a policy is the scope for inefficient entry into the subsidized industry. This is a powerful argument against the use of export subsidies to producers of primary agricultural products. The idea here is that when a subsidy is made available to producers, it makes it feasible for relatively

inefficient firms to continue to produce output, and for potential entrants to come into the market to take advantage of the subsidy. This means that inefficient producers who should have been driven out of the market by competition will continue to produce output and use up government subsidies. Also, entry into the market of new firms will reduce or even reverse the beneficial effects of reduced average costs due to increasing returns to scale, since inefficient entry will lead to more firms each with a smaller market share.

Finally, even if entry into the market is restricted, the subsidy is removed after a period of time, and the Canadian hockey stick producers are able to take advantage of increasing returns to scale and lower average costs, the effect of the short-term subsidy will have been to give Canadian hockey stick producers more monopoly power in the hockey stick market. With a larger share of the world hockey stick market, these producers may now have the ability to price discriminate, which as we saw in Chapter 4 may lead to lower consumer welfare. That is, the reduction in average cost may lead to a reduction in the market price of hockey sticks, but the increase in monopoly power as the hockey stick producers gain more market share may enable the producers to increase the market price. And what about the Russian hockey stick producers? Surely they won't be happy about this sort of outcome, and will lobby their government to retaliate against the Canadian subsidy.

In short, any application of strategic trade policy must be viewed with caution and careful evaluation of all potential effects of the policy being considered. As we saw, any one policy like an import tariff or an export subsidy will generally have many different effects. While some economic agents may be made better off, others may be made worse off, and the threat of retaliation must always be acknowledged.

12.3   Trade liberalization

Since the end of the World War II, there have been many efforts at liberalization of international trade, particularly between developed economies. These efforts typically fall into two distinct categories:

- Preferential Trade Agreements
- Multilateral Trade Negotiations

The NAFTA and the EU are two examples of PTAs. These are agreements negotiated between a few countries, with the aim of liberalizing trade between members. On the other hand, Multilateral Trade Negotiations have been conducted under the auspices of the General Agreement on Tariffs and Trade (GATT) and the WTO, and involve trade liberalizing negotiations between a large group of nations. The most recent *Round* of trade negotiations under the GATT, known as the Uruguay Round, involved 117 participants. As of July 2001, membership of the WTO included 142 countries.[4] There are strategic advantages and disadvantages to both types of trade liberalizing mechanisms.

12.3.1   Preferential trade agreements

The objective of a trade liberalization agreement like the NAFTA or the EU is to limit the ability of member nations or governments to apply strategic trade policy, to affect the structure of the competitive trading environment. For example, the principal objective of the NAFTA is to liberalize trade between Canada, the United States, and Mexico in a number of sectors, including trade in goods, services, investment, and

many others. This agreement commits member governments to not applying any trade policy tools like import tariffs which would distort the trading environment between these three countries. We want to consider the implications of these PTAs for two groups of economic agents: the government of the member country which actively negotiated the agreement, and the manager of a firm within the member country.

By committing to the rules and regulations contained in a PTA, the government of a member country is committing itself to the principle of liberalized trade with other members. This limits the ability of the government to use strategic trade policy to give domestic exporters and import-competing producers a competitive advantage against firms in other member countries. However, it is very important to note that the ability of *all* member governments to use strategic trade policies against each other is limited by a PTA.

This means that we can identify one of the most important strategic effects of a PTA by viewing the PTA as a forum for cooperation between member countries. Individual countries on their own recognize that trade policies may have positive terms of trade effects. But by taking into account how countries will respond or retaliate against each other, we see that without any cooperation, application of strategic trade policies can ultimately result in a prisoner's dilemma outcome, where countries do not realize the full gains from trade. A PTA is a mechanism whereby countries can cooperate to limit the application of distortionary trade policies to benefit as much as possible from the gains from trade.

Another important issue relates to the relative bargaining power between member governments. In many PTAs there are some member countries (like the US in the

Honda Manufacturing Canada

Honda Canada Manufacturing began producing Honda Civics at its plant in Alliston, Ontario in 1986, producing 507 vehicles. Plant output was 106,000 vehicles in 1995, with the majority of these units being exported to the US. What would motivate Honda to set up a plant to produce Honda Civics in Canada, when these cars were already being produced in Japan?

Both Canada and the US maintain tariffs on imports of motor vehicles from other countries, including Japan. But under the Auto Pact between Canada and the US which came into effect in 1965, cars and parts can be traded duty-free between Canada and the US. So managers at Honda in Japan faced the following problem: produce vehicles in Japan which are subject to import tariffs when exported to the US, or set up a plant in Canada so that Honda motorcars can be produced in Canada and exported duty-free to the US. Setting up a production facility overseas is a costly venture, but being able to avoid tariff charges in export markets may make such a venture worthwhile.

When evaluating the manager's problem, it is important to consider the climate of trade relations between the US and Japan in the early 1980s. This was a period of growing trade tensions between Japan and the US, which saw the negotiation of VER Agreements between Japan and the US, whereby Japan voluntarily agreed to limit automobile exports to the US. Such an environment makes producing in Japan and exporting to the US relatively more expensive, and very likely influenced Honda's decision to expand production facilities into Canada and the US.

Source: Data for this case can be found in Ward's *Automotive Yearbook.*

NAFTA and Germany and the UK in the EU) which are significantly larger than other members (like Canada and Mexico in the NAFTA or Greece and Portugal in the EU). It is possible that smaller members are worse off negotiating in a forum like a PTA because their relative bargaining power is smaller than the bargaining power of larger members. To illustrate this point, suppose that Mexico wants to pursue a liberalized trade policy with the US. This policy was pursued within the NAFTA, wherein Mexico was one of three member countries. As an alternative, Mexico could bargain with the US within the WTO. In the WTO, Mexico and the US are only two of 142 other member countries, so their bargaining power would be limited, and Mexico's relative bargaining position would be stronger. This issue of relative bargaining power is explored more fully in Section 12.3.2.

This argument is complicated and difficult to evaluate. We must also keep in mind that the trade liberalizing initiatives implied by the NAFTA are generally much broader than those implied by the Uruguay Round of trade negotiations. As such, the potential gains from trade liberalization from the NAFTA may be much more significant.

From the point of view of the manager of a firm, trade liberalizing initiatives of PTAs like the NAFTA or the EU are important because the structure of international competition between member countries will be affected. Managers in industries which had previously been afforded protection from import tariffs, for example, must prepare for increased competition from competing firms in other member countries. These managers may have to adopt a strategy like the *puppy dog* strategy described in Chapter 10, as

Table 12.8   GATT rounds of multilateral trade negotiations

1947	Geneva	tariffs
1949	Annecy	tariffs
1951	Torquay	tariffs
1956	Geneva	tariffs
1960–1	Dillon Round	tariffs
1964–7	Kennedy Round	tariffs and anti-dumping
1973–9	Tokyo Round	tariffs, non-tariff barriers, and *framework* agreements
1986–93	Uruguay Round	tariffs, agriculture, services, investment, intellectual property, etc.

import-competing firms in other member countries become stronger competitors.

On the other hand, PTAs also imply that access to markets of other member countries will open up. This represents an opportunity for expansion for producers who already were in a strong competitive position, and who may want to adopt a *top dog* strategy of expanding into new markets.

12.3.2 Multilateral trade liberalization

The *multilateral trading system* is governed by rules and regulations which make up the *GATT*. The GATT itself is made up of a series of *Articles* which describe a set of principles which govern international trade. Since its inception in 1948, the GATT has sought to liberalize trade through expansion of its membership and through trade negotiations. When the GATT was formed in 1948, membership consisted of 23 nations. At the conclusion of the Uruguay Round of trade negotiations at the end of 1993, there were 117 nations who were *signatories* to the GATT. GATT negotiations have typically been conducted as *GATT Rounds*, formal negotiations with relatively well-defined objectives between countries which subscribe to the principals of the GATT. The recently completed *Uruguay Round* was the most

ambitious GATT Round thus far, with negotiations on many aspects of international trade which were previously beyond the scope of the GATT. All GATT Rounds and a very brief list of negotiation topics are listed in Table 12.8.

One of the results of the Uruguay Round was the creation of the WTO. The WTO was to assume the responsibilities of the GATT, and all other initiatives described in the Uruguay Round which were typically beyond the scope of the GATT. As of July 2001, there were 142 member countries or *contracting parties* to the WTO. In order to be a contracting party to the WTO, nations must commit to observing and applying the rules and regulations implied by the WTO. Nations do this voluntarily, and as such are committing to a policy of liberalized trade when they become contracting parties to the WTO.

While there are a number of Articles and Agreements which describe how international trade is governed by the WTO, the first three Articles have arguably been the most important in affecting how international trade has been liberalized through the GATT and WTO since 1948:

- *Article I*: guarantees *most-favored-nation* treatment between contracting parties, commonly referred to as *MFN*. Under *MFN*, any contracting party must grant treatment to any other contracting party consistent with treatment granted to its most-favored trading partner. For example, any tariff concessions negotiated between the Argentina and Brazil must be extended to all other contracting parties under *MFN*.

- *Article II*: a series of Annexes to the GATT which list the tariff bindings and concessions of each of the contracting parties. Every contracting party submits a list of MFN tariffs to the GATT, and commits to ensuring that actual import tariffs can never be raised above these MFN tariffs. In this way, the GATT ensures that tariffs do not escalate, and through subsequent GATT Rounds, contracting parties negotiate reductions in these MFN tariffs, resulting in trade liberalization.

- *Article III*: guarantees that all contracting parties afford *national treatment* to all imports, once all tariffs and GATT-consistent duties have been paid at the border. Any imported good must be afforded treatment as favorable as that granted any domestically produced good. As such, domestic measures (other than tariffs) which discriminate against imports are prohibited.

Through application of these three Articles, the GATT (now the WTO) ensures that all contracting parties do not discriminate between imports and domestically produced goods, and do not discriminate between imports from different nations. Also, by binding tariffs and then negotiating reductions in these tariff bindings, significant liberalization of trade has been achieved by the GATT. So for all members of the WTO, the Articles and Agreements which make up the WTO effectively change the *rules of the game* when the strategies played are trade policy tools. Instead of a non-cooperative setting where individual countries apply trade policy tools like import tariffs, the WTO provides a cooperative setting where members commit themselves to limited and well-defined application of strategic trade policy. Agreements for the settlement of disputes (described in the case on Howe Leather earlier in this chapter) ensure that a mechanism is in place to deal with WTO members who fail to abide by the *rules of the game*.

It is also interesting to see how the most-favored-nation article affects relative bargaining power between WTO members. Let's return to the example of the previous section where Mexico was bargaining with the US. Within the NAFTA, Mexico might have relatively little bargaining power against a trading partner like the US which is so much larger. But in the WTO, any agreements which Mexico makes with the US, and which the US makes with Mexico, are automatically extended to *all* WTO members through MFN. This has the effect of leveling the playing field between any WTO members when it comes to strategic trade policy.

Finally, we should note how liberalized trade through the GATT and the WTO has changed the competitive environment which the manager faces. Greater trade liberalization through reductions of tariff bindings and an increase in the number of members of the GATT and the WTO have resulted in a considerable increase in international competition. All managers must be aware of these changes, in order to formulate the appropriate strategic responses to changes in the international competitive environment. The decision to invest in plant and equipment, as described in the case on Honda Canada Manufacturing, will certainly change as trade is liberalized and WTO members commit

Canada–EU Dispute over Trade in Beer

Some strategies which affect international competition can be illustrated by considering a recent dispute between Canada and the EU on trade in beer. The EU argued that listing practices by provincial liquor boards in Canada were inconsistent with Article III (National Treatment) of the GATT. In Canada, provincial governments have monopoly control over the sale and distribution of alcoholic beverages. This control allowed provincial governments to require that brewers producing beer outside of a province obtain a *listing* from the provincial liquor board in order to legally sell in that province. This strategy provided a barrier to entry, limiting competition within provincial beer markets. Note that this strategy applied to beer imported from outside of Canada, and also to beer "imported" from other Canadian provinces. In some provinces, foreign producers (but not domestic producers) were required to provide proof of demand for their product to the liquor board in order to obtain a *listing*.

These listing practices affected the strategy of foreign beer producers like Anheuser-Busch in the US, who allowed Canadian producers to sell their beer in Canada under license. Instead of trying to export Budweiser to Canada directly through provincial liquor boards, Anheuser-Busch sells a license to Labatt's, a Canadian beer producer, which allows Labatt's to produce and sell Budweiser in Canada.

These discriminatory listing practices also induced Canadian producers like Labatt's and Molson's to set up production facilities in different Canadian provinces, instead of having a small number of production facilities supplying the entire Canadian market.

Source: A more detailed description of Canadian discriminatory practices in the beer industry is available in Knieling (1993).

themselves to restricted application of strategic trade policies. A more liberalized trade environment is certainly important when considering entry and exit problems, such as those described in Chapter 10. Another example is presented in the above case, where beer producers decide where to set up production plants and whether or not to license production of their products internationally.

Summary

- As trade barriers are reduced, firms are exposed to greater competition from firms in other countries, but also have the opportunity to take advantage of greater access to markets in other countries.
- Nations can experience *gains from trade*, which can arise from many sources, including international differences in production technology and relative factor endowments, and increasing returns to scale.
- Trade distortions like import tariffs have different effects on different agents within the country applying the distortion and its trading partners.
- The effects of trade distortions can be broken into a volume of trade effect and a terms of trade effect.

Summary contd

- On its own, a nation has an incentive to apply trade distortions if it can take advantage of a positive terms of trade effect.
- The strategic effects of trade distortions take account of retaliation by trading partners, so that application of strategic trade policy can leave all trading partners worse off.
- The negative prisoner's dilemma outcome which can be associated with application of strategic trade policies can be avoided by increased cooperation between trading partners.
- Cooperation can be encouraged through PTAs like the EU and the NAFTA, and through Multilateral Trade Organizations like the WTO.

Notes

1 Of course, a complete description of motivations for trade between countries could form the subject for a semester-long course in International Trade. There exist many excellent references for such material, including Appleyard and Field (2001), and Markusen *et al*. (1995).

2 You should be able to verify that all 80 units of labor in North and all 800 units of labor in South are fully employed in this example.

3 *Restraint Utilization Quota Year 1995 – Country Report*, published by the Special Trade Policy Division, Department of Foreign Affairs and International Trade Canada.

4 In July 2001, Moldova became the 142nd country to accede to the WTO.

Exercises

1 The following table shows the unit labor requirements for two commodities in two countries, Home and Foreign.

Country \\ Commodity	Home	Foreign
Guns	8	6
Roses	4	12

(a) Which country has the absolute advantage rose production, and gun production?

(b) Which country has the comparative advantage in rose production, and gun production?

(c) If the terms of trade are $e = p_{guns}/p_{roses} = 1$, are there gains from trade? What will be the pattern of trade?

(d) If e rises from $e = 1$ to $\tilde{e} = 1.5$, is Home better off or worse off? Is this an improvement or a deterioration in Home's terms of trade?

2 Suppose that the world price of wine $p_{wine} = \$10$ per bottle, and that Canada is a net importer of wine. To promote and protect wine production in the Niagara peninsula, suppose that the Canadian government charges a 20 percent tariff on wine imports.

(a) Using a graph like Figure 12.1, illustrate this initial trading equilibrium in the Canadian wine market using the Canadian demand and supply curves for wine.

(b) Suppose that the government removed the tariff on imported wine. What would happen to:

- the volume of wine imports
- Canadian wine production
- the price of wine in Canada
- welfare of Canadian wine consumers
- surplus of Canadian wine producers
- government tariff revenue

3 Until recently, some countries including Australia, Canada, and South Korea used supply management programs to control production and pricing in a number of agricultural sectors. Marketing Boards in these sectors controlled production and distribution of primary agricultural products like chicken and wheat, and restricted imports, so that these programs operated like very strict import quotas.

(a) Given discussions of entry and exit problems in Chapter 10, discuss whether these Marketing Boards provide a barrier to entry. If so, what effect would this have on the structure of competition in the primary agricultural markets in Australia, Canada, and South Korea?

(b) The Uruguay Round included Articles which explicitly prohibited supply management programs. As a result, these countries were required to replace the import restrictions implied by Marketing Boards with tariffs, such as listed by Canada in the following table:

Commodity	WTO tariff equivalents (%)
Butter	351
Cheddar cheese	289
Milk	284
Chicken	280
Skimed milk powder	237
Eggs	192
Turkey	182

* Tariff Equivalents of Canadian Marketing Board Distortions.
Source: *Globe and Mail*, July 10, 1995.

If the world price of chickens is $1 per kilogram, what would the price be in Canada?

(c) Do these tariff data support or contradict your answer to part (a)? What effect would a reduction in the tariff on imported chickens have on the price of chickens in Canada? Use a graph to answer this question, if necessary.

4 Australia and New Zealand entered into the "Closer Economic Relations (CER) Trade Agreement" on January 1, 1983. Given your understanding of PTAs and Game Theory, try to describe the Agreement between Australia and New Zealand as a Game. Who are the players? What are the strategies and payoffs to each player? Would you describe this as a non-cooperative or a cooperative game? How does entering into the CER change the rules of the game?

5 The US and EU both use export subsidies to support producers in their agriculture sectors.

(a) Use a graph like Figure 12.1 to describe the effects of an export subsidy on a country which exports agricultural products.

(b) What are the terms of trade and volume of trade effects of such an export subsidy in the United States or the EU?

(c) Now consider a country which imports agricultural products from the US or the EU. What are the terms of trade and volume of trade effects of these export subsidies in this importing country?

(d) The Cairns Group includes countries like Australia and Canada which export agricultural products but have very limited domestic support programs for producers of agricultural products. Considering the strategic effects of the export subsidies by the US and the EU, what do you expect would be the attitude of the Cairns Group toward these export subsidies?

References

Appleyard, Dennis R. and Alfred J. Field, Jr. *International Economics,* 4th edn (New York: McGraw Hill, 2001).

Export and Import Controls Bureau. *Restraint Utilization Quota Year 1995: Country Report* (Ottawa: Department of Foreign Affairs and International Trade Canada, 1996).

International Monetary Fund. *The World Economic Outlook,* December 2001. Washington, DC: IMF, 2001.

Knieling, Derek. *Canadian Brewing: An Industry Facing International Competition* (unpublished manuscript, Wilfrid Laurier University, 1993).

Markusen, James R. *et al. International Trade: Theory and Evidence* (New York: McGraw Hill, 1995).

Ward's Communications, *Ward's Automotive Yearbook* (Southfield, MI: Intertec Publishing Corp., various issues).

World Bank. *World Development Indicators,* Washington, D.C: International Bank for Reconstruction and Development/World Bank, 2000.

Part III

Strategic Interaction within Firms

Chapter 13

Vertical and horizontal integration

●●

When you are finished with this chapter you should understand:

- The difference between vertical and horizontal integration
- How a multiplant firm allocates output between its various production facilities
- How a multi-output firm prices goods with related demands
- Outsourcing and the role of transfer pricing in the multidivisional firm

Everything we have looked at in this book so far – from pricing to advertising, from location to regulation – has dealt with how the firm interacts with other firms, the marketplace, or the government. In other words, all the interactions we have looked at take place between the firm and an entity outside the firm. For the last four chapters of the book we are going to leave behind the outside world and look at decisions that are made to deal with issues inside the firm.

So far we have assumed that the firm produces a single output. But practically all modern corporations produce multiple products. BP, for example, is involved in oil exploration, production, transportation, refining, and retail marketing. General Motors makes cars, light trucks, railroad locomotives, airplanes, refrigerators, air conditioners, and aerospace products as well as being involved in such diverse activities as consumer financing and satellite television. The Korean giant Lucky-Goldstar corporation produces everything from cosmetics to toothbrushes, televisions,

computers, cellular phones, and fibre optic cable in addition to running oil refineries, chemical plants, a tanker-shipping service, and an insurance business. Controlling firms with such a vast range of activities is a major challenge for management systems.

Modern corporations by and large follow the multidivisional form of organization. Managers that control individual divisions are responsible for performance of their division. They report to higher-level managers, who monitor the division managers, coordinate their activities, and plan the overall strategy of the firm. The degree of autonomy for the division managers varies from firm to firm. In some organizations, the head office keeps a very tight rein on the management of divisions; in others, divisional managers have so much autonomy that they are effectively running firms within firms. Divisions may be defined by geographic area, the technology used, the type of product produced, or the market being served. The divisional structure that is chosen depends on the particular needs of the company. In general, the structure of divisions minimizes coordination problems and facilitates the flow of information within the corporation.

One way to characterize the multidivisional structure of a firm is the degree of *vertical integration*. A vertically integrated enterprise is involved in successive stages of the production of a particular good or service. BP is a vertically integrated firm. It is involved in exploration, drilling and extraction, and transportation of crude oil to refineries; refining crude oil into petroleum, airplane fuel, heating oil, and so on; transportation of these products to retail outlets, and ownership of the outlets. The degree of vertical integration may change over time as technology changes. As recently as the 1970s, Ford manufactured steel for its automobiles and trucks at the Rouge River plant in Detroit. Today, Ford purchases all the steel it uses from outside suppliers.

A firm's divisional structure may also be characterized by the degree of *horizontal integration*.[1] A horizontally integrated firm produces different kinds of the same broadly defined good or service. BP makes many kinds of petroleum products, including heating oil, engine oil, diesel fuel, gasoline, kerosene, and so on. And General Motors produces dozens of different types of cars and trucks. Firms may be both horizontally and vertically integrated, as the example of BP suggests.

In this chapter, we're going to look at the issues and problems that arise in vertically and horizontally integrated firms. The basic problem is how to coordinate different divisions so that profit is maximized for the firm as a whole. This problem is particularly acute in the case of vertically integrated firms. When one division in the firm supplies another, the *upstream* (supplying) division may overcharge the *downstream* (buying)

division, in order to raise profit at the upstream division. But this may not be in the interest of the firm as a whole. Before we get to the problem of vertical integration, however, we look at the issues arising in a horizontally integrated enterprise.

13.1 Horizontal integration

There are two ways you can think of horizontal integration. One way is a firm with several divisions producing the same product. Toyota, for example, builds its Corolla model at Van Nuys, California factory and at Cambridge, Ontario plant. Heineken has breweries in more than 50 countries around the world. Another kind of horizontal integration arises when a firm has several divisions producing different products. For example, Toyota produces its Corolla and Camry models at three different factories in North America. Some Heineken-owned breweries produce the Amstel brand, while others produce the Murphy's brand of beers.

Of course, many firms combine both aspects of horizontal integration, as the example of Toyota suggests. To keep things simple we discuss the problems that arise in these cases separately. The next section looks at the problem of allocating output in a firm with several divisions, or plants, producing the same product, which we call the multiplant firm. The section after that looks at the issues that arise in a firm with divisions producing different products, which we call the multiproduct firm.

13.1.1 The multiplant firm

An important question that arises in the multiplant firm is: how does the firm choose production levels at the various plants? To focus the discussion, let's assume that the

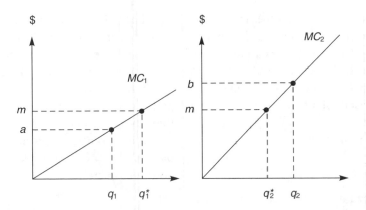

Figure 13.1 Marginal cost curves at two plants

firm is a monopoly and that it is operating just two plants. The rule we derive doesn't depend on these assumptions: it applies to any market structure and any number of plants. Let the total cost of producing the good at plant 1 be given by the function $c_1(q_1)$, where q_1 is the amount of output produced at plant 1. Similarly, let $c_2(q_2)$ be the total cost function for producing q_2 units of output at plant 2. There is no reason to expect the total cost functions at each plant to be exactly the same. The cost functions could be different, for example, because one plant is newer than the other. Because the total cost functions are different, the marginal cost functions are different as well. Figure 13.1 shows possible marginal cost curves for the two plants.

Given that the marginal cost functions are different, you might think that the firm should just pick the plant with the lower costs and close the other one down altogether. In the example of Figure 13.1, plant 1 looks more efficient because it has a lower marginal cost for the same given level of output. While this is true, it doesn't make sense to shut plant 2 down altogether. In fact, the firm should set the level of production such that output equalizes the marginal cost in the

two plants. In other words, the firm should choose q_1 and q_2 such that:

$$MC_1(q_1) = MC_2(q_2)$$

To see why this works, suppose the output levels in the two plants didn't equalize the marginal costs. Suppose the firm is producing q_1 units in plant 1 and q_2 units in plant 2 for a total output of $q = q_1 + q_2$. At output levels q_1 and q_2 in Figure 13.1, marginal cost in plant 2, given by b, is higher than marginal cost in plant 1, given by a. If the firm produces one *less* unit in plant 2, total cost falls by b. At the same time, if the firm produces one *more* unit in plant 1, total cost rises by a. Since $a < b$, switching production from plant 2 to plant 1 results in a cost saving to the firm. Total output hasn't changed, so the output levels q_1 and q_2 are not the lowest-cost way of producing the total output level of q.

This argument applies in general. If the marginal cost levels in the two plants are not equal, the firm can save money by switching production from the plant with the higher marginal cost to the plant with the lower marginal cost. Once the firm's output level is decided, therefore, the firm allocates production among its plants to equalize marginal costs. But how does the firm decide the total level of output in the first place? Since we've assumed the firm is a monopoly, it just chooses the level of total output to equate marginal revenue to the marginal cost level in each plant. To see this, we'll just write down the profit-maximization problem for a monopoly:

$$\max_{q} p(q)q - c(q)$$

Here, $p(q)$ is the inverse demand curve for the monopoly and q is the total level of output. Since $q = q_1 + q_2$ and since $c(q) = c_1(q_1) + c_2(q_2)$, we can write the two-plant monopoly profit-maximization problem as:

$$\max_{q_1, q_2} p(q_1 + q_2)(q_1 + q_2) - c_1(q_1) - c_2(q_2)$$

(13.1)

The first-order conditions (using the chain rule) for the two output levels are:

$$\frac{\partial p}{\partial q_1}(q_1 + q_2) + p - \frac{\partial c_1}{\partial q_1} = 0$$

(13.2)

$$\frac{\partial p}{\partial q_2}(q_1 + q_2) + p - \frac{\partial c_2}{\partial q_2} = 0$$

(13.3)

The first two terms in each of these equations are simply the firm's marginal revenue from producing another unit of output at plant 1 (13.2) or plant 2 (13.3). Because the output produced at the two plants is identical, it follows that:

$$\frac{\partial p}{\partial q_1}(q_1 + q_2) + p = \frac{\partial p}{\partial q_2}(q_1 + q_2) + p = MR$$

In other words, marginal revenue to the firm is the same whether the last unit of output is produced at plant 1 or plant 2. The last terms in equations (13.2–13.3) are just the marginal cost in the respective plants. We can, therefore, rewrite the first-order conditions:

$$MR - MC_1 = 0$$
$$MR - MC_2 = 0$$

In other words, the firm produces a level of output such that the marginal costs at the two plants are equal to the marginal revenue. For example, q_1^* and q_2^* in Figure 13.1 are the profit maximizing output levels at the two plants given a marginal revenue of m. Notice that, because plant 1 has lower marginal costs, more output is produced there than at plant 2 ($q_1^* > q_2^*$). But plant 2 is not shut down completely.

13.1.2 Economies of scope

Why do firms become horizontally integrated in the first place? One reason is to eliminate competition. By merging or acquiring firms that produce competing products, firms can increase their market power.[2] But it doesn't make sense to buy or merge with a firm unless profits are going to increase as a result. This depends in part on whether *economies of scope* exist. Economies of scope exist when it is cheaper to produce two or more products in the same firm than it is to produce them in separate firms. For example, gas stations often also have convenience stores. Thus, oil companies have expanded into the business of selling groceries and snack foods as well as retailing gasoline. Oil companies have, thus, realized economies of scope in supplying the services of gasoline sales and grocery sales. Since the gas station is already effectively a retail outlet, it is relatively inexpensive for the owners to add a few shelves and a couple of fridges and go into the grocery business.

Suppose the firm produces two separate goods. Economies of scope can be defined using the following measure:

$$\frac{[c(q_1) + c(q_2)] - c(q_1 + q_2)}{c(q_1 + q_2)}$$

(13.4)

Here, $c(q_1) + c(q_2)$ is the cost of producing the two goods separately. Using the example of the oil company, $c(q_1) + c(q_2)$ could represent the cost of having a corner store a few blocks away from the gas station rather than in the same physical location. The expression $c(q_1 + q_2)$ is the cost of producing the two outputs together. For example, $c(q_1 + q_2)$ could represent the cost to the oil company from having the convenience store and the gas station in the same place.

Equation (13.4) just measures the proportionate difference in costs between separate production and joint production. If there is no difference between the costs of separate and joint production, that is $c(q_1) + c(q_2) = c(q_1 + q_2)$, then there are no economies of scope. The larger the difference between separate and joint production, the larger are the economies of scope, and the greater the incentive to the firm to carry out production in combination rather than separately.

Of course, there have to be limits to economies of scope or firms would eventually swallow up the entire economy. One limit placed on the horizontal growth of firms arises from the increased coordination problems that come with firm size. As firms add more divisions, the amount of information that flows into the head office increases. Top-level managers may become overburdened with work, or they push many decisions down to the division level. In the former case, the quality of decision making will suffer. In the latter case, coordination between divisions is reduced. The firm's performance suffers either way. Creating more levels of management may not necessarily be the answer. More layers of management may further restrict the flow of information, thereby compounding the coordination problem. There is also a possibility that the further managers are removed from head office, the more time they will spend protecting their domains and furthering their own ends rather than those of the firm. Such activities, referred to as *influence costs*, are another limit to the size to which firms can grow.

13.1.3 The multiproduct firm

The multiproduct firm produces an array of products. As we've just seen one reason for this may be the existence of economies of scope. Economies of scope arise when the production of some goods or services are related. But besides being interrelated on the production side, a firm's products may be related on the demand side as well. In this section, we look at the pricing decision facing a firm producing two products with related demand. To keep things simple, we'll stick with the case of a monopoly and ignore possible economies of scope. The demand equation for the two goods may be written:

$$q_1 = D_1(p_1, p_2) \tag{13.5}$$

$$q_2 = D_2(p_1, p_2) \tag{13.6}$$

Hence, the demand for the first good depends not only on its own price (p_1), but on the price of the other good produced at the firm (p_2). The same applies for the second good. For example, demand for the Chevrolet Cavalier depends not only on its price, but also on the price of the Pontiac Sunfire, and vice versa. And the demand for the Microsoft computer program Word depends on its price and on the price of the Windows operating system: the reverse is also true.

The profit-maximization problem for the monopoly is:

$$\max_{p_1, p_2} \; p_1 q_1 + p_2 q_2 - c_1(q_1) - c_2(q_2)$$

This is just the revenue from sales of the first good plus revenue from sales of the second good minus the cost of producing goods 1 and 2.[3] By substitution from (13.5–13.6), the problem may be written:

$$\max_{p_1,p_2} p_1 D_1(p_1,p_2) + p_2 D_2(p_1,p_2)$$
$$-c_1(D_1(p_1,p_2)) - c_2(D_2(p_1,p_2))$$

Since there are only two goods and they appear symmetrically in the problem, let's focus on just one good. The first-order condition for good 1 is:

$$p_1 \frac{\partial D_1}{\partial p_1} + D_1 + p_2 \frac{\partial D_2}{\partial p_1} - \frac{\partial c_1}{\partial D_1}\frac{\partial D_1}{\partial p_1} - \frac{\partial c_2}{\partial D_2}\frac{\partial D_2}{\partial p_1} = 0$$

Using the fact that $q_1 = D_1$ and $q_2 = D_2$ and after re-arranging we have:

$$\left(p_1 - \frac{\partial c_1}{\partial q_1}\right)\frac{\partial D_1}{\partial p_1} = -D_1 - \left(p_2 - \frac{\partial c_2}{\partial q_2}\right)\frac{\partial D_2}{\partial p_1}$$

By definition, $MC_1 = \partial c_1/\partial q_1$ and $MC_2 = \partial c_2/\partial q_2$. Using these and dividing both sides of the equation by $p_1 \partial D_1/\partial p_1$, thus preserving the equality, gives:

$$\frac{p_1 - MC_1}{p_1} = -\frac{D_1}{p_1 \partial D_1/\partial p_1}$$

$$-(p_2 - MC_2)\frac{\partial D_2/\partial p_1}{p_1 \partial D_1/\partial p_1}$$

The first expression on the right-hand side is the negative of the inverse of the own elasticity of demand for good 1 (ε_1), so the first-order condition for good 1 ends up looking like:

$$\frac{p_1 - MC_1}{p_1} = \frac{1}{\varepsilon_1} - (p_2 - MC_2)\frac{\partial D_2/\partial p_1}{p_1 \partial D_1/\partial p_1}$$

(13.7)

Let the price that solves this equation be denoted p_1^*.

Recall from Chapter 3 that a monopoly producing a single good sets the price such that the markup over marginal cost is equal to the inverse of the own elasticity of demand. Suppose the division producing good 1 in our multiproduct monopoly were to follow this rule. The price of good 1 would be set according to:

$$\frac{p_1 - MC_1}{p_1} = \frac{1}{\varepsilon_1}$$

(13.8)

Let the price that solves this equation be called p_1^m.

Comparing equations (13.7) and (13.8), you can see that equation (13.7) has an extra term on the right-hand side. This extra term can be interpreted as a spillover effect between goods 1 and 2. This spillover effect means that the optimal price for good 1, p_1^*, will not equal the simple monopoly price determined by equation (13.8), p_1^m.

Consider first the case of goods that are *substitutes*. In this case, an increase in the price of good 1 increases the demand for good 2, or $\partial D_2/\partial p_1 > 0$. Together with the fact that $\partial D_1/\partial p_1 < 0$ (the demand curve for good 1 has a negative slope), this means that the second term on the right-hand side of (13.7) is positive, thus equation (13.7) can be written:

$$\frac{p_1 - MC_1}{p_1} = \frac{1}{\varepsilon_1} + \text{a positive number}$$

In other words, when goods 1 and 2 are substitutes, the markup for good 1 is higher than if the division producing good 1 sets the monopoly price. In other words, $p_1^* > p_1^m$. Why is this? Because goods 1 and 2 are substitutes, an increase in the price of good 1 increases demand for good 2. If the division producing good 1 doesn't take this effect into account and instead sets the price according to (13.8), it sets too low a price from the point of view of the aggregate firm. In effect, a division acting alone treats the other division as a competitor, which forces down the price. But the divisions are not in competition because they are in the same firm, so they must raise their prices to maximize overall profits at the firm.

As an example, consider the case of the Chevrolet Cavalier and the Pontiac Sunfire. The cars are substitute goods produced by two divisions of General Motors. If Chevrolet acted alone when setting the price of the Cavalier, it would set too low a price from the point of view of General Motors. Since the two cars are substitutes, an increase in the price of the Cavalier increases demand for the Sunfire. From GM's perspective, it is important to take this effect into account. Thus the Chevrolet division will raise its price higher owing to the spillover effect on demand for the Pontiac Sunfire.[4]

A second possibility is that the goods are *complements*. In this case, an increase in the price of good 1 decreases the demand for good 2, or $\partial D_2/\partial p_1 < 0$. Since $\partial D_1/\partial p_1 < 0$, the second term on the right-hand side of (13.7) is negative and equation (13.7) can be written:

$$\frac{p_1 - MC_1}{p_1} = \frac{1}{\varepsilon_1} + \text{a negative number}$$

In other words, when goods 1 and 2 are complements, the markup for good 1 is lower than if the division producing good 1 sets the monopoly price. In other words, $p_1^* < p_1^m$. Because goods 1 and 2 are complements, an increase in the price of good 1 decreases demand for good 2. If the division producing good 1 doesn't take this effect into account and instead sets the price according to (13.8), it sets too high a price from the point of view of the aggregate firm. An interesting possibility in this case is that one of the goods may be sold at less than marginal cost in order to boost demand for the other good.

The Microsoft software products Windows and Word provide an example of com-

plements produced by the same firm. If the spillover effects between the two products were ignored, Microsoft would set the price of the products too high. Because the products are complements, a decrease in the price of Windows raises demand for Word. This effect must be taken into account to maximize profit at Microsoft. There is also a possibility that Windows might be sold at less than marginal cost in order to boost sales of Word, and, indeed, all Microsoft products that run under Windows.

Although the mathematics has been done in terms of a monopoly, the general message of this section applies to any firm which has some degree of market power. The lesson is this: a firm producing more than one product must take into account the effect the price of each product has on all the other products. Failure to take account of substitute or complement relationships between the goods leads to lower profit. In a large firm, therefore, where different products are produced by separate divisions, coordinating prices across divisions is an important aspect of the overall performance of the firm.

13.2 Vertical integration

One of the most important coordination problems within a multiproduct firm arises when divisions transact with one another. Although this may occur in a horizontally integrated organization, interdivisional transactions are the rule in a vertically integrated firm. By definition in a vertical structure, the upstream division supplies the downstream division. In an oil company, for example, the refining division sells gasoline to the retailing division. In an automobile manufacturing company firm, the division building engines sells them to the division that assembles the car. In order to measure the performance of each division, these transactions have to be recorded and, more importantly, priced. The prices for interdivisional transactions are referred to, not surprisingly, as *transfer prices*.

Transfer prices are probably the single most important element in a division's financial performance. For example, consider an oil company in which the refining division sells to the retailing division. The transfer price between the two divisions determines the revenue of the refining division and is a major component in the cost of the retailing division. The transfer price does not have a direct impact on the overall profit at the oil company, but it is a major determinant of the financial performance of the two divisions.

Although transfer prices do not directly affect the firm's profit, they can affect profit indirectly. Inappropriately set transfer prices will reduce overall profit at the firm. To see this, consider what happens if the divisional managers are free to determine the quantities they buy and sell from other divisions or from outside suppliers. If the managers at the refinery division are judged by the profit at the division, they may have an incentive to charge the retailing division too much. In this case, the retailing division might seek outside suppliers. If the transfer price is set too low, the refining division may decide to sell to other retailing firms rather than the retailing division in the same company. Either way, the transfer prices adversely affect transactions within the firm to the detriment of the overall performance of the firm. Even if there are no outside suppliers or buyers for the divisions, an incorrect transfer price may lead quantities to be transacted between divisions that are not consistent with maximizing the firm's total profit.

To see the problem more clearly, consider the example of a firm with two divisions: a production (upstream) division, and a marketing (downstream) division. Assume that each unit of output from the production division is produced at constant marginal cost MC_P. The production division sells its output to the marketing division, which sells the product to consumers. Assume that the marginal cost of the marketing division is constant and equal to MC_M. Figure 13.2 shows the demand and marginal revenue curve for the firm as a whole, and the marginal cost curves for the two divisions.

Ignore the issue of transfer pricing for the moment, and consider what is optimal for the overall firm. One unit of the final good sold by the marketing division requires one unit of the good from the production division. The marginal cost to the firm, therefore, is equal to the sum of the marginal costs at each division. The firm's marginal cost curve is shown in Figure 13.2 as MC_F, where $MC_F = MC_P + MC_M$. Profit is maximized where marginal revenue (MR) equals marginal cost to the firm (MC_F), resulting in an output level of q^*.

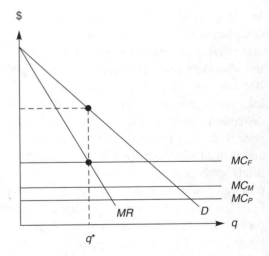

Figure 13.2 Optimal output at a firm with two divisions

The question is, given that q^* is the profit-maximizing output level for the firm, what transfer price would result in the output level of q^*? Because the marketing division sells the final product, the demand curve for the firm as a whole is also the demand curve for the marketing division. To maximize the firm's profit, therefore, the transfer price T must be set so that the marketing division sells q^* units. This will occur as long as the marginal cost to the marketing division equals the marginal revenue curve at q^*. Each extra unit purchased from the production division adds T to the cost of the marketing division, so the marginal cost to the marketing division equals $MC_M + T$. Therefore, if the transfer price is set so that $T = MC_P$, then the marginal cost to the marketing division will be $MC_M + MC_P = MC_F$, and the marketing division will sell q^* units. The transfer price effectively makes the marginal cost of the marketing division equal to the marginal cost of the firm. As a result, the optimal amount is transferred from the production to the marketing division, and profit for the firm as a whole is maximized. Therefore, the optimal transfer price is the marginal cost to the production division.

Figure 13.3 shows what happens if the wrong transfer price is set. Consider what happens if the transfer price is set too high, say at T^1. In this case, the marginal cost to the marketing division is $MC_M + T^1$. The marketing division will sell q^1 units, where $MR = MC_M + T^1$, which is not the profit maximizing output for the firm. If the transfer price is set too low, say at T^0, the marginal cost to the marketing division is $MC_M + T^0$, and again the resulting output q^0 does not maximize the firm's profit.

Incorrectly specified transfer prices may adversely affect the performance of the firm

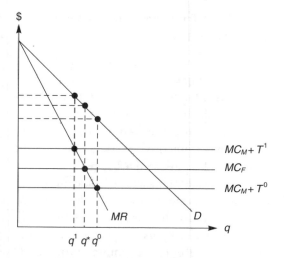

Figure 13.3 The importance of correct transfer pricing

in the long-run as well as reduce the short-run profits. A badly chosen transfer price will tend to overstate the profit of one division and understate the profit of another division. If head office decides to reward the managers of the profitable divisions and transfer prices are not correctly chosen, it might reward the wrong people because measured profits will not truly reflect the performance of the division. Moreover, if investment decisions are based on divisional profitability, artificially inflated profits from incorrect transfer prices may lead the firm to expand activities that are not really worthwhile. Alternatively, low profits or even losses resulting from wrongly specified transfer prices may lead to efficient divisions being shut down.

The example above illustrated that an incorrect transfer price may reduce overall corporate profits. We now look into the transfer pricing problem in more detail. We will see that the existence of a supplier outside the firm is an important factor in the transfer pricing decision.

13.2.1 Transfer pricing with a competitive outside market

When there are other firms that also produce the good being transferred between divisions and provided these firms constitute a competitive market, the transfer pricing problem is straightforward. The optimal transfer price equals the competitive market price for the product. The outside market price results in interdivisional transactions that maximize overall corporate profit and it provides the right signals for the firm's investment decisions. As we demonstrate below, it doesn't matter to overall corporate profitability whether the good being transferred between divisions is produced outside the firm or produced by one of the firm's upstream divisions, as long as the competitive market price is used as the transfer price.

Let's continue with the example of a firm with two divisions: the upstream division supplying an input for the downstream division. In addition, suppose there is a group of firms outside the two-division conglomerate that also make the good produced by the upstream division. Suppose these firms constitute a competitive market and that the market price of the upstream good is p_1. Inside the firm, the supply curve of the good is just the marginal cost curve of the upstream or selling division, shown in Figure 13.4 as MC^U.[5] The marginal revenue curve of the downstream or buying division, labeled MR^D, is also the demand curve for the buying division.[6]

The price that clears the internal market at the firm is p_2. One might be tempted to think that p_2 will be the optimal transfer price. At this transfer price, revenue to the upstream division is $p_2 q_2$. Cost to the upstream division is the area under the marginal cost curve up to q_2. Profit to the upstream division, therefore, is represented by the area of the rectangle $p_2 q_2$ minus the area under MC^U up to q_2, or the area of the triangle ABC. Given a transfer price of p_2, cost to the downstream

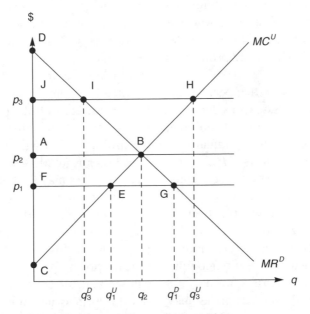

Figure 13.4 Transfer pricing with a competitive outside market

248

division is $p_2 q_2$. Revenue to the downstream division is the area under the marginal revenue curve up to q_2. Profit to the downstream division, therefore, is represented by the area under MR^D up to q_2 minus the area of the rectangle $p_2 q_2$, or the area of the triangle ABD. Total profit at the firm is the sum of profits at each division. Adding together the triangles ABC and ABD, yields a total profit to the firm represented by the area of the triangle BCD.

There is no reason to expect that the price that clears the internal market at the firm, p_2, is equal to the outside market price. In fact, p_2 will be the outside market price only by a fluke. In general, the market price will be higher or lower than p_2. Suppose the market price is p_1. If this is chosen as the transfer price, the upstream division produces q_1^U where price equals marginal cost. Profit to the upstream division in this case is the area of the triangle CEF. The downstream division buys q_1^D where marginal revenue equals marginal cost (the transfer or market price p_1). Profit to the downstream division is the area of the triangle DFG. Adding the two areas together gives total profit at the firm. Total profit is higher than when the transfer price is p_2 by the area of the triangle BEG. In other words, if p_1 is the market price, the firm maximizes profit by setting a transfer price of p_1 and not the price that equates supply and demand for the internal market, p_2. In this case, the upstream division produces only a small amount, much less than the amount the downstream ends up selling. The difference, $q_1^D - q_1^U$, is purchased by the downstream division from outside firms.

The phenomenon wherein firms purchase inputs from outside suppliers is commonly called *outsourcing*. Notice that if the market price p_1 is below the point C, then the mar-

keting division will purchase nothing from the upstream division. In fact, the firm will shut down the production division altogether at a market price of p_1 and the firm will outsource all of its input to the marketing division. Because outside suppliers can produce the good at a lower marginal cost than the production division, there is no point operating the production division at all. Recent years have seen more and more firms favor outsourcing over in-house divisions. This is especially true in the automotive industry. One explanation for this trend is increased competition at the upstream level which has forced down the prices of output produced by automobile parts manufacturers.

A similar argument may be used if the market price is p_3. In this case, with a transfer price of p_3, the upstream division produces q_3^U and the downstream division sells q_3^D. Profit at the upstream division is the area of the triangle CHJ and profit at the downstream division is the area of the triangle DIJ. Combined profits are larger than when the transfer price is p_2 by the area of the triangle BHI. In this case, the upstream division produces way more than the downstream division sells, with the excess being sold to outside firms. Once again, the optimal profit-maximizing transfer price is not the price that clears the internal market. The optimal transfer price is the outside market price.

In 2001, Acer, Taiwan's largest producer of personal computers, responded to a downturn by re-evaluating its own manufacturing branch. As a result of the exercise, the entire manufacturing division was renamed (Wistron) and sold off. The new firm will have to compete to build Acer's computers in the same way that it bids to build computers for other firms.

Outsourcing by the Military

By the late 1990s, following a decade of cuts to defense spending, many NATO countries considered outsourcing various "non-strategic" services. The US Air Force, for example, stated that it wants to save $4 billion by 2005 through outsourcing all activities that are "not inherently governmental." Estimates suggested that private contractors could perform logistical operations – like setting up tents and toilets, washing uniforms, pumping gas, and so forth – for about two-thirds the cost of the military.

Lower labor costs are the primary source of the contractors' cost advantage. For one thing, private firms rely much less on permanent staff, hiring cheaper part-time workers on a contract basis as they are needed. Second, the service firms tend to hire local workers and pay local wages rather than hire, say, American or British workers that would have to be paid more to travel to dangerous foreign venues. The security concerns that arise from hiring locally in ethnically torn regions seem to have been unfounded. Local recruits can be vetted with the help of military security and have been used without incident in Angola, Somalia, and the Balkans.

Besides reducing the costs in the field, domestic military operations may also be subject to cost-savings. Britain has handed over the daily operation of a naval dockyard to a private firm. And private firms maintain military aircraft and bases in Australia. In future, private firms could even provide training and education for armed services personnel. At the extreme, armies and war itself could be outsourced, as it was by the city-states of medieval Italy!

Source: "War and piecework." *The Economist*, July 9, 1999.

13.2.2 Transfer pricing with no outside market

Of course, it is very rare that a competitive outside market exists for products transferred within firms. Competitive markets for products that have exactly the specifications any particular firm needs exist for only a few very standardized products, like wheat. For instance, it is unlikely that an automobile manufacturer will be able to find a competitive market that produces exactly the kind of air conditioners it needs for its cars. Competitive outside suppliers should, therefore, be considered the exception rather than the rule. More realistically, the market producing inputs for a firm's downstream divisions either won't exist, or it will be oligopolistic.

At the beginning of this section, we briefly discussed the transfer price within a corporation for which there was no outside firm producing the upstream good. We concluded that the optimal transfer price in this case is the marginal cost of the upstream division. Let's look at this problem in a little more detail using a numerical example.

Suppose that demand for the good produced by the downstream or marketing division is $p = 20 - q/12$. The marginal costs of the production and marketing divisions are, respectively, $MC_P = 2$ and $MC_M = 4$. From above, we know that the optimal transfer price for the firm is the marginal cost of the production division, implying $T = 2$. The marginal cost of the marketing division is thus $MC_M + T = 6$. Total revenue ($p \times q$) is $20q - q^2/12$, so marginal revenue is $20 - q/6$.

The marketing division maximizes profit by equating marginal revenue and marginal cost:

$$20 - \frac{q}{6} = 6 \rightarrow q = 84$$

Substituting 84 for q into the demand function yields a final price of $p = 13$.

Now consider what happens if the manager of the production division is allowed to set the transfer price. Suppose that head office judges the manager's performance by the profitability of the division. In this case, the production manager seeks to maximize profit of the production division. This is done by equating the division's marginal revenue and marginal cost. Marginal cost is $MC_P = 2$. Marginal revenue is determined from the demand curve for the production division output. To determine demand, the manager has to look at the profit maximization problem of the marketing division, the only customer of the production division. Given a transfer price of T, the marginal cost at the marketing division is $4 + T$. Marginal revenue at the marketing division is, from above, $20 - q/6$. Since the marketing division manager also maximizes profit, output of that division is determined where marginal revenue equals marginal cost:

$$20 - \frac{q}{6} = 4 + T \rightarrow T = 16 - \frac{q}{6}$$

The production division manager knows that this equation determines marketing division output, or equivalently, production division demand.[7] Total revenue at the production division $(T \times q)$ is, therefore, $16q - q^2/6$, implying marginal revenue is $16 - q/3$. Equating marginal revenue and marginal cost at the production division:

$$16 - \frac{q}{3} = 2 \rightarrow q = 42$$

Substituting 42 for q into the production division demand function yields a transfer price of $T = 9$. Therefore, a transfer price of $T = 9$ maximizes the profit of the production division. The marketing division buys 42 units from the production division, which it sells to consumers for $P = 16.5$.

Of course, a transfer price of $T = 9$ does not maximize overall profit at the firm because the profit-maximizing transfer price is $T = 2$. This is easy to check. For a transfer price of $T = 9$, revenue at the production division is $9 \times 42 = 378$ and cost is $2 \times 42 = 84$,[8] giving a profit of $378 - 84 = 294$. Revenue at the marketing division is $16.5 \times 42 = 693$ and cost is $4 \times 42 + 9 \times 42$,[9] giving a profit of $693 - 546 = 147$. Total profit for the firm when $T = 9$ is, therefore, $294 + 147 = 441$. When $T = 2$, revenue and cost at the production division are both equal to 168, giving a profit of zero. Revenue at the marketing division is $13 \times 84 = 1,092$ and cost is $4 \times 84 + 2 \times 84 = 504$, giving a profit of $1,092 - 504 = 588$. When $T = 2$, therefore, the firm's profit is 588, which is higher than the profit for $T = 9$, as expected.

The problem is, of course, the incentive structure at the firm encourages the production division manager to consider only profit at the production division. The implications for the downstream marketing division are completely ignored. The manager ends up charging a monopoly price to the downstream division, reducing the firm's output below the optimal level. The manager is given an incentive in the first place to encourage optimal performance. But in this case, the incentive backfires and the firm ends up with lower profits as a result. This is a very important lesson for any integrated organization. The incentives for the division managers must be consistent with the goal of profit maximization at the firm as a whole.

One response to this example might be: why not just order the manager at the production division to transfer 84 units to the marketing division? There are a couple of reasons. For one thing, the whole idea of the multidivisional firm is to reduce the amount of decision-making that goes on at head office. Division managers are closer to the level where decisions have an impact, so it makes sense for them to have control. The cost of the multidivisional structure, as we have already pointed out, is a potential lack of coordination. Transfer pricing is a way to coordinate divisions. Firms with appropriately set transfer prices will, therefore, be able to take advantage of the benefits that come from a multidivisional structure.

Another reason for using the transfer pricing mechanism over direct orders lies in managerial autonomy. Simply feeding mounds of information to a head office that may not even be in the same country is likely to be far less effective than giving a divisional manager with knowledge and expertise about a specific technology or market some control. Transfer pricing gives managers the freedom to adjust the amount they buy or sell in interdivisional transactions. The advantage of this system is its flexibility. It allows managers to respond to incentives within the firm and provides competitive pressure to maintain costs and quality. A list of orders from head office does not provide the same incentives.

Rather than quantity controls, another solution may be to order the upstream division to set the transfer price equal to its marginal cost. In other words, head office could just unilaterally require that all transactions take place at the transfer price $T = 2$. The only problem with this is, in practice, the marginal cost at the production division is unlikely to be known by either head office or the downstream division. Indeed, the production manager has an incentive to overstate the costs of the production division in order to get a higher transfer price and, thereby, boost the profit of the division. While this would improve the apparent performance of the upstream division, it is detrimental to the profit of the overall firm. Merging the two divisions isn't really a solution either, because it just converts an external problem between two divisions into a problem internal to a single division.

13.2.3 Transfer pricing with a non-competitive outside market

Even if there is a market outside the firm producing an input for the downstream division, it is unlikely that the market is competitive. An interesting case occurs when the upstream or supplying firm is a monopoly. In this case, if the upstream firm exercises monopoly power over the price of the input used by the downstream firm, a lower than optimal amount of the input will be purchased by the downstream firm. The result is that total profits at the two firms will be lower than they could otherwise be. There is an incentive, therefore, for the two firms to join together (or one firm to take over the other) in order to take advantage of the higher potential profits. In other words, a non-competitive outside market is a potential reason for vertical integration to occur in the first place.

This argument is easy to follow, because it is just an application of the example used in the previous section. In the example, we looked at what an upstream division in the same firm would do if allowed to set the transfer price. We saw that if the manager at the upstream division were to set the transfer price to maximize profit at the division, profits at the firm as a whole would be lower.

The upstream manager would set a monopoly price and, as a result, the downstream division would purchase an inefficiently low amount of the input. Overall profits can be increased if the transfer price is set equal to the marginal cost.

Now consider what happens if the upstream operation is a separate firm altogether rather than a division of the same firm. The same scenario will be played out. The manager of the upstream firm maximizes profit by setting a monopoly price. As a result, the downstream firm buys less of the input. Profits at the two firms together would be higher if the upstream firm were to supply the input at marginal cost rather than at the monopoly price.

The problem, however, is that marginal cost pricing reduces profits at the upstream firm to zero. In the example in the previous section, profit at the upstream (production) division fell from 294 to zero under marginal cost pricing, while profit at the downstream (marketing) division rose from 147 to 588. The firm's total profit from marginal cost pricing was 588, or 147 higher than when the upstream division charged a monopoly price.

When the upstream and downstream operations are in separate firms, however, the managers at the upstream firm will have to be given some of the profits at the downstream firm, otherwise it is not in the interest of the upstream firm to supply the input at marginal cost. The extra profit to the two firms resulting from marginal cost pricing means there is room for the firms to reach an agreement. For example, the downstream firm could transfer profits of 295 to the upstream firm, which is higher than the 294 profit the upstream firm earns through monopoly pricing. This leaves a profit of 293 for the downstream firm (588 − 295), which is higher than the profit of 147 to the downstream firm with monopoly pricing.

Negotiating an agreement of this type may be tricky, however. For one thing, we have assumed that there is perfect information about the marginal cost of production at the upstream firm. But if costs at the upstream firm are not known by the manager of the downstream firm, the upstream firm has an incentive to overstate costs and charge the downstream firm a monopoly price. This way, the upstream firm gets the profit from monopoly pricing in addition to the profit transferred from the downstream firm. Knowing this, the manager of the downstream firm may be reluctant to enter into an agreement with the upstream firm.

Another problem arises because the downstream firm is the only customer of the upstream firm. In this case, the monopoly power of the upstream firm is countered by the monopsony power of the downstream firm. The downstream firm can exploit the fact that the upstream firm has no other customers and hold out for a low price, a phenomenon referred to as the *hold-up problem*.

For example, suppose the upstream firm agrees to invest $1 million in machinery to produce a part for the downstream firm at a variable cost of $10 per unit. Suppose that the machinery is specific to producing the particular part and cannot be used to make anything else. The machinery also has a useful life of 100,000 parts and has no scrap value. In order to recover the investment cost and cover the variable cost of production, the supplier must get at least $20 per part from the downstream firm ($10 per part to cover variable cost and $10 per part to cover the cost of machinery and equipment). But, once the machinery is in place, it pays the upstream firm to operate the machinery as long as the variable cost of $10 per part is covered because the investment of $1 million is a sunk cost. Once the machinery is in place, therefore, the downstream firm can bargain for a price reduction. Because the machinery has no other use, the downstream firm is in a very strong position. But any price reduction below $20 per part means the upstream firm won't recover the cost of the investment. Knowing this, the upstream firm, will not invest in the machinery in the first place.

Thus, hold-up problems exist in both directions: a monopoly supplier may hold key inputs back from a downstream firm in order to get a high price, or a downstream firm might take advantage of specific capital at a supplier in order to hold out for a lower price. In either case, the problem can be controlled by vertical integration. The downstream firm can purchase the specific machinery and equipment and produce the good or service internally. Alternatively, the two firms could negotiate a contract that specifies a price and quantity to be transferred. The choice depends on the relative costs of vertical integration versus the costs of writing and enforcing contracts.

Electric Utilities and Coal Suppliers

A classic case of the interplay between assets and the hold-up problem concerns that of coal-burning electricity generating plants. Since the amounts of coal required to fuel power stations are so large and the resulting transportation costs so high, it is often economical to locate them right at the site of the coal mine. The characteristics of the coal, such as the sulfur content, often differ from mine to mine. Thus, once the decision to locate a power station at a mine has been taken, the construction of the boilers is often optimized precisely for the grade of coal available. The generating company may also undertake expensive investments in transmission capacity in order to deliver power to its customers.

The electric utility thus invests heavily in capital specific to the mine site and is vulnerable to hold-up by the mining company. In response to the potential hold-up, mine-mouth generating plants are much more likely to own the coal mine compared with plants that are not located near mines. And in those cases where mine-mouth plants were not vertically integrated, generating companies much more heavily on long-term contracts rather than on the spot market or short-term contracts.

Source: Paul Joskow. "Vertical integration and long-term contracts: the case of coal-burning electric generating plants." *Journal of Law, Economics, and Organization*, 33 (Fall 1985), pp. 32–80.

Summary

- Vertically integrated firms are involved in successive stages of the production process for a good or service.
- Horizontally integrated firms produce different kinds of the same broadly defined good or service.
- A multiplant firm produces the same good at more than one location. The firm allocates output between plants so that the marginal cost of production is equal across the plants.

Summary Contd

- Economies of scope exist when it is cheaper to produce two or more products in the same firm than it is to produce them separately.
- When pricing its goods, a multiproduct firm producing goods which have related demands must take into account the effect the price one good has on the demand for another.
- Correct transfer prices are key to the performance of a vertically integrated firm. Incorrectly set transfer prices provide the wrong indicators about the performance of upstream and downstream divisions.
- If there is a competitive market producing the upstream good, the optimal transfer price equals the price in the competitive market.
- If there is no market producing the upstream good, the optimal transfer price equals the marginal cost of the upstream division.
- If there is a non-competitive market producing the upstream good, the fact that joint profits of the upstream and downstream firm will be greater if the transfer price is set equal to the marginal cost of the upstream firm is a reason for the two firms to merge.

Notes

1 In business writing, the term *horizontal* is used to describe any activity that is not vertically related. The definition here is narrower because it refers to related activities, following the definition used in antitrust law and economics.

2 Of course, this presumes antitrust regulators allow the merger or acquisition to go ahead.

3 Total cost appears as two separate cost functions owing to the assumption that there are no economies of scope.

4 Strictly speaking, of course, GM does not have a monopoly in the market for compact cars, so this example does not completely match the conditions of the theoretical model.

5 Recall that the marginal cost curve of a competitive firm, which is effectively the role of the upstream division, is also its supply curve.

6 If the buying division were to pay more than the marginal revenue it gets when it sells the final product, it would be making a loss. Therefore, marginal revenue represents the maximum the buying division will pay for a given quantity from the selling division, or, in other words, it represents the demand curve of the buying division.

7 Recall that one unit from the production division is required for every one unit sold by the marketing division.

8 Assuming fixed cost is zero, total cost is the area under the marginal cost curve, which, because marginal cost is constant, is just $MC_P \times$ (output).

9 The marketing division incurs selling cost of $MC_M \times$ (output) plus the cost associated with the transfer price $T \times$ (output).

Exercises

1 Consider a multiplant monopoly facing demand given by:

$$q = 480 - 4p$$

The firm operates two plants with total cost functions given by:

$$c_1(q_1) = \frac{2}{3}q_1^2 - 12q_1$$
$$c_2(q_2) = 2q_2^2 + 36q_2$$

(a) State the profit maximizing rule that determines how much output the monopoly will produce at each plant.

(b) Use the profit maximizing rule to determine the output produced at each of the two plants and, hence, the total output of the firm.

(c) Show that the profit maximizing rule for output allocation between the plants is satisfied.

(d) Determine the price charged by the firm. Compute costs at the two plants and, hence, determine profits at the firm.

2 Consider a multiplant monopoly facing demand given by:

$$q = 4100 - 25p$$

The firm operates two plants with total cost functions given by:

$$c_1(q_1) = 0.1q_1^2 + 40q_1$$

$$c_2(q_2) = 0.05q_2^2 + 50q_2$$

(a) State the profit maximizing rule that determines how much output the monopoly will produce at each plant.

(b) Use the profit maximizing rule to determine the output produced at each of the two plants and, hence, the total output of the firm.

(c) Show that the profit maximizing rule for output allocation between the plants is satisfied.

(d) Determine the price charged by the firm. Compute costs at the two plants and, hence, determine profits at the firm.

3 Consider a multiproduct firm that has a monopoly in the production of each of the two goods. Suppose the demand functions are given by:

$$D_1(p_1, p_2) = 100 - 2p_1 - p_2$$
$$D_2(p_1, p_2) = 200 - p_1 - 4p_2$$

The total cost functions for production of each of the two goods are given by:

$$c_1(q_1) = 2q_1$$
$$c_2(q_2) = 4q_2$$

(a) Are these two goods substitutes or complements? Explain.

(b) Suppose the firm ignores the relationship between the two goods and uses the inverse elasticity formula to set the prices of the two goods as a markup over marginal cost. Calculate p_1 and p_2.

(c) Now suppose that the firm takes into account the relationship between the two goods and sets the prices accordingly. Determine p_1 and p_2. Are the prices higher or lower than the prices using the inverse elasticity rule? Explain the reason for your answer.

(d) Show that total profit is higher for the optimal prices than it is for the prices using the inverse elasticity rule.

4 Consider a multiproduct firm that has a monopoly in the production of each of the two goods. Suppose the demand functions are given by:

$$D_1(p_1, p_2) = 10 - 0.2p_1 + 0.1p_2$$
$$D_2(p_1, p_2) = 20 + 0.1p_1 - 0.3p_2$$

The total cost functions for production of each of the two goods are given by:

$$c_1(q_1) = q_1$$
$$c_2(q_2) = 4q_2$$

(a) Are these two goods substitutes or complements? Explain.

(b) Suppose the firm ignores the relationship between the two goods and uses the inverse elasticity formula to set the prices of the two goods as a markup over marginal cost. Calculate p_1 and p_2.

(c) Now suppose that the firm takes into account the relationship between the two goods and sets the prices accordingly. Determine p_1 and p_2. Are the prices higher or lower than the prices using the inverse elasticity rule? Explain the reason for your answer.

(d) Show that total profit is higher for the optimal prices than it is for the prices using the inverse elasticity rule.

5 Suppose there is a firm with two divisions: an upstream division and a downstream division. One unit of output from the upstream or production division is used for each unit of output of the downstream division. The upstream division is the only producer of the input for the downstream division. The cost functions for the two divisions are given by:

$$c_P(q) = 5q$$
$$c_M(q) = q^2$$

where P and M stand for the production and marketing divisions, respectively. The inverse demand for output produced by the marketing division is given by:

$$p = 10 - 0.25q$$

(a) Determine the profit maximizing transfer price for the firm.

(b) Calculate the output of the two divisions and the price the marketing division charges its customers if the production division sets the optimal transfer price.

(c) Suppose the firm allows the manager of the production division to set the transfer price. Determine the transfer price the manager will charge the marketing division, assuming the manager maximizes profits at the production division.

(d) Demonstrate that the firm's profits are greater when the optimal transfer price, as opposed to the transfer price set by the manager of the production division, is set.

6 Suppose there are two separate firms. The upstream firm is the only producer of an input required by the downstream firm and the upstream firm has no other customers. One unit of input at the downstream firm is required to produce one unit of output at the downstream firm. The cost functions for the two firms are:

$$c_U(q) = 4q^2 - 2q$$
$$c_D(q) = q^2 + 10q$$

where U and D stand for the upstream and downstream firms, respectively. The inverse demand for output produced by the downstream firm is given by:

$$p = 100 - q$$

(a) Determine the demand for output at the upstream firm from the downstream firm as a function of the price charged by the upstream firm.

(b) Determine the price the upstream firm will charge the downstream firm for the output produced by the upstream firms

(c) Suppose the two firms were to merge and maximize joint profits. Determine the price the upstream division will charge the downstream division, i.e. determine the optimal transfer price.

(d) Show that profits are greater at the merged firm than at when the two firms were operating as separate entities. What problems is the merger likely to face?

Reference

Milgrom, Paul and Roberts, John. *Economics, Organization and Management* (Englewood Cliffs, NJ: Prentice Hall, 1992).

Chapter 14

Labor markets

• •

When you are finished with this chapter you should understand:

- The determination of wages in a competitive labor market
- How changes in output prices and worker productivity affects wage levels
- The effect of payroll taxes on wage and employment levels
- The difference between labor demand in the short run and the long run
- The definition of a "compensating differential" and its effect on the wages a firm must pay

In this chapter and the remaining chapters in the book, we will focus on the firm's most important resource: its workers. We will look at things like hiring and firing workers, training and promoting workers (Chapter 15), wages and salaries, and unions (Chapter 16).

At the beginning of the book, before we discussed the strategic issues facing the firm, we went over the basics of perfect competition and monopoly, where strategy doesn't come into play. The idea was to get the basics out of the way before proceeding to more complex issues. The discussion of firms and their workers will follow similar lines. In this chapter, we'll look at the basics behind the most fundamental decision the firm makes, namely how many workers to hire. In fact, we'll start off by returning to the hot-dog vendor on Wasaga Beach and analyze the decisions she will have to make about how many people to hire and how much to pay them. This relatively simple starting point can be used to explain several aspects of the

employer–employee relationship, the most important being how wages are determined. We'll also use the model to illustrate other issues like why some firms will have to pay more than other firms to hire the same type of worker.

While important, the basic model is far too simple to deal with the complex issues that arise in a modern corporation which has employees at many different levels doing many different jobs. With so many employees, it is difficult to keep track of exactly what each worker is doing at every point in time. This raises the very important issue of how the company can motivate workers to work hard even if they are not under direct supervision all the time. The issue of worker motivation is discussed in the next chapter. Another important issue that arises in large firms is how to fill positions further up in the management hierarchy. One option is to promote workers from within the firm, another option is to hire from outside the firm. The issues surrounding promotion are also discussed in the next chapter.

In many countries, a significant proportion of the labor force belongs to a trade union. This means that many managers have to deal with employees through the union that represents the workers, rather than directly with the workers themselves. In the final chapter of the book, we'll look at the unique issues that arise in a unionized work place, focusing on the impact of unions on wages and conditions of employment. We will also discuss collective bargaining, that is, negotiating labor contracts between firms and unions. Not surprisingly, issues of bargaining power and strategy that we have seen elsewhere in the book arise naturally in the context of firms and unions bargaining over labor contracts. Thus, collective bargaining will provide our last application of game theory in the book.

14.1 Perfectly competitive labor market

The first thing to note is that all of the situations we have dealt with so far have looked at the firm as a supplier. But firms buy things too, namely the services of workers and capital equipment. Just as the manager will work hard to get the best deal for the things that the firm sells, the manager will work hard to get the best deal for things that the firm buys. In terms of hiring workers, getting the best deal means hiring the most productive workers for the lowest wage the firm can get away with.

By and large, the wage the firm will pay is determined by the market. Since individual firms hire only a small fraction of the total number of workers, firms have no market power over the wage they pay their workers. This is just saying that firms are price takers in the labor market. Workers also have little say over the price they can sell their services because individually they make up such a tiny fraction of the total number of workers in the market. So workers are price takers as well. To keep things simple for the time being, let's ignore how firms might try to distinguish the most productive workers from everyone else by assuming that all available workers are equally productive. It also makes sense to assume that workers won't be fooled into working for less than the going wage and firms won't be duped into paying more than the going wage, which is akin to assuming that there is perfect information in the market. Lastly, since slavery is illegal, it is safe to assume that workers are free to enter or leave the labor market as they choose.

Clearly, what we have described is a labor market that is perfectly competitive, so that the price of labor (the wage) is determined by supply and demand. To summarize, a perfectly competitive labor market is described by the following assumptions:

- firms and workers have no market power
- firms and workers have perfect information
- workers are identical in every respect
- workers are free to enter or exit the industry

Notice that these conditions are analogous to those discussed in Chapter 3 for a market for goods or services. Really, the only difference between the labor market and markets for other goods and services is that the firms are the source of demand (rather than consumers) and the workers are the source of supply (rather than firms).

14.1.1 The firm's hiring problem

Even though the firm has no control over the wage, it does have control over the number of workers it hires. Therefore, the manager's problem boils down to how many workers to hire at the going or market wage. To illustrate the basic ideas involved in the hiring decision, let's return to the hot-dog vendor on Wasaga Beach.

After a great deal of thought, the location of the cart on the beach has been chosen and the price and quality of the hot dogs has been set. It's a nice hot weekend, the barbeque has been fired up and the hot dogs are selling briskly. Pretty soon the vendor is furiously putting hot dogs in buns, handing them to customers, getting drinks from the cooler, adding up the bill, taking the money, making change at the same time as getting more hot dogs from the cooler and trying to barbeque the hot dogs without burning them. It's really too much for one person to do. Inevitably, a long line-up begins to form.

A bit later, the vendor notices out of the corner of her eye that people are beginning to leave the line-up. It can't be the quality of the food, everyone munching the hot dogs around the stand is complimenting her on how delicious they are. Besides, the people in the line-up haven't bought any of the hot dogs yet, so they couldn't know how good or bad they are. She soon realizes with horror that the people are leaving the line-up because they are fed-up waiting so long to be served. She's a victim of her own success. The worst thing is, since the people leaving the line-up are obviously hungry, they are just going to go somewhere else to get food: they won't be back. And who knows how many people further down the beach have seen the length of the line-up and haven't even bothered to come over to her stand?

Later in the afternoon, when things have quieted down, she ponders what to do about the lost customers. One option would be to cook dozens of hot dogs in advance. But there is a limit to how many can be kept warm on the grill, and there's no point serving cold hot dogs. If the quality of the food suffers, she loose all her customers. Another grill perhaps? No, she couldn't possibly operate both and do everything else at the same time. The solution is obvious: she has to hire some help. The question is, of course: how much help does she need? Naturally, it all comes down to profit. She has to figure out what is the profit-maximizing number of workers to hire.

She knows that the minimum wage in Ontario is C$6.85 per hour, so the hourly cost of each extra worker is easy to figure out: one worker will cost her $6.85 an hour, two workers $13.70 an hour, and so on. But what about the revenue side? This requires a bit more thought.

That night, she sits down and works out how many customers she served that day working on her own. If she had someone to get the drinks, add up the bills, take the money and make change, she would be able to serve more customers. But why hire just one helper? With a second helper, one could be responsible for taking the orders and dealing with the money, while the other could get the drinks and keep the grill supplied with hot dogs. Even more customers could be served that way. With a fourth helper, the tasks could be even more specialized and likely more customers could be served. Of course, it won't work this way forever. If she adds too many helpers, they will start to get in one another's way or spend half their time standing around with nothing to do. After all, there is only so much space around the grill. After a great deal of thought, she decides to try to come up with some estimates relating the number of helpers hired to the number of customers served and, thus, the amount of money the stand can take in. Suppose that she pays $1.00 for each hot dog and

Table 14.1   Helpers' contribution to the hog-dog stand

Helpers	Customers served	Extra customers served	Extra (net) revenue ($)
0	20	–	–
1	22	2	8.00
2	26	4	16.00
3	29	3	12.00
4	31	2	8.00
5	33	1	4.00
6	32	−1	−4.00

$0.50 for each can of soft drink. Hot dogs sell for $4.00, implying a net revenue of $3.00 per hot dog, and soft drinks sell for $1.50, implying a net revenue of $1.00 per can.[1] Using these numbers, she ends up with Table 14.1.

On her own, with no helpers, she managed to serve 20 customers per hour. With one helper, she figures she could serve 22 customers per hour, or two customers per hour more than she can serve working on her own. On average, each customer buys one hot dog and a drink, so an extra customer represents an increase in net revenue of $4.00 ($3.00 from the hot dog and $1.00 from the can of soft drink). Thus, an extra two customers represent an increase in net revenue of $8.00 over what she can take in by herself. A second helper would result in a further four customers served per hour and an extra $16.00 in net revenue over what she and one helper could achieve. A third helper would result in three extra customers being served and a further $12.00 in net revenue over what she and two helpers could take in. Similarly, a fourth helper adds $8.00 to net revenue and a fifth helper adds $4.00 to net revenue. The sixth helper actually results in a decrease in net revenue. The sixth helper makes the crowding around the cart so severe that the helpers get in each other's way and the total number of customers served actually falls.

Because profit is the difference between revenue and cost, it makes sense to hire helpers as long as they add more to revenue than to cost. Since the hourly cost of helpers is $6.85, the vendor figures that as long as an extra helper results in an increase of more than $6.85 in revenue, her profit goes up if she hires the helper. For example, the first helper adds $6.85 to hourly cost and $8.00 to hourly revenue, thus increasing profit by $1.15. The second helper adds $16.00 to revenue and $6.85 to cost, resulting in an extra $9.15 in profit to the vendor. The third and fourth helper add $5.15 and $1.15, respectively, to profit. But a fifth helper results only in an extra $4.00 of revenue at a cost of $6.85, or a loss of $2.85, so it doesn't make any sense to hire a fifth helper. She decides to hire four helpers. She finds an easy way to check how much the four helpers will boost her profit: all she has to do is add up how much each of them separately adds to profit. So, adding $1.15, $9.15, $5.15, and $1.15, she calculates that profit is $16.60 per hour higher with four helpers than if she works alone.

There are a couple of things she's still concerned about. First of all, her estimates of the number of customers that can be served per hour with helpers might be wrong. But the numbers can easily be adjusted after a few days experience with the new help. She knows she'll find out pretty soon if something is way off: all she has to do is compare her daily profit with the profit she made when she worked alone. If it's lower with helpers, she should probably try a slightly smaller staff. There's bound to be a bit of hit and miss in this operation, but she's a quick learner. The important thing is, the fundamental reasoning is sound. The other thing she's worried about is the weather: if it rains, she'll be stuck paying four helpers to stand around doing nothing, whereas if she were on her own it wouldn't cost her as much. But there's nothing she can do about the weather. And, in any case, what if she sends home workers on the basis of a forecast of rain that turns out to be wrong? Then she'll be back in the situation she was on the first day with long line-ups resulting in lost customers.

14.1.2 Equilibrium at the firm

The fundamental hiring rule used by the beach hot-dog vendor is applied by any firm, large or small. The basic condition is: hire workers as long as they add more to revenue than to cost. To firm-up this idea, we're going to derive the condition formally using calculus and a bit of notation.

To keep things focused, we're going to assume that everything our hypothetical firm uses to produce output, except the number of workers, is fixed. The amount of plant and equipment (physical capital) in place cannot be altered by the firm and the contracts to purchase given amounts of energy, materials and any other inputs needed are all signed and cannot be changed.[2] Because all the other inputs are pre-determined, the only thing the firm has left to do is choose the number of workers to hire.

As is the case for the hot-dog vendor, the key thing for the firm is the relationship between the number of workers (the vendor's helpers) and the amount of output produced (customers served). Typically, this relationship is represented by a *production function*. If L denotes the number of workers hired and y the amount of output that can be produced, the production function is written:

$$y = f(L) \tag{14.1}$$

The production function shows the maximum amount of output that a given amount of labor can produce. In fact, you have already seen a production function earlier, although it was in the form of a table: the first two columns of Table 14.1 represent a production function because they show the relationship between customers served (output) and the number of helpers (labor).

The production function is plotted with y on the vertical axis and L on the horizontal axis, as shown in Figure 14.1. The production function is often assumed to have the shape shown in Figure 14.1. Over most values of L, it has a positive slope, which means that output increases as more workers are hired. But the slope of the production function changes as L is increased. For low numbers of workers, the slope becomes steeper as the number of workers are increased, but, after a point, the slope becomes flatter as the number of workers are increased. This reflects the *law of diminishing returns* and follows from the fact that labor is the only input that isn't fixed. The idea is that

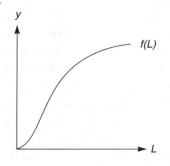

Figure 14.1 The firm's production function

the first few workers can increase output significantly because they can specialize in well defined tasks. But as more and more workers are hired to work with the fixed capital stock, the gains from specialization decrease. And if too many workers are hired the congestion caused may actually result in lower output. The hot-dog vendor was aware of this kind of behavior: she knew the first few helpers would add a lot to output, but eventually hiring more workers would be counter-productive because they would just end up getting in one another's way.

The production function represents a constraint on the firm. The constraint is a result of the firm being stuck with a particular technology, which cannot be changed because the physical capital is assumed to be fixed. For a given number of workers, points above the production function cannot be achieved because the production function gives the maximum amount of output the workers can produce. Points below the production function can obviously be achieved: if the firm can produce a certain amount of output with a given number of workers, it can certainly produce less output with the same number of workers. The production function is really just the boundary between what is technologically *feasible* at the firm – the area on and below the production function – and what is infeasible – the area above the production function.

For reasons that will become clear below, we are actually more interested in the slope of the production function than the production function itself. The slope of the production function is called the *marginal product of labor* or MP_L for short. Taking the derivative of (14.1):

$$\frac{df}{dL} = MP_L$$

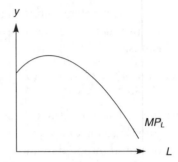

Figure 14.2 The firm's marginal product of labor function

In words, df/dL or the marginal product of labor is the extra output the firm gets from hiring an extra worker. You have seen the marginal product of labor before in Table 14.1: the third column gives the extra customers served for each extra helper, or the marginal product of each helper. Figure 14.2 plots MP_L against L for the production function shown in Figure 14.1. Because the slope of the production function at first rises, then falls, the marginal product of labor function initially increases, then decreases as more workers are hired by the firm. It should be clear that the marginal product of labor function changes from a positively to a negatively sloped function because of the law of diminishing returns.

Of course, the firm is really only interested in profit. The firm's profit (π) is the difference between revenue and cost. Assuming a fixed output price p for each unit of output y, revenue is py. Cost is made up of expenditures on the fixed inputs (F) and expenditure on labor, which is just the number of workers hired times their wage w, or wL. It follows that profit is:

$$\pi = py - wL - F$$

The firm's hiring decision is based on profit-maximizing behavior. The firm is also constrained by its technology, which is represented by the production function. So, the hiring problem is:

$$\max_{L} \quad \pi = py - wL - F \quad \text{subject to} \quad y = f(L)$$

which just says that the firm chooses the amount of labor L to maximize profit π subject to the constraint imposed by the production function. Notice that we can substitute the production function in place of y in the profit function, giving:

$$\max_{L} \quad \pi = pf(L) - wL - F \tag{14.2}$$

Putting the production function directly into the maximization problem just incorporates the constraint into the function to be maximized, thereby guaranteeing the solution will satisfy the constraint. In other words, substituting the production function into the profit function guarantees that the solution will be technologically feasible.

We are left with the straightforward problem of maximizing an unconstrained function of a single variable. The solution is found by taking the derivative of (14.2) with respect to L and setting it equal to zero. Thus:

$$\frac{d\pi}{dL} = p\frac{df}{dL} - w = 0 \tag{14.3}$$

which we can rewrite as:

$$p\frac{df}{dL} = w$$

let's write this condition as:

$$p \cdot MP_L = w$$

The left-hand side of this equation, price times the marginal product of labor, is just the amount of revenue an extra worker

brings to the firm (the extra output times the price the output is sold for). This is referred to as the *value of marginal product of labor* or VMP_L for short. The right-hand side of this equation, the wage, is just the amount an extra worker adds to the firm's cost. Let's rewrite the equation:

$$VMP_L = w \tag{14.4}$$

This gives the first part of the firm's profit-maximizing hiring rule: hire workers until the value of their marginal product equals the wage. To see why this works, recall that the hot-dog vendor hired more helpers as long as they added more to revenue than to cost and stopped hiring only when the helpers started adding more to cost than to revenue. Equation 14.4 says that the firm should hire to the point where the last worker adds just as much to revenue as to cost, which is exactly the rule used by the hot-dog vendor.

It's worth stressing that the hiring rule in (14.4) *does not* say that the firm should choose the wage equal to the value of the marginal product of labor. The wage is set in the market, which means that the firm can't set the wage at all. All the firm can do is, by hiring the right number of workers, ensure the value of marginal product of labor equals the market-determined wage. Let L^* be the number of workers that solves (14.4).

The hiring rule stated in (14.4) is actually incomplete. As with any optimization problem, it is important to check the second-order condition to be sure the solution is a maximum and not a minimum. The second-order condition is satisfied if the second derivative of the profit function is negative at L^*, that is:

$$\frac{d^2\pi}{dL^2} < 0 \text{ at } L^*$$

Taking the derivative of the first derivative of the profit function (14.3), gives the second derivative:

$$\frac{d^2\pi}{dL^2} = p\frac{d^2f}{dL^2}$$

Since the first derivative of the production function is the marginal product of labor, the second derivative of the production function is the derivative of the marginal product of labor. We can, therefore, write the second derivative of the profit function as:

$$\frac{d^2\pi}{dL^2} = p\frac{dMP_L}{dL}$$

In other words, the second derivative of the profit function is just the price times the first derivative of the marginal product of labor function. Since the price is positive, the second derivative of the profit function will be negative if:

$$\frac{dMP_L}{dL} < 0 \text{ at } L^*$$

So, provided that the derivative of the marginal product of labor function is negative at L^*, the second-order condition is satisfied, and we can be certain the hiring rule represented by (14.4) corresponds to maximum profit for the firm. In other words, the hiring rule corresponds to maximum profit for the firm as long as the marginal product of labor function has a negative slope at L^*. To summarize, the hiring rule requires two things:

1 the wage equals the value of marginal product of labor;
2 the marginal product of labor function has a negative slope at the level of employment at which the wage equals the value of marginal product of labor.

This two-part hiring rule is fundamentally important to the firm, so it's worth looking

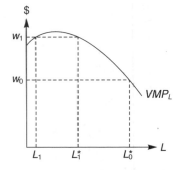

Figure 14.3 The firm's hiring decision

at another way. Multiplying every value on the marginal product of labor function in Figure 14.2 by the price p gives the value of marginal product of labor function, shown in Figure 14.3 as the curve labeled VMP_L. Since the price p is a constant, the VMP_L curve has the same shape as the marginal product of labor function.

Suppose the market wage is w_1. Part 1 of the hiring rule states that workers are hired until the VMP_L of the last worker equals the wage. Reading across the graph in Figure 14.3 we see that w_1 equals VMP_L at two different levels of employment, L_1 and L_1^*. Which one maximizes profit? This is where part 2 of the hiring rule comes in. At L_1, the marginal product of labor function has a positive slope. At L_1^*, the marginal product of labor function has a negative slope. Therefore, if the wage is w_1, the firm will hire L_1^* workers, not L_1 workers.

To see this another way, recall that profit can be increased as long as the VMP_L of an extra worker is greater than their wage. Starting with L_1, the VMP_L of an extra worker is greater than w_1, which means profit would increase if that extra worker were hired, so L_1 cannot be a profit-maximizing employment level. In fact, all the workers between L_1 and L_1^* have VMP_L's greater than w_1, so it makes sense to hire all of them. However, starting

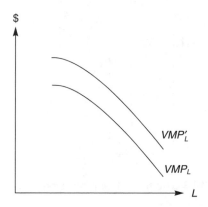

Figure 14.4 The firm's demand for labor

with L_1^*, the VMP_L of an extra worker is lower than the wage, so profit would fall if that worker were hired. By this argument, L_1^* is the profit-maximizing employment level. The same argument can be used for any wage. For example, if the wage is w_0, then L_0^* is the profit-maximizing number of workers for the firm to hire, where the wage intersects the downward-sloping portion of the VMP_L curve.

It should be clear now that the two-part hiring rule means that the firm's employment level is determined where the wage intersects the downward-sloping part of the VMP_L curve. In other words, the downward-sloping portion of the VMP_L curve is the firm's *labor demand curve* because it shows how many workers the firm would hire for any given wage. The firm's labor demand curve or the downward-sloping portion of the VMP_L curve is illustrated in Figure 14.4.

The position of the firm's labor demand curve depends on two things: the price of output and the marginal product of labor. An increase in the price of output raises the value of marginal product of labor at every level of employment, causing the VMP_L curve to shift upward, shown in Figure 14.4 as VMP_L'. And if the marginal product of workers increased at every level of employment, the VMP_L curve would also shift upward.

Wages and Productivity

In the early 1990s, there was a spirited debate in North America over the effects of adding Mexico to the Free Trade Agreement between the US and Canada. Opponents of the North American Free Trade Agreement were concerned that many American and Canadian firms would be unable to compete with Mexican firms paying much lower wages. This competitive disadvantage, it was claimed, would result in job losses for Americans and Canadian workers. At first glance, the concern may appear to be valid: in 1989 the average hourly manufacturing wage in Canada, for example, was C\$17.43 compared with C\$2.31 in Mexico – over seven times higher in Canada.

However, the hiring condition $w = p \times MP_L$ says that wages are determined by output prices and the marginal product of labor. Assuming that output prices are the same in Canada and Mexico (after all, Canadian and Mexican firms involved in trade will be competing in the same output market, so their prices will be similar) and that wages in both countries are determined by competitive market forces, it follows that wages in Canada and Mexico might be different in part because the marginal product of the workers is different.

In fact, studies at the time suggested that Canadian manufacturing workers were 6.46 times more productive than their Mexican counterparts, which goes a long way to eliminating the perceived wage advantage of Mexican workers. It follows that Canadian firms can pay their workers 6.46 times as much as Mexican workers, or C$14.92 per hour, and not be at any competitive disadvantage. Of course, this doesn't completely eliminate the wage differential, but it goes a long way. And even though Canadian workers are still relatively more expensive after accounting for productivity differences, it turns out that capital was relatively cheaper in Canada, implying that Canadian firms could simply substitute capital for labor in order to compete with Mexican firms. Why were Canadian workers more productive? Well there are many reasons including higher capital per worker, better education, a superior health system, and so on.

There is a lesson here for any firms, not just those involved in international trade. The lesson is: the competitive position of firms depends not only on the wage, but also on the productivity of workers. Firms paying high wages can compete with firms paying much lower wages as long as the workers at the high-wage firms are productive enough to compensate for the higher wages. Put another way, firms can improve their competitive position by getting more productivity from their workers for any given wage level.

14.1.3 Equilibrium in the labor market

So far, we have only looked at hiring by a single firm. But it is the joint hiring of all the firms that determines the market demand for labor. Deriving the market labor demand curve from the labor demand curves of individual firms is relatively straightforward: for any given wage, determine the amount of labor each firm will hire and add up these values to get total market labor demand for that particular wage. Then, simply plot the wage against total labor demand to get a point on the market labor demand curve.

To derive the whole market labor demand curve, just repeat the process for different wages: choose a wage, add together the number of workers each individual firm would hire to get total labor demand at that wage, and plot the wage against total labor demand.

Mathematically, it's easiest to see how this works if all the firms in the labor market are using the same technology, i.e. they have the same production function. Suppose the labor market has n firms with the same technology. Then total labor demand at a given wage is simply:

$$n \times (\text{labor demand at a single firm})$$

Because each firm's labor demand curve slopes downward, it follows that the market labor demand curve slopes downward as well. A representative market labor demand curve is shown in Figure 14.5.

We won't say much about the origins of the market labor supply curve except to explain briefly why it has a positive slope. An individual has many options how to spend her time: leisure, school, volunteer work, work for pay, and so on. Everything else being equal, higher wages make working for pay a relatively more attractive option.

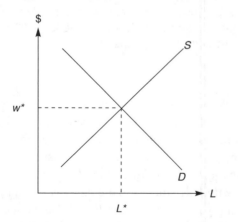

Figure 14.5 Labor market equilibrium under perfect competition

Put another way, the opportunity cost of not working increases as the wage rises. Thus, we can expect that as wages increase, more people will choose to look for work. In other words, as wages rise more people will be induced to supply their labor to the market, giving rise to a positively sloped labor supply function as shown in Figure 14.5.

As usual, equilibrium in the market is determined at the intersection of the supply and demand curves. As shown in Figure 14.5, this results in an equilibrium wage of w^* and an employment level of L^*.

Since the position of the labor demand curves of individual firms is determined by output price and the marginal product of the workers, changes in either of these variables will affect the position of the market labor demand curve and, hence, the equilibrium wage. For example, an increase in output prices raises the demand for labor, shifting the market labor demand curve upward and, everything else equal, raising the equilibrium wage. Alternatively, an increase in the marginal product of the workers also raises the demand for labor and, everything else equal, increases the equilibrium wage.

Of course, changes in labor supply also affect the equilibrium wage. Increases in labor supply depress the market wage, everything else being equal, and reductions in supply increase the market wage.

Wages of Baby Boomers

Following the end of the World War II, the fertility rate of Canadian and Australian women began to rise substantially, continuing at high levels until it began to tail off in the mid-1960s. The resulting bulge in the number of births has become known as the "baby boom." The huge increase in the number of births over this period translated into a huge increase in the number of labor market entrants during the mid-1960–80s period, when the baby boomers became old enough to enter the labor force. Effectively, these new entrants to the labor market shifted the supply curve of new workers to the right in Canada and Australia and, as a result, the wages of new workers fell.

Studies based on the US, where a similar phenomenon occurred, suggest that the increased supply of new workers reduced entry-level wages by about 10 percent. Moreover, there is evidence that the depressing effect of boomers on wages has persisted. By the late 1980s, baby boomers in the US earned 5–10 percent less than other age groups.

14.1.4 Payroll taxes

In many developed countries, national pension plans and workers' compensation plans are funded partly through a payroll tax assessed on firms. In the United States, the payroll tax is 7.65 percent, and it is even higher in other countries: in Germany the payroll tax is 18.7 percent, in Sweden it is 34.1 percent, and in Italy it is 45.2 percent.

We're interested in two aspects of payroll taxes. First, the effects of payroll taxes on wages and employment levels. Second, who ends up paying the tax. These issues can be answered using Figure 14.6. In the absence of the tax, the labor demand curve is D_0 and the supply of labor is given by S. The competitive equilibrium wage is w_0 and L_0 workers are hired.

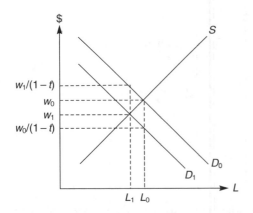

Figure 14.6 The impact of a payroll tax on labor demand

the tax is shifted to the worker. While the hiring cost of a worker has increased (from w_0 to $w_1/(1-t)$), the wage received by the worker has decreased (from w_0 to w_1). Therefore, the firm and the worker share the burden of the tax. Whether the firm or worker bears the larger burden of the tax depends on the relative elasticities of demand and supply. If demand is relatively inelastic, the firm will bear the brunt of the tax; if supply is relatively inelastic, the worker will bear the brunt of the tax. The point is that the actual burden of the tax bears little relation to who officially pays the tax.

Points on the demand curve give the number of workers firms want to hire at different wages. For instance, firms are willing to hire L_0 workers if each worker costs w_0. Now if the government imposes a tax of t percent on the firm's payroll, the firm will pay tw_0 in payroll taxes for each worker. Because firms are only willing to pay a total of w_0 for each of the L_0 workers, they will only be willing to pay $w_0 - tw_0$ or $w_0(1-t)$ to each of the workers after the tax is imposed. For example, suppose the payroll tax is 10 percent. Then a gross hiring cost of w_0 to the firm will be split between the government, which gets $0.10 \times w_0$, and the worker, who gets $0.90 \times w_0$.

In this way, the payroll tax effectively shifts the labor demand curve to D_1. Firms are willing to hire L_0 workers only if their wage falls to $w_0(1-t)$. Therefore, the demand curve shifts down proportionately by $(1-t)$. The equilibrium level of employment falls to L_1 and the equilibrium wage (the wage that workers receive) falls to w_1. The hiring cost paid by the firm is $w_1/(1-t)$.

Notice that, even though the payroll tax is assessed on the firm, some of the burden of

14.1.5 Short run versus long run

The discussion so far has been based on the assumption that all the firm's inputs except labor are fixed at predetermined levels. This corresponds to the *short run*. If the firm wants to increase output in the short run it hires more workers, or if it wants to reduce output it lays workers off.

The *long run* refers to the period of time when inputs that are fixed in the short run can be varied. For example, a Toyota plant in central Canada was recently expanded to increase its output of Toyota Corollas. The time between the announcement of the project in April 1993 and when the cars began rolling off the expanded production line was almost five years. Thus, the long run is around five years for Toyota, because that is the time it takes for the fixed input, plant size, to be changed. The actual length of time for the long run will vary enormously from one industry to the next. Think of the hot-dog vendor. For hot-dog grilling, the fixed input is the grill cart. It may be possible for the vendor to get hold of another grill cart within a couple of days, maybe even sooner. In this case, the long run is a matter of days rather than years.

We won't cover the long run in any great depth, suffice to say that Part 1 of the hiring rule applies separately to each of the inputs. That is, the firm will hire each input up to the point where the extra revenue to the firm from the input (holding all other inputs fixed) is just equal to the extra cost of the input.

The firm also has a lot more options in the long run compared with the short run. In the short run the firm can only vary the labor input, whereas in the long run all inputs can be varied. Because the firm has more options in the long run, long-run demand for inputs is more elastic than short-run demand. To see why this is the case, think about what happens when, say, the wage increases relative to other input prices. In the short run, the firm will layoff a few workers because costs have risen, but it can't layoff too many workers because output would fall too much. In the long run, however, the firm can substitute away from the relatively more expensive workers by shifting to more capital-intensive production methods, like using robots for example. This will enable the firm to maintain its output level as, essentially, some workers are replaced by machines. So, for a given wage change, there are more layoffs in the long run than in the short run, which is just the same thing as saying long-run demand is more elastic than short-run demand, as illustrated in Figure 14.7.

14.2 Compensating wage differentials

So far, we have assumed that all jobs are equally pleasant or unpleasant, equally dangerous or safe, either fulfilling or non-rewarding, and so on. But this is clearly not the case. Workers on an oil rig off the Scottish coast have a much tougher job than oil rig workers

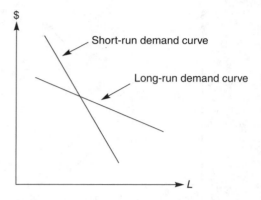

Figure 14.7 The short- and long-run demand curves for labor

outside Houston, Texas. The off-shore oil rig worker spends several weeks at sea; the inland worker can drive home to have supper with the family. While working on any oil rig is dangerous, offshore oil rig workers have to contend with problems that simply don't arise when working on land, like the possibility of falling overboard in heavy seas or of the rig getting hit by icebergs. As a result of these additional hardships, even if the workers inland have exactly the same VMP_L as the offshore worker, we would expect the offshore worker to get paid more to compensate for the hardships. A wage difference between otherwise identical workers that arises to adjust for unique characteristics of the working environment is referred to as a *compensating wage differential*.

Generally speaking, compensating differentials arise to compensate workers for particularly dangerous or unpleasant tasks: cab drivers in large cities like London could be expected to be paid more than in a small place like Cambridge; airplane test pilots will be paid more than commercial airline pilots, and so on. In these cases, the dangerous or unpleasant nature of the task gives rise to a higher wage. Alternatively, the job in question could be particularly pleasant or fulfilling, in which case the task gives rise to a lower wage. For example, environmental lawyers with a commitment to green causes may accept lower pay than regular trial lawyers; sports journalists could be expected to be paid less than their counterparts covering business news.

To sum up, firms with dangerous or unpleasant working conditions will have to offer higher wages to attract workers, while firms with pleasant working conditions will be able to pay lower wages.

Summary

- A perfectly competitive labor market is defined by price-taking on the part of the firm and worker, perfect information, homogeneous workers, and freedom of entry and exit.
- In a perfectly competitive labor market the wage is determined by the forces of supply and demand and not by individual firms.
- The firm's hiring rule states workers should be hired so that $w = VMP_L$ on the downward-sloping portion of the VMP_L curve.
- The firm's labor demand curve is the downward-sloping portion of the VMP_L curve.
- Changes in output prices and the marginal product of workers shift the firm's demand for labor.
- Even though payroll taxes are officially collected from firms, both workers and firms share the incidence of the tax.
- In the short run, the firm can only alter the number of workers. In the long run, the levels of all other inputs can be changed as well.
- The short-run demand for labor is steeper than the long-run demand for labor because the firm has more options in the long run.
- Firms with particularly dangerous or unpleasant working conditions will have to pay a compensating differential in order to attract workers.

Notes

1 In what follows, we'll simply refer to net revenue as revenue.
2 The hot-dog vendor was basically in the same situation: the grill cart, propane, hot dogs, buns, and drinks had been purchased by the vendor – all she had to do was choose the right number of helpers.

Exercises

1 A manufacturing firm produces bicycles using labor as the only input according to the following weekly production table. The bicycles are sold in a competitive market for a price $P = \$200$ each.

Number of workers	Output of bicycles
0	0
1	5
2	12
3	18
4	21
5	23

(a) Calculate, and record in a table, the marginal product of labor (MP_L) and the value of marginal product of labor (VMP_L) at each level of employment.

(b) If the wage of workers is set at $600 per week, how many workers will the firm hire? Draw a diagram to illustrate your answer.

(c) Suppose the price of bicycles rises to $300. Determine the new VMP_L and, hence, determine the number of workers the firm will hire after the price increase. Illustrate your answer on the diagram. What characteristic of labor demand have you just illustrated?

(d) Suppose the wage rises to $800 per week, how many workers will the firm hire? (Assume $P = 300$.) Again, illustrate the answer on a diagram. What have you just shown?

2 A firm uses labor as its only variable input. Its daily production function is given by:

$$Q = -0.01L^3 + L^2 + 36L$$

where L is measured in hours of labor time per day. All markets are perfectly competitive. The price of output is 10 cents per unit and the wage rate is $4.80 per hour.

(a) Determine the profit-maximizing hours of labor input the firm hires per day and, hence, the firm's total daily output.

(b) Assuming that the cost of the fixed inputs is $40 per day, calculate the firm's total daily profit.

3 If a firm's short-run production function is $f(L) = 2L^{1/2}$, the price of output is $p = 1,000$, and the market wage of workers is $w = 100$, determine the profit-maximizing number of workers the firm will hire. Be sure to check the second-order condition.

4 Suppose 100 firms in a labor market all have an identical short run production function given by $f(L) = 4L^{1/2}$, and that the price of output is $p = 100$. Determine the market labor demand curve. If the supply of workers to the market is given by $L = 1,000\,w$, determine the equilibrium wage in the market.

5 Suppose that the (inverse) demand for labor in a competitive market is given by:

$$W = 20 - 0.01L$$

and that the supply of labor is given by:

$$W = 0.03L$$

(a) Determine the equilibrium wage and level of employment in the labor market.

(b) Suppose a payroll tax of 25 percent is introduced. Determine the equation of the labor demand curve incorporating the tax. Hence, determine the wage paid by the firms, the wage received by the workers, and the total tax revenue.

(c) Compare the workers wage before the payroll tax to the wage they receive after the tax is imposed. Likewise, compare the wage firms paid before the tax to the wage they pay after the tax is imposed. Who bears the higher burden of the tax proportionately?

(d) Explain why the group that bears the higher burden of the tax does so. What is the intuition behind your answer? (Hint: compute the elasticities of demand and supply at the pre-tax equilibrium.)

6 Suppose that the (inverse) demand for labor in a competitive market is given by:

$$W = 40 - 0.1L$$

and (inverse) labor supply is given by:

$$W = 0.3L$$

(a) Determine the equilibrium wage and level of employment in the labor market.

(b) Now suppose that a new study reveals that the work has previously unknown harmful health effects to the extent that each worker now requires a compensating differential of $10 in order to work in the industry. Find the new equation for the labor supply curve.

(c) Determine the new equilibrium wage in the labor market. Why do you think the wage does not rise by the full $10 required to compensate workers to work in these jobs?

Chapter 15

Training and motivating workers

••

When you are finished with this chapter you should understand:

- The difference between general and specific training and how it affects whether the firm or the worker pays the costs of training
- How performance-based pay schemes can affect worker productivity
- The role of risk aversion in influencing the choice of pay scheme
- How tournaments can affect worker productivity
- How deferred wages can increase worker productivity and reduce turnover
- How efficiency wages can increase worker productivity and reduce turnover

The last chapter described the perfectly competitive labor market. This is useful for getting across the basic condition that firms hire workers until the value of the marginal product of the last worker hired equals the wage. The competitive market also fixes the notion that wages are, by and large, determined in the market and not by individual firms. But apart from these insights, the perfectly competitive labor market isn't very realistic.

According to the competitive model, if the price of output falls, the value of the marginal product falls, and the firm immediately cuts back on employment. If output price rises, employment is increased. At the market level, the resulting fluctuating demand for labor causes frequent wage changes. Workers are very mobile in this market, moving from firms where they are laid off to firms hiring workers, perhaps every day. In short, the competitive labor market is just like any other market where prices and quantities

adjust to equate supply and demand. The perfectly competitive model of the labor market, therefore, treats workers just like any other economic commodity.

In essence, the competitive model of the labor market treats workers just like machines. But workers are different from machines. For one thing, when a machine becomes obsolete, the firm can throw it away and buy a new one. With workers, however, the firm has the option of upgrading obsolete skills through training. And if the firm decides not to retrain workers, workers can decide to undertake training on their own, which is impossible for a machine. In this chapter, we're going to look into the issues that surround training from both the firm's and the worker's point of view. We will look at why training is undertaken and who pays for it. Along the way, we'll distinguish between skills that are useful only in a specific firm and skills that are in demand at many firms.

Another difference between workers and machines is that machines can be counted on to behave more or less the same way day after day. Workers, on the other hand, are human. Some like hard work, others don't. Some are able to carry out their jobs efficiently and effectively, others are incompetent. Of course, if the firm can identify the slackers and the incompetent, it can get rid of them. But problems arise when it is difficult for the firm to monitor its workers. We are going to look carefully in this chapter at ways to motivate workers to do their jobs properly especially when constant supervision is impossible or too costly. We'll see, not surprisingly, that appropriately designed compensation schemes can provide the right incentives for employees even when they aren't closely monitored by the firm.

15.1 Training

At any point in time, a worker has a set of knowledge, skills, and abilities referred to as the worker's *human capital*. A worker's human capital determines the worker's productivity: greater knowledge, skills, and abilities makes for a more productive worker. Human capital is not simply a matter of genetic build-up. It isn't fixed like the worker's height. A worker's human capital can be changed through *experience* or through *training*.

Experience, which is acquired simply by spending time in a particular job, enables a worker to learn how to perform tasks more quickly. Thus, experience increases a worker's productivity. Of course, this is the reason employers are so keen to hire people with experience: they are more productive. However, the rate at which a worker's productivity increases through experience may be too slow for the firm. The firm, therefore, may turn to methods that increase worker productivity more rapidly. This is where training comes in.

Training may take different forms. It may be quite formal. It is not unusual for firms to send employees on courses that involve a few weeks of classes followed by an examination. In other cases, training can be informal. For example, the new employee might just sit down at a computer for a couple of hours with a more experienced employee to "learn the ropes."

For our purposes, the key aspect of training is that it is costly. In the case of formal training, fees must be paid to the college or university providing the training. If the courses are supplied in-house, the salaries of the trainers have to be paid and classroom facilities provided for. With informal training, the costs are measured in the time that experienced employees spend training new workers. The time takes away from the normal work of employees resulting in lost output to the firm.

Nobel prize-winning economist Gary Becker pointed out that it is extremely important to make the distinction between *general* training and *specific* training.[1] General training increases the productivity of the worker at *any* firm. General training, therefore, gives the employee skills that can be applied usefully at many firms. Examples of general training are learning how to drive, university degrees, and knowledge of widely-used software packages like Microsoft Word. On the other hand, specific training increases the productivity of workers only at the firm where the training takes place. Specific training, therefore, gives the employee skills that are useful only at a single firm. Examples of specific training are learning how to drive an Abrams tank, or knowledge of a software package that is unique to a particular firm.

In many cases, it may be impossible to make a precise distinction between general and specific training.[1] For instance, knowledge of a software package that is unique to a single firm clearly has a specific training element to it. But knowledge of the package might provide the employee with programming skills that are in demand at other firms. Nevertheless, the dichotomy is a useful way to fix ideas.

Both general and specific training increase the productivity of the worker at the firm where the training takes place. Both general and specific training are costly. The question is: who pays for the training? As we shall see, the answer depends on whether the training is general or specific. This can be illustrated using a simple two-period model. The worker is hired and trained in the first period. In the second period, the fully-trained employee works at the firm.

Suppose MC_1 is the marginal cost of the worker in period 1 and MC_2 is the marginal cost of the worker in period 2. Likewise, VMP_1 and VMP_2 are the values of marginal products in periods 1 and 2, respectively. The discount rate is r. The profit-maximizing employment condition for the firm is just an adaptation of the hiring rule from the last chapter. Owing to the two-period timeframe, the condition is that the present value of the marginal cost associated with hiring the worker equals the present value of the worker's value of marginal product:

$$MC_1 + \frac{MC_2}{1+r} = VMP_1 + \frac{VMP_2}{1+r}$$

Suppose it costs the firm T dollars to train each worker. The costs include the salaries of the trainers, classroom costs, and so forth. The firm also pays the trainee a wage during the training period. Since training only takes place in the first period, call the training wage

w_1. It follows that the marginal cost of the worker in the first period is the training cost plus the training wage, or $MC_1 = T + w_1$. There is no training in the second period, so the marginal cost of the worker is just their second period wage, implying $MC_2 = w_2$. Substituting for the two marginal cost expressions into the profit-maximizing condition:

$$w_1 + T + \frac{w_2}{1+r} = VMP_1 + \frac{VMP_2}{1+r}$$

Subtracting $w_2/(1+r)$ from both sides:

$$w_1 + T = VMP_1 + B$$

where:

$$B = \frac{VMP_2 - w_2}{1+r} \tag{15.1}$$

Clearly, B is the discounted benefit to firm of a trained worker in the second period. To this point we haven't said whether the training gives the worker general or specific skills.

General training

Suppose the worker goes through general training. By definition, the general skills picked up by the worker during the training are valuable at any firm. Since the trained worker is worth VMP_2 to the firm where training took place, the worker's value of marginal product at any firm is VMP_2. This means the worker's market wage in the second period is VMP_2. The firm has no choice but to set $w_2 = VMP_2$, or risk losing the worker to another firm. From (15.1) it follows that $B = 0$, so the benefit to the firm of a trained worker in the second period is zero. Since $B = 0$, (15.1) can be written:

$$w_1 = VMP_1 - T$$

In words, the firm pays the worker their market wage in the first period minus the cost of training. The worker, therefore, pays all of the training cost. This isn't really very surprising. The worker's market wage rises to capture all of the benefits of the training. Because the firm can't reap any benefits from the training, it's no wonder the firm won't pay for the training.

Any firm that provides general training will simply not pay for it. Workers receiving general training will pay for it through low wages during the training period. Apprentice plumbers and electricians learn valuable skills from contracting firms that the apprentices pay for with low wages. Medical interns at hospitals and interns at law firms also learn valuable skills that they pay for with low wages until their training is complete. Neither the hospital nor the law firm are willing to bear training costs they will be unable to recoup. Lastly, many companies say to young workers they will pay for the worker to get an MBA. But the MBA degree is really general training. Although the firm may actually write a cheque for the tuition fees, it should be clear now that it is really the young workers that will bear the cost of the MBA through lower wages while they are studying for the degree.

Specific training

The key aspect of specific training is that the productivity gains from training vanish if the worker leaves firm. The specific skills are of no use to other firms, so the worker cannot reap any benefits by leaving the firm to work elsewhere. And the firm won't be able to receive any of the benefits of the training if the worker leaves. If the trained worker stays at the firm, however, the firm will gain from the worker's increased productivity. Again, the issue is: who pays for the training?

One possibility is that the firm pays the entire cost of the training, T. The workers can always earn VMP_1 elsewhere, so the firm has to pay workers at least VMP_1 in both periods implying $w_1 = w_2 = VMP_1$. Since $w_2 = VMP_1 < VMP_2$, the firm can recoup the cost of the training with a low wage in the second period. The only problem is, the firm has no assurance that the worker will not quit after the first period. If the worker quits, the firm suffers a loss. It will have paid for the training but have no opportunity to receive the benefits of the higher second-period productivity.

Another possibility is that the worker pays T with a low first period wage, just like the case for general training. The training cost could be recouped by the worker if the second period wage is set sufficiently high enough. In this case, $w_1 = VMP_1 - T$ as the worker pays for the training, and $w_2 > w_1$, which allows the worker to recoup the training cost. Notice that the firm is paying $w_1 < VMP_1$ in the first period, thus making a profit on each worker. In principle, the profit is repaid in the second period wage to compensate the worker for the training cost. But there is nothing stopping the firm from firing the worker. In effect, the firm could become a "training" factory, hiring workers, paying them low wages in the first period on the promise of a high second period wage, then reneging on the promise by firing the workers at the end of the first period. Unless the worker can get assurance that no firing will take place, having the worker pay for the training isn't going to work either.

Both the firm and the worker are reluctant to invest in specific training because the system doesn't provide any incentive for either party to behave in the other party's interest in the second period. In principle, the firm and worker could agree to a contract that would bind them together for two periods. In practice, such contracts are illegal because they represent indentured labor.

The way out of the difficulty, of course, is for the worker and the firm to share in the returns from specific training. In other words, the second period wage can be set higher than the worker could earn elsewhere, but less than the value of the worker's marginal product:

$$VMP_1 < w_2 < VMP_2$$

This way the worker has no incentive to quit the firm because the second period wage is greater than what they could earn elsewhere ($w_2 > VMP_1$). The firm has no incentive to fire the worker because it is paying a second period wage which is less than the value of the worker's marginal product ($w_2 < VMP_2$).

Since worker and firm are sharing the returns, they will share the training costs as well. Thus, the worker pays for part of the first-period training cost and the rest is paid by the firm. Costs are shared in the same proportion as the returns. For example, if the firm pays 70 percent of the training cost, then it will receive 70 percent of the returns from training. If it took a greater share of the returns, the firm would find it difficult to attract job applicants. Potential employees would be reluctant to invest in training costs for which they weren't being adequately compensated. On the other hand, if the firm paid a greater share of the costs, it would find itself swamped by applicants eager to be overcompensated for their training costs.

The existence of firm-specific training has several implications for the work place. Because quits and fires are lower in firms with specific training, workers on average will stay longer with their firms than they would with firms providing little or no speci-fic training. Specific training, therefore, may be one of the reasons that many employees stick with the same firm for so long. Neither the firm nor the worker has an incentive to terminate the employment relationship. Once trained, the worker is getting paid more than they could earn at another job. And the firm is getting more out of its trained workers than it is paying them.

Specific training also could explain the "last hired, first fired" rule exercised by many firms during an economic downturn. When demand for output drops and a firm decides to trim its labor force, it has to decide who to get rid of. Workers who have been at the firm longer are likely to have more specific training than recent hires. It is the older workers, therefore, who are getting paid less than their value of marginal products. The difference between their pay and value of marginal product acts as a buffer zone for the older workers. As long as the value of marginal product remains greater than the wage, the firm has no incentive to fire older workers. In a recession, when the value of marginal product falls, therefore, the firm is more likely to lay off recently hired workers.

15.2 Motivation

As we have seen, training raises the productivity of the workers. Another way the firm can increase the productivity of its workers is to motivate them to work harder. In fact, the firm's problem may be even more basic than that. In some circumstances, it may be a question of how the firm can get its employees to do any work over the bare minimum.

For example, sales representatives at many firms spend much of their time away from the office. It's very difficult, therefore, for the firm to keep an eye on them. It would be far too costly for the firm to hire someone to check that the sales representative had made all their calls. And, in any case, there is no guarantee that the person doing the checking would do a thorough job either. Of course, the firm could hire someone to check on the person checking on the sales representative. But hiring even more monitors doesn't address the fundamental question: who monitors the monitors? Far better to design a system to make it in the sales representative's best interests to make all the calls in the first place. Carefully designed, such a system could significantly reduce the amount of monitoring.

Of course, these issues are not unique to sales representatives. It is very difficult for any firm to monitor its employees all the time. Some workers might take long breaks. Others might close the office door and read the paper or surf the net. In all these cases, the workers behavior results in lost output to the firm. From the firm's point of view, the issue is how to get employees to keep on-the-job leisure to a minimum. If monitoring is relatively easy, as on a production-line, then it is relatively easy to control on-the-job leisure. But in many instances, monitoring is simply not an option, except at periodic intervals. So the question is what the firm can do to motivate its employees to work as hard as the firm wants them to when constant monitoring isn't possible.

These issues are not just confined to workers. In firms where ownership is separate from management, as in most firms with publicly traded shares, the issue is how the owners can motivate the managers to work hard. The owners want the firm's profit maximized. The managers may have other goals, like amenities and prestige. Corporate jets, chauffeurs, plush office suites, executive dining rooms, health clubs, golf-club memberships, and so on do not come cheaply. Shareholders, therefore, may be interested in ways to keep perks in check. This raises the issue of how to get the manager to pursue the same profit-maximizing goal that the shareholders would like them to.

There are several *control mechanisms* in place to keep managers in line. The threat of takeover, or bankruptcy, provides incentives for managers to work hard and keep costs down. Boards of directors or shareholders have the power to fire incompetent managers. But these mechanisms don't always work perfectly. For many large corporations bankruptcy simply isn't a real threat. Managers can also devise "poison pill" schemes that make takeovers difficult. A board of directors may be reluctant to fire a manager that the board itself appointed. And it is difficult to organize dispersed shareholders in sufficiently large numbers to achieve anything, let alone firing an executive. Many shareholders will find it easier simply to sell their shares. Given that the control mechanisms won't always fully control managers, the question is what other mechanisms can the shareholders use.

At a basic level the issue of motivating managers to maximize profit is the same as motivating workers to work hard. Both are just another example of the *principal–agent* relationship. A *principal* (owner or manager) hires an *agent* (manager or worker) to perform a task (maximize profit or work hard). Since the task is not easily monitored by the principal, the question is what mechanisms can the principal design to ensure that the task is satisfactorily carried out. In the next section, we will look at how compensation schemes can be used to motivate managers and workers to do what their employers want.

15.2.1 Principal–agent model

If you recall, the hot-dog vendor at Wasaga Beach also has a few carts in Toronto. The problem is, Toronto is two hours drive from Wasaga Beach (on a good day!). Since she can't be in two places at the same time, she's going to have to put someone else in charge of running the stand at Wasaga Beach while she's in Toronto. Of course, there are the issues of who to hire and how much to pay them. But what really troubles her is how to get whoever she does hire to do a good job when she isn't there to watch over them.

For example, suppose she pays the cart manager a straight hourly wage like her other employees. It would make sense to pay the manager more than her other employees because of the extra responsibilities the manager must bear. But even if she sets the manager's wage at the appropriate level, she's still troubled that the manager won't really have an incentive to get the most from the hot-dog cart. The fixed hourly wage means that the manager will get the same take-home pay regardless of how hard they work. Since the owner can't be there checking all the time, it's even possible that the manager may decide to take it easy. After all, when she's away in Toronto, who's to say whether low sales at Wasaga Beach are a result of bad luck, poor weather, or a lazy manager more interested in getting a suntan than selling hot dogs?

When she thinks about why she got into the business in the first place, the way to resolve the problem becomes clear. She decided to run her own business because that way she could make a lot of money if she worked really hard. So why not set the managers pay to work the same way? In other words, she could just pay the manager a percentage of the profit at the cart on Wasaga Beach. That will bring the objectives on the manager exactly in line with her own objectives: both will get more money the more profitable is the cart.

What the hot-dog vendor has hit on is the classic resolution to the principal–agent problem in the context of the employer–employee relationship: a *performance-based compensation* scheme.

To see how this works, let's model the vendors problem as follows. Suppose the hot-dog cart will be open for business from 11 am to 7 pm Wednesday through to Sunday, a total of 40 hours per week. The hired manager can divide those 40 hours between work effort e and shirking (leisure) s so that:

$$e + s = 40$$

Since most people would rather relax than work, everything else being equal, assume that the manager is better-off the more he shirks. To fix ideas, let the manager's utility function be given by:

$$U(m, s) = m + 20s^{1/2} \qquad (15.2)$$

where m is the manager's pay. This function captures the key aspects of the problem: utility increases with pay and increases with the amount of shirking by the manager.

Let's suppose that the manager can get a job elsewhere for $400 per week. However, assume shirking is impossible in this job. (Perhaps the owner works along side the manager in this other job.) In order to get the manager to work at the hot-dog cart, he must get as much utility from working at the hot-dog cart as at the other job. The manager's utility at the other job is $U(400, 0) = 400$, because shirking is not possible there ($s = 0$). The manager will be indifferent between working at the hot-dog cart and working at the other job if his utility at the hot-dog cart equals his utility at the other job. In equation form:

$$m + 20s^{1/2} = 400$$

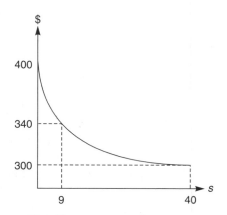

Figure 15.1 The pay constraint

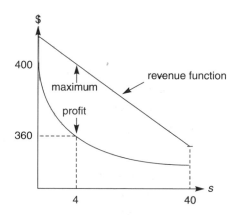

Figure 15.2 Revenue and profit at the hot-dog stand

Solving this equation for *m* gives the amount of income the manager must be paid to induce him (just) to work at the hot-dog stand:

$$m = 400 - 20s^{1/2} \qquad (15.3)$$

We'll call this equation the *pay constraint*, since it reflects the minimum pay that someone will accept to the manage the hot-dog cart.

The pay constraint is shown in Figure 15.1. Since the manager likes shirking, he will accept less pay at the hot-dog stand for every extra hour he can shirk. Thus, the pay constraint slopes downward. For example, the manager is indifferent between $340 per week and 9 hours of shirking at the hot-dog stand and working a solid 40 hours at the other job for $400. In effect, the manager is willing to accept lower pay for a more relaxed work environment. The pay constraint also has a convex shape. The first few hours of shirking are really worth a lot to the manager, so he is willing to give up quite a lot of pay to be able to shirk. But if his shirking is already high, an extra couple of hours doesn't make him that much better off, so it takes less pay to compensate for the ability to shirk.

Sales at the hot-dog stand obviously decrease the more the manager shirks. For the sake of argument, let's suppose that sales will be $500 if the manager doesn't shirk at all and that sales decline by a constant $5 for every extra hour the manager shirks. In equation form, the owner's *revenue function* is given by:

$$R(s) = 500 - 5s \qquad (15.4)$$

Figure 15.2 shows the revenue function and the pay constraint. For a given level of shirking, the owner's revenue is represented by the point on the revenue function. Also, for a given level of shirking, the owner's cost is represented by the point on the pay constraint, because it gives the minimum amount the manager must be paid in order for him to work at the hot-dog stand. The owner's profit, therefore, is represented by the vertical distance between the revenue function and the pay constraint.[2]

Before we discuss compensation schemes, let's examine the situation facing the owner if she could somehow observe the amount of shirking by the manager. Because the owner aims to maximize profit, the owner simply solves the following problem:

$$\max_{s} \quad 500 - 5s - (400 - 20s^{1/2}) \qquad (15.5)$$

The solution to the maximization problem will give the amount of shirking that maximizes the difference between revenue, substituted from (15.4), and the manager's pay, substituted from (15.3). Taking the derivative of the objective function in (15.5), and setting it equal to zero:

$$-5 - (-10s^{-1/2}) = 0 \qquad (15.6)$$

which can be solved to yield $s = 4$. In this case, revenue is $500 - (5 \times 4) = 480$, the manager's pay is $400 - 20\sqrt{4} = 360$, and profit is $480 - 360 = 120$. The maximum profit to the owner occurs when the manager shirks four hours per week and is paid $360. This is perhaps surprising, for you might think that profits would be maximized when there is no shirking at all. However, recall that the manager is willing to accept lower pay if he's allowed to shirk. The owner can, therefore, pay the manager less than $400 as long as the manager is allowed to shirk. Of course, sales will decrease too much if a lot of shirking occurs. Profits are maximized when just the right balance between pay and shirking is achieved.

Flat salary scheme

In reality, the owner is unable to observe how much the manager is shirking, because the owner is in Toronto all day. This means the owner has no idea if the manager is shirking the profit-maximizing four hours per week. Given that she has no idea how much the manager is shirking, it is not obvious that paying the manager $360 per week will result in four hours of shirking. To see this, suppose the manager were paid a flat salary of $360 per week. By definition, the flat salary means that manager gets paid the same amount regardless of the sales at the cart. In other words, it means the manager will get paid

$360 regardless of how much he shirks. Since there is no opportunity cost to shirking, the manager will shirk the maximum 40 hours per week. He can get away with it because the owner is not able to observe how much the manager is working or not working. For all she knows, low sales may be the result of customers that, for some unknown reason, aren't interested in eating hot dogs. When the manager shirks 40 hours per week, revenue is $500 - (5 \times 40) = 300$. Given the manager's pay of $360, the owner takes a loss of $60 per week under the flat pay scheme.

Of course, the owner could always pay the worker less than $360 and perhaps make a positive profit. For example, the manager would be willing to accept pay of $273.51 and shirk 40 hours per week.[3] In this case, the owner's profit would be $300 - 273.51 = 26.49$, which is positive but a long way from the owner's maximum level of profit. In fact, under a flat salary scheme, $26.49 is the highest profit the owner can make: if she pays the manager any less than $273.51, he will take the other job.

The point is, shirking will amount to 40 hours per week regardless of the fixed salary paid because, under a flat salary scheme, there is no penalty for shirking. Since the owner cannot tell how much the manager is shirking, the manager can get away with shirking the entire work week.

Performance-based salary scheme

Clearly, the flat salary isn't very satisfactory. The problem arises because the manager is not penalized for shirking. The owner needs to come up with a scheme that penalizes shirking. One possibility is to tie pay to profits. Suppose the owner were to offer the manager the following scheme: the manager

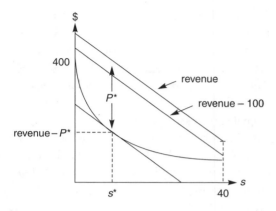

Figure 15.3 Manager's pay under the residual claimant scheme

gets to keep all the revenue the manager is able to generate from the cart minus a fixed amount P that the manager pays the owner. Thus:

manager's income $=$ revenue $- P$

To see how this works, suppose $P = 100$. The manager's pay is, therefore, equal to revenue minus $100. Figure 15.3 shows that the manager's pay schedule is effectively just the revenue function shifted down by $100. In this case, the manager is penalized for shirking: the more the manager shirks, the lower are sales, and the lower is his pay. The owner gets paid $100 regardless of how much the manager decides to shirk. The manager gets to keep whatever is left over, so we say the manager is a *residual claimant*.

Given that P can be set by the owner, the question is whether $P = 100$ the best the owner can do. It should be clear from Figure 15.3 that the answer to this question is: no. Raising P increases the return to the owner and shifts the manager's pay schedule toward the origin. Of course, a higher P implies lower pay to the manager and there is the matter of the pay constraint to take

into account. The owner can't set P so high that it is not in the manager's interest to work at the hot-dog cart. As long as the pay schedule doesn't slip entirely below the pay constraint when P is increased, the manager has no reason to quit the hot-dog cart. In essence, the owner simply shifts the pay schedule toward the origin (by increasing P) until the pay schedule is tangent to the pay constraint. In this way, P is maximized at P^* in Figure 15.3. The manager has no incentive to quit the cart because the combination of pay and shirking with P^* lies on the pay constraint.

It should be clear from Figure 15.3 that the level of shirking s^* corresponding to P^* is exactly equal to the level of shirking in the original case when the owner could observe the amount of shirking. Maximizing P is the same as maximizing the distance between the revenue function and the pay constraint. Since profit is maximized at s^*, it follows that profit at any other level of shirking is lower. In particular, the profit generated with the flat salary scheme (where $s = 40$) must be lower than with the residual claimant scheme. In this example, the owner is much better-off offering the manager a performance-based compensation scheme.

Another way of looking at the scheme is to consider the manager's options when facing a fixed payment of P. The manager's income is revenue minus P, or $m = 500 - 5s - P$. The manager's utility is given by (15.2). Given P, the manager aims to maximize his utility. In other words, the manager solves the following problem:

$$\max_{s} \quad 500 - 5s - P + 20s^{1/2} \qquad (15.7)$$

which just says that the manager maximizes utility by choosing s subject to P. Taking the derivative of the utility function in equation (15.7) and setting it equal to zero, we have:

$$-5 - (-10s^{-1/2}) = 0 \qquad (15.8)$$

But this is exactly the same condition as before, when we assumed that the owner could observe the amount of shirking (see equation (15.6)). Thus, the solution to the manager's utility maximizing problem is $s = 4$. Hence, the performance-based pay scheme produces the profit-maximizing level of shirking. It's easy to see that the reason this scheme works is because it makes the manager's utility maximizing problem (15.7) basically the same as the owner's profit-maximizing problem (15.5). Thus, the interests of the manager are brought into line with the interests of the owner.

There is one last detail: how is P determined? From Figure 15.3, you can see P is equal to the distance between the revenue function and the pay constraint at $s = 4$. Thus, $P = 500 - (5 \times 4) - 400 - (20 \times \sqrt{4})$ $= 120$. The manager pays the owner $120, shirks four hours, thereby making a revenue of $500 - (5 \times 4) = 480$. Once the payment to the owner is made, the manager is left with an income of $480 - 120 = 360$.

This example illustrates the basic idea behind profit sharing schemes. Employees paid a flat salary have little incentive to work harder for their employer because their pay won't increase as a result. There is little point working harder when you're not getting paid for it. Giving employees a share of the profit means that their pay goes up along with the employer's profit. Thus, profit sharing schemes potentially induce employees to work harder. As a result, the owners see profits increase.

Franchising arrangements are another example of a performance-based scheme. An entrepreneur pays the franchise-owner a fixed fee and takes whatever is left from operating the business. Sales representatives, real estate agents, lawyers, and many other occupations also have a performance-based salary schemes. Sales staff and real estate agents are paid a commission when they make a sale. Lawyers in civil suits take a percentage of the damages. All these schemes have the simple motivating factor: the harder you work, the more you get paid. And the end result is that employees work harder and owners' profits are higher.

Although it doesn't work well in principle it turns out that many managers are paid a flat salary and not as residual claimants. Why is that? For one thing, many people are not simply out to shirk at every possibility. Many workers take pride in a job well done and will not take advantage of inadequate supervision by wasting time at work. Others are motivated to work hard because they feel a degree of loyalty toward their employer. Still others may feel guilty if they don't work hard. In all these cases, the employers are self-motivated to work hard. In other cases, periodic performance reviews followed up with lazy employees getting fired may be sufficient to discourage shirking. Nonetheless, performance-based pay schemes like profit-sharing are on the rise in the work place.

15.2.2 Risk aversion

Another, more fundamental, reason that performance-based schemes are relatively rare has to do with the amount of risk they place on the worker. In our example, the manager's pay is as variable as hot-dog sales. The manager makes the fixed payment to the owner from the weekly sales at the hot-dog cart and keeps what's left over. If the weather happens to be poor one week, or more people than usual stay in Toronto to watch the Molson Indy, it's just tough luck on the manager. The resulting variability in his pay may be unacceptable to the manager. He may prefer a job with a lower average pay than the hot-dog cart if it provides more a more certain income.

For example, suppose that there are "good weeks" with sales of $1,000 and "bad weeks" with sales of $500. Suppose also that good weeks are just as likely to happen as bad weeks. The expected pay of the manager is:

$$0.5 \times (1000 - P^*) + 0.5 \times (500 - P^*)$$
$$= 750 - P^*$$

If $P^* = 550$, then the manager will expect to make, on average, $200 per week. On good weeks the manager makes $450 and on bad weeks the manager loses $50. Since the owner gets $550 no matter what, the manager bears all the risk of the enterprise.

If the manager is *risk averse*, this arrangement is not efficient. An alternative arrangement could make both the owner and the manager better-off. A risk averse individual prefers a stable income to a variable income with the same average value. Put another way, a risk averse manager will accept a stable income with a lower average value than a variable income. For example, a risk averse manager would be willing to accept less than $200, say $180, as long as the $180 were guaranteed. Thus, the manager would be better-off, because he prefers the stable income, and the owner would be better-off, because her profits would go up.

The same argument applies in many situations. Risk averse workers prefer stable incomes over the variability that comes with a residual claimant scheme. This means workers are willing to take lower average fixed pay in return for the owners of the firm bearing the risk. This is even true if the firm's owners are themselves risk averse. The owners are able to reduce their risk by investing in more than one firm. Workers, on the other hand, don't have this opportunity because the bulk of their income comes from only one source.

Of course, if the wages of workers are guaranteed then the ability of wages to act as a motivational force are lost. The fact is, for a compensation scheme to motivate workers it necessarily implies some risk. In other words, there is a trade-off between incentives and risk. Well-designed compensation schemes have to balance the workers' needs for stable income versus the firm's needs to motivate its work force.

Although not very common at lower levels in organizations, profit-sharing is quite common at the executive level. We have seen the rationale for profit-sharing. But what about profit-sharing in practice? We have argued essentially that executives will work harder if their pay is based on the firm's profit. In principle, the harder-working executives will result in higher profits for firms. But is this the case in practice? The answer is: yes.

15.3 Motivating managers

There are other performance-based compensation schemes besides profit-sharing. If you look at the salary of many top executives, they are often paid two- or three-times the salary of the person next-highest in the ranks. Large salary increases of this type are extremely difficult to justify in terms of the individual's value of marginal product. Moving from executive vice-president to president only results in a small change in the nature of the job and the level of responsibility. But if salary increases aren't justified by changes in the individual's value of marginal product, what explains such huge salary differences for promotions at very high levels in firms?

15.3.1 Tournaments

One approach compares the large salary increases to prizes for winning a *tournament*. The basic idea is that the senior executives are implicitly engaged in a tournament that serves to rank them in terms of their productivity. Once the ranking is established, rewards are distributed to the executives according to their rank, just as in tournaments in professional sport like tennis or golf. By paying a very large prize to the top-ranked executive and much smaller prizes to the lower ranks, the firm motivates every vice-president to work extremely hard. The tournament, therefore, has the effect of motivating everyone who might be considered for promotion to work very hard, just like the golfers in a major PGA tour event. It's worth paying a fat reward to only one individual even if it doesn't equal their value of marginal product, because the value of marginal product of everyone competing for the position increases their value of marginal product. The prize pays for itself by motivating all the managers at the executive level. The larger the prize, the harder the executives will work to get the promotion.

Tournaments break the link between an individual's pay and their value of marginal product. In the basic hiring problem of Chapter 14, pay was linked to an individual's *absolute* performance in the firm. A more productive individual has a higher value of marginal product and gets paid more. With tournaments, however, pay is linked to *relative* performance. The best worker gets the promotion and the pay increase, even though they may be only slightly better than the second-ranked employee.

There is a potential problem with using tournaments to rank executives, however. When the prize is so high, there is the poten-

tial that the competition becomes destructive rather than productivity-enhancing. One way to win a tournament, after all, is by cheating. In some cases cheating may be an easier option than trying hard. There are stories of pre-medical students in the US competing so fiercely for places in medical school that they sabotage the experiments of their classmates or remove pages from library books containing important readings. The explanation could be that the high incomes doctors earn in the US are such that admission to a medical school is just like a prize. In a competition where being near the top of the class becomes so important, it is possible that some will stoop to desperate measures.

In the context of tournaments among executives, it is not inconceivable that sabotage may occur. Suppose, for example, that the heads of two divisions know that one of them is going to be the next president and may expect a hefty pay increase if promoted. Because they are competing against one another on the basis of how their divisions perform, there is an incentive for either candidate to sabotage the output of the rival's division. Key reports and information could be delayed, or outside firms may be given preference over the rival division, and so on. Thus, far from enhancing the firm's total productivity, the tournament has the opposite effect. As the rivals strive to win the promotion, the sabotage is detrimental to the overall performance of the firm.

Thus, there is a trade-off between establishing incentives on the one hand and creating sabotage on the other. Very likely, the size of the prizes in the tournament will have to be adjusted depending on the circumstances. In a firm where rival divisions are relatively autonomous, it is difficult for one division to sabotage the work of another. In these cases, it is probably safe to install a tournament with a very large prize for the winner. However, in organizations where team-work is important, the possibility of sabotage becomes a concern. In these cases, the tournaments should have very low prizes in order to minimize the potential for sabotage. In very extreme cases like this, the firm may prefer to choose its president from out-side the firm rather than run the risk of ruining the firm.

There is evidence at the CEO level that large salary increases are common, suggesting that firms use tournament like schemes to motivate upper-level managers. A study of 200 large US firms found that the average pay increase for a promotion from vice-president to CEO was 142 percent.[4]

Incentives in PGA Tournaments

The main purpose of tournaments in firms is to motivate managers to work harder. Presumably, if tournaments don't work to motivate professional athletes, then there is little hope that they will work in the firm. Professional athletes' income depends solely on winning, not only because of the prize money, but also because lucrative endorsement contracts tend to go only to the winners. A study of professional golfers attempted to find out whether tournaments increased the performance of the competitors.

There were 45 tournaments in the 1984 US PGA tour. On average, the prize money for placing first was 66 percent larger than the prize money for second place, which was 59 percent greater than the prize money for coming third. The difference between first and second, and between second and third was, therefore, substantial. In contrast, the difference between the prize money for the twenty-second and twenty-third places was only 10 percent.

The theory of tournaments says that players will be motivated to work harder in events with larger total purses. In fact, this was found to be the case: each extra $100,000 in total prize money at a tournament reduced average scores by 1.1 strokes. The structure of prize money also suggests that the closer a player is to being among the top finishers, the harder he should try. Thus, players who were within a few strokes of the lead heading into the final round are predicted to try harder than players who are a long way off the lead. This prediction was also supported in the PGA tour data.

Source: Ronald G. Ehrenberg and Michael L. Bognanno. "Do tournaments have incentive effects?" *Journal of Political Economy*, 98 (December 1990), pp. 1307–24.

15.4 Motivating non-managers

While tournaments might help motivate upper-level managers, not every worker at the firm will aspire to become president. Many workers lower in the management hierarchy don't have the ability or the ambition to participate in a tournament. What are the issues involved in trying to motivate workers at lower levels?

15.4.1 Piece rates and time rates

A common form of remuneration for employees in developed economies is a *time rate*. A time rate is simply a fixed amount of pay for a given amount of time spent working. It could be an hourly wage, or a weekly or monthly salary. As discussed earlier in this chapter, a fixed time rate provides employees with no incentive to work harder because their pay is fixed regardless of how hard they work. However, because the pay is guaranteed, the firm can pay risk averse workers less than they would have to under a performance-based scheme.

An alternative payment scheme to time rates that is becoming more popular recently is the *piece rate*. Piece rates pay workers exactly according to their productivity. In some industries, the piece rate is literally a payment that is made for each unit of output the worker produces. For example, garment workers may be paid for each shirt they sew together, telemarketers may be paid by the phone call, and sales personnel are paid commission. Clearly, piece rates will be effective at motivating employees to work hard: the more they produce, the more they get paid.

But there are several problems with using piece rates to pay workers. One problem has already been discussed earlier in the chapter. Risk averse workers may not like the amount of variability in their income that piece rate simply. Sales commissions, especially on expensive items like houses and cars, will rise and fall over the business cycle. The incomes of sales representatives will vary accordingly. Garment workers will not be able to produce shirts if their machines break down or the material from suppliers is behind schedule. In both cases, the employee bears the risk for events that are out of their control. Risk averse workers will, therefore, choose to work at firms that offer time rates. In order to attract risk averse workers, firms paying piece rates will have to pay more than firms offering time rates and, as a result, profits will be lower.

Piece rates are not very suitable in firms where production depends on team effort. On a production line, for example, the effort of one worker has very little impact on the overall productivity of the line. Thus, it is difficult for the firm to measure the individual contribution of a worker, which is the whole basis of the piece rate system. In contrast, it is easy to measure the output of sales people. This partly explains why piece rate systems in the form of sales commission are so common for sales people.

Still another problem with piece rates is the incentive for workers to produce as many physical units as possible without regard to quality. One way around this is to inspect the product of each worker. But this adds extra monitoring costs to the piece rate system and reduces its attractiveness to firms. Some clothes manufacturing firms have addressed the quality problem by relying on the final consumer to do the inspecting. A tag with the name of the worker is included with the final product. The idea is that, if a consumer is dissatisfied with the product, the complaint will get back to the firm who can root out the worker responsible. Since the workers know that they may be found out, they may try harder to produce a quality product in the first place. This reduces monitoring costs to the firm.

Lastly, many workers under a piece rate system may be wary of the *ratchet effect*. Piece-rate workers face a dilemma. The harder they work and the more they get paid, the more likely that the firm will think it has overestimated how difficult the task is. To avoid over-paying its workers, therefore, the firm may consider reducing the piece rate. But then the workers will have to work even harder just to maintain their pay.

15.4.2 Deferred wages

So far, we have talked about how compensation schemes can be used to motivate workers and managers over relatively short-time frames. In spite of recent accounts that the

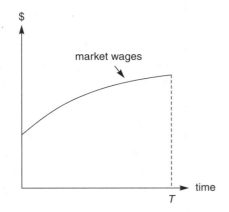

Figure 15.4 The worker's age-earnings profile

length of tenure of employees with firms has radically decreased, most workers in developed countries can expect to work with the same employer for about 20 years. As we shall see, this opens up a more subtle way for firms to motivate workers.

Suppose that a worker and firm expect the employment relationship between the two to last for many periods until the worker reaches the age of *mandatory retirement*. Assume that the productivity of the worker rises over time as the employee gains more experience at the firm. To keep things simple, we will ignore the possibility of firm-specific training. Assuming a competitive labor market, as the productivity of the worker rises, the market wage of the worker rises as well. If we graph the wage of the worker against time, we get the *age-earnings profile* illustrated in Figure 15.4.

Let w_t be the wage the worker is paid in each period t, VMP_t be the worker's value of marginal product, and mandatory retirement take place at the end of period T. Over the worker's tenure with the firm, the present value of the wage paid to the worker must equal the present value of the worker's value of marginal product:

$$\sum_{t=0}^{T} \frac{VMP_t}{(1+r)^t} = \sum_{t=0}^{T} \frac{w_t}{(1+r)^t} \qquad (15.9)$$

This condition is trivially true if the firm pays the worker the market wage in each period since $w_t = VMP_t$. However, even if the worker were not paid the market wage in every period, so $w_t \neq VMP_t$ for all t, this condition still must be true. If it were not, firms would be systematically under-paying or over-paying workers during their tenure with the firm. Under-paying would result in all the workers leaving for other firms where their lifetime income would be rewarded at the market rate. Over-paying would result in such a flood of job applicants that the firm would soon realize it could cut the wage.

As long as (15.9) is satisfied, the firm can choose any particular sequence of wages it suits. In particular, there is nothing that prevents the firm from tilting the worker's age-earnings profile so that it becomes steeper. As shown in Figure 15.5, tilting the age-earnings profile means that early in their careers workers are paid less than the market wage. Later in their careers, workers are paid more than the market wage. The worker, therefore, is paid *deferred wages*.

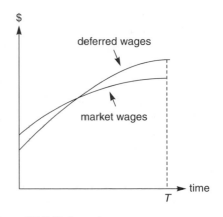

Figure 15.5 Deferred wages

Why would the firm want to tilt the worker's age earnings profile? Deferred wages give workers a strong incentive to work hard throughout their time with the firm. Although young workers are paid less than their market wage, they know that in the future their wages will rise above market level to compensate them for low initial wages. The only way young workers can receive what the firm owes them when they get older, of course, is if they stay at the firm. This gives young workers a strong incentive to work hard to avoid being fired. Old workers are paid more than their market value, which gives them plenty of incentive to work hard. If they are fired for shirking, the best they can hope for is another job at the their market wage, which is lower than they are currently getting paid.

In effect, the deferred wages scheme gets young workers to post a bond. The bond is represented by the wages young workers receive that are below the market level. If the young worker is caught shirking and fired, the worker can't realize high wages in the future. Therefore, the bond is forfeited if the young worker doesn't perform satisfactorily at the firm. Because deferred wages act as a powerful motivational device, they reduce the need for costly monitoring of workers. Periodic performance reviews backed up with the threat of firing shirkers will be sufficient to produce the right amount of effort from the workers. Moreover, since the worker must stay at the firm until retirement to collect their bond, older workers are much less likely to leave the firm. This reduces turnover as well.

Although deferred wages benefit the firm, workers may be concerned that the firm will fire them when they get old. Since young workers are paid less than their value of marginal product and old workers are paid more, the firm has an incentive to lay-off old workers. In effect, the firm could simply specialize in collecting bonds from young workers. What stops the firm from doing this? Perhaps the most important factor is the firm's reputation. If the firm were known for exploiting young workers in this fashion, it would find it very difficult to attract any young job applicants. For firms that will be in existence a lot longer than most of their workers, it is not viable in the long run to take advantage of young workers.

An interesting side effect of a deferred wages scheme is the need for a mandatory retirement date. Without a mandatory retirement date T, the firm will be unable to compute the schedule of deferred wages to ensure that the condition (15.9) holds. Recent debate over removing mandatory retirement provisions may meet with opposition from firms using deferred wages to discipline their workers.

15.4.3 Efficiency wages

In this chapter we have argued that there is a link between compensation schemes and worker productivity. Performance-based schemes, tournaments, and deferred wages are all ways of motivating workers. However, not one of these schemes results in the firm paying higher than market level wages over the workers' tenure with the firm. According to these schemes, firms that pay workers more than their fair market wage will have higher costs than other firms and soon be forced out of business or taken over. Another observation is that the link between pay and productivity in these schemes has to do with how or when the wages are paid, not with the level of the wages *per se*.

The basic idea behind an *efficiency wage* is that there is a direct link between pay and

Did Ford Pay Efficiency Wages?

In the period before World War I, The Ford Motor Company of Detroit was building the most successful model in automotive history, the Model-T. Yet annual labor turnover at Ford was 370 percent in 1913 and the daily rate of absenteeism was 10 percent. A report commissioned by management in the summer of 1913 concluded that there was a serious morale problem among production-line workers. In January 1914, the working day at the Ford plant was reduced from nine to eight hours and minimum daily pay was more than doubled, from $2.34 to $5.00.

There is plenty of evidence that the "five-dollar day" was in excess of prevailing market levels. Other automobile manufacturers in Detroit at the time were paying between $2.00 and $3.00 per day. There were also massive queues for jobs at the Ford factory gate.

After the introduction of the five-dollar day, annual labor turnover declined to 54 percent in 1914 and 16 percent in 1915, productivity increased by over 30 percent, and profits increased.

Source: D. Raff and L. Summers. "Did Henry Ford Pay Efficiency Wages?" *Journal of Labor Economics* 5 (October 1987): S57–S86.

productivity: the more workers are paid, the more productive they will be.[5] In fact, for efficiency wages to work, the firm must pay its workers more than the market wage. However, firms paying efficiency wages will not have higher costs than other firms as long as there is a direct link between pay and productivity. Firms paying efficiency wages will have more productive workers than other firms. The high-wage costs are offset by increased productivity. Efficiency wages can affect productivity in a variety of ways: reducing turnover, reducing shirking, and attracting more productive employees to the firm.

It is easy to see why efficiency wages reduce turnover and shirking. Workers paid an efficiency wage are getting paid more than they can receive at another firm. As a result,

they have an incentive to try to stay with the firm paying the efficiency wage. The workers will, therefore, be less likely to shirk, because they don't want to be fired. Everything else being equal, they will also be less likely to quit.

It is more difficult to see how efficiency wages can result in a better pool of job applicants. The argument is based on the assumption that workers differ in ability. Higher ability workers have better opportunities and will need a higher wage offer to attract them to any particular firm. Firms paying low wages will attract mostly low ability workers. Firms paying high wages will attract more high ability workers. Offering high wages, therefore, resolves the firm's problem of *adverse selection* among job seekers.

Summary

- Training increases a worker's productivity. General training increases worker productivity at any firm. Specific training increases worker productivity only at the firm where training takes place.

> ## Summary contd
>
> - Because the firm can't capture any of the benefits from general training, the worker pays all the training cost. In order to reduce turnover, firms and workers share in the costs and benefits of specific training.
> - Motivating workers to give more effort is another way to increase worker productivity. Flat salary schemes lead to large amounts of shirking. Performance-based schemes can reduce shirking to zero.
> - Risk averse workers prefer flat salary schemes over performance-based schemes that make their incomes too variable.
> - Tournaments that give large salary increases to promoted upper-level managers can motivate all managers to give more effort.
> - Piece rates can be used to motivate non-managers but may be difficult to implement because of worker risk aversion, trouble measuring output, and quality considerations.
> - Deferred wages may motivate workers and reduce turnover. Mandatory retirement is necessary for a deferred wages scheme to be operational.
> - Efficiency wages are the practice of raising wages to improve worker productivity. Efficiency wages may help reduce turnover and shirking, and provide a better pool of job applicants.

Notes

1 Much of Gary Becker's important work in the area of worker training is discussed in Becker (1993).
2 Again, the revenue function is, strictly speaking, a net revenue function: it represents the revenue to the owner net of costs paid to other workers, soft-drink manufacturers, hot-dog manufacturers, and so on.
3 This is the value of m given $s = 40$ in equation (15.3).
4 Brian G. M. Main, Charles A. O'Reilly III, and James Wade. "Top executive pay: tournament or team work?" *Journal of Labour Economics*, 4 (October 1993), pp. 606–28.
5 For a survey of the literature on efficiency wages, see Weiss (1990).

Exercises

1 In each of the following cases, state whether the case is an example of general or specific training and give a brief explanation.

(a) A Bachelor of Arts in Economics.

(b) Flight training on a Boeing 767.

(c) Training in the Registrar's Office at the University of London.

(d) Training to operate mail-sorting machinery at Australia Post.

2 Suppose that the value of marginal product of an untrained worker is $25,000 per year. One year of worker training costs $12,500 and raises the worker's value of marginal product to $50,000. Suppose the worker will only remain with the firm two years and that the interest rate is 10 percent. Assume that the firm and the worker decide to split the training costs equally.

(a) Determine the worker's wage in the first year.

(b) Determine the worker's wage in the second year.

(c) Does the present value of the benefit from training exceed the present value of the cost?

3 Suppose that the value of marginal product of an untrained worker is $20,000 per year and that one year of worker training raises productivity by 20 percent. Suppose training costs are $3,500 and that the worker will stay with the firm for two years. Assume that the worker agrees to pay three-quarters of the training costs and that the interest rate is 10 percent.

    (a) Determine the worker's wage in the first year.

    (b) Determine the worker's wage in the second year.

    (c) Does the present value of the benefit from training exceed the present value of the cost?

    (d) Suppose the interest rate rises 15 percent. Will the training still be undertaken? Explain.

4 Suppose the owner of a small business is considering hiring a manager and has decided to opt for a performance-based scheme for the manager's pay. Suppose a manager's utility function is given by $U(m, s) = m + 40s^{1/2}$, where m is the manager's income and s the number of hours of shirking the manager takes. In the absence of shirking, suppose that the small business will achieve revenue (net of all costs except the manager's pay) of $1,200 and that, for every hour of shirking, revenue is reduced by $25.

    (a) Derive the revenue function of the small business.

    (b) Derive the pay constraint for the small business. What does the pay constraint represent?

    (c) Assuming for the moment that the owner can observe the amount of shirking, derive the profit-maximizing hours of shirking at the business.

    (d) Assuming the pay scheme takes the form of a fixed payment P to the owner with all residual revenues from the business going to the manager, calculate the value of P.

    (e) What potentially important aspect of the manager's pay does this compensation scheme ignore? Explain.

5 Suppose that a worker is expected to stay with a firm for two years. The worker's value of marginal product is $20,000 in the first year, rising to $25,000 in the second year owing to experience gained in the job. Suppose that the interest rate is 10 percent and the worker is paid $18,000 in her first year at the job.

    (a) What condition must be true in order for the firm not to overpay or underpay the worker during her tenure at the firm?

    (b) Using this condition, calculate the wage the worker will be paid in the second year of the job.

    (c) The worker is paid less in her first year at the job than her market value. Why do you think a worker would opt for such an arrangement?

6 Suppose the value of marginal product for all workers in a firm is $20 per hour. Shirking is a major problem in the firm, so the manager of the firm proposes to institute a scheme of deferred wages. Assume that the wage of a worker is determined by the formula:

    wage = $12 + (0.5 \times$ years at the firm)

Assuming that the discount rate is zero and that all workers enter the firm at the age of 25. What will be the mandatory retirement age in this firm?

7 A study by an economics consulting firm finds the following relationship between wages and output at a small firm hiring a fixed number of workers.

Wage rate ($)	Units of output
8.00	60
10.00	80
11.25	90
12.00	95
12.50	98

(a) Calculate the percentage change in the wage and the corresponding percentage change in output as the wage is increased from $8.00 to $10.00. Given that all other inputs at the firm are fixed, would you recommend the wage increase? Explain.

(b) Compute the percentage wage changes and corresponding percentage output increases for the wage pairs $10.00 and $11.25, $11.25 and $12.00, and $12.00 and $12.50.

(c) Based on your calculations, what wage do you think the firm should adopt? Explain.

(d) What do economists call the wage you have determined?

References

Gary S. Becker. *Human Capital*, 3rd edn (Chicago: University of Chicago Press, 1993).

Andrew Weiss. *Efficiency Wages: Models of Unemployment, Layoffs, and Wage Dispersion* (Princeton, NJ: Princeton University Press, 1990).

Chapter 16

Trade unions

··

When you are finished with this chapter you should understand:

- The meaning of the term "union density"
- The three kinds of industrial relations systems followed around the industrialized world
- Supply and demand explanations for the reduction in union density observed in many countries
- The implications of the Rubinstein bargaining model for firm–union negotiations
- Measures of union power and the factors causing strikes
- The effects of unions on worker pay and productivity and the effect of unions on firm profits

In the last two chapters, we have discussed issues of employment and compensation at the firm. It was implicitly assumed in this discussion that the firm could make employment and compensation decisions unilaterally, without any input from the workers. If the work force at the firm is unionized, however, then there are many things that the firm cannot do without first negotiating with the union. And this is not simply a matter of courtesy. Agreements between firms and unions are legally binding contracts, so a firm acting unilaterally may be breaking the law.

In this chapter we are going to discuss issues that managers have to face when their employees, or some of the employees, are members of a union. There are important differences between the degree of unioniza-

tion across countries as well as differences in the role unions play in the workplace. Thus, we'll begin with a comparison of the extent of unionization and the industrial relations systems in various countries and try to draw some general conclusions about union behavior. We then go on to discuss union objectives and what happens when a previously non-union work place becomes unionized. While the general view is that unions are bad for business, we'll see that unions may have some positive impacts on the firm. With the background on the effects of unions, we turn to the contract negotiation problem. Here we will see that the primary source of union power over the firm is the ability to withdraw labor services from the firm, i.e. the strike.

16.1 Unions around the world

The usual way to measure the degree of union organization in a region or industry is the *union density*, defined as:

$$\frac{\text{total number of union members}}{\text{total number of organizable workers}} \times 100$$

The "number of organizable workers" excludes workers that would typically never join a union, such as the self-employed, military personnel, and agricultural workers. Table 16.1 gives you an idea of union density around the world in 1995 and the change in union density over the previous ten-year period.[1] As a rule, most European countries have higher rates of unionization, while the United States and Japan have lower rates.

As well as differences in rates of unionization across countries, there are substantial differences in the economic and political role played by unions across countries. By and large, unions in the United States, and to varying degrees in other English-speaking countries, have a long tradition of *business unionism*, where the main goal of the union is to improve the wages and working conditions of its members through *collective bargaining*. Bargaining is highly decentralized in these countries, most often being conducted at the firm or enterprise level. While the union density in Canada has actually grown slightly over the 1985–95 period, union density in the other English-speaking countries has fallen drastically over the same period – by a fifth in the US, almost a third in the UK and Australia, and by over half in New Zealand.

On the other hand, unions in western Europe have much stronger political ties and place more emphasis on wider economic and social issues, like poverty or the environment. Bargaining in these countries is typically at the industry-wide level. In 1995, for example, enterprise agreements covered only eight percent of the private sector in the Netherlands

Table 16.1   Union density and change in union density for various countries

	Union density (1995)	Change in density (1985–95)
Africa		
Egypt	38.8	−9.1
South Africa	40.9	130.8
America		
Argentina	38.7	−42.6
Canada	43.5	1.8
Costa Rica	37.4	−43.0
Cuba	70.2	−29.8
Mexico	42.8	−28.2
United States	14.2	−21.1
Venezuela	17.1	−42.6
Asia		
Japan	24.0	−16.7
Korea, Rep. of	12.7	2.4
Philippines	38.2	84.9
Thailand	4.2	−2.5
Oceania		
Australia	35.2	−29.6
New Zealand	24.3	−55.1
Europe		
Austria	41.2	−19.2
Denmark	80.1	2.3
Finland	79.3	16.1
France	9.1	−37.2
Germany	28.9	−17.6
Greece	24.3	−33.8
Hungary	60.0	−25.3
Israel	23.0	−77.0
Italy	44.1	−7.4
Netherlands	25.6	−11.0
Poland	33.8	−42.5
Portugal	25.6	−50.2
Spain	18.6	62.1
Sweden	91.1	8.7
Switzerland	22.5	−21.7
United Kingdom	32.9	−27.7

compared with 75 percent for industry-wide agreements and in France the figures are 25 percent and 80 percent, respectively. In industry-wide bargaining, the union representing all the workers in a particular industry bargains with an employers' association over wages for various job categories, overtime pay, hours of work and so forth.

A third kind of industrial relations system, which combines element from both the English-speaking countries and the European model, is prevalent in Japan. While enterprise-level bargaining is the norm for most workers and firms, there are various forms of national coordination that may have an influence on bargaining outcomes. The "shunto" is the most prominent form of national coordination, organizing annual wage bargaining for 25 percent of all Japanese workers. In fact, the influence of the shunto is more widespread than this figure would suggest, since it acts as a benchmark for wage increases in small- and medium-sized firms where there may be no unions at all. Another common feature of the industrial relations system in Japan are the worker–employer cooperation committees. Set up to address productivity problems in the aftermath of the 1970s oil shocks, they continue today and have been emulated by many non-Japanese firms. Unions seem to have played an important role in maintaining the committees: 81 percent of unionized firms have the committees, compared with only 32 percent of non-union enterprises.

16.1.1 Factors affecting union membership

One of the most striking aspects of Table 16.1, is that union density has dropped in the vast majority of countries over the 1985–95 period. Only seven countries have shown an increase in union density over the ten-year period: the other 25 countries have

all witnessed a decline in union density. To see why this has occurred, we need to investigate the reasons why workers form and join unions.

One way to look at the motivation behind unions is to think of unions as selling a package of services – a grievance procedure, a seniority system, higher wages, better job security, and so forth – that workers pay for through union dues. Thus, we may think of the economy as having a market for union services with an equilibrium determined by the balance between the "supply" and "demand" for the services unions have to offer. The demand side is determined largely by the number of the workers that may require union services and the preferences of those workers. The supply side is determined by the costs of producing union services, which in particular is related to the cost of organizing workers into unions. Viewed within this framework, a number of recent events helps explain why the drop in union density is so widespread internationally.

On the demand side, four forces have been at play: technological change, globalization, shrinking public sectors, and attitudes toward unions. Especially in the developed world, the rate of technological change has accelerated over the last decade. Information technology, in particular, has spread rapidly through many industries. As a result, the types of workers firms need to hire have changed and, in particular, the number of *blue-collar* jobs has fallen while the number of *white-collar* jobs has risen. Since a traditional source of union demand has been among blue-collar workers, the shift in the worker composition at firms has resulted in a lower demand for unions.

Along with technological change, another major impact on economies around the world through the 1980s and 1990s was the rapid increase in global trade and the influence of capital markets, often referred to collectively as *globalization*. For example, competition from developing countries with low wages has led to a steady decline in the number of low-skilled, labor-intensive jobs in high-wage countries. Certain manufacturing industries in developed countries, like textiles and consumer electronics, have seen large employment losses. Given that the manufacturing sector has traditionally been a source of strength for unions, the resulting decline in the sector has decreased the demand for unions.

Likewise, the public service has been another source of union growth in many countries since World War II. From about the mid-1980s on, however, governments have decreased in size as many countries around the world have tackled budget deficits. Fewer government workers translate into another source of reduced demand for union services.

Lastly, the general attitude toward unions, especially in the US and the UK, became less favorable over the 1985–95 period. In the US, air-traffic controllers were fired *en masse* after refusing to take pay cuts. In the UK, there was a bitter struggle between the government and the miners union over the closing of coal mines. In both cases, the government prevailed in part due to public opinion supporting their position. To the extent that public opinion also reflects the tastes for unions in general, demand for unions has fallen as a result.

On the supply side, two forces have played a role: changing structure of the workforce and government legislation. Throughout the last 30 years, the service-producing sectors of developed economies around the world have grown while the goods-producing sector has declined. At the same time, there has been a massive increase in the number of part-time workers, women workers, and younger workers in the labor forces of these countries. It turns out that part-time workers are much more costly for unions to organize than full-time workers. Also, men were traditionally much more likely to be unionized, and unions have been much less able to organize women or younger workers. In both cases, the effect has been to reduce the supply for union services over 1985–95 time period.

Second, government legislation in many countries has become less union-friendly in recent years, perhaps reflecting the attitudes of the population in general. In the economies of central and eastern Europe, a huge drop in union size can be attributed to the end of compulsory union membership.[2] In the US, UK, New Zealand, Canada, and Australia, legislation outlawing various union practices, like third-party picketing, have made union policies less effective, thus raising the cost of union services and reducing union supply. Other legislation not directly related to unions can also impact union membership. For example, much of the original demand for unions was to get decent wages and working conditions. Now most developed countries have minimum wage laws ruling out very low wages and labor codes that protect workers from unreasonable working conditions. Thus, the demand for unions to protect wages and the working environment has been reduced by other legislation.

16.2 Collective bargaining and union power

As noted above, the norm in English-speaking countries is the negotiation of a single agreement between an employer and the union local at a single site. Contract negotiations are at the heart of the firm–union relationship. The outcome of negotiations is a *contract* that establishes the terms and conditions of employment at the firm. In this section, we'll examine the factors that influence the outcome of negotiations. In particular, we will examine what factors determine whether union workers get a large pay increase, or a small pay increase.

There is no widely accepted theory of collective bargaining. But there are several fundamental features of any bargaining situation that a theory should try to capture. A fundamental characteristic of any bargaining situation is that there are gains from cooperation, but there is conflict over the division of those gains. Cooperation is necessary for an agreement to be reached. In buying a house or negotiating a labor contract, the final agreement is voluntary for both bargaining agents.[3] Since agreements are voluntary, each side must accommodate the other to some degree or risk not reaching any agreement and, thereby, forfeit potential gains. On the other hand, conflict arises because one side's gain is the other side's loss. A higher selling price for the house makes the vendor better off and the buyer worse off. A low wage settlement makes the union worse off and the firm better off.

Another common feature of bargaining is that there is a minimum acceptable outcome for each side. The worst that can happen to a house vendor is that the sale isn't made to the prospective buyer, so the vendor has to wait for another buyer to come along. If a union and firm aren't able to reach an agreement, they can just keep negotiating. If that doesn't work, the lack of a contract may lead the union to go on strike or the firm to lockout the workers. The outcome that obtains if no

agreement is reached is called a *disagreement point*. Because the disagreement point can be obtained if no agreement is reached, no side will settle for less than their disagreement point. For this reason, the disagreement point is sometimes called the "threat point," because it is the outcome one side can threaten the other side with if no agreement is reached.

Someone selling house has a minimum price they are willing to accept, and someone buying a house has a maximum price they are willing to pay. A union may have a minimum acceptable wage increase, and a firm may have a maximum increase that it is prepared to pay. In other words, all bargaining situations have a range of possible outcomes, referred to as the *bargaining set*. Suppose the minimum acceptable wage increase is two percent and the maximum the firm is willing to pay is four percent. Then the bargaining set contains all wage increases between two and four percent. Of course, if the bargaining set is empty, there is no possibility of an agreement.

16.2.1 Rubinstein's bargaining theory

We are going to look at the bargaining model of Rubinstein.[4] This is a general model of the bargaining process and, as such, it can be applied to any bargaining situation. It can just as well model negotiations over selling a house or a car as model collective bargaining between a firm and union. In the context of Chapter 5, the Rubinstein model is an example of non-cooperative game theory. Of course, bargaining is a very complex problem, so the model has to make some simplifying assumptions.

Labor contracts can be very detailed. For example, the contract between Wilfrid Laurier University and its Faculty Association runs over 70 pages. It covers everything from salaries, pensions, rules for promotion, tenure, and appointment of new faculty, teaching loads, employment equity, and sexual harassment to name just a few of the 40 articles in the contract. Negotiating such a complex agreement can itself be a very complex task.

We'll simplify things by assuming that the firm and the union are bargaining over a fixed dollar amount. Assume the excess economic profits generated by the activity of the firm are π. The union and firm bargain over how π is going to be split: 50–50, 60–40, 90–10, or whatever.

For example, let's suppose the firm has 500 unionized employees that were paid $40,000 each under the terms of the old contract, representing a total wage bill of $20 million. A minimum acceptable wage increase to the union of two percent would add $400,000 to the firm's wage bill. A maximum wage increase the firm is willing to pay of four percent would add $800,000 to the wage bill. In essence, the firm and union are bargaining over $400,000. If the union gets just its minimum wage increase, it gets nothing from the $400,000; the firm gets it all. If the firm ends up paying its maximum acceptable wage increase, it gets nothing from the $400,000; the union gets it all. A 50–50 split of $200,000 to the union and the firm represents a $400,000 + $200,000 = $600,000 increase in the wage bill, or a three percent increase.

Although this is a highly simplified version of what actually is going on, it does go straight to the heart of the matter. At the end of the day, even a very complex collective agreement represents a bottom-line cost to the firm. It's easy to see how wages, rates of overtime pay, pensions, health and dental plans, and so on represent a dollar cost to the firm. But other things like rules for lay-offs and promotion are costly to the firm. The cost is reflected in direct administrative costs to ensure the rules are followed. The rules may also prevent the firm from doing exactly what it wants, representing an implicit cost to the firm. When the contract is being negotiated, therefore, the managers of the firm will always have in mind the dollar cost of their offers to the union and be well aware of the dollar cost of the union's counter-offers. So bargaining is really over the cost terms of the contract represent. The question is then: how much of π these costs will eat up?

Because actual contracts are so detailed, negotiations may take months. In the Rubinstein model, contract negotiations are characterized as follows. A rational firm and rational union bargain in a series of rounds. Each side faces a cost from delay. That is, the time between rounds is costly to the firm and the union. The firm and union take turns making offers to the other side. If an offer is accepted, bargaining ends. If an offer is rejected, bargaining continues in the next round and both sides bear their respective delay costs.

The delay costs are made up from two components. First, there are the direct negotiation costs to both sides. The firm and the union must pay for negotiators (or at least bare the cost of the time they spend away from their regular jobs) and lawyers. In addition, there are the costs associated with the strike or lockout that occurs if the first offer in negotiations is not accepted. The direct negotiation costs will be much smaller than the costs to both sides of a strike or lockout. Continuing with our example, let's suppose that the delay costs amount to $200,000 each for the firm and the union. There's no reason that the costs should be equal, of course, but let's suppose they are for the time being.

Another key assumption is that there is full information and no uncertainty. This means that there is no doubt about the size of π. A more realistic model would take into account that there may be some uncertainty over the size of π on one or maybe both sides of the bargaining table. For example, even if the firm is aware of the ongoing profits from working with the union, there is no reason to suppose that the union also knows what these profits are. Without seeing the firm's accounts, the order books for the next few months, and so on, the union might not be nearly as well-informed about the size of π at the firm. However, bargaining with uncertainty is a considerably more difficult problem than we need to take on here. We will assume, therefore, that the union is as equally well-informed about the size of π as the firm.

Figure 16.1 illustrates the Rubinstein model when the firm and union are bargaining over $400,000 and delay costs

are $200,000 to each side. The vertical axis shows the amount the union gains from bargaining, and is labeled π_U. Similarly, the horizontal axis shows what the firm gets from bargaining, and is labeled π_F. If the union takes all the money, it ends up with $400,000 and the firm ends up with nothing. Each dollar firm gets from bargaining means one dollar less for the union. Thus, all the possible outcomes to bargaining are described by a line from the point $(0, 400,000)$ with a slope of -1. The horizontal intercept of the line must occur at $400,000, representing the outcome if the firm ends up with the $400,000 and the union with nothing.

The line furthest from the origin is called the bargaining frontier. All the points inside the line represent the bargaining set. Since delay costs are $200,000 per side for each round, the bargaining frontier shifts inwards by $200,000 after every round in which no agreement is reached. Since each side can gain at most $400,000 from an agreement, all the possible gains from bargaining will

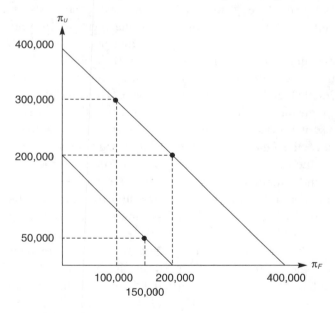

Figure 16.1 Solution to the Rubinstein bargaining model

be exhausted if no agreement is reached after two rounds of bargaining. The origin, therefore, represents the disagreement point for both the union and the firm.

"Empty threats" are ruled out because both the firm and the union are rational. For example, suppose the union makes the first offer to the firm. The union could offer the firm $100,000, thereby taking $300,000 for itself, and threaten to refuse to accept any future offers from the firm. If the firm believed the union's threat, it would accept the $100,000 because the firm would receive nothing in the event that no agreement is reached (the disagreement point). But the union's threat is not believable. If the firm rejects the union's offer, both sides incur delay costs of $200,000, shifting the bargaining frontier inwards. Now the firm can offer the union $50,000, taking $150,000 for itself. The union will accept the $50,000 because it is better than nothing, which is what the union will receive if it rejects the $50,000 and the union and firm end up at the disagreement point. Since the firm won't believe the union's threat, there is no point in the union making the threat in the first place.

Let's suppose the union makes the first offer. The model predicts the union will offer the firm $200,000 and the firm will accept the offer immediately. To see why this happens we use a process called *backward induction*. Since the union makes the first offer, it will be the firm's turn to make an offer in the second round. In the third round of bargaining there is nothing left for either side. In the second round, the firm knows that the union will accept anything equal to or better than its disagreement point, which is what the union will get if it rejects the firm's offer. Therefore, the firm will offer the union nothing, taking $200,000 for itself, and the union will accept

the firm's offer. In the first round, the union knows the firm will accept anything equal to or better than $200,000, because the firm can always get $200,000 by rejecting the union's offer and waiting to the second round. Therefore, the union offers the firm $200,000 in the first round, and the firm accepts the offer.

In the Rubinstein model, agreement occurs without delay. Rational behavior by both sides combined with delay costs result in an agreement where neither side incurs any delay costs. Delay costs reduce the size of the surplus to be split between the firm and the union. Since both sides are rational, they can follow through the consequences of rejecting each other's offers to the end of the game where both receive nothing if no agreement is reached. Working backwards from this point yields the solution to the bargaining game.

Delay costs are clearly a very important part of the picture. The desire of both sides to avoid delay costs provide the impetus to both sides to finish the bargain quickly. In some sense, delay costs, or at least the threat of using them, are a weapon that each side can use against the other. For this reason, the size of the delay costs can have an important influence on the outcome of the firm-union bargain. However, it is the *relative* size of the delay costs that matter, not their *absolute* size. The next two figures illustrate this point.

In Figure 16.2, the absolute size of the delay costs is changed from the initial bargaining game. The delay costs to both the firm and the union are reduced to $100,000 per round from $200,000 per round. In absolute terms, delay costs have been cut in half. But, in relative terms, delay costs are the same as they were before. The union and the firm have equal delay costs. The halving of delay costs now means that it takes four rounds of bargaining until the $400,000

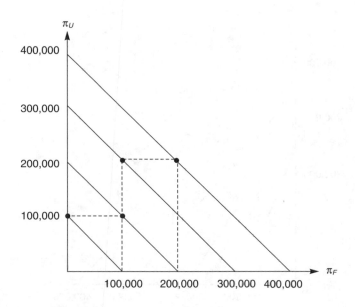

Figure 16.2 The effect of a change in absolute delay costs

surplus to be split between the two sides has been eliminated.

Let's stick with the case where the union makes the first offer. This means the firm makes the offer in the second round, the union in the third round, and the firm in the fourth round. Again we use backward induction to solve the bargain. In the fourth round, it's the firm's turn to make an offer to the union. The union will get nothing if it rejects the firm's fourth round offer (the disagreement point). Therefore, the firm can offer the union nothing in the fourth round and take $100,000 for itself. In the third round, the union need offer the firm no more than the firm will get in the fourth round, which is $100,000. Thus, the union will take $100,000 and offer the firm the same. In the second round, the firm will offer the union $100,000, which is what the union will get in the third round, and take $200,000 for itself. In the opening round, therefore, the union will offer the firm $200,000 and take $200,000. Of course, both

sides know that the offers will follow this path. The solution to the bargain, therefore, is for the union to offer the firm $200,000 in the first round. The firm will accept the offer.

Cutting delay costs in half has had absolutely no effect on the bargaining outcome. When delay costs were $200,000 to each side, the $400,000 was split equally. And when delay costs were cut in half to $100,000 each, the $400,000 was again split equally. The conclusion is that a change in absolute delay costs that leave relative delay costs the same will have no impact on the bargaining outcome.

In Figure 16.3, the relative size of the delay costs are changed from the previous bargaining game. The delay costs to the firm remain at $100,000 per round. But the delay costs to the union are reduced to $50,000 per round. As a result, the disagreement point changes. After four rounds of unsuccessful negotiation, the firm's delay costs will have exhausted all its potential gains from bargaining. But if no agreement is reached after

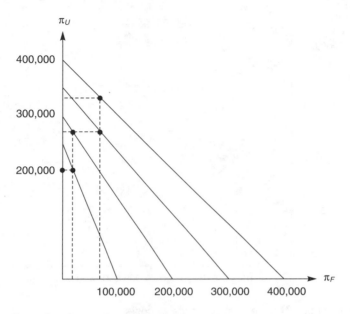

Figure 16.3 The effect of a change in relative delay costs

four rounds of bargaining, the union has lost only $200,000. The disagreement point is, therefore, (0, 200,000) and not the origin as before.

In relative terms the costs of the union have fallen by 50 percent. Delays are now relatively more costly for the firm than they are for the union. Put another way, the penalty for not reaching an agreement in any given round is greater for the firm than it is for the union. In this sense, there is more pressure on the firm to settle. The firm may be willing to give up more than the union in order to avoid delay. In other words, the union ought to be able to get more from the firm with the new delay costs. Let's see if it turns out this way.

Again, let the union make the first offer. As before, this means the firm will make the offer in the fourth round. The union will get $200,000 (the disagreement point) if it rejects the firm's fourth round offer. The firm will offer the union $200,000 in the fourth round, leaving $20,000 for the firm. The union will, therefore, offer the firm $20,000 in the third

round, taking $270,000 for itself. The firm will offer the union $270,000 in the second round, taking $68,571 for itself. Hence, in the first round, the union will offer the firm $68,571 and take $331,429 for itself. The firm will, of course, accept this initial offer.

When delay costs were equal, both sides gained equally from an agreement. When delay costs for the union fell relative to those of the firm, the agreement moved in favor of the union. The union's gain from an agreement rises to $331,429 when its delay costs fall to $50,000 per round. Conversely, the firm's gain from an agreement falls to $68,571 from $200,000. As we suspected, the relative change favors the side with the lower delay costs, which in this case is the union. Because its delay costs are relatively higher, the firm is willing to forgo relatively more of the bargaining surplus. Put simply, the side with the lower delay costs gains a better settlement.

The Rubinstein model has two important implications for collective bargaining. First, the relative delay costs of the two sides are an important determinant of the negotiated settlement. The side with the higher delay costs has more to lose from not reaching an agreement and, therefore, is willing to give up more to reach a settlement. This could explain why union wage gains tend to be procyclical – higher when the economy is expanding and lower when the economy is contracting. When business is booming, the firm has more to lose from not reaching a quick settlement than when business is slow. Also, when the economy is growing, union workers will find it easier to get alternative work in the event that no agreement is reached. Thus, relative delay costs shift in favor of the union when the economy is expanding. Consequently, unions may be able to reach more favorable agreements during upswings in the business cycle.

The second important lesson from the Rubinstein is more subtle. It is not necessary for a delay to occur in order for delay costs to affect the negotiated settlement. In other words, it is not necessary for a strike or lockout to occur in order for the costs of strikes and lockouts to influence the outcome of bargaining. Rational firms and unions with full information are able to see through the implications of delay costs for the eventual agreement. If there is a relative difference in delay costs that favor one side, both sides will be fully aware that the final agreement will necessarily favor the side with the lower costs. According to the Rubinstein model, strikes and lockouts are not necessary to communicate differences in delay costs to the two sides.

For example, unionized retail workers and their employers are both well aware that a strike before Christmas could be extremely punishing to the firm. Unionized baseball players and their employers are well aware that a strike during the World Series is extremely costly to the team owners. In each case, these costs will be reflected in the terms of the negotiated settlement and not necessarily in the occurrence of strikes or lockouts. Of course, the 1994 baseball season ended with a lockout that caused the cancellation of the World Series. Strikes and lockouts are a costly side-effect of real-world collective bargaining. They are examined in a separate section below.

16.2.2 Union bargaining power

There are two ways to think of union bargaining power. In the Rubinstein game analyzed above, the firm and union were bargaining over $400,000. In this case, the union's most preferred outcome is to get all the $400,000. One way bargaining power can be defined is how close to the union's preferred outcome is the negotiated outcome. In the context of the example, therefore, the closer the negotiated outcome is to $400,000, the more powerful the union. We noted above that when the delay costs changed giving the union relatively lower costs, the negotiated outcome shifted to the union's favor. A change in delay costs, therefore, shifts bargaining power toward the side whose costs have decreased relatively.

In the Rubinstein game, the employment level at the firm is assumed to be fixed. The firm and union simply bargain over a pot of money. In principle, however, the firm and union can bargain over the wage rate and the level of employment. Alternatively, they may bargain over the wage rate and leave the firm to set the employment level once the wage has been set by negotiations.[5] In fact, this is how negotiations typically proceed: the firm and union bargain over the wage, then employment is set unilaterally by the firm.

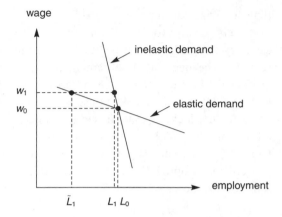

Figure 16.4 Bargaining power and the elasticity of labor demand

In this case, the wage rate is taken as given by the firm when the employment decision is made. Because the firm chooses the profit-maximizing employment level given the wage, it follows that the employment level is determined from the firm's labor demand curve. This corresponds to the situation we examined in Chapter 14, except that here the wage is set through negotiations between a single firm-union bargaining pair rather than in the labor market.

Of course, the firm's labor demand curve slopes downward. Higher wages, therefore, result in lower employment levels. Wage increases inevitably result in some of the union workers losing their jobs. As Figure 16.4 illustrates, however, the extent of layoffs depends on the elasticity of the firm's labor demand. If labor demand is relatively inelastic, a wage increase from w_0 to w_1 results in an employment reduction from L_0 to L_1. But if labor demand is elastic, the same size wage increase reduces employment from L_0 to $\tilde{L}_1$. This brings us to the second way of thinking about union bargaining power. The union facing an inelastic labor demand is, in a sense, in a much more powerful position than a union facing an elastic demand

curve. The union at a firm with an inelastic demand curve can pursue wage increases without the fear that many of its members will lose their jobs.

Thus, bargaining power can be measured in terms of how close the union can get to its preferred outcome or in terms of the elasticity of the demand curve. Unions can be powerful in one sense and not in the other. The union may be able to get a very large wage increase from the firm because, for example, the union has relatively low delay costs. But the union may not be willing to pursue a large wage increase because labor demand at the firm is very elastic. Gaining a large increase, although possible, would come only at the cost of losing many of the union members through layoffs. Alternatively, a union may be at firm with a very inelastic labor demand curve and yet only be able to raise wages a small amount.

Whatever the relative size of the union's bargaining power, there is no doubt about its origins. The union gets its bargaining power from its ability to strike. By withholding labor services from the firm, for an indefinite period, the union is able to impose delay costs on the firm. As we have seen, these delay costs are an important determinant of bargaining power.

Before turning to the topic of strikes, there is one very important observation that must be understood. There is a popular misconception that an increase in union bargaining power leads to more strikes. For example, it is said that more strikes occur during economic booms because unions have more bargaining power. This power follows because workers can easily get jobs elsewhere and firms are reluctant to lose business when the economy is booming. But the Rubinstein model clearly shows that this reasoning is false. A change in one side's bargaining

Beetle Delay Costs

The highly successful New Beetle model, launched by Volkswagen (VW) AG in 1998, is produced at only one factory in the world. The plant is located in Puebla, Mexico, which is about 60 miles (100 km) east of Mexico City. The plant also produces the classic Beetle, which is sold only in Mexico, and the Jetta and Golf Cabrio models, which are manufactured primarily for the American and Canadian markets. Almost 80 percent of the 425,073 vehicles produced at the Puebla plant in 2000 were exported.

A strike by 12,500 workers started on August 18, 2001 over the issue of pay. Initially, the two sides were far apart: VW's opening offer was a pay increase of 7 percent, while the union was asking for a pay rise of 30 percent. By the second week of the strike, the union reduced its demands to a wage increase of 19 percent, while VW held firm with its offer of a 7 percent increase.

The VW stated the cost of the strike in terms of the market value of forgone production was $30 million per day. The 12-day strike, therefore, cost $360 million in terms of lost production. To put this into perspective, VW AG's profit for 2000 was €824 million ($750 million). In other words, the cost of the strike to VW represented almost half its profits for the previous year.

But do lost sales represent the delay costs to VW? There are a couple of reasons why lost sales exaggerate the cost of the strike. First, VW does not have to pay any wages during the strike, which saves money. Second, the strike occurred when the economies of Mexico, the United States, and Canada were entering a recession, meaning that production would have been scaled back in any case. Third, production lost during any strike can be made up either from inventory accumulated prior to the strike or from increased production through overtime after the strike. In fact, it is possible that the delay costs to VW were actually quite small, a fact that the union may have misjudged thereby leading to the strike in the first place.

Source: "Striking VW Mexico workers vote on new offer," Reuters, August 28, 2001.

power will be recognized by both sides, implying that the bargaining outcome, and *not* strike activity, is affected. Since the firm knows that the union has more bargaining power in a boom, it has an incentive to increase its wage offers in order to avoid a strike. Differential bargaining power explains how wages are determined, not what causes strikes.

16.3 Strikes and lockouts

A strike occurs when the union workers refuse to work. A lockout occurs when the firm prevents the workers from working. There are basically three types of strike. The *first-contract* strike occurs when the union is fighting to be recognized by the firm. The *contract-renewal* strike occurs during negotiations. The *wildcat* strike occurs during an existing contract. Wildcat strikes are illegal in many jurisdictions, like the United States, but not in others, such as France. We will focus on contract-renewal strikes, which account for the majority of strikes by number and almost all strikes by working-days lost. Before we go on, one thing is worth mentioning: despite the large amount of media coverage that strikes generate, they are actually quite rare. In 1995, the fraction of working time lost to strikes in most developed countries was less than one-tenth of one percent.

Economists have a hard time explaining why strikes occur. The Rubinstein model shows why this is. Let's go back to our original example with the firm and union bargaining over $400,000, illustrated in Figure 16.5. If an agreement is not reached in the first round of negotiations, both sides incur delay costs of $200,000 and the bargaining frontier moves toward the origin, as before. The delay costs, of course, result from a strike (or lockout).

Because the bargaining frontier shifts inwards, *any* agreement reached in the second round is inferior to a first round agreement. For example, if point A is achieved in the second round, any point inside the dashed box on the first-round bargaining frontier is superior because it leaves both sides with more money. Indeed, this was a main point of the Rubinstein model: agreement occurs in the first round because both parties can see that if they don't agree right away they stand to lose money. In other words, when the parties have infor-

mation about the costs of a strike, no strike will occur. Put simply, strikes are irrational.

Nobel prize-winning economist John Hicks put the problem of strikes another way. If a theory existed that successfully explained the outcome of a strike, then the firm and union could presumably agree to the outcome without the bother of a strike. But then strikes would never occur. A theory which "explained" strikes, therefore, would have the effect of explaining away the occurrence of strikes altogether. The observation that a decent theory of strikes implies that strikes would never occur is referred to as the "Hicks paradox" and explains why a satisfactory theory of strikes is so elusive.

This is all very well, but obviously strikes do occur. Clearly, in real-world collective bargaining, agreement does not necessarily occur without delay. This seems to fly in the face of the Rubinstein model. However, recall two assumptions of the Rubinstein model: perfect information and rational behavior.

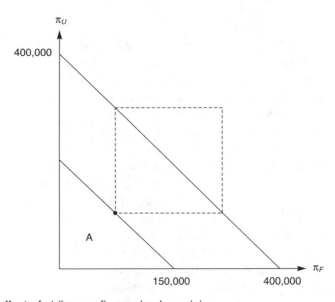

Figure 16.5 The effect of strikes on firm–union bargaining

In real-life bargaining situations, there is very probably some private information on at least one side of the bargaining table. This means that the delay costs of one side may not be perfectly known by the other side. In this case, a misinterpretation by one side of the other's delay cost may lead to a misunderstanding between the two over the relative delay costs. As a result, each side may have a different expectation about the outcome of the bargaining. Differing expectations severely complicate bargaining and may lead to a break-down in negotiations. In such cases, strikes or lockouts may be necessary to communicate private delay costs to the other side.

Another possibility is that the agents, and in particular the union, may be motivated by forces other than rational economic behavior. Union leaders carrying out negotiations are typically elected by union members. Because the leaders are elected, political considerations, like a desire to hold onto office, may come into play during negotiations with the firm. For example, suppose union workers are convinced they should be able to get a large wage increase from a firm. Even if the union leaders know the workers' expectations are unrealistic, they may wish to appear tough rather than accept a low wage offer from the firm. Thus, a desire to be re-elected as union leaders may lead them to behave in an apparently "irrational" manner.

16.4 Effects of unions

The discussion so far has focused on theoretical aspects of union behavior. In this last section, we look at the effects of unions that economists have been able to document. The primary concern in this area has been measuring the effect of unions on wages. But, like many other things in economics, focusing on just one effect of unions ignores potentially offsetting effects. For example, if unions raise wages, firms may respond by selecting employees more carefully. By choosing more productive workers, the firm may be able to offset increased wages from unionization.

16.4.1 Wages

The effect of unions on wages is usually captured by the *union–nonunion wage differential*. If $w_U =$ is the union wage, and $w_N =$ the nonunion wage, the union–nonunion wage differential is given:

$$\delta = \frac{w_U - w_N}{w_N}$$

Therefore, δ is just the proportionate difference between union and nonunion wages. It is very important that the wage measures w_U and w_N are taken from workers that are identical in every respect other than their union membership status. Not using comparable workers results in a wage differential that captures other factors that may not be anything to do with unions.

A commonly held view is that unions raise nonunion wages. This happens, so the argument goes, because nonunion firms are forced to compete with union firms for the same workers. Moreover, it is claimed that all firms try to maintain traditional wage differentials between occupations. Thus, if the wages of production-line workers are raised by a union, the firm will have to raise the wages of nonunion management workers to maintain the traditional wage differential between the two groups. The problem with these arguments is that they ignore market forces. If unions raise wages, firms will layoff workers. The laid-off union workers are then forced to look for work in nonunion firms, thereby driving down the nonunion wage.

In other words, there is no need for the non-union firms to compete with union firms for workers. The workers laid off from unionized firms represent an increase in supply to the nonunion firms.

One factor that may reduce the impact of market forces on nonunion wages is the possibility that nonunion firms raise wages in order to discourage their workers from joining a union. This is known as the *threat effect* of unionization. The threat effect will be higher the larger is the union–nonunion wage differential. The size of the threat effect also depends how averse firms are to unions, how aggressive unions are at organizing nonunion workers, and the cost to unions of organizing workers in nonunion firms. For example, if the firm is extremely averse to unionization, it may pay its workers the same or even more than comparable union workers. In North America, for example, Toyota pays its nonunion work force roughly the same as unionized employees with similar qualifications at Ford and General Motors. Another factor that may mitigate market forces is *queue unemployment*. Because wages are higher in union firms, laid-off workers may prefer to wait for a job to become available at a unionized firm rather than seek employment in nonunion firms. In this case, the increase in the supply of ex-union workers to nonunion firms will be reduced and the resulting fall in the nonunion wage will be smaller.

The fact that identical workers must be used for the wage comparison makes it very difficult to get an accurate measure of δ. Simply put, other factors besides unions can affect wages. Just because there exists a wage differential between a union and a nonunion employee doesn't mean that the wage difference is due to the presence of a union. For example, union firms may hire better quality workers or they may make unionized employees work harder. Some determinants of labor quality can be quantified and controlled for in an empirical study, like education, experience, and training. But other factors that determine labor quality, like motivation, work effort, and morale are not easy to control for. Even if the economist can get groups of union and nonunion workers that are comparable it terms of education, experience, and training, it still is possible that an observed differential arises because the union workers are more highly motivated or have better morale on the job.

Another problem measuring δ arises because it is difficult to separate the cause of unions from the effect of unions. The conventional view is that unions cause higher wages. But it is possible that high wages result in unionization. Unions may find it easier to organize workers in high-paying jobs and these workers may be more willing to join unions. If this is the case, then a union-nonunion wage differential would have existed even if the union weren't present. In other words, the presence of a union merely signals that wages are high, but it doesn't mean that the union is the cause of the high wages.

Empirical measures of δ vary in the range 10–25 percent. Crude measures that simply compare union to nonunion workers, but that take no account of differences in worker quality or training levels estimate δ to be around 10 percent.[6] More accurate studies based on cross-sections of workers with similar qualifications and characteristics estimate the differential to be around 25 percent.[7] A problem with cross-sectional differences, however, is the inability to control for factors that can't be measured, like motivation and morale. A clever way around this problem is to follow the same individual over time as the worker moves between union and nonunion jobs. Assuming that the unobservable characteristics of the worker, such as their desire to work hard, and their innate ability, remain constant over time, comparing the worker's union and nonunion wages should provide a more accurate measure of the actual size of δ. Interestingly, these studies estimate δ to be in the range of 10 percent.[8] This would suggest that an inability to control for unobserved differences between union and nonunion workers does lead to inaccurate estimates of the wage differential.

16.4.2 Non-wage variables

Many workers receive monetary benefits from employment that are not reflected in their hourly wage or salary. Pensions, dental plans, vacations, and any other forms of compensation the worker receives over and above regular pay are referred to as *fringe benefits*. Ignoring the size of fringe benefits understates the cost of labor to the firm. This is potentially significant because there is evidence that unions have an even greater effect on benefits than on wages. Thus, if estimates of the effect of unions were to take into account fringe benefits, they would probably be larger than estimates of the union-nonunion wage differential.

Another effect of unions is measured in terms of resource allocation and economic welfare. If unions are able to raise wages above competitive market levels, in essence they have the same effect that a monopoly firm in the output market has. As such, the impact of unions on economic welfare can be judged according to the same set of criteria that we used to evaluate monopolies in Chapter 11 on regulated industries. As a simple example, consider what happens if a union successfully increases the wage in a particular industry above the competitive

market level. The result is that workers in the industry are laid off and employment drops below the competitive level. At this lower level of employment, the marginal benefit to society from hiring an additional worker is greater than the marginal cost of the worker. Because the extra worker isn't hired, there is an unrealized gain to society, or a *deadweight loss*. Obviously, the higher the union is able to raise the wage, the larger the deadweight loss. The loss can be interpreted in exactly the same way as that of a monopoly in the output market raising price above the competitive level. Although present in theory, the deadweight loss is estimated to be quite small in reality. Estimates typically amount to less than 0.2 percent of GNP per year for the United States.

Suppose we accept that unions result in higher wages for their members than otherwise comparable nonunion workers. In principle, it is possible that the union workers are more productive than their nonunion counterparts. Indeed, union workers may be sufficiently more productive to completely offset the higher wage they receive. The effect of unions on productivity is an old debate in economics. A commonly held view is that unions decrease productivity essentially by imposing restrictive rules on the firm. For example, promotion in unionized firms may be determined by seniority rather than by ability. Or unions may bargain for, and receive, rules that make the firm hire more workers than it would choose itself.

An alternative view is proposed by American economists Richard Freeman and James Medoff.[9] Their argument is based on the *exit-voice hypothesis*. In a nonunion work place, the argument goes, a dissatisfied worker has very little option but to leave, or exit, the firm. The complaints of one worker are unlikely to get the attention of management and may even get the worker fired for being trouble-maker. The presence of a union, and the griev-ance procedures that go along with it, gives the dissatisfied worker the ability to voice their concerns with the feeling that something might be done and the security that they can't be punished for saying it. As a result, union firms should have lower rates of turn-over, because dissatisfied workers won't be forced to leave. Even after controlling for the fact that wages are higher in unionized firms, which alone would make union workers less likely to quit, there is evidence that turnover rates are lower in unionized firms. Turnover is costly to firms because workers have to be screened, hired, and trained. A reduction in turnover, therefore, saves costs at the firm and increases productivity.

At the end of the day, regardless of the effects of unions on wages, fringe benefits, turnover, or productivity, what really mat-ters to the owners of the firm is the impact of unions on profits. The fact that most firms resist attempts by unions to organize their workers suggest that the owners anticipate that the presence of a union will decrease profits. Evidence from the United States indi-cates that unionized firms, on average, achieve a 19 per cent lower rate of return on their capital than similar nonunion firms.[10] Thus, even if the presence of a union raises the productivity of the workers, it seems unli-kely that the increase in productivity would be sufficient to offset the higher costs that go along with unionization. Evidence from Canada, however, is less clear cut. In firms where union representation is granted by the Labor Relations Board without a certifica-tion vote, profitability actually increases. This is consistent with the exit-voice hypoth-

---

Does Unionization Affect a Firm's Profits?

Any "event" that reduces a firm's profit will eventually be reflected by a fall in the firm's share price. A procedure in financial economics known as *event study methodology* tracks share prices for several months before and after the occurrence of the event in order to compute the effect of the event on the firm's profitability. In order to study the impact of unions on profits, the "event" to be considered is the unionization of a firm that previously had nonunion employees. By analyzing share prices before and after a union organizes a firm, event study methodology can be used to determine the impact of unionization on a firm's level of profit.

A recent paper uses event study methodology to determine the effect of unions on the profit-ability of 66 Ontario firms listed on the Toronto Stock Exchange. The event studied is union *certification*. In order to legally represent employees at a particular firm, a union must apply to the Ontario Labor Relations Board.

Surprisingly, the study finds there is no appreciable drop in share prices for firms where unions are certified. Although there is a drop in share prices in the month the union organization attempt is announced, the value is recouped in the following months. For firms where the union's application is rejected, there is no significant impact on the share price. The results are different from the United States, where studies consistently find profits fall when unionization takes place.

Source: Felice Martinello, Robert Hanrahan, Joseph Kushner, and Isidore Masse. "Union certification in Ontario: its effect on the value of the firm." *Canadian Journal of Economics*, 28 (November 1995), pp. 1077–95.

esis that unionization brings beneficial effects to the firm. But in firms where workers vote on union representation, the profits of the firms are estimated to fall.

Summary

- There are basically three kinds of industrial relations system in developed economies: English-speaking countries, the rest of Europe, and Japan.
- A simple supply and demand model of the market for union services can be used to explain why union density has dropped in so many countries between 1985 and 1995.
- The Rubinstein model shows that a rational firm and union bargaining under conditions of perfect information about the delay costs of each side will reach a contract agreement without delay.
- Relative changes in delay costs will shift the terms of the agreement in favor of the side with a relative decrease in delay costs. It is not necessary for delay (a strike or lockout) to occur in order for delay (strike or lockout) costs to influence the outcome.
- Union bargaining power can be measured in terms of proximity to the union's preferred outcome or in terms of the elasticity of labor demand. Changes in union bargaining power will be reflected in the terms of the agreement and not in more strikes.
- In actual contract negotiations, political concerns of union leaders or insufficient information on the delay costs of opposing parties can lead to disagreement in the form of strikes and lockouts.
- Unions are estimated to raise the wages of otherwise comparable workers by 10–25 percent.
- The exit-voice hypothesis argues that unions may increase productivity by reducing turnover at firms.

Notes

1 Source: *World Employment Report 1996–97*, Geneva: International Labor Office, 1997. Mexico's union density is from 1991 and its change in density is for 1981–91.
2 Table 16.1 shows that union density has declined 25 percent in Hungary and 43 percent in Poland.
3 This is not true of contracts that are determined by arbitration, where a third party imposes a settlement. However, arbitrated settlements are relatively rare.
4 The bargaining model is discussed more thoroughly in Rubinstein (1982).
5 Agreements resulting from bargaining over wages and employment are referred to as "effi-cient contracts"; agreements resulting from negotiations over the wage alone are referred to as "right-to-manage contracts."
6 For example, see Pradeep Kumar and Thanasis Stengos. "Measuring the union relative wage impact: a methodological note." *Canadian Journal of Economics*, 18 (February 1985), pp. 182–9.
7 See Chris Robinson and Nigel Tomes. "Union wage differentials in the public and private sectors: a simultaneous equations specification." *Journal of Labor Economics*, 2 (January 1984), pp. 106–27.
8 See David A. Green. "A comparison of estimation approaches for the union–Nonunion Wage Differential." University of British Columbia Department of Economics Discussion Paper 91–13, May 1991.

9 See the reference at the end of the chapter for the book upon which this discussion is based.

10 See Kim B. Clark. "Unionization and firm performance: the impact on profits, growth, and productivity." *American Economic Review*, 74 (December 1984), pp. 893–919.

Exercises

1 Suppose the bargaining frontier is given by the following equation:

$$U = 20 - \pi$$

where U is the union's utility and π is the firm's profit. Let the delay cost to the union be 10, i.e. $C_U = 10$ and the delay cost to the firm also be 10, i.e. $C_F = 10$.

(a) Sketch the bargaining frontier on a diagram with U on the vertical and π on the horizontal axis. Indicate the horizontal and vertical intercepts of the frontier.

(b) On the same diagram, sketch the bargaining frontier after a one-period delay. Again, indicate the horizontal and vertical intercepts on the diagram.

(c) If the *union* makes the first offer, what is the Rubinstein solution to the bargaining problem?

(d) If the *firm* makes the first offer, what is the Rubinstein solution to the bargaining problem?

(e) Is there a first-offer advantage in this game?

2 Suppose the bargaining frontier in a firm-union contract negotiation is given by:

$$U = 200 - \pi$$

where U is the union's utility and π is the firm's profit. Let the delay cost to the union be 100, i.e. $C_U = 100$ and the delay cost to the firm also be 100, i.e. $C_F = 100$.

(a) Sketch the bargaining game, showing the bargaining frontier, the effects of delay, and the disagreement point.

(b) Assuming the firm makes the first offer, compute the Rubinstein solution to this bargaining problem.

(c) Now suppose that delay costs fall to 50 for the union and the firm, i.e. $C_U = C_F = 50$. Sketch the bargaining diagram and compute the Rubinstein solution to the game.

(d) Compare the solutions from the two sets of bargaining costs. What feature of the Rubinstein model have you illustrated? Explain.

3 Suppose the bargaining frontier in firm-union contract negotiations is given by:

$$U = 400 - \pi$$

where U is the union's utility and π is the firm's profit. Let the delay cost to the union be 200, i.e. $C_U = 200$ and the delay cost to the firm also be 200, i.e. $C_F = 200$.

(a) Sketch the bargaining game, showing the bargaining frontier, the effects of delay, and the disagreement point.

(b) Assuming the union makes the first offer, compute the Rubinstein solution to this bargaining problem.

(c) Now suppose that the delay costs fall to 100 for the firm only, i.e. $C_F = 100$, while the delay costs for the union remain unchanged at 200. Sketch the bargaining diagram and compute the Rubinstein solution to the game.

(d) Compare the solutions from the two sets of bargaining costs. What feature of the Rubinstein model have you illustrated? Explain.

4 Suppose a union has so much bargaining power over a firm that the union can set any wage it wants. In addition, suppose the union membership has collectively decided that their objective should be to maximize the total wages received by employed union members from the firm. In other words, suppose that the union decides to maximize the firm's wage bill. Assume that the firm's (inverse) labor demand curve is given by:

$$w = 20 - 0.01L$$

where w is the wage received by each employed union member, and L is the total number of union members employed by the firm.

(a) Write down an algebraic expression for the firm's total wage bill.

(b) Using this expression for the wage bill, write down the union's maximization problem assuming the union maximizes the firm's wage bill.

(c) Compute the first-order condition from the union's maximization problem. Use the demand curve and the first-order condition to solve for the wage and level of employment at the firm.

(d) Compute the firm's total wage bill.

5 Suppose a union has so much bargaining power over a firm that the union can set any wage it wants. In addition, suppose the union membership has collectively decided that their objective should be to maximize the wage differential times the number of employed union members at the firm. (The wage differential is the difference between the union wage and the wage available to union members that quit the firm.) Assume that the wage union members can get if they quit the firm is $10 and that the firm's (inverse) labor demand curve is given by:

$$w = 20 - 0.01L$$

where w is the wage received by each employed union member, and L is the total number of union members employed by the firm.

(a) Write down an algebraic expression for the wage differential times the number of employed union members.

(b) Using this expression, write down the union's maximization problem assuming the union maximizes the wage differential times the number of employed union members.

(c) Compute the first-order condition from the union's maximization problem. Use the demand curve and the first-order condition to solve for the wage and level of employment at the firm.

(d) Compute the firm's total wage bill.

References

Richard B. Freeman and James L. Medoff. *What Do Unions Do?* (New York: Basic Books, 1984).

Ariel Rubinstein. "Perfect equilibrium in a bargaining model." *Econometrica*, 50 (January 1982), pp. 97–110.

World Employment Report 1996–97 (Geneva: International Labor Office, 1997).

Answers to odd-numbered problems

•••

Chapter 1

1 (a) The first equation is demand. (b) $P = 1.6$, $Q = 68$. (c) $\eta = 0.47$ (inelastic), $\eta_S = 1.88$ (elastic). (d) $P = 1.8$, $Q = 64$. (e) 80%, 20%.

3 (a) $P = 50$, $Q = 1{,}000$. (b) 240. (c) 52, $11,520.

Chapter 2

1 The license fee $\hat{p}$ is a *fixed cost* to the firm. As we'll see in Chapter 3, the presence of fixed costs gives rise to the existence of increasing returns to scale. All other things being equal, we saw that the existence of increasing returns to scale suggests that firms would grow very large. If the license fee $\hat{p}$ were very large, this would make it very difficult for any new ISPs to compete against any large established ISPs, so if $\hat{p}$ was very large, we'd expect there to be very few ISPs in the market. If the government reduced $\hat{p}$, then this fixed cost of doing business for ISPs would fall, making it easier for new smaller firms to compete in this industry, reducing the degree of returns to scale, and increasing the number of ISPs we'd expect to see in the market.

3 Many companies produce more than one product, so it is important to begin by identifying a particular good associated with each producer:

Microsoft Corporation

- *Product*: Microsoft Internet Explorer Web Browser
- *Industry competitors*: Netscape Navigator
- *Buyers*: personal computer wholesalers and retailers, individual PC consumers
- *Suppliers*: markets for major inputs in this industry tend to be very competitive
- *Substitutes*: other media to download (digital) information, cellular (mobile) telephones
- *Potential entrants*: high fixed costs of entry imply that this is likely not the most important element of this market environment
- *Government*: the recent anti-trust case in the United States makes the relationship between Microsoft and the government very important

How might your answer change if you considered a different Microsoft product, like the word processor *MSWord* or the Operating System *Windows 2000*?

Seagate Technology

- *Product*: hard disk drives
- *Industry competitors*: Maxtor, Western Digital, IBM
- *Buyers*: personal computer manufacturers, wholesalers and retailers
- *Suppliers*: markets for major inputs in this industry tend to be very competitive
- *Substitutes*: portable media storage devices, CD-ROMs
- *Potential entrants*: high fixed costs of entry imply that this is likely not the most important element of this market environment
- *Government*: government regulation is likely not the most important element of this market environment

Qantas Airlines

- *Product*: domestic air travel within Australia
- *Industry competitors*: Ansett, Virgin Blue
- *Buyers*: tourists, business travelers, travel companies and tour groups
- *Suppliers*: many important inputs into production of airline services, such as pilots and flight attendants, are unionized, so the relationship between Qantas and the unions which represent its workers is very important
- *Substitutes*: rail or road travel
- *Potential entrants*: recent entry and exit in the market for domestic air travel in Australia has been very important, leading to intense price competition
- *Government*: since the airline industry is regulated by the government, Qantas must be aware of any potential changes to government regulation of the airline industry

What parts of your answer would change if you looked at Qantas international flights instead of domestic flights?

Italian Restaurants

- *Product*: sit-down meals
- *Industry competitors*: other Italian restaurants and other restaurants in the neighborhood
- *Buyers*: consumers going out for dinner
- *Suppliers*: markets for major inputs in this industry tend to be very competitive
- *Substitutes*: eating at home, take-away meals
- *Potential entrants*: turnover in the restaurant industry can be very high, so entry and exit is potentially important
- *Government*: government regulation is likely not the most important element of this market environment

Chapter 3

1 Homogeneous products, many firms (sellers): personal computers, commodities, shares in a company. Homogeneous products, few firms: aluminum smelting, nickel smelting. Differentiated products, many firms: doctors, dentists, lawyers. Differentiated products, few firms: electronics products, airlines, beer.

3 (a) Short run (fixed cost of 5). (b) $c_F = 5$, $c_V = q$. (c) $AFC = 5/q$, $AVC = 1$, $AC = 1 + 5/q$. (d) $MC = 1$.

5 (a) $r(q) = 10q - 2q^2$. (b) $q^* = 9/4$. (c) $p^* = 22/4$. (d) $c = 29/4$, $r = 99/8$, $\pi = 41/8$.

7 (a) $q^M = 1$. (b) $p^M = 19$, $\pi = -90$. (c) No, because the firm is making an economic loss. (d) Not unless they have access to a technology that can produce at a lower cost, or unless they are able to price discriminate. In either case, the question arises as to why the existing firm could not have done the same thing.

Chapter 4

1 (a) $Q = 1,000 - 200p$. (b) $p = 2$. (c) Consumer surplus (fixed fee per consumer) is 9. (d) $r = 2$, 100, $c = 1,200$, $\pi = 900$. (e) No. All the available consumer surplus has been extracted by the firm from every consumer, so an attempt to extract any more will result in lower profit.

3 (a) No resale between markets. (b) $Q_1 = 25$, $Q_2 = 15$, so total output is 40. (c) $P_1 = 30$, $P_2 = 20$. (d) $r = 1,050$, $c = 200$, $\pi = 850$.

5 (a) $Q_1 = 8$, $Q_2 = 7$, so total output is 15. (b) $P_1 = 60$, $P_2 = 110$, $\pi = 875$. (c) $Q = 15$, $P = 70$, so $Q_1 = 4$, $Q_2 = 11$. (d) $\pi = 675$.

Chapter 5

1 (a) *Players*: OPEC members are Algeria, Indonesia, Iran, Iraq, Kuwait, Libya, Nigeria, Qatar, Saudi Arabia, United Arab Emirates, Venezuela
Strategies: level of crude oil production
Payoffs: profits from crude oil sales

Rules of the game: OPEC decides on oil production quotas for each member, and members produce no more than their assigned quota

(b) This is likely best modeled as a cooperative game, since OPEC members meet to assign production quotas for each member. However, there have been periods where member countries *cheated* by producing oil to a level greater than their production quota. In a non-cooperative setting, each individual OPEC member can increase its payoff by producing beyond its quota. How can OPEC keep members from *cheating*?

3

Supervisor \ Laborer	Work	Shirk
Monitor	v-h-w, w-g	-h, 0
Not monitor	v-w, w-g	-w, w

(a) *Supervisor*. If laborer works, best response is not to monitor. If laborer shirks, best response is to monitor as long as $h < w$. Supervisor has no dominant strategy.
Laborer. If supervisor monitors, best response is to work as long as $w - g > 0$. If supervisor does not monitor, best response is to shirk. Laborer has no dominant strategy.

(b) There is no Nash equilibrium in pure strategies. Neither player has a best-response strategy, as in the matching pennies game described in Section 5.4.2.

5 (a) The following figure shows the Nash equilibrium N when actions are strategic complements:

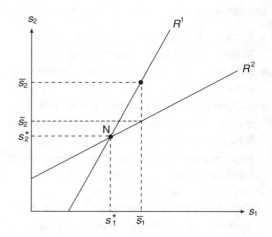

If firm 2 chooses strategy $\bar{s}_2$, firm 1's best-response is $\bar{s}_1$.

(b) $\bar{s}_2$ is not firm 2's best response to $\bar{s}_1$ because firm 2 is not on its reaction function at $(\bar{s}_1, \bar{s}_2)$. Firm 2 would rather decrease $\bar{s}_2$ to $\tilde{s}_2$.

Chapter 6

1 (a) Profit functions:

$$\pi^1 = q_1[750 - 15q_1 - 15q_2] - cq_1$$
$$\pi^2 = q_2[750 - 15q_1 - 15q_2] - cq_2$$

First-order conditions:

$$\pi_1^1 = 750 - 30q_1 - 15q_2 - c = 0$$
$$\pi_2^2 = 750 - 15q_1 - 30q_2 - c = 0$$

(b) Reaction functions:

$$R^1 = 25 - \frac{c}{30} - \frac{q_2}{2}$$
$$R^2 = 25 - \frac{c}{30} - \frac{q_1}{2}$$

(c) Cournot equilibrium:

$$q_1^c = q_2^c = \frac{50}{3} - \frac{2c}{90}$$

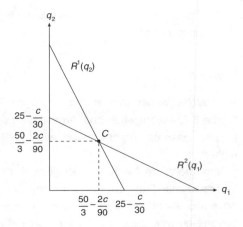

(d) Equilibrium price and firm profits:

$$p^* = 250 + 2c/3$$

$$\pi^1 = \pi^2 = 2500 - \frac{100c}{9} + \frac{c^2}{135}$$

3 Price competition would result in an equilibrium where price equals marginal cost, so each firm would charge $p_1^b = p_2^b = c$. Each firm would produce and sell output $q_1^b = q_2^b = 25 - c/30$. Each firm earns zero profits in equilibrium. Compared to the Cournot and Stackelberg equilibria, market price and firm profits are lower, and equilibrium market output is higher in the Bertrand equilibrium when firms compete in prices.

5 The following figure shows the Cournot equilibrium C when firm 2's reaction function is steeper than firm 1's reaction function:

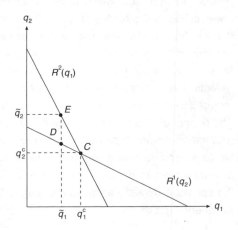

The Cournot equilibrium remains at point C where the reaction functions intersect. However, if either firm chooses a strategy different from the Cournot equilibrium, the model becomes unstable. For example, if firm 1 chooses $\tilde{q}_1 < q_1^c$ at point D firm 2's best response is to choose $\tilde{q}_2$ at point E which moves the market away from the Cournot equilibrium.

Chapter 7

1 Suppose we arrange different types of beer according to how heavy they taste. Light beer would be at the extreme left end of the horizontal line representing product differentiation, and very heavy-tasting beer like stout would be at the extreme right end:

Lager beers might be near the middle of this line, while ales, which are heavier-tasting than lagers, would be somewhat farther to the right end of this product line. Ice beer is meant to be lighter-tasting with no after-taste, so it may be located between lager and light beers.

Even if consumers are uniformly distributed along this interval representing product differentiation, positioning ice beer between light and lager beer is meant to attract a share of the beer market, either light beer drinkers who might prefer a somewhat stronger beer, or lager drinkers who might prefer a lighter-tasting beer. Beer producers who sell nationally, like Anheuser-Busch and Miller in the United States or Labatt and Molson in Canada, would not want to have a competitor introduce a new product and capture market share, so firms would introduce a new product like ice beer at the same time.

3 (a) From the previous question, each firm's reaction function is given by:

$$p_1 = R^1(p_2) = \frac{15 + 2c_1 + p_2}{4}$$

$$p_2 = R^2(p_1) = \frac{30 + 2c_2 + p_1}{4}$$

If firm 1's costs c_1 rise due to a strike, then the intercept in firm 1's reaction function increases, so firm 1's reaction function shifts to the right.

(b) From the previous question, each firm's equilibrium price is given by:

$$p_1^b = 6 + \frac{8c_1}{15} + \frac{2c_2}{15}$$

$$p_2^b = 9 + \frac{2c_1}{15} + \frac{8c_2}{15}$$

If c_1 rises, firm 1's price rises by $\partial p_1^b / \partial c_1 = 8/15$ and firm 2's price rises by $\partial p_2^b / \partial c_1 = 2/15$.

(c) From the previous question, each firm's equilibrium quantity is given by:

$$q_1^b = 24 - \frac{28c_1}{15} + \frac{8c_2}{15} = 4$$

$$q_2^b = 36 + \frac{8c_1}{15} - \frac{28c_2}{15} = 16,$$

so firm 1's market share was 20 percent and firm 2's market share was 80 percent. As c_1 rises, firm 1's output falls by $\partial q_1^b / \partial c_1 = 28/15$ and firm 2's quantity rises by $\partial q_2^b / \partial c_1 = 8/15$, so firm 1's market share must fall, and firm 2's market share must rise. From the previous question, each firm's equilibrium profits are given by:

$$\pi_1^b = \left[6 - \frac{7c_1}{15} + \frac{2c_2}{15} \right] \left[24 - \frac{28c_1}{15} + \frac{8c_2}{15} \right]$$

$$\pi_2^b = \left[9 + \frac{2c_1}{15} - \frac{7c_2}{15} \right] \left[36 + \frac{8c_1}{15} - \frac{28c_2}{15} \right],$$

so as c_1 rises, firm 1's profits fall and firm 2's profits rise.

Chapter 8

1 All payoffs would remain the same as in Figure 8.2, except when both firms advertise, in which case each firm's payoff would be $2 higher:

Now there are Nash two equilibria in this game: neither firm advertises, or both firms advertise. All other things being equal, more advertising now causes a bigger increase in revenue, relative to the example in Figure 8.2. This means demand is more elastic with respect to advertising, or that advertising has become more effective.

Apple grower \ Orange grower	Not advertise	Advertise
Not advertise	**10, 10**	12, 9
Advertise	9, 12	**13, 13**

3 The studies cited in the case on Optometric Services in the United States support the conclusion that advertising leads to increased competition, so that firms which advertise charge lower prices and offer lower quality services. If advertising makes the market for dentist's services more competitive, this should lead to a lower price for dentist's services, a reduction in quality of dentist's services and reduced profitability in the dentist industry. The degree of effectiveness of advertising, and whether advertising is predatory or cooperative, would depend upon whether and to what extent advertising would cause more people to visit the dentist. A dentist's services are likely to be experience goods.

Chapter 9

1 (a) An LSAT score gives the Law School the ability to deduce information about whether an applicant is more or less qualified to study Law. If we simplify and suppose that applicants are either high-aptitude or low-aptitude Law students, applicants know whether they are high- or low-aptitude types, but the Law School does not. LSAT scores can correct this adverse selection problem between applicants and Law Schools.

(b) A high-aptitude type applicant may score well on an LSAT exam without having taken a preparation class. A low-aptitude applicant may score much higher after having taken a preparation class, so the Law School may not be able to distinguish between a high-aptitude type applicant who did not take the preparation class, and a low-aptitude type applicant who took the preparation class.

(c) A Law School can use other information, such as performance in other university courses, or letters of reference written by university faculty to support an applicant.

(d) A Law School which used LSAT scores would be better able to distinguish between high-aptitude and low-aptitude students, and should therefore have a higher share of high-aptitude students, making it a higher quality School.

3 (a) A moral hazard problem exists between wine producers, who know and can control the level of quality of wine, and the wine consumer who does not know the level of quality.

(b) As more consumers become aware of wine quality, the fraction of informed consumers ψ increases, creating a stronger incentive for the producer to provide higher quality.

(c) More wine magazines and wine appreciation courses would result in some consumers having more information about wine quality, increasing ψ and reducing the informational asymmetry between the wine producer and some consumers.

(d) The higher the cost of wine magazines or wine appreciation courses, the higher the cost to consumers for information about wine, the smaller will be the increase in the share of informed consumers ψ.

(e) Such a newsletter can have two effects: it would increase the number of informed consumers, causing the market to become more competitive. But it may also increase the overall size of the market, if more consumers buy more wine as they become better informed.

Chapter 10

1 (a) When $c = 60$, $\pi^{1d} - \pi^{1a} = -4F + 120\sqrt{F} - 450$.

(b) Note that the solution to $\pi^{1d} - \pi^{1a}$ is a quadratic in $\sqrt{F}$, which can be solved for $\sqrt{F} \approx (25.6, 4.4)$, or $F \approx (655.36, 19.36)$. When $F = 655.36$, profits are negative under both entry deterrence and accommodation, so $\pi^{1d} = \pi^{1a}$ when $F \approx 19.36$. As long as $F > 19.36$, $\pi^{1d} > \pi^{1a}$.

(c) As the fixed cost F gets larger, the incumbent is more likely to deter entry.

3 (a) This is an example of *bundling*, a *top dog* strategy which should increase competition.

(b) The clothing store is *underinvesting* by stocking only a particular type of clothing. This is a *puppy dog* strategy, appropriate when firms are competing in prices.

(c) The optometrist is adopting a *top dog* strategy of overinvesting in capacity.

Chapter 11

1 (a) $Q^M = 1{,}000$, $P = 40$. (b) $Q^* = 1{,}333.33$, $P^* = 36.67$.

3 (a) 100. (b) $MC_S = 14 + 0.1\,Q$. 60. (c) 50. (d) No, it reduces newsprint output too much. Set tax at $4 (equal to marginal external social cost).

Chapter 12

1 (a) Home has an absolute advantage in production of roses since its unit labor requirement for rose production is lower ($4 < 12$). Foreign has an absolute advantage in production of guns ($6 < 8$).

(b) Home has a comparative advantage in production of roses, since 4/8 < 12/6. Foreign has a comparative advantage in production of guns.

(c) Both countries gain from trade at $e = 1$. Countries trade according to their pattern of comparative advantage, so Home exports roses to Foreign and imports guns from Foreign.

(d) As e rises from 1.0 to 1.5, the relative price of guns rises. Home imports guns, so this is a deterioration in Home's terms-of-trade, leaving Home worse off.

3 (a) Import quotas restrict the quantity of imports. This would lessen the degree of competition in primary agricultural markets.

(b) If the tariff is t and the domestic price (world price) is $p\,(p^*)$, then $p = (1 + t)p^*$. So if the Canadian tariff on chickens is 280 percent and the world price is $p^* = \$1$, $p = (1 + 2.80) \times 1 = \$3.80$.

(c) Very high tariffs imply that domestic prices remain very high. This limits price competition, making a market less competitive. A reduction in tariffs would reduce the domestic price, increasing price competition and increasing the market share of imports. This can be illustrated using Figure 12.1, where a reduction in the tariff from t to 0 causes the domestic price to fall from \$55 to \$50, and imports to rise to $q_c - q_p$.

5 (a) The following figure shows the effects of an export subsidy s charged when the world price is p^*.

(b) The volume of exports increases from $q_p - q_c$ to $q_p^s - q_c^s$. The increase in domestic production and decrease in domestic consumption results in an excess world supply of agricultural commodities at p^*, causing the world price p_{agr} to fall below p^*, so the terms-of-trade effect would be negative.

(c) For an agricultural importer, the decrease in p_{agr} represents an improvement in the terms of trade. Also, as the world price falls, the volume of imports would rise, so the terms-of-trade and volume-of-trade effects would both be positive.

(d) The terms-of-trade effect for agricultural exporters would be negative, leaving such countries worse off.

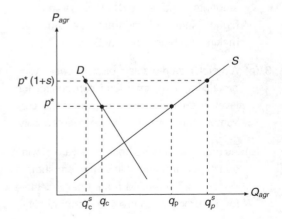

Chapter 13

1 (a) $MC_1 = MC_2 = MR$. (b) $q_1 = 69$, $q_2 = 11$, so total output is 80. (c) Show $MC_1 = MC_2 = MR = 80$. (d) $p = 100$, $c_1 = 2,346$, $c_2 = 638$, $\pi = 5,016$.

3 (a) Complements, because an increase in the price of one brings about an increase in demand for the other. (b) $p_1 = 19.87$, $p_2 = 24.52$. (c) $p_1 = 15.29$, $p_2 = 23.43$. The prices are lower than (b) because the goods are complements. The formula used in (b) ignores the effect that increasing the price of one good decreases demand for the other. (d) Using (b), $\pi = 2,322.39$. Using (c), $\pi = 2,379.14$.

5 (a) $T = 5$. (b) $q_M = q_P = 2$, $p = 9.5$. (c) $T = 7.5$. (d) Correct transfer price profits are 5, incorrect transfer price profits are 2.75.

Chapter 14

1 (a)

L	MP	MRP ($p = 200$)	MRP ($p = 300$)
0	0	0	0
1	5	1,000	1,500
2	7	1,400	2,100
3	6	1,200	1,800
4	3	600	900
5	2	400	600

(b) 4. (c) 5. As output price rises, employment rises (assuming a constant wage), i.e. labor demand is a *derived* demand. (d) 4. As the wage rises, employment falls (assuming a constant output price).

3 $L^* = 10$. Second order condition is satisfied.

5 (a) $L = 500$, $W = 15$. (b) $W = 16 - 0.008L$. Firms pay $W = 300/19$, workers receive $W = 240/19$, tax revenue is $480,000/361$. (c) Workers wage falls by 45/19, wage paid by firm rises by 15/19, so workers bear a higher burden. (d). Workers bear 75 percent of the tax burden, firms bear 25 percent. At the initial equilibrium, the elasticity of demand is 3.0 and the elasticity of supply is 1.0. Tax burden falls on the group with the lower elasticity, which is the workers in this case.

Chapter 15

1 (a) General training since skills are useful in many employers. (b) General training since skills are useful in many airlines (at least those that have 767s in their fleets). (c) Specific training if there are procedures at University of Toronto that are unique to that university. May have a general component to the extent that skills used in the registrar are applicable at other universities. (d) Specific training since the machinery is probably not used anywhere else in Canada.

3 (a) The worker's net wage is $20,000 minus the chares of training costs ($2,625) for a net wage of $17,375. (b) The worker pays 75 percent of the costs, so must receive 75 percent of the benefits from training. Since the benefit of the training is $4,000 in the second year, the worker must receive $3,000 of this, implying a wage of $23,000 in the second year. (c) Present value of the benefit is $4,000/1.1, which is greater than the present value of the costs, $3,500. (d) Present value of the benefit is $4,000/1.15, which is less than the present value of the costs, $3,500. Thus, the training will not be undertaken.

5 (a) The present value of *VMP* must equal the present value of *MC*. (b) $27,200. (c) Because she is paid more than the value of her marginal product in the second period of the job.

7 (a) Wages increase 25 percent and output increases 33 1/3 percent. Since nothing else changes, profits must increase, justifying the wage increase. (b) Respectively, the wage increases are 12.5 percent, 6 2/3 percent, and 4 1/6 percent compared with output increases of 12.5 percent, 5 5/9 percent, and 3 3/19 percent, respectively. (c) A wage

of $11.25, since any larger wage results in a greater proportional wage increase than output increase. (d) An efficiency wage.

Chapter 16

1 (a, b) Two parallel lines with vertical and horizontal intercepts at 20 and 10, respectively. (c) 10 each. (d) 10 each. (e) No.

3 (a) Two parallel lines with vertical and horizontal intercepts at 400 and 200, respectively. The origin is the disagreement point. (b) 200 each.

(c) One line with vertical and horizontal intercepts at 400 and a second line with vertical intercept at 200 and a horizontal intercept at 300. The disagreement point is at $(200, 0)$. The solution is 100 to the union and 300 to the firm. (d) The side with the lower relative delay costs has more bargaining power, i.e. can extract more from the game.

5 (a) $(w - 10)L$. (b) Maximize $(w - 10)L$ subject to $w = 20 - 0.01L$. (c) $L = 500$, $w = 15$. (d) $7,500.

Index

●●